MOON 月詠 PHASE 3

つくよみ

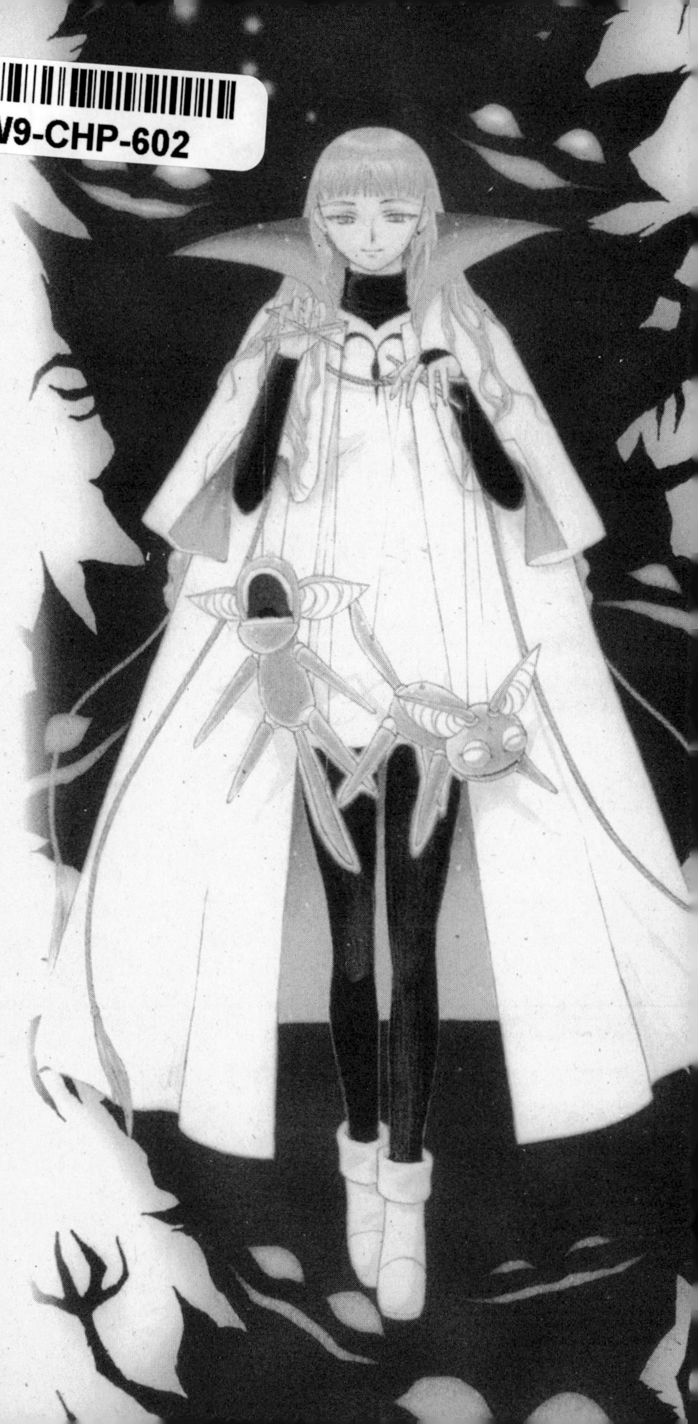

Keitaro Arima

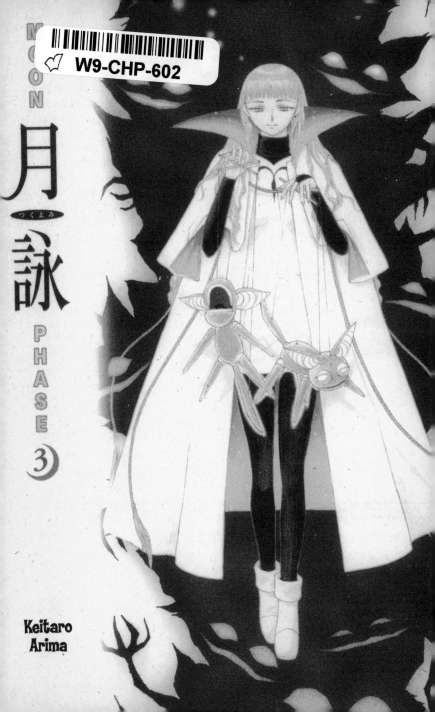

THE STORY SO FAR

Kouhei Mido has no power to see or feel ghosts, yet every picture he takes contains a ghost. (What's up with that?) He meets a vampire girl named Hazuki at an old German castle haunted by a supernatural phenomenon. Although she tries to turn Kouhei into a vampire slave by biting him, she finds that he is immune to her powers. Darn! A medium is called to the castle to exorcise all these supernatural spirits. Soon thereafter, Kouhei returns to Japan. Hazuki goes after Kouhei and stays at his house. Kouhei discovers the reason Hazuki has come to Japan is to look for her mother. He promises to help her in her quest. Although Hazuki tries to control the people around her with her vampire power, Kouhei advises her against this. She's determined to learn how to make friends without using her power. Elfriede (who works for Count Kinkel) appears in front of Kouhei and Hazuki. She explains that Hazuki is the "mistress" who has "blue blood" (the pure blood of a vampire) and asks her to come back to Germany...

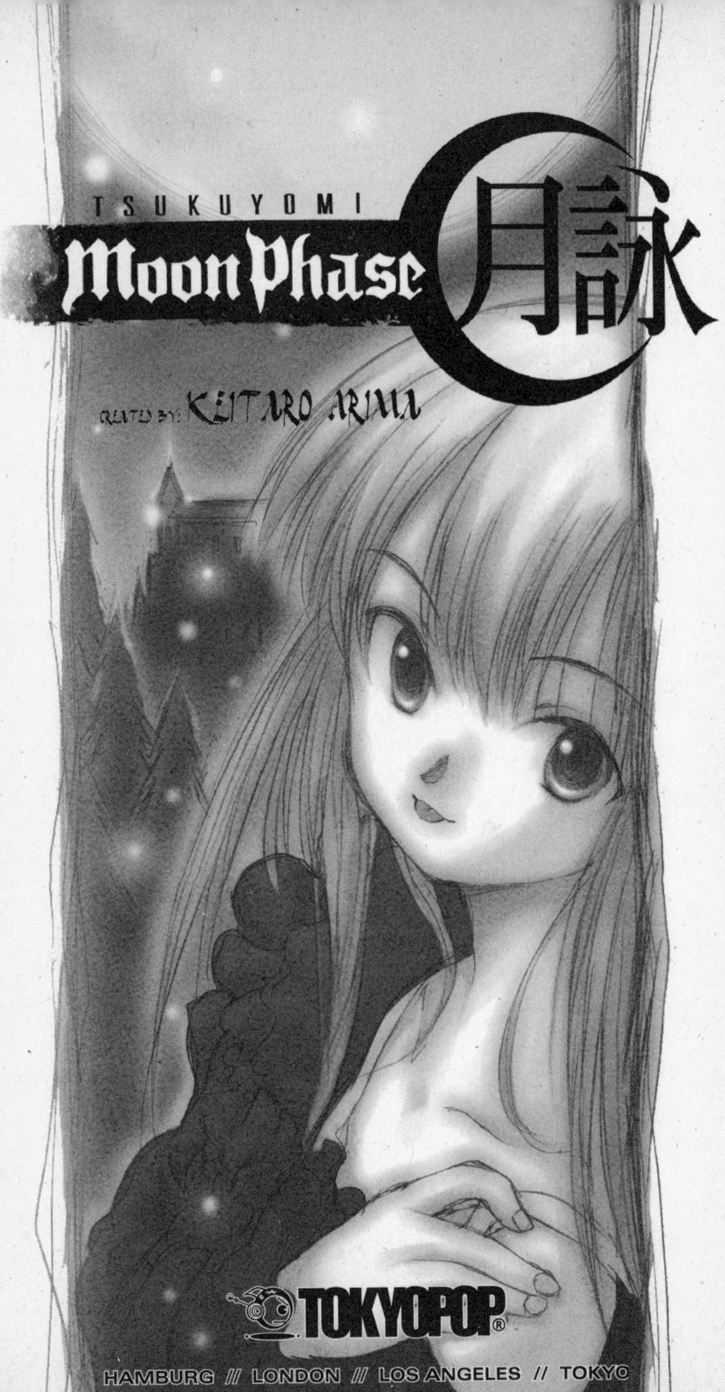

TSUKUYOMI

Moon Phase 月詠

CREATED BY: KEITARO ARIMA

TOKYOPOP®

HAMBURG // LONDON // LOS ANGELES // TOKYO

Tsukuyomi - Moon Phase Vol. 3
created by Keitaro Arima

Translation - Yoohae Yang
English Adaptation - Jeffrey Reeves
Retouch and Lettering - Fawn Lau
Production Artist - Lucas Rivera
Cover Design - Kyle Plummer

Editor - Julie Taylor
Digital Imaging Manager - Chris Buford
Managing Editor - Lindsey Johnston
VP of Production - Ron Klamert
Editor-in-Chief - Rob Tokar
Publisher - Mike Kiley
President and C.O.O. - John Parker
C.E.O. and Chief Creative Officer - Stuart Levy

A  Manga

TOKYOPOP Inc.
5900 Wilshire Blvd. Suite 2000
Los Angeles, CA 90036

E-mail: info@TOKYOPOP.com
Come visit us online at www.TOKYOPOP.com

© 2001 Keitaro Arima. All Rights Reserved. All rights reserved. No portion of this book may be
First published in 2001 by Wani Books., Tokyo, Japan. reproduced or transmitted in any form or by any means
without written permission from the copyright holders.
English text copyright © 2006 TOKYOPOP Inc. This manga is a work of fiction. Any resemblance to
actual events or locales or persons, living or dead, is
entirely coincidental.

ISBN:1-59532-950-1

First TOKYOPOP printing: June 2006
10 9 8 7 6 5 4 3 2 1
Printed in the USA

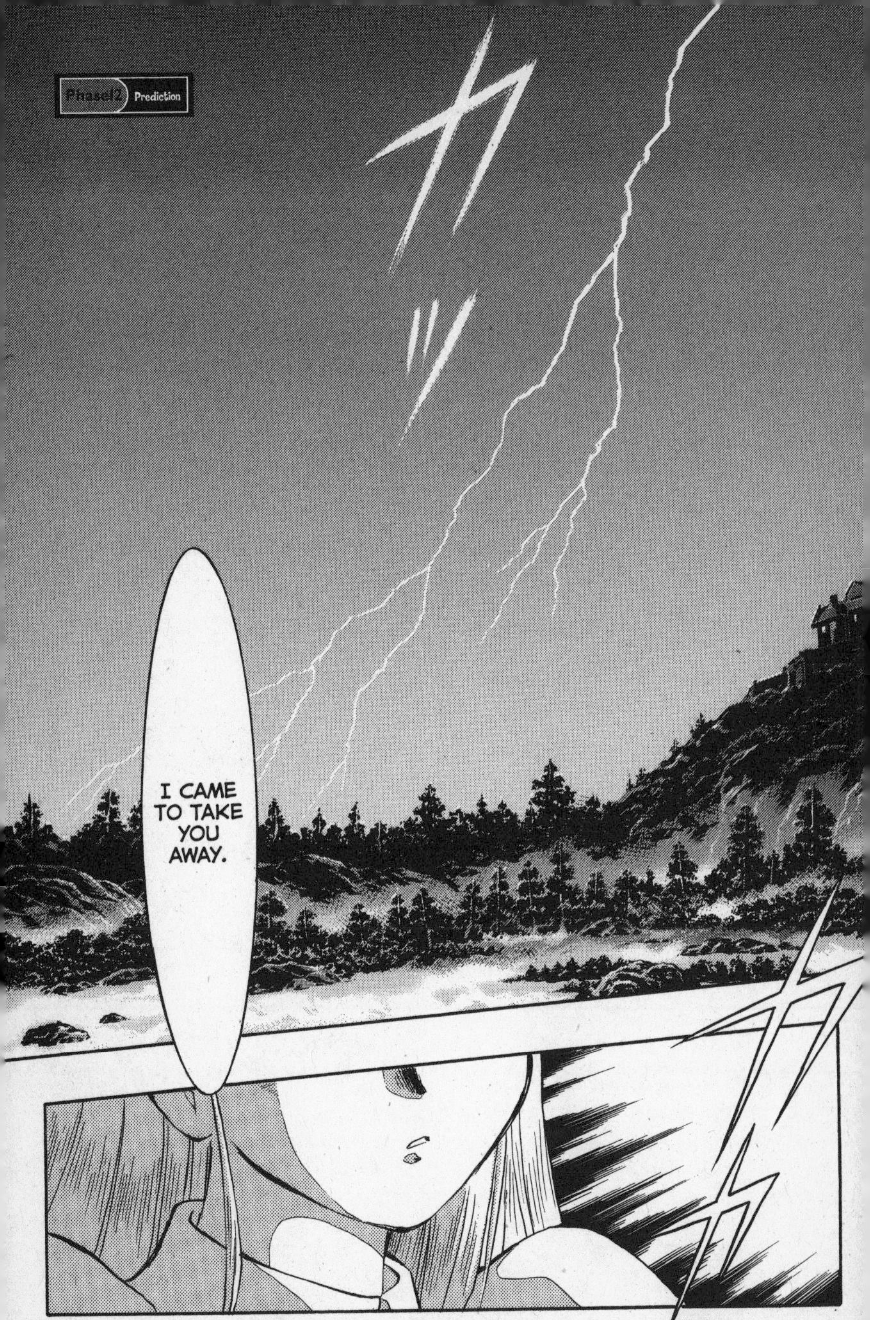
I CAME TO TAKE YOU AWAY.

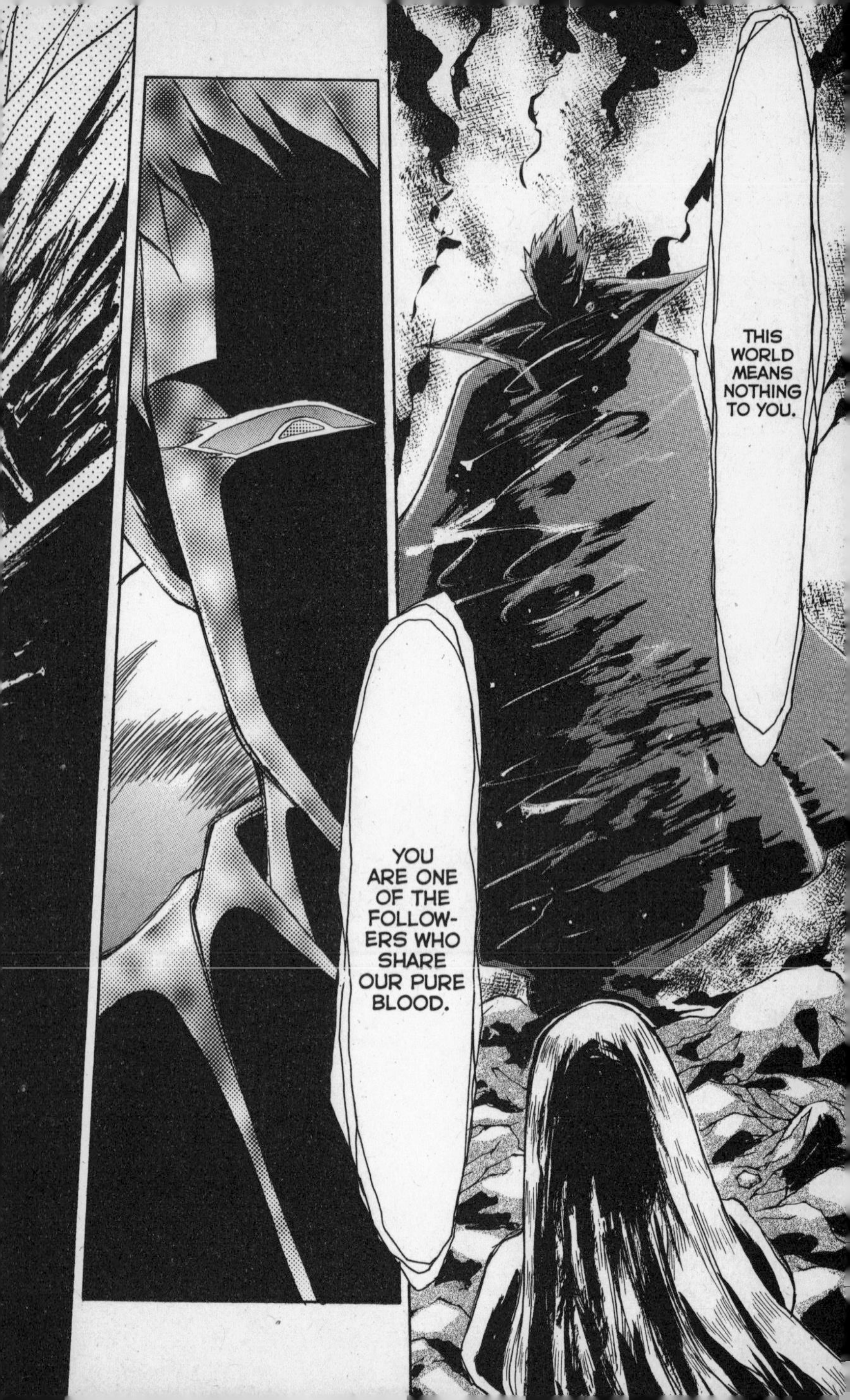
THIS WORLD MEANS NOTHING TO YOU.
YOU ARE ONE OF THE FOLLOW-ERS WHO SHARE OUR PURE BLOOD.

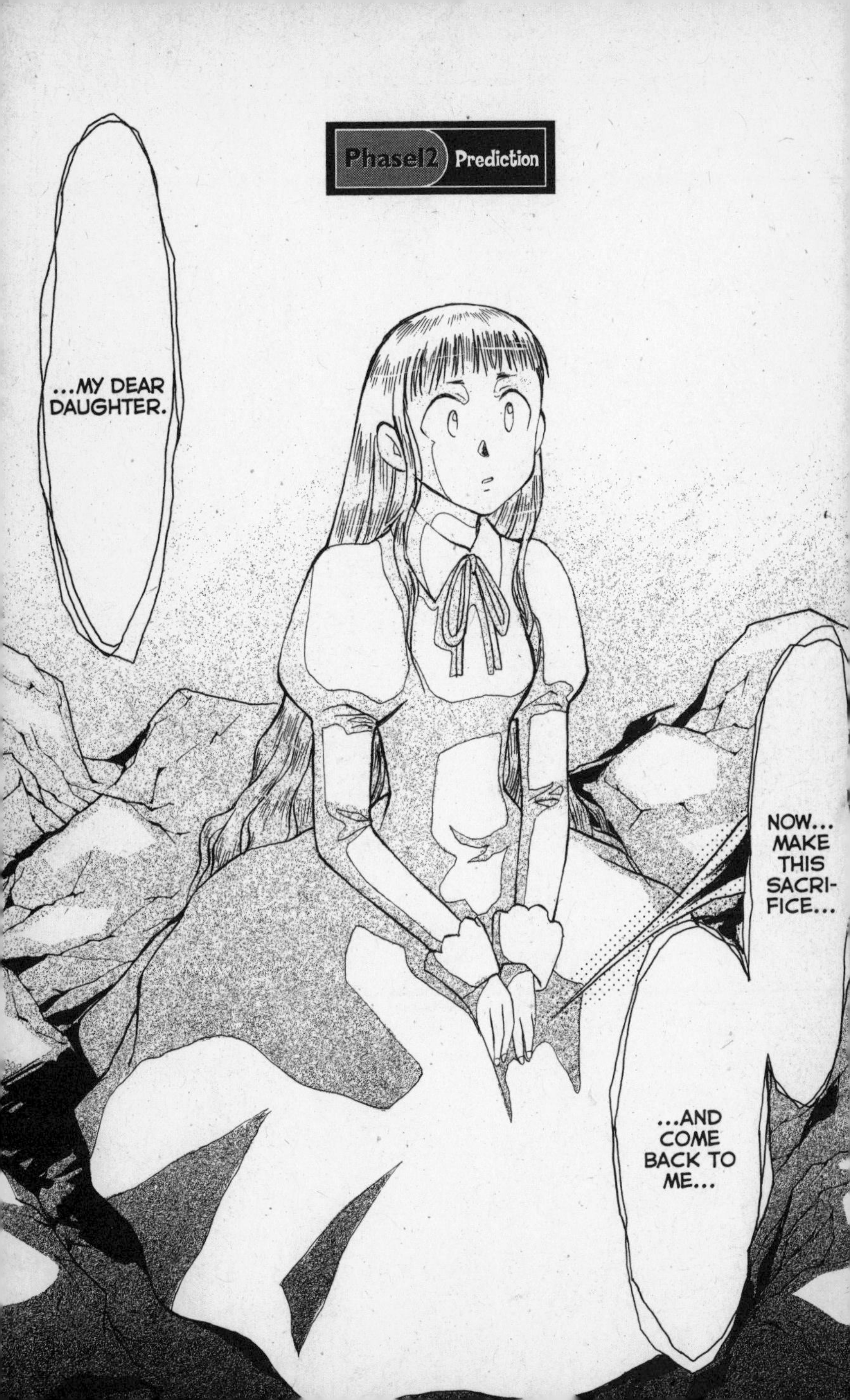
Phase12 Prediction
NOW... MAKE THIS SACRI-FICE...
...AND COME BACK TO ME...
...MY DEAR DAUGHTER.

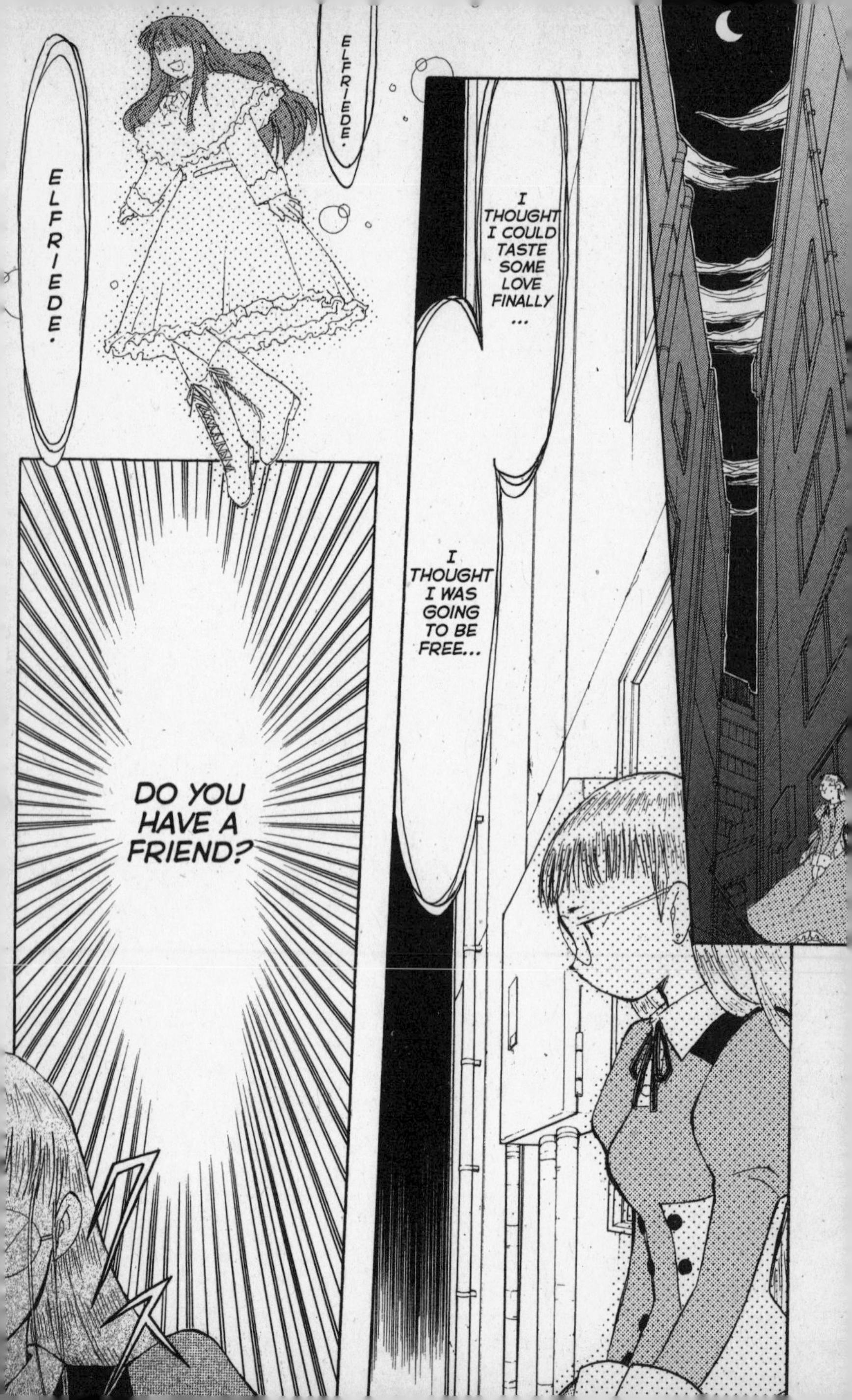
I THOUGHT I COULD TASTE SOME LOVE FINALLY ...
I THOUGHT I WAS GOING TO BE FREE...
ELFRIEDE.
ELFRIEDE.
DO YOU HAVE A FRIEND?

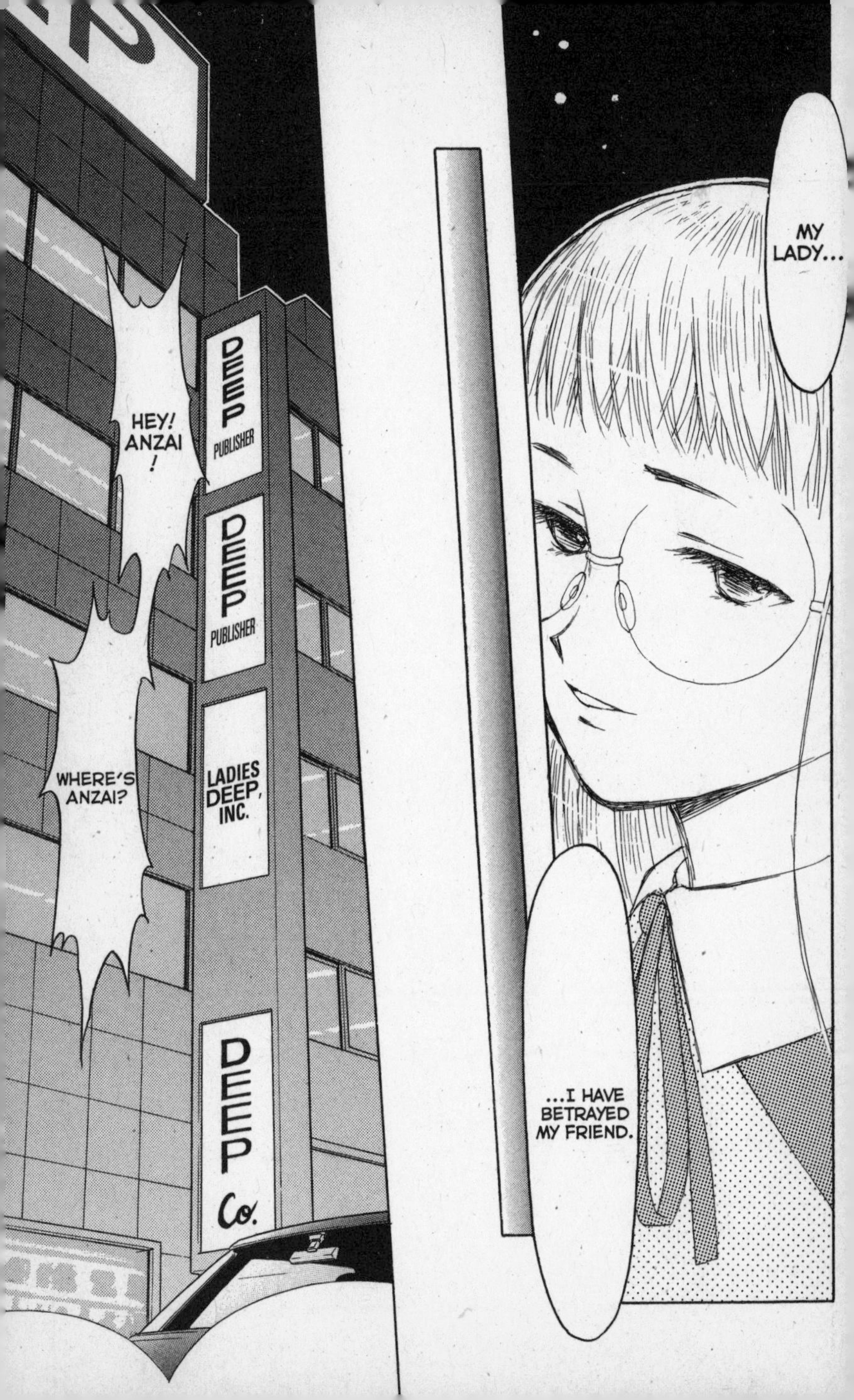
MY LADY...
...I HAVE BETRAYED MY FRIEND.
DEEP PUBLISHER
DEEP PUBLISHER
LADIES DEEP, INC.
DEEP Co.
HEY! ANZAI!
WHERE'S ANZAI?

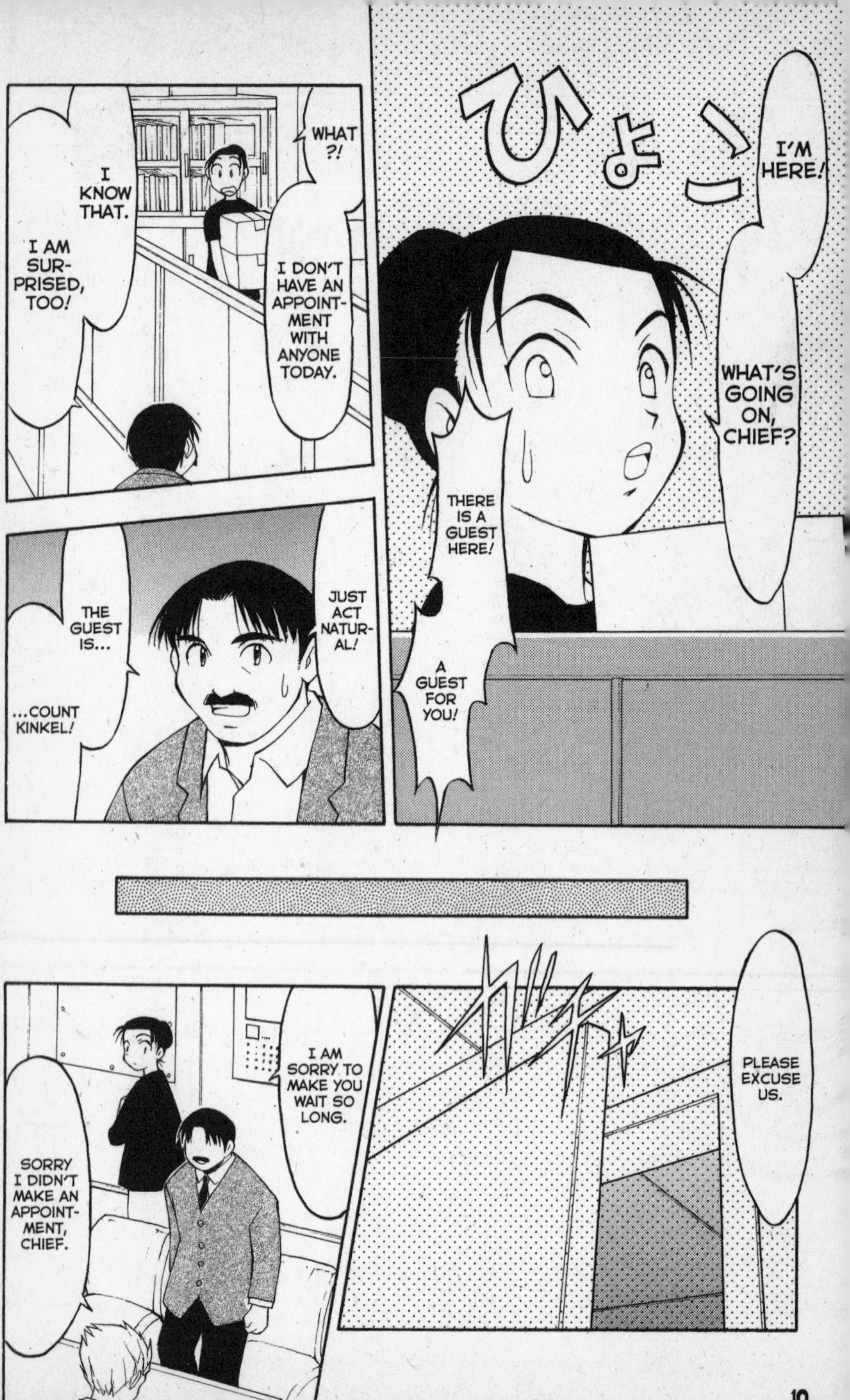
ひょこ
I'M HERE!
WHAT'S GOING ON, CHIEF?
THERE IS A GUEST HERE!
A GUEST FOR YOU!
WHAT ?!
I DON'T HAVE AN APPOINTMENT WITH ANYONE TODAY.
I KNOW THAT.
I AM SURPRISED, TOO!
JUST ACT NATURAL!
THE GUEST IS...
...COUNT KINKEL!
ガチャ
PLEASE EXCUSE US.
I AM SORRY TO MAKE YOU WAIT SO LONG.
SORRY I DIDN'T MAKE AN APPOINTMENT, CHIEF.

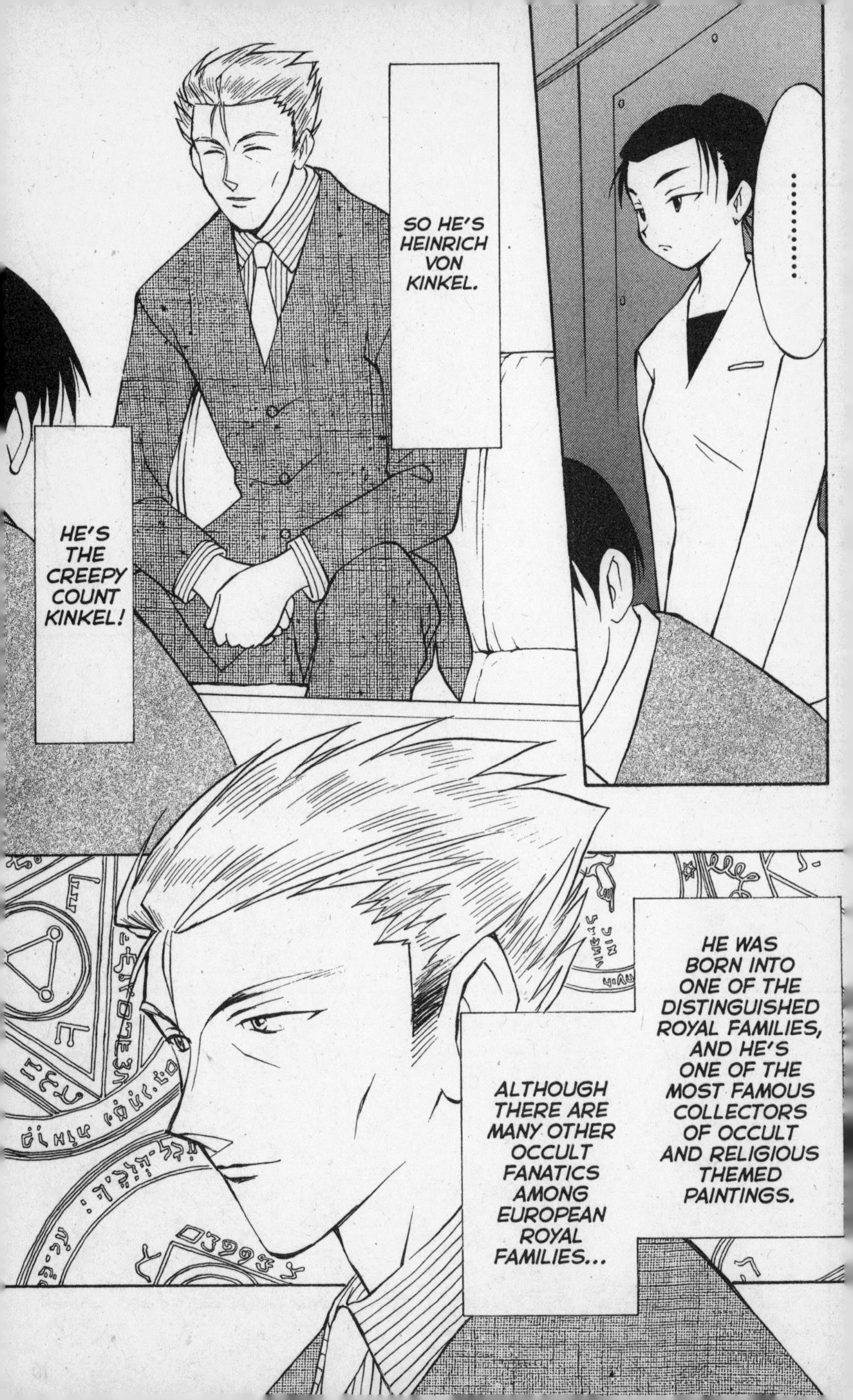
......
SO HE'S HEINRICH VON KINKEL.
HE'S THE CREEPY COUNT KINKEL!
HE WAS BORN INTO ONE OF THE DISTINGUISHED ROYAL FAMILIES, AND HE'S ONE OF THE MOST FAMOUS COLLECTORS OF OCCULT AND RELIGIOUS THEMED PAINTINGS.
ALTHOUGH THERE ARE MANY OTHER OCCULT FANATICS AMONG EUROPEAN ROYAL FAMILIES...

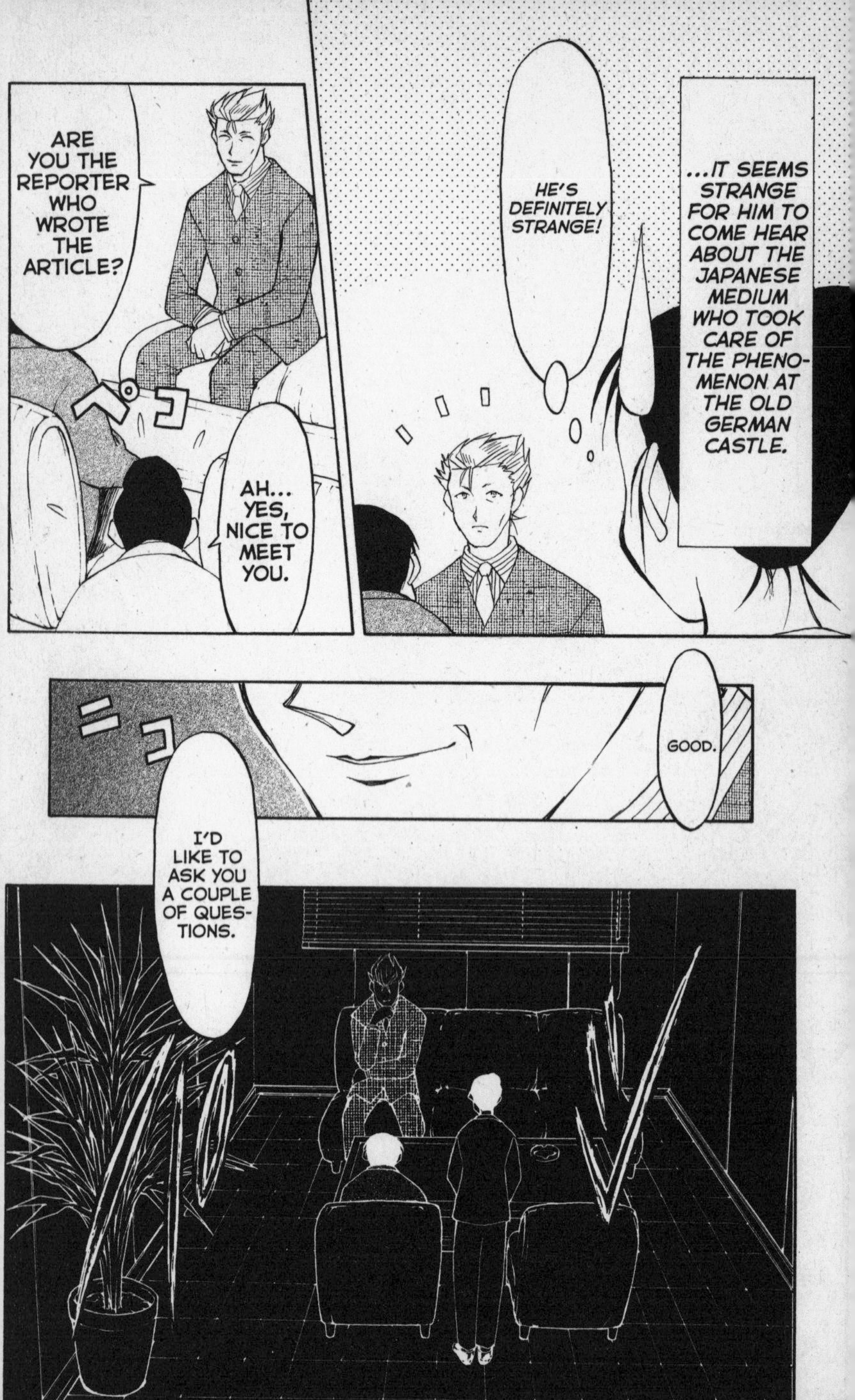
...IT SEEMS STRANGE FOR HIM TO COME HEAR ABOUT THE JAPANESE MEDIUM WHO TOOK CARE OF THE PHENOMENON AT THE OLD GERMAN CASTLE.
HE'S DEFINITELY STRANGE!
ARE YOU THE REPORTER WHO WROTE THE ARTICLE?
ペコ
AH... YES, NICE TO MEET YOU.
GOOD.
ニコ
I'D LIKE TO ASK YOU A COUPLE OF QUES-TIONS.

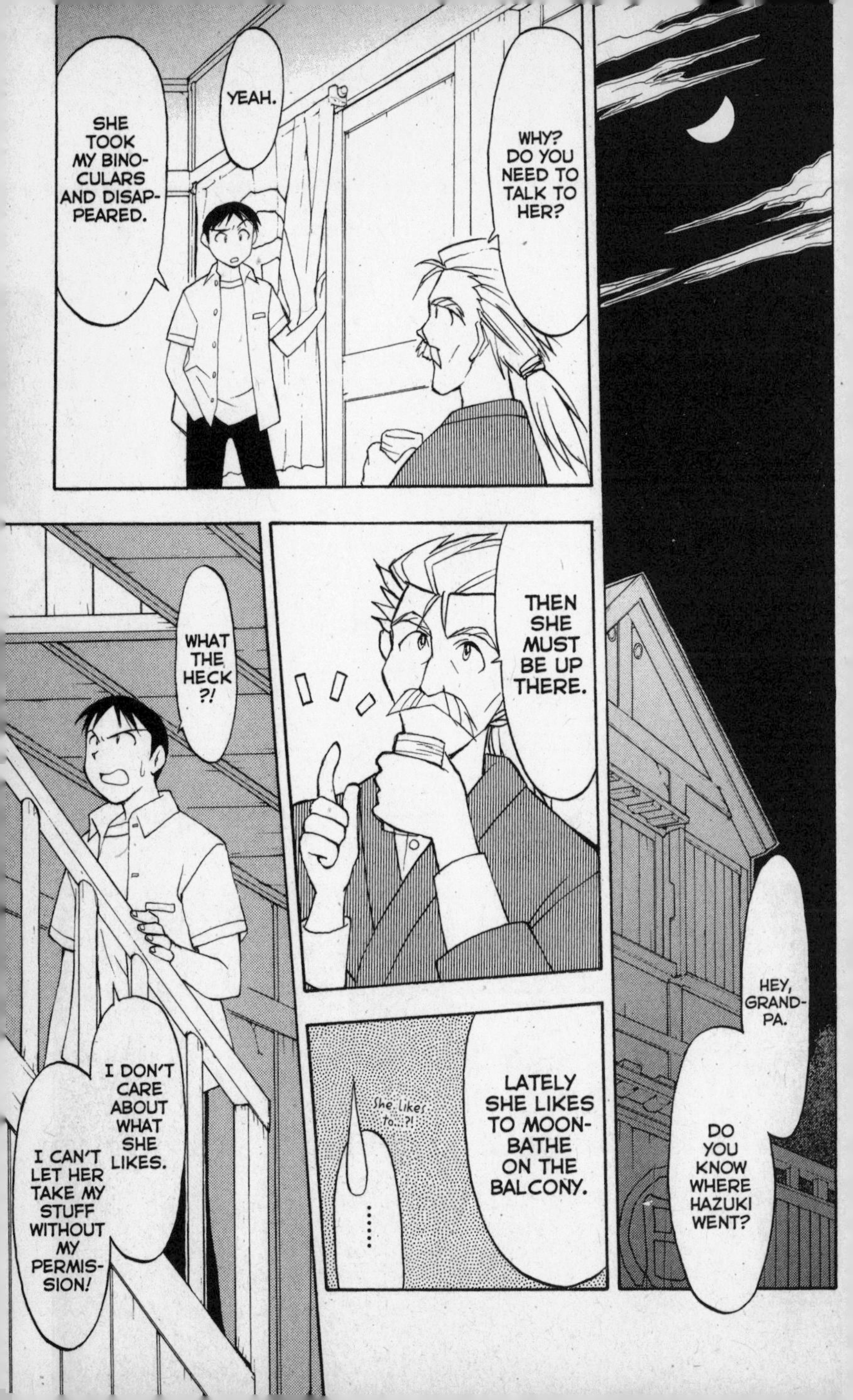
HEY, GRAND-PA.
DO YOU KNOW WHERE HAZUKI WENT?
WHY? DO YOU NEED TO TALK TO HER?
YEAH.
SHE TOOK MY BINOC-ULARS AND DISAP-PEARED.
THEN SHE MUST BE UP THERE.
LATELY SHE LIKES TO MOON-BATHE ON THE BALCONY.
She likes to...?!
......
WHAT THE HECK ?!
I DON'T CARE ABOUT WHAT SHE LIKES.
I CAN'T LET HER TAKE MY STUFF WITHOUT MY PERMIS-SION!

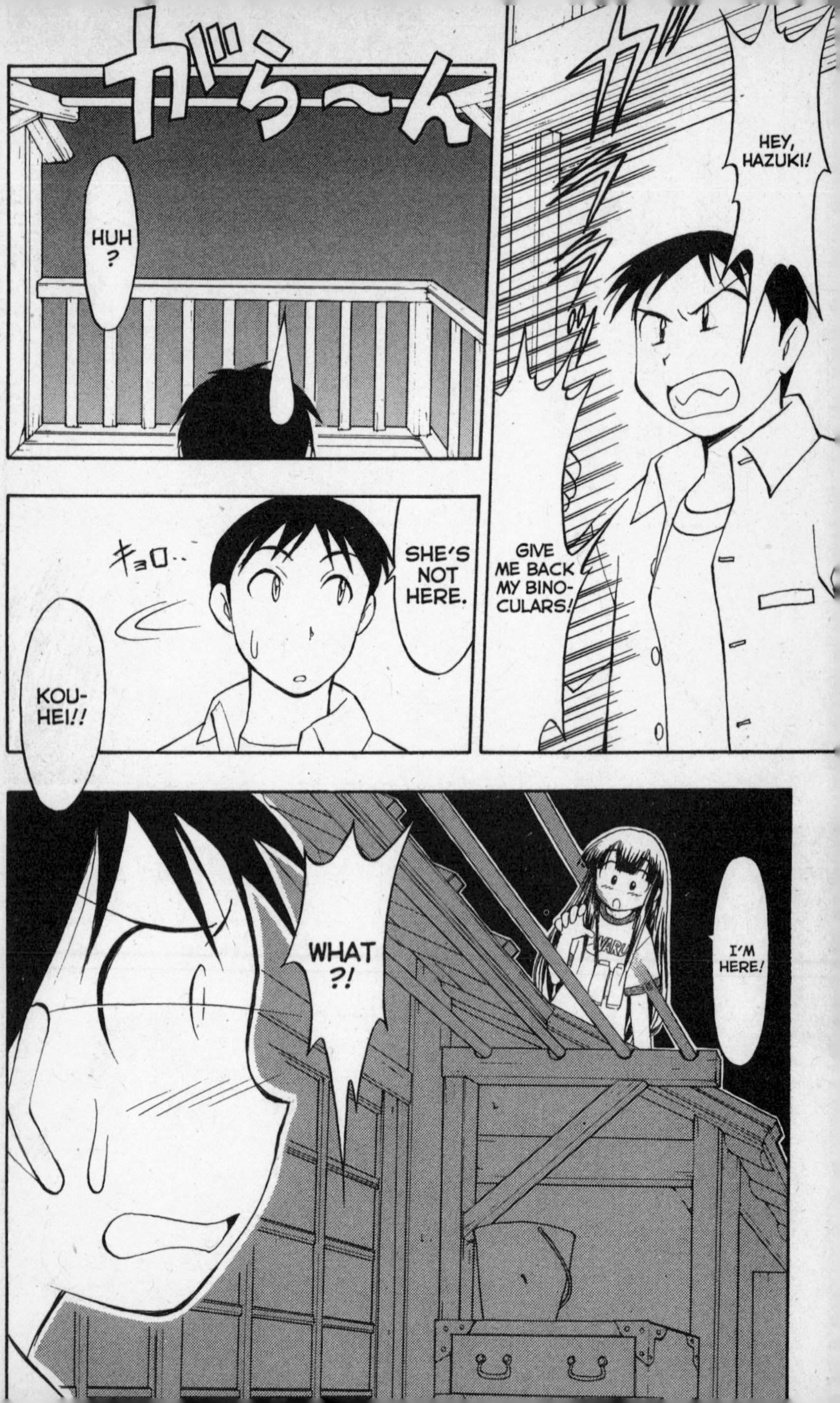
ガラッ
HEY, HAZUKI!
GIVE ME BACK MY BINOCULARS!
がら～ん
HUH?
キョロ..
SHE'S NOT HERE.
KOU-HEI!!
I'M HERE!
WHAT?!

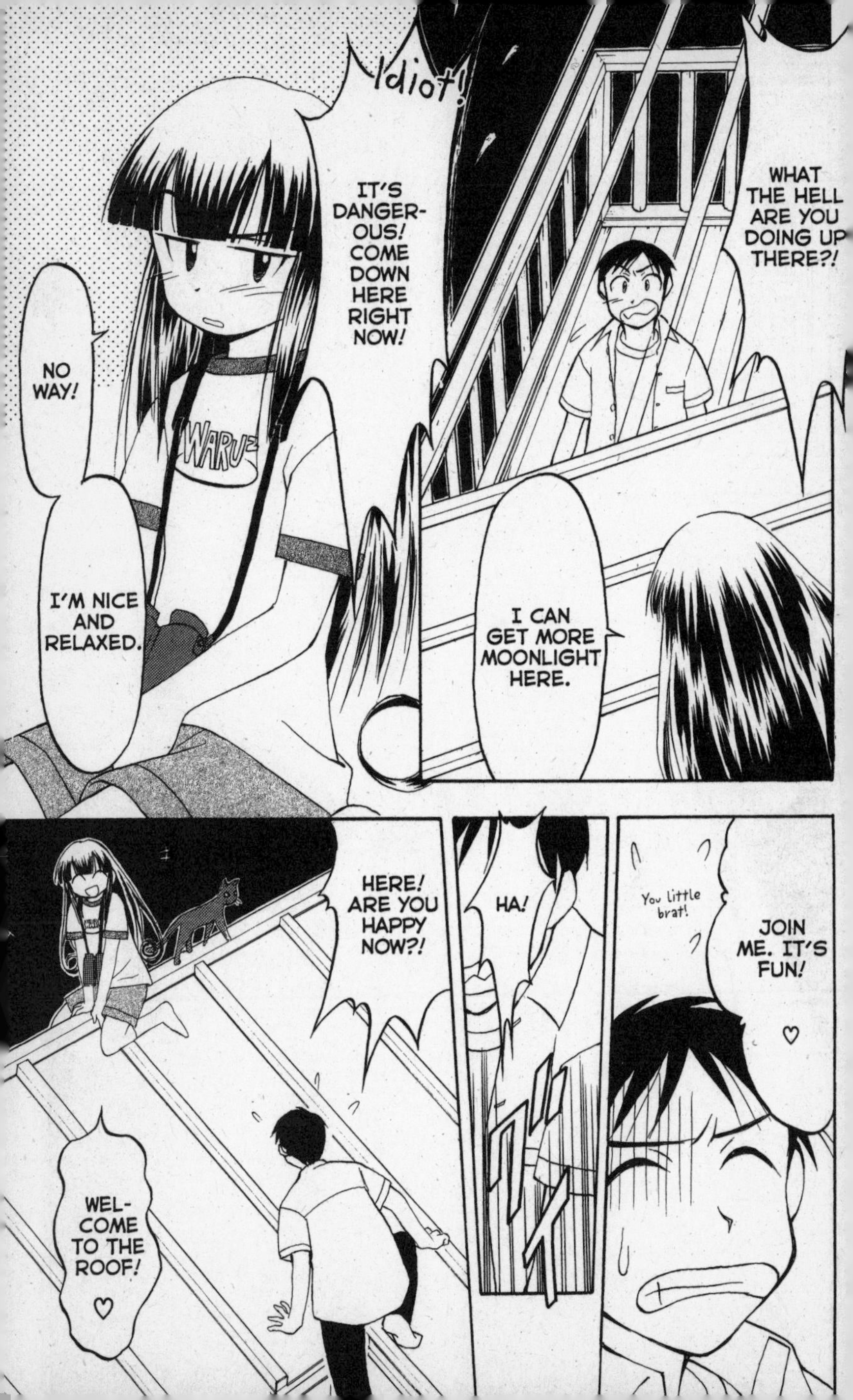
WHAT THE HELL ARE YOU DOING UP THERE?!
I CAN GET MORE MOONLIGHT HERE.
Idiot!
IT'S DANGER-OUS! COME DOWN HERE RIGHT NOW!
NO WAY!
I'M NICE AND RELAXED.
JOIN ME. IT'S FUN! ♡
You little brat!
HA!
HERE! ARE YOU HAPPY NOW?!
WEL-COME TO THE ROOF! ♡

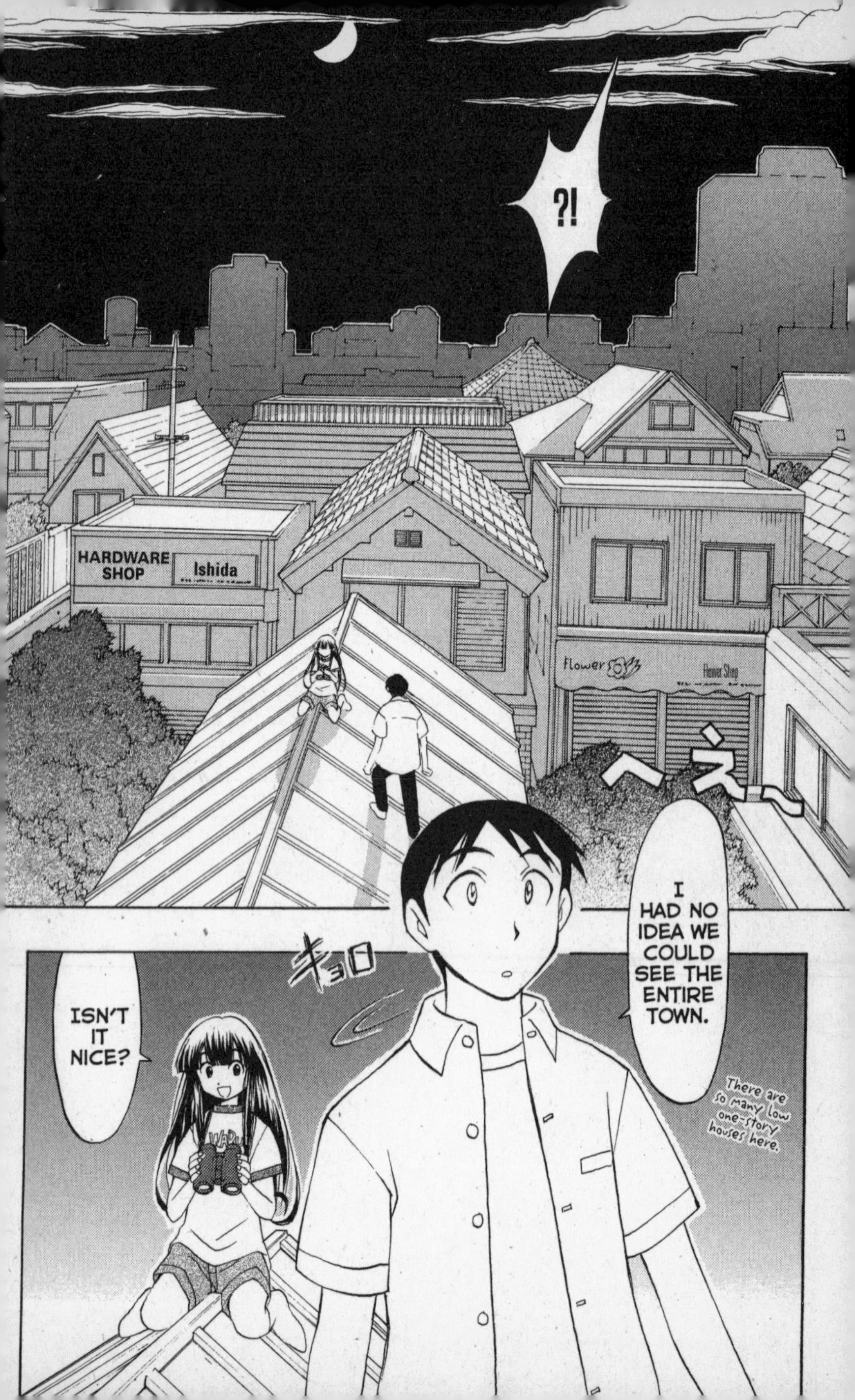
?!
HARDWARE SHOP
Ishida
Flower
I HAD NO IDEA WE COULD SEE THE ENTIRE TOWN.
へえ~
There are so many low one-story houses here.
キョロ
ISN'T IT NICE?

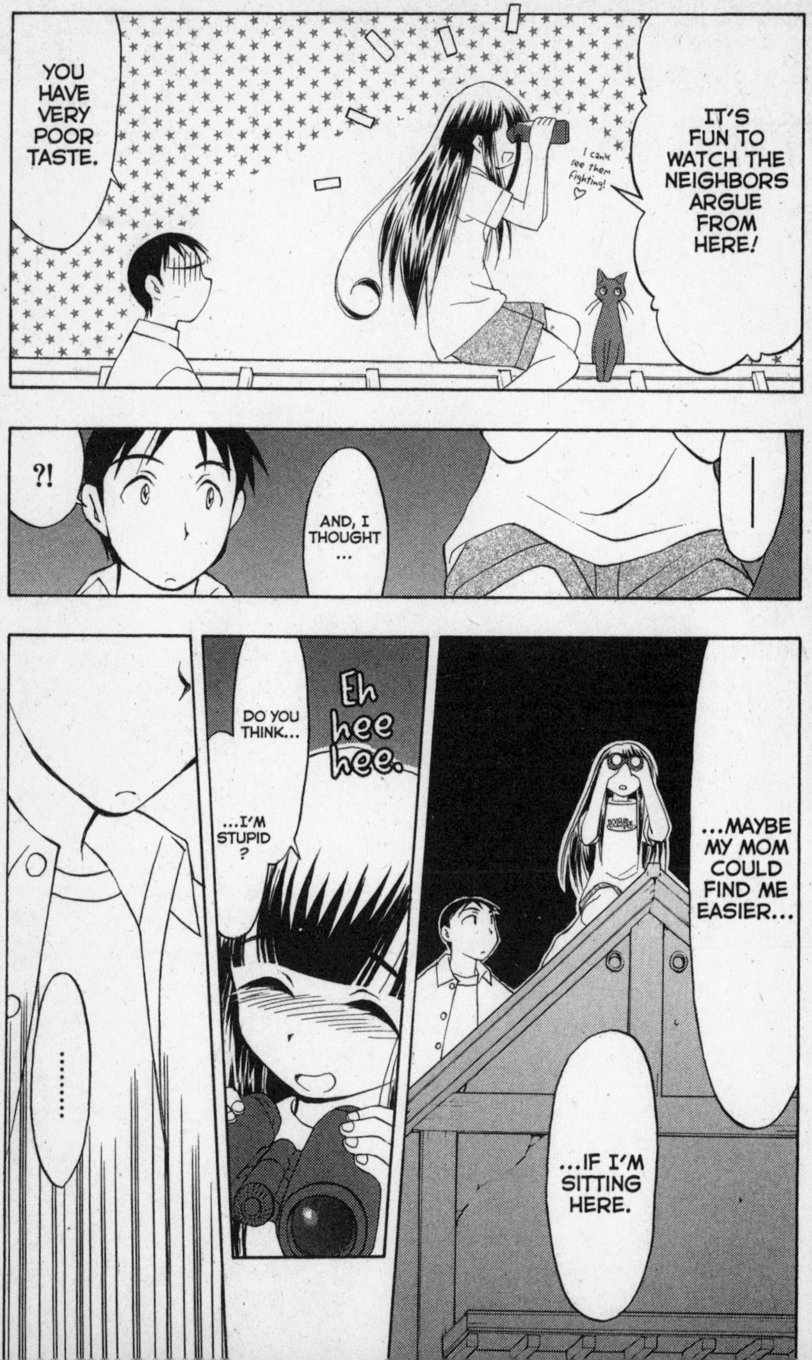
IT'S FUN TO WATCH THE NEIGHBORS ARGUE FROM HERE!
I can't see them fighting! ♡
YOU HAVE VERY POOR TASTE.
—
AND, I THOUGHT ...
?!
...MAYBE MY MOM COULD FIND ME EASIER...
...IF I'M SITTING HERE.
Eh hee hee.
DO YOU THINK...
...I'M STUPID ?
....

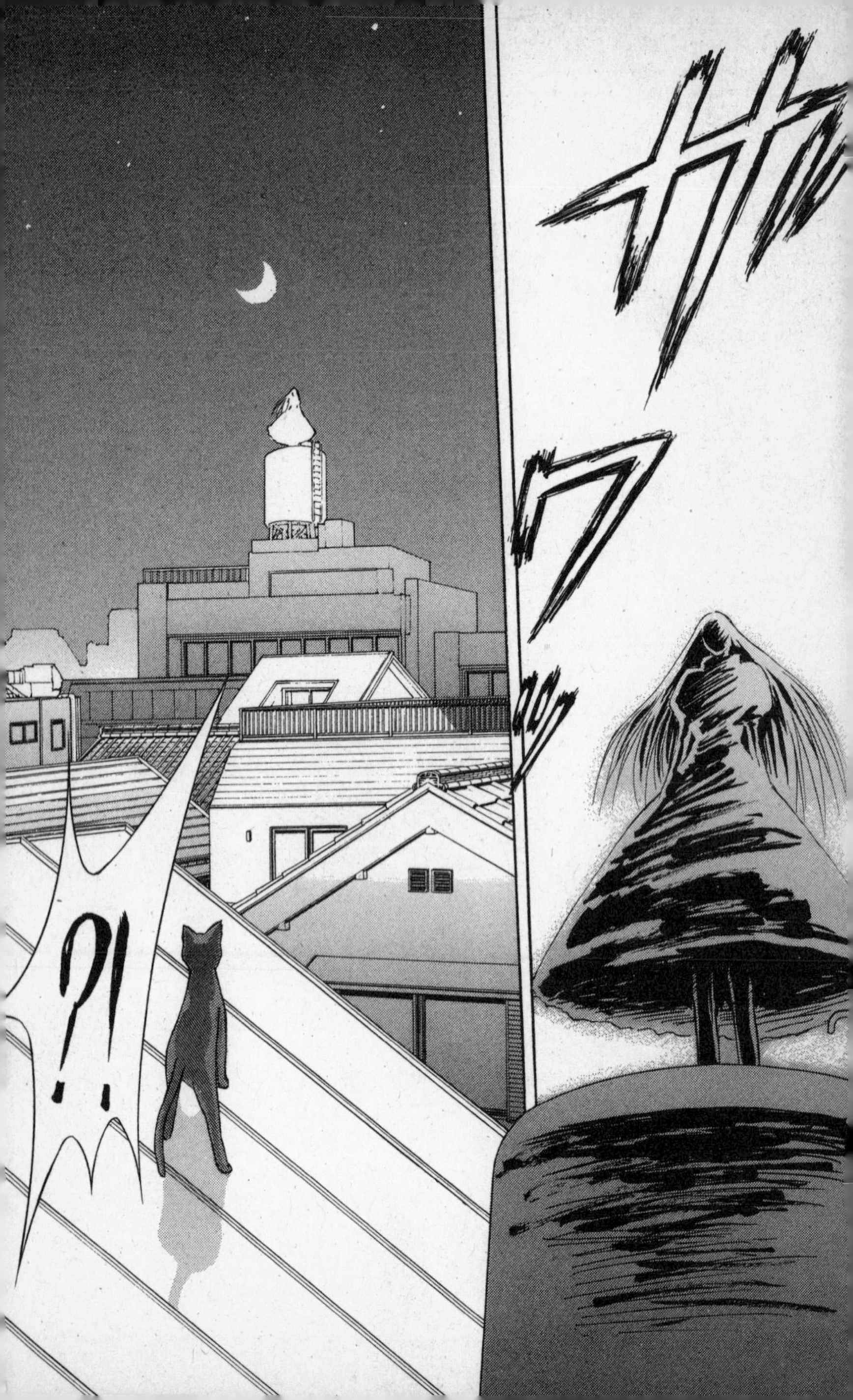
?!

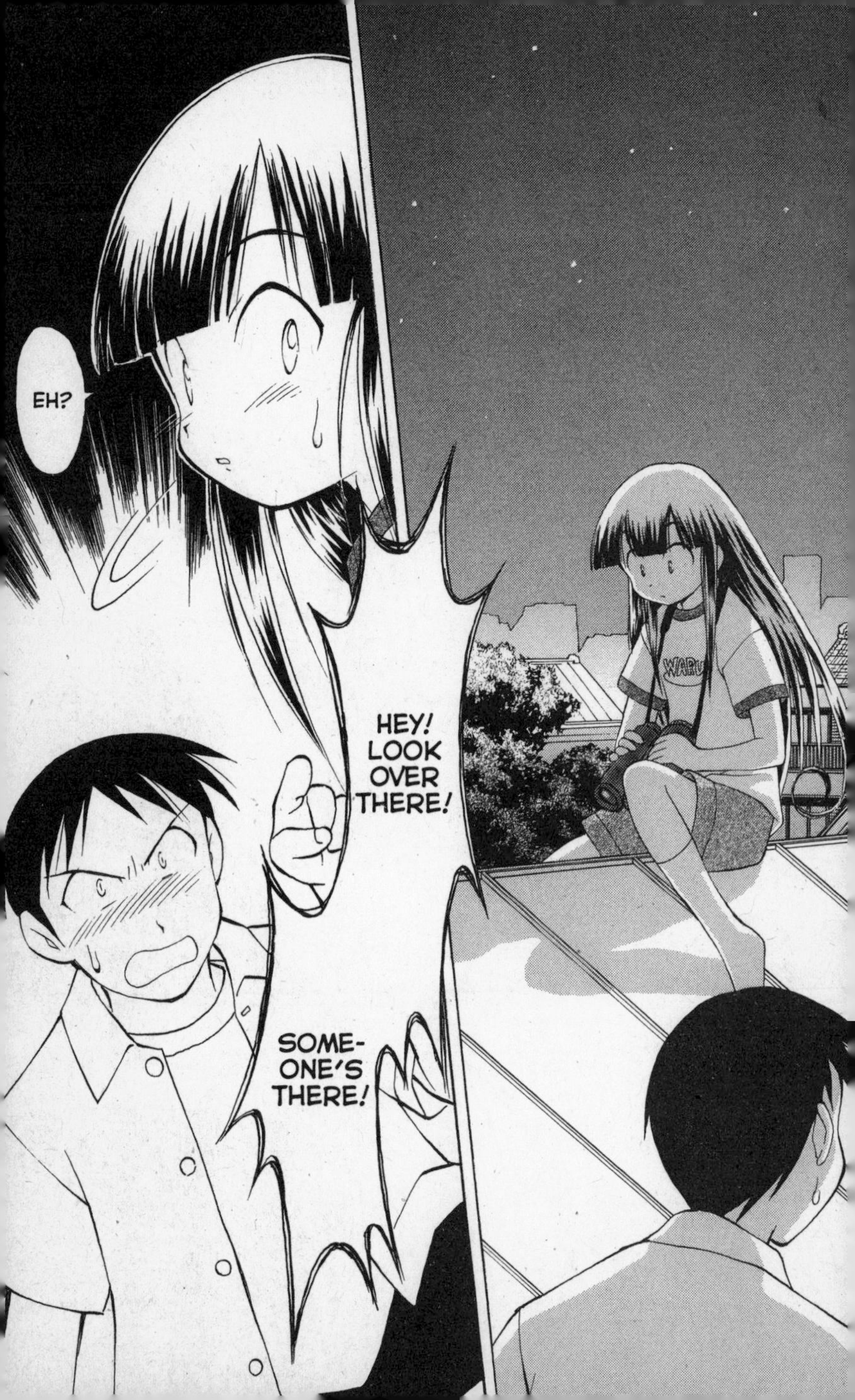
HEY! LOOK OVER THERE!
SOME-ONE'S THERE!
EH?
WARU

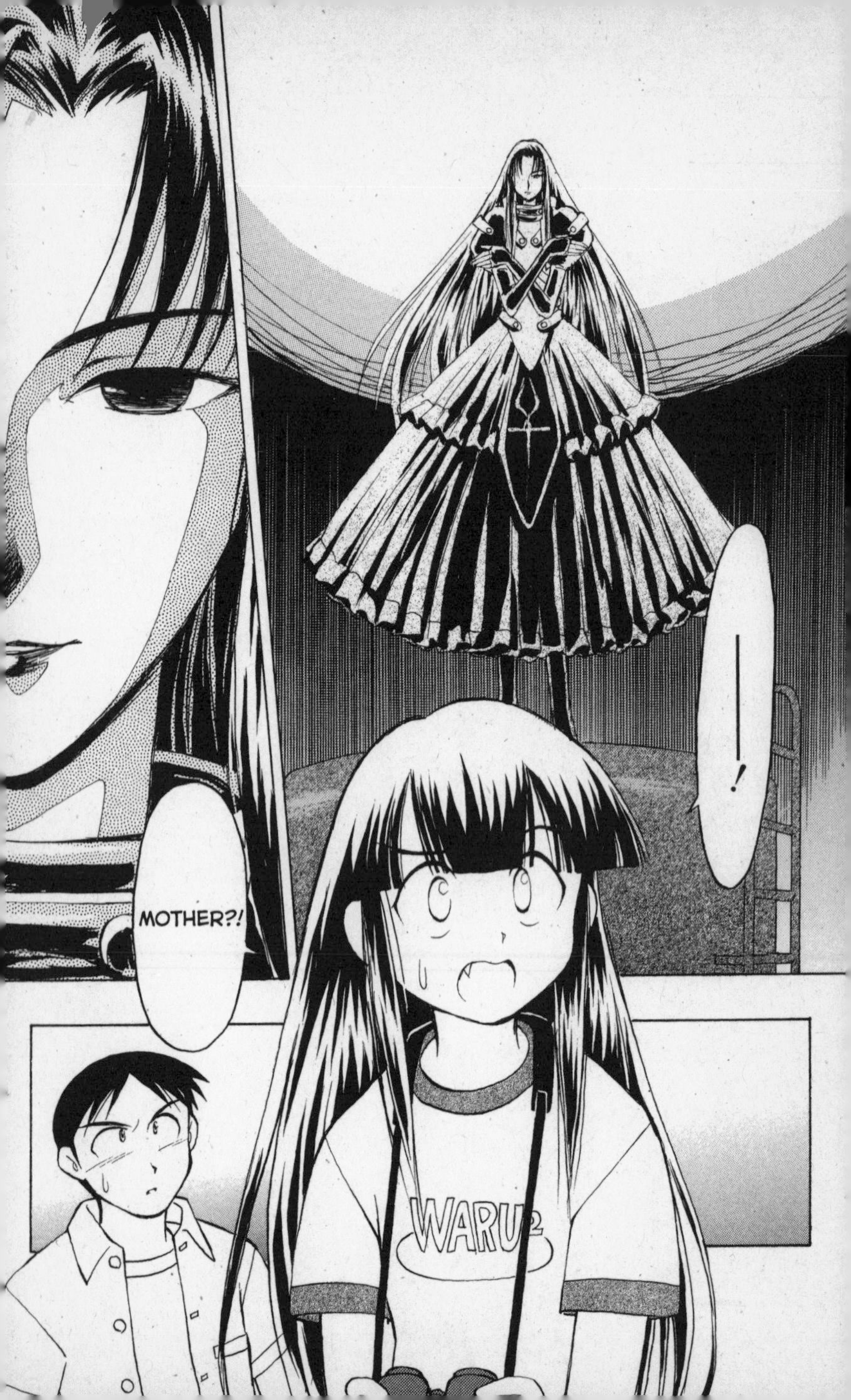
—!
MOTHER?!
WARU2

MOON·PHASE·STORY

I CAN REVEAL SECRETS WITHOUT
THE FEAR OF CONSEQUENCES.

CUTE MAID

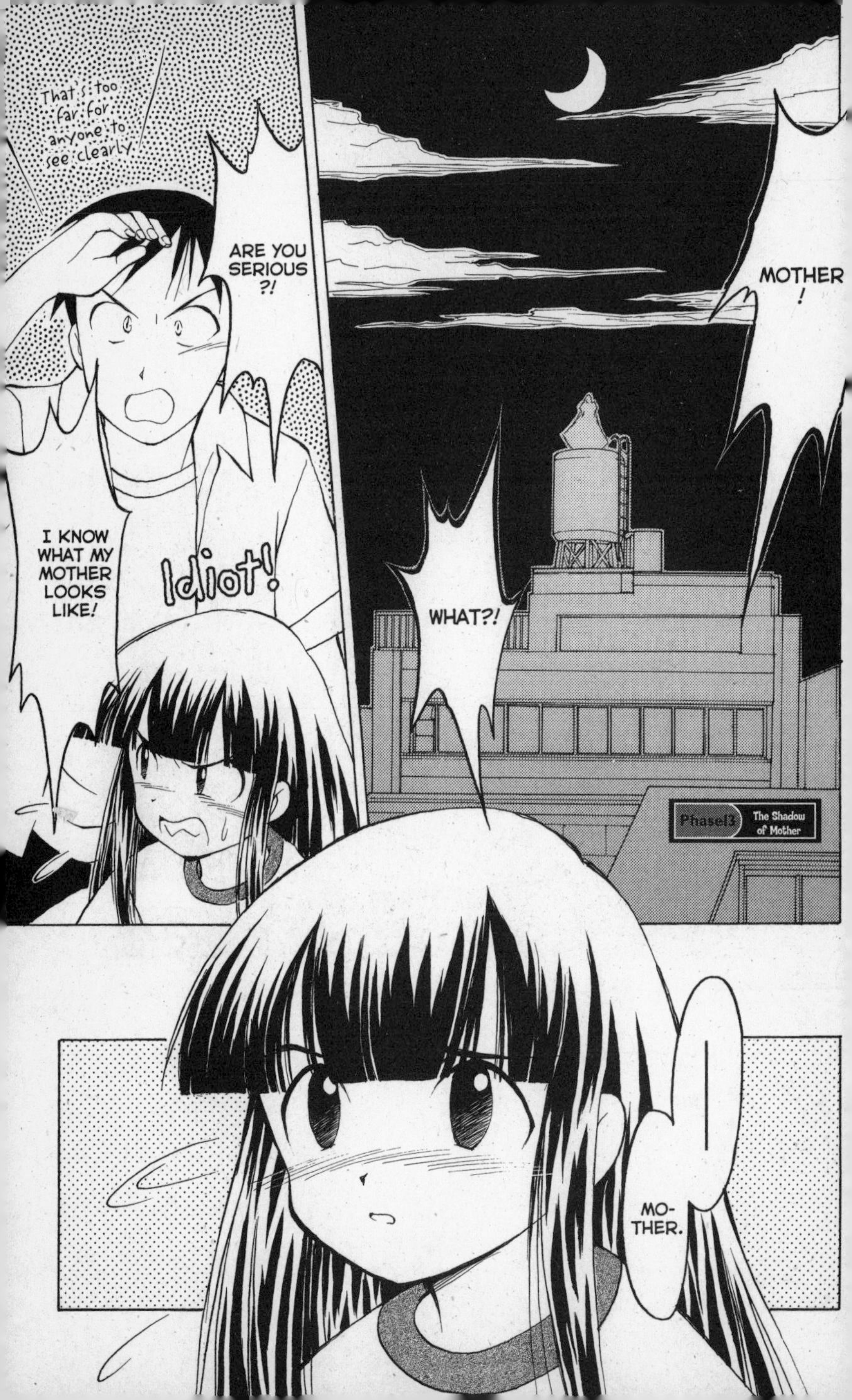
MOTHER!
WHAT?!
Phase13 The Shadow of Mother
ARE YOU SERIOUS?!
That's too far for anyone to see clearly.
Idiot!
I KNOW WHAT MY MOTHER LOOKS LIKE!
MO-THER.

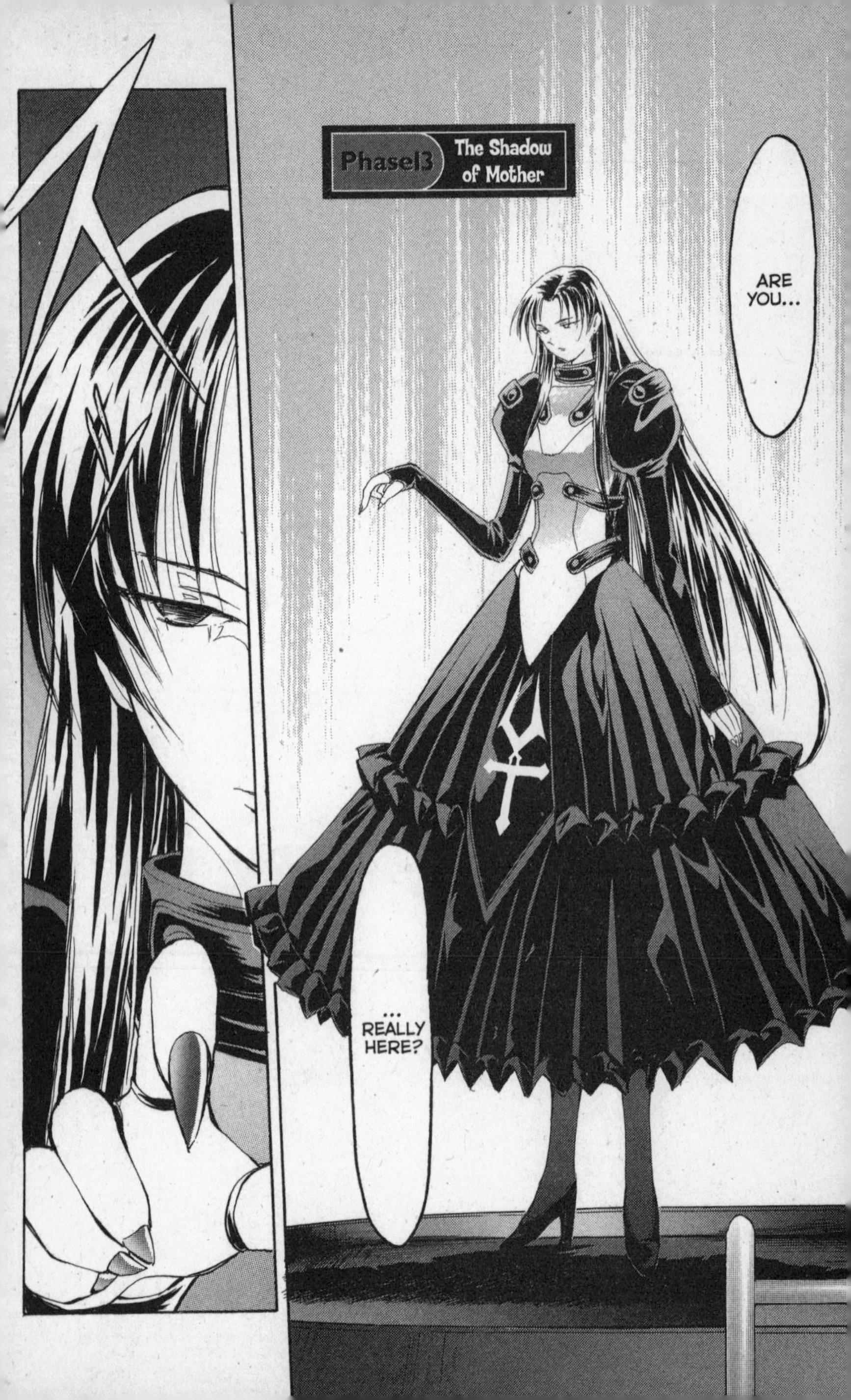
Phase13 The Shadow of Mother
ARE YOU...
...REALLY HERE?

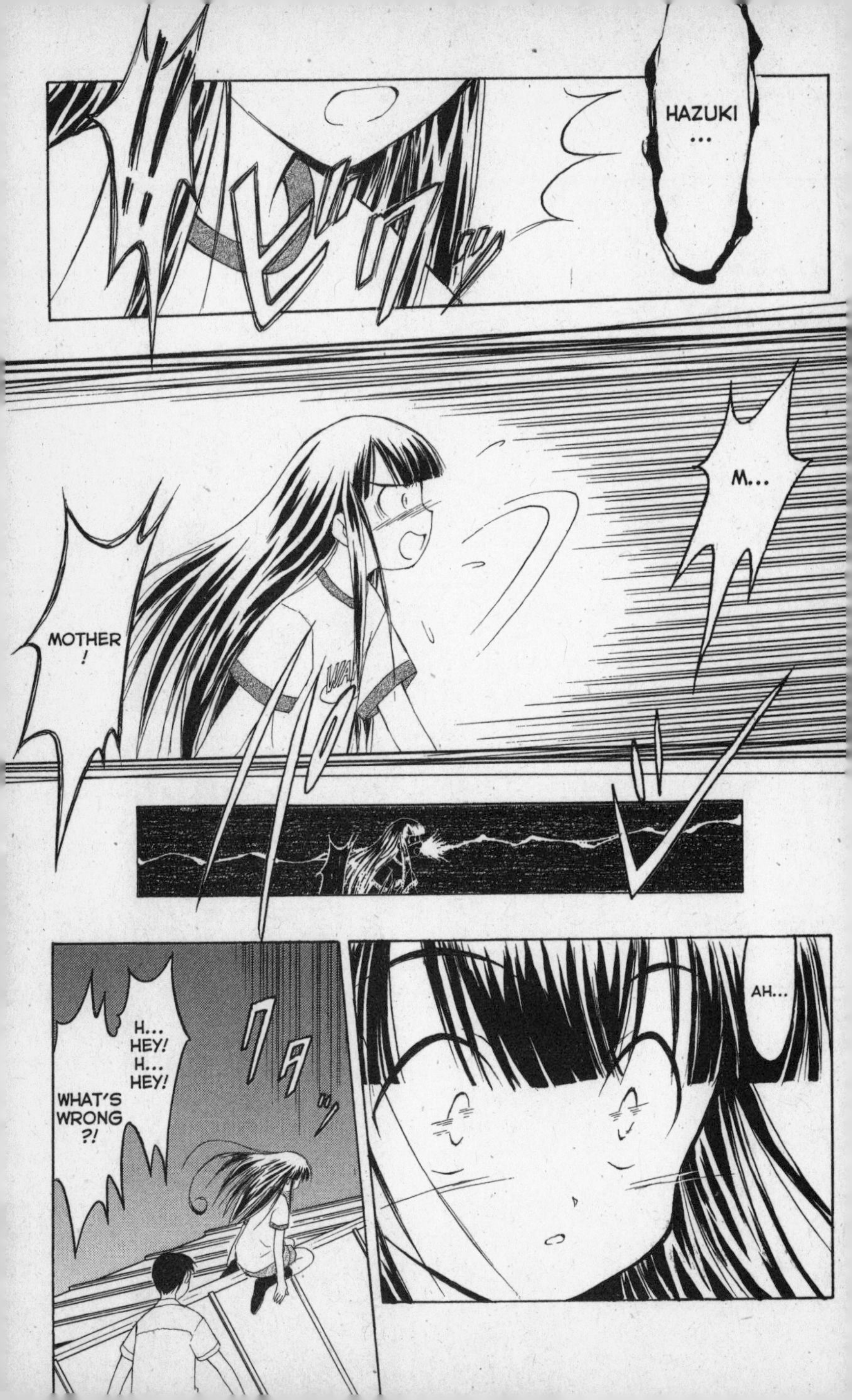
HAZUKI ...
M...
MOTHER !
AH...
H... HEY! H... HEY! WHAT'S WRONG ?!

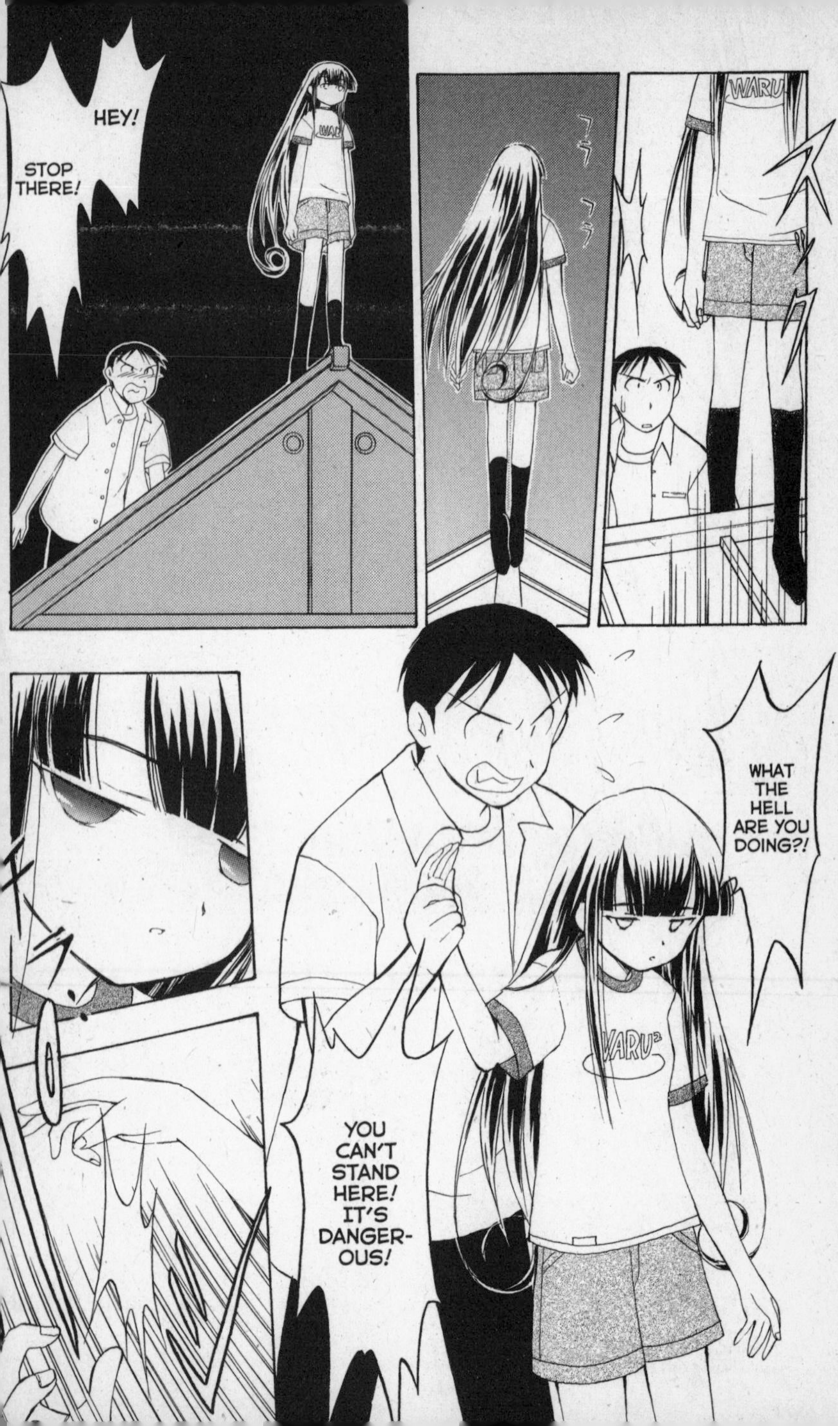
HEY!
STOP THERE!
WHAT THE HELL ARE YOU DOING?!
YOU CAN'T STAND HERE! IT'S DANGER-OUS!

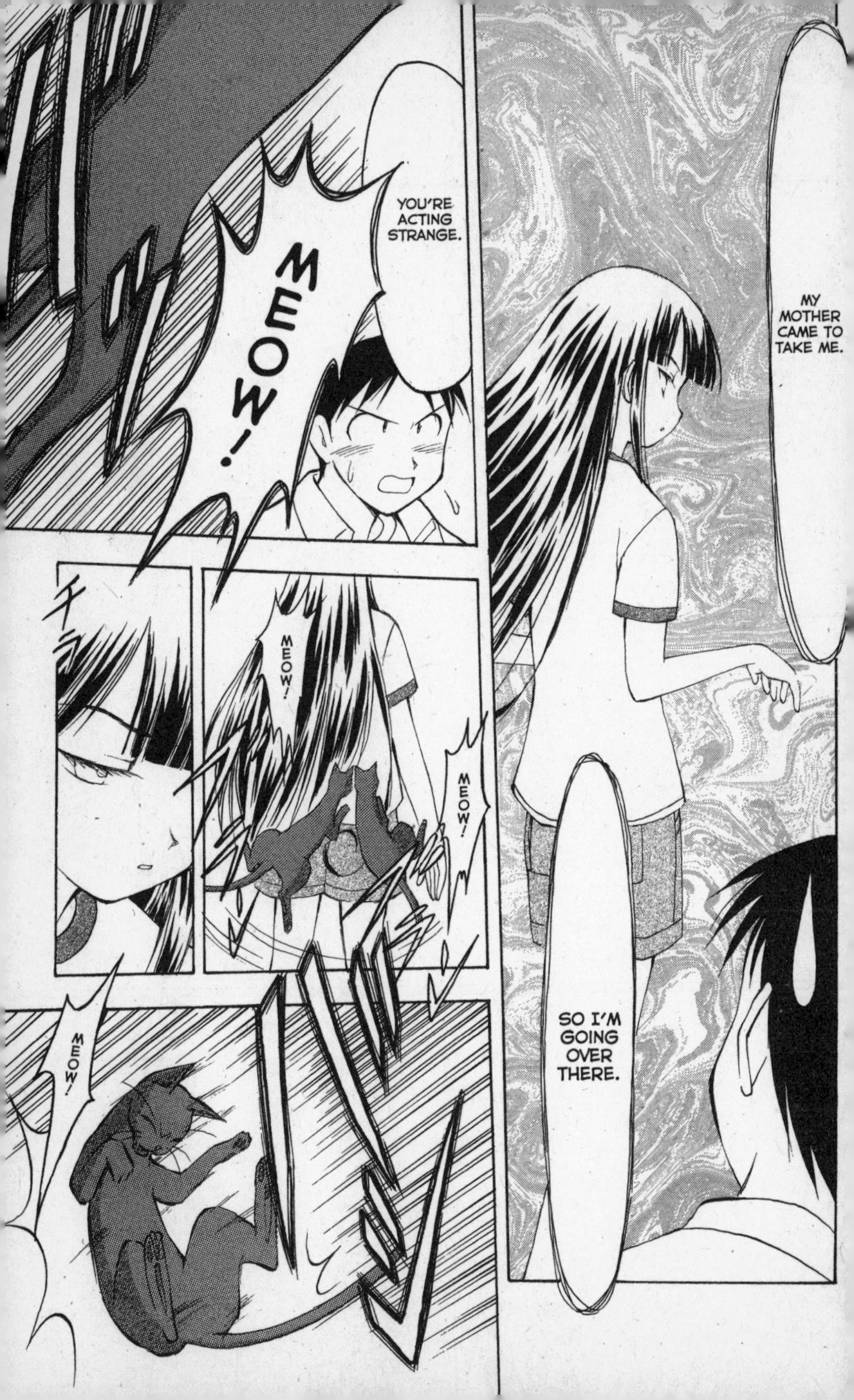
MY MOTHER CAME TO TAKE ME.
SO I'M GOING OVER THERE.
YOU'RE ACTING STRANGE.
MEOW!
MEOW!
MEOW!
チラ
MEOW!

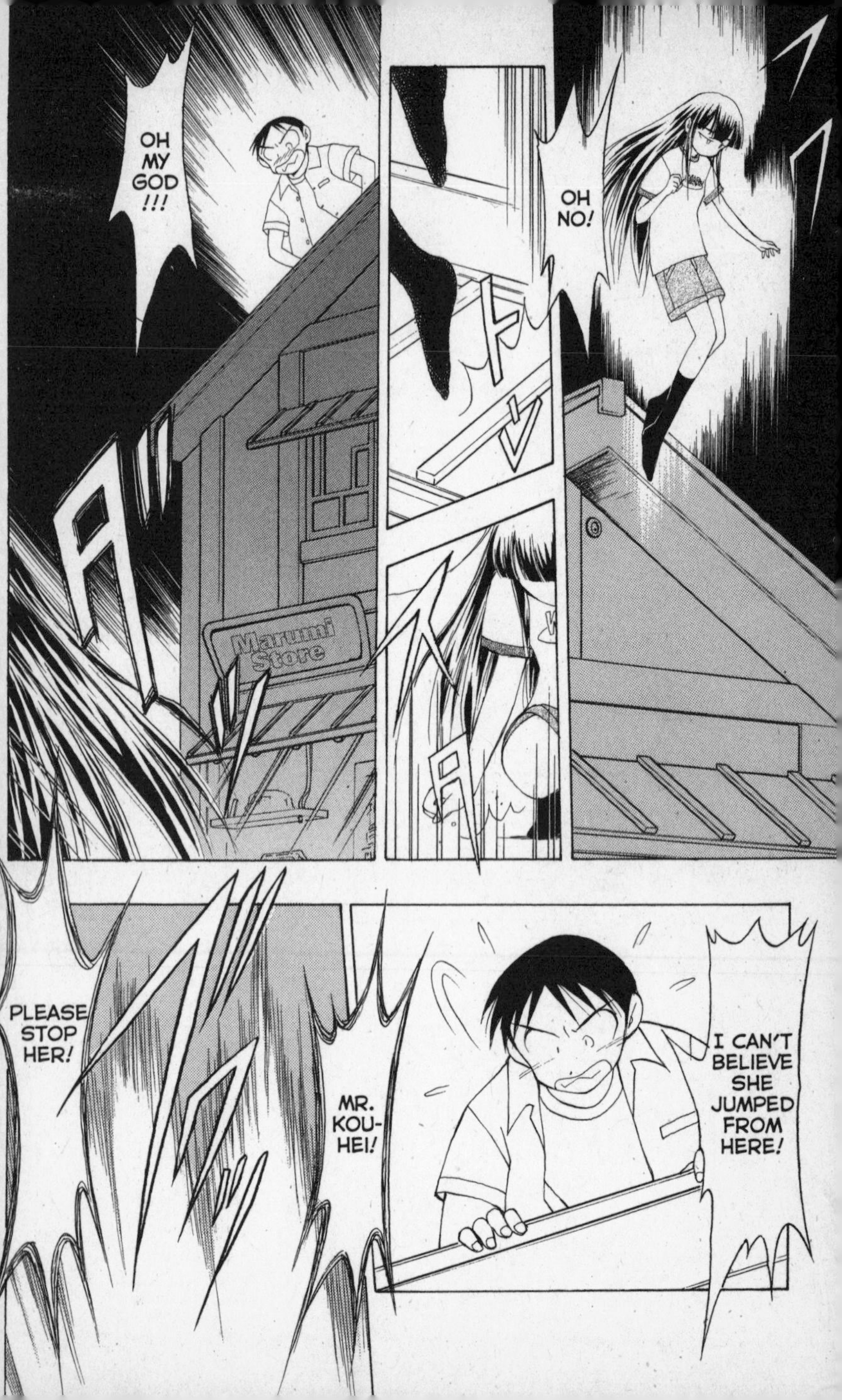
OH NO!
OH MY GOD!!!
Marumi Store
I CAN'T BELIEVE SHE JUMPED FROM HERE!
MR. KOU-HEI!
PLEASE STOP HER!

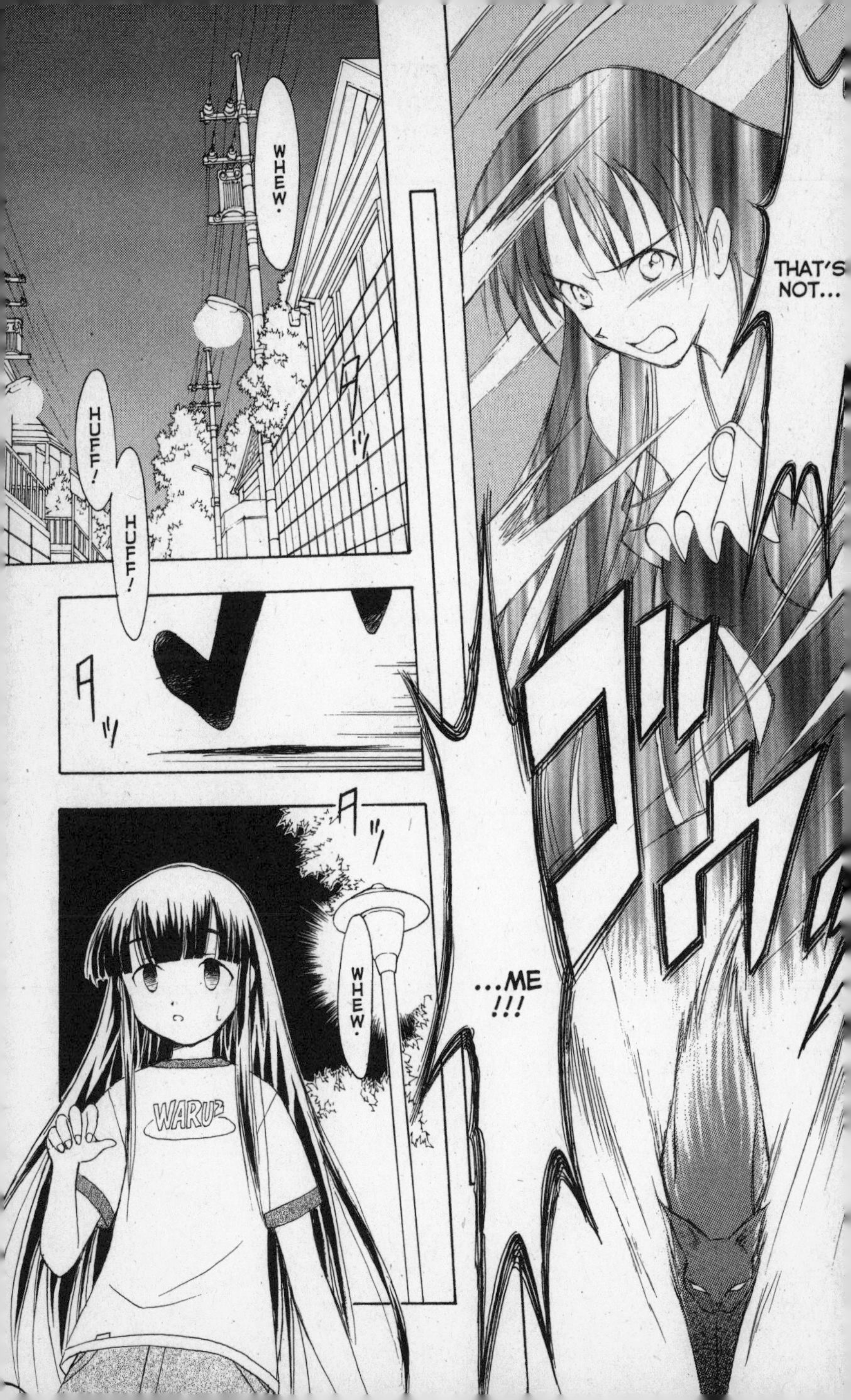
THAT'S NOT...
...ME !!!
WHEW.
HUFF! HUFF!
WHEW.
WARU²

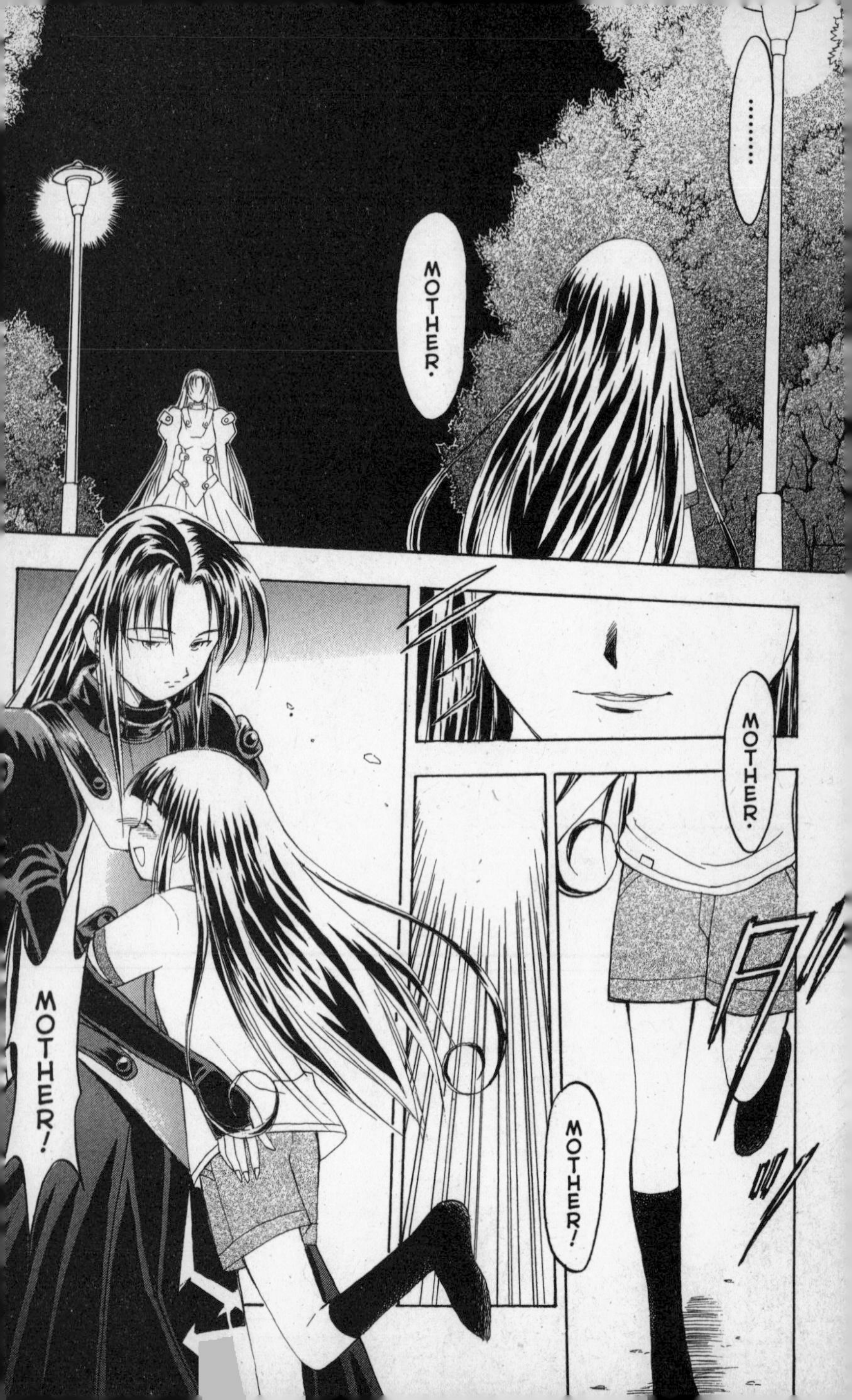

....
MOTHER.
MOTHER.
MOTHER!
MOTHER!

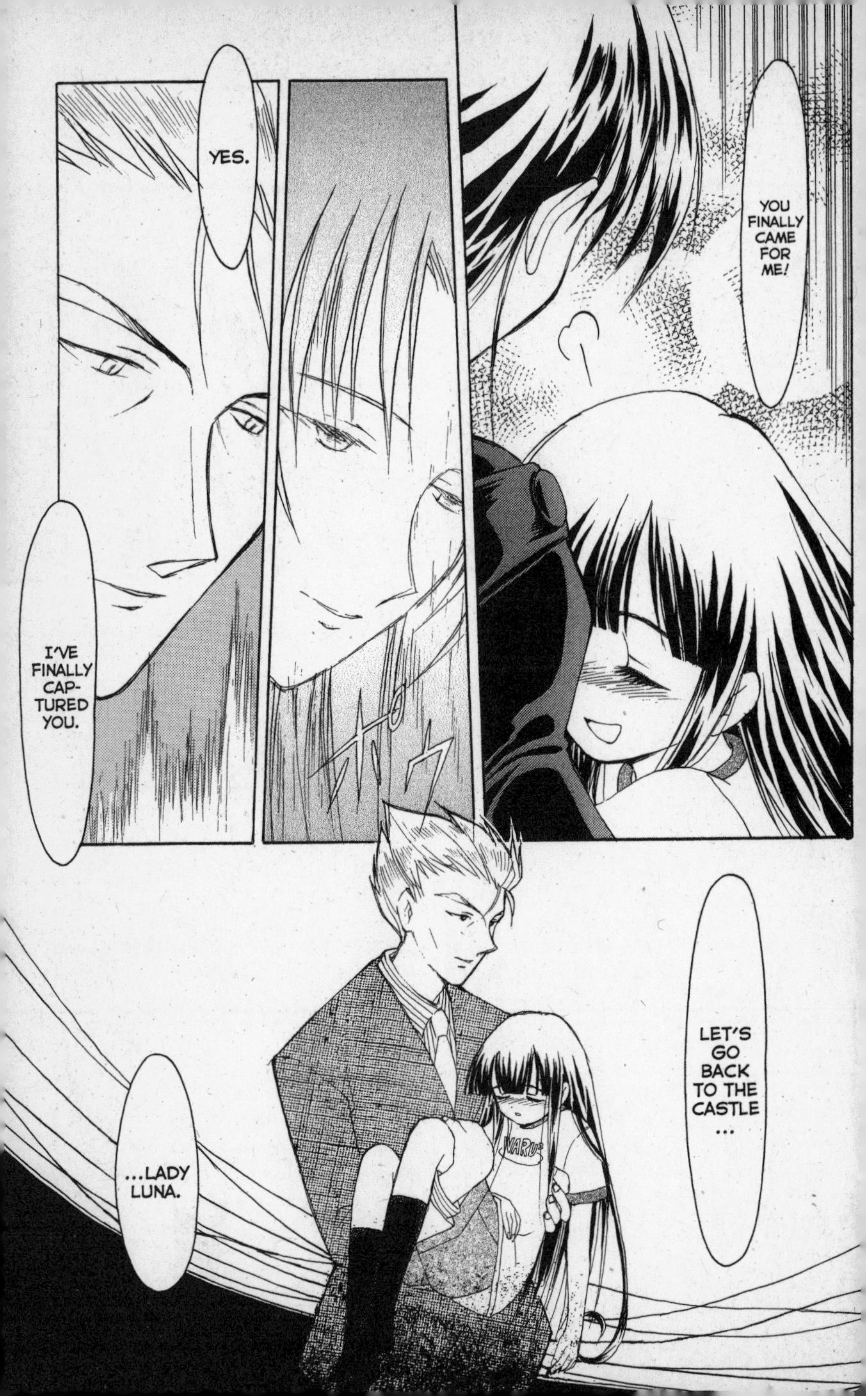
YOU FINALLY CAME FOR ME!
YES.
I'VE FINALLY CAP-TURED YOU.
LET'S GO BACK TO THE CASTLE...
...LADY LUNA.

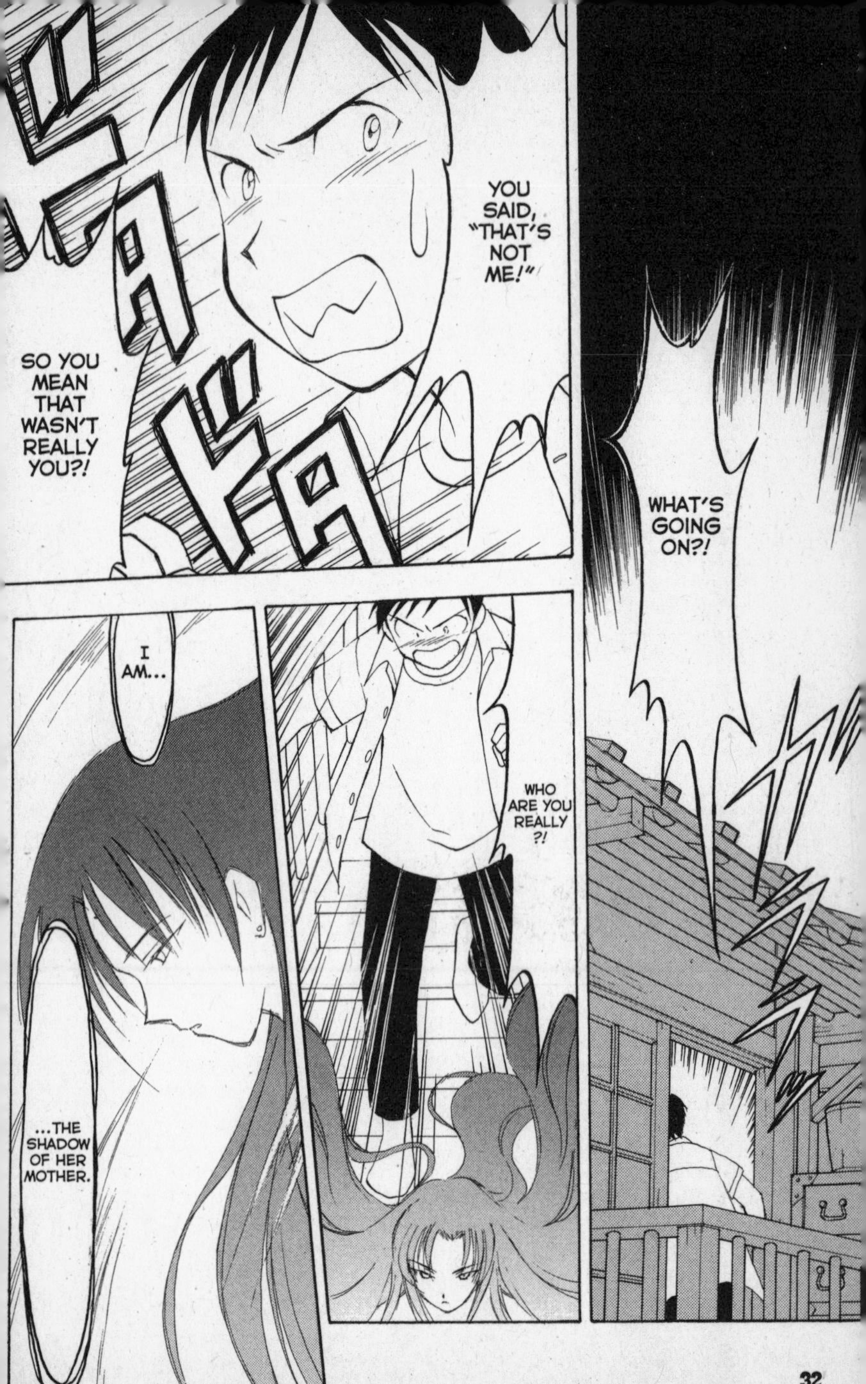
WHAT'S GOING ON?!
YOU SAID, "THAT'S NOT ME!"
SO YOU MEAN THAT WASN'T REALLY YOU?!
WHO ARE YOU REALLY ?!
I AM...
...THE SHADOW OF HER MOTHER.

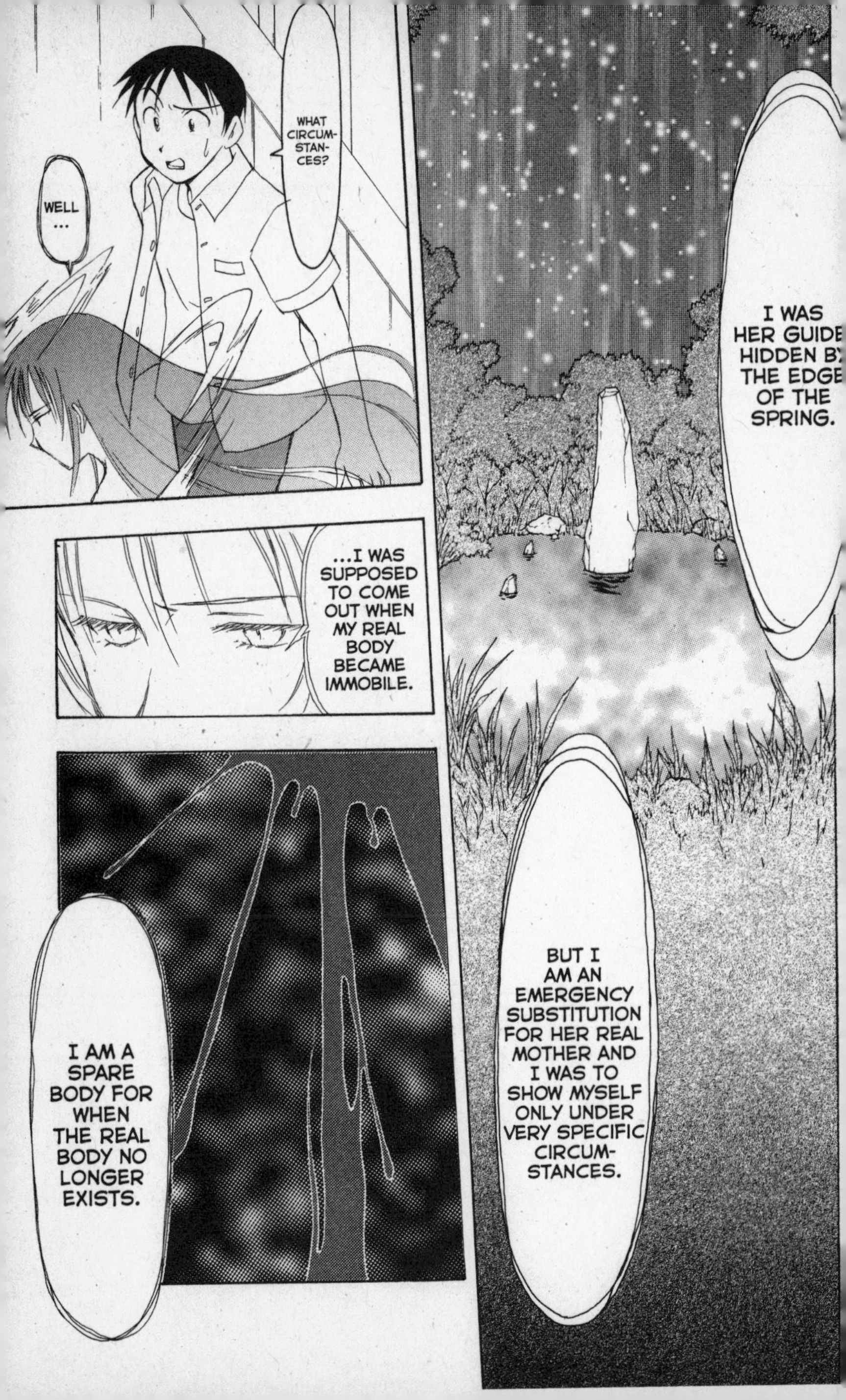
I WAS HER GUIDE HIDDEN BY THE EDGE OF THE SPRING.
BUT I AM AN EMERGENCY SUBSTITUTION FOR HER REAL MOTHER AND I WAS TO SHOW MYSELF ONLY UNDER VERY SPECIFIC CIRCUM-STANCES.
WHAT CIRCUM-STAN-CES?
WELL ...
...I WAS SUPPOSED TO COME OUT WHEN MY REAL BODY BECAME IMMOBILE.
I AM A SPARE BODY FOR WHEN THE REAL BODY NO LONGER EXISTS.

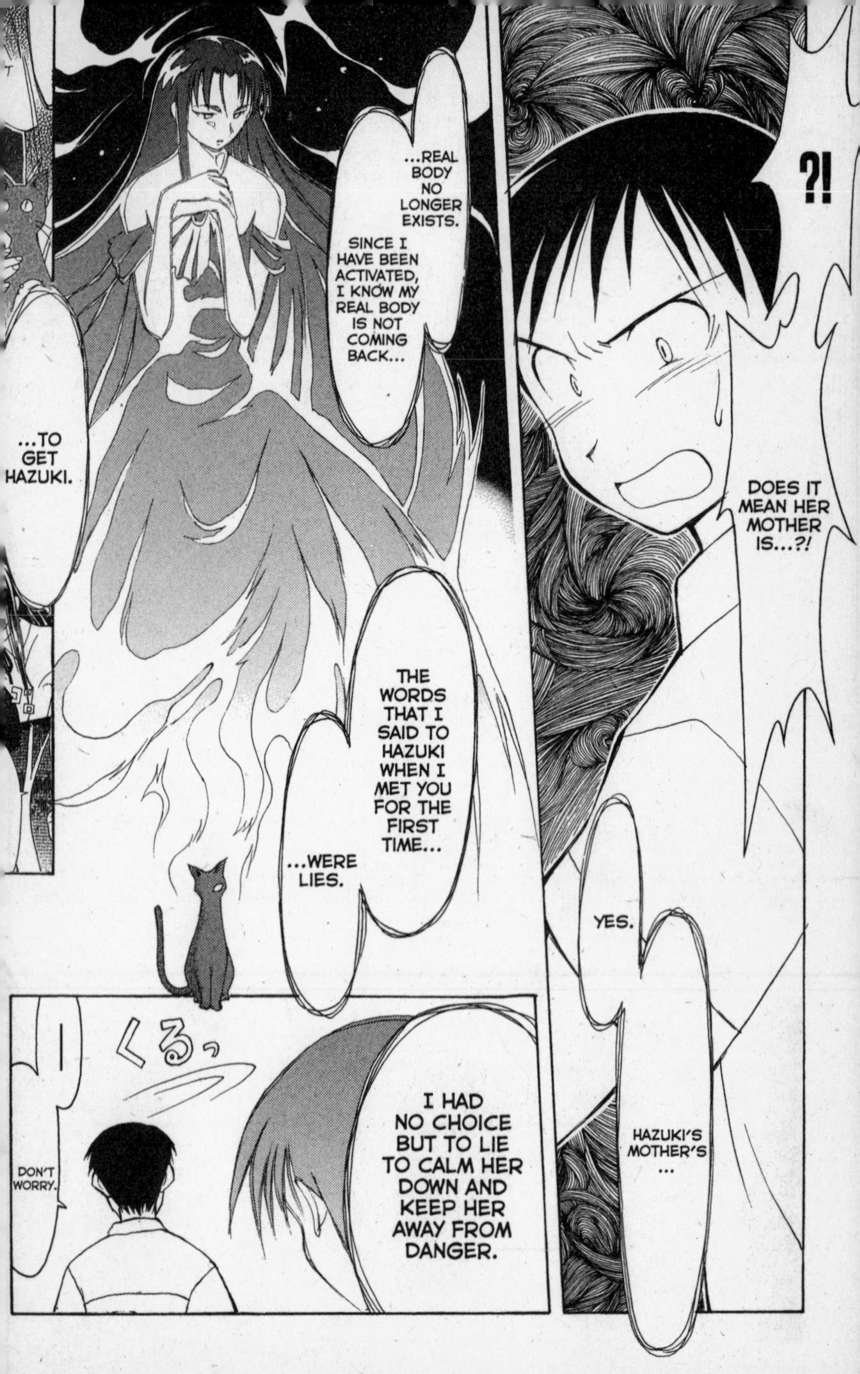
?!
DOES IT MEAN HER MOTHER IS...?!
YES.
HAZUKI'S MOTHER'S ...
...REAL BODY NO LONGER EXISTS.
SINCE I HAVE BEEN ACTIVATED, I KNOW MY REAL BODY IS NOT COMING BACK...
THE WORDS THAT I SAID TO HAZUKI WHEN I MET YOU FOR THE FIRST TIME...
...WERE LIES.
...TO GET HAZUKI.
くるっ
I HAD NO CHOICE BUT TO LIE TO CALM HER DOWN AND KEEP HER AWAY FROM DANGER.
DON'T WORRY.

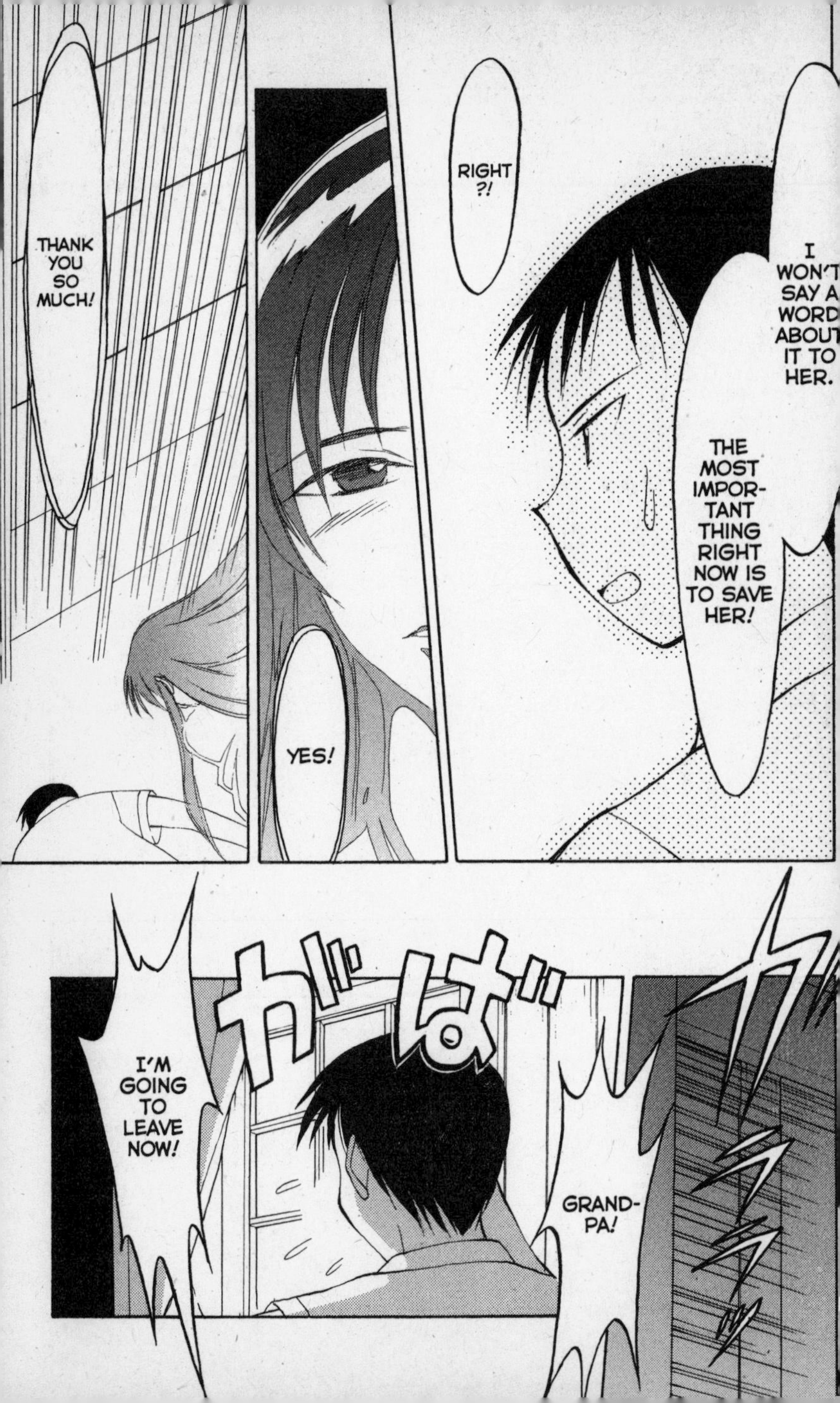

I WON'T SAY A WORD ABOUT IT TO HER.
THE MOST IMPORTANT THING RIGHT NOW IS TO SAVE HER!
RIGHT ?!
YES!
THANK YOU SO MUCH!
GRAND-PA!
がば
I'M GOING TO LEAVE NOW!

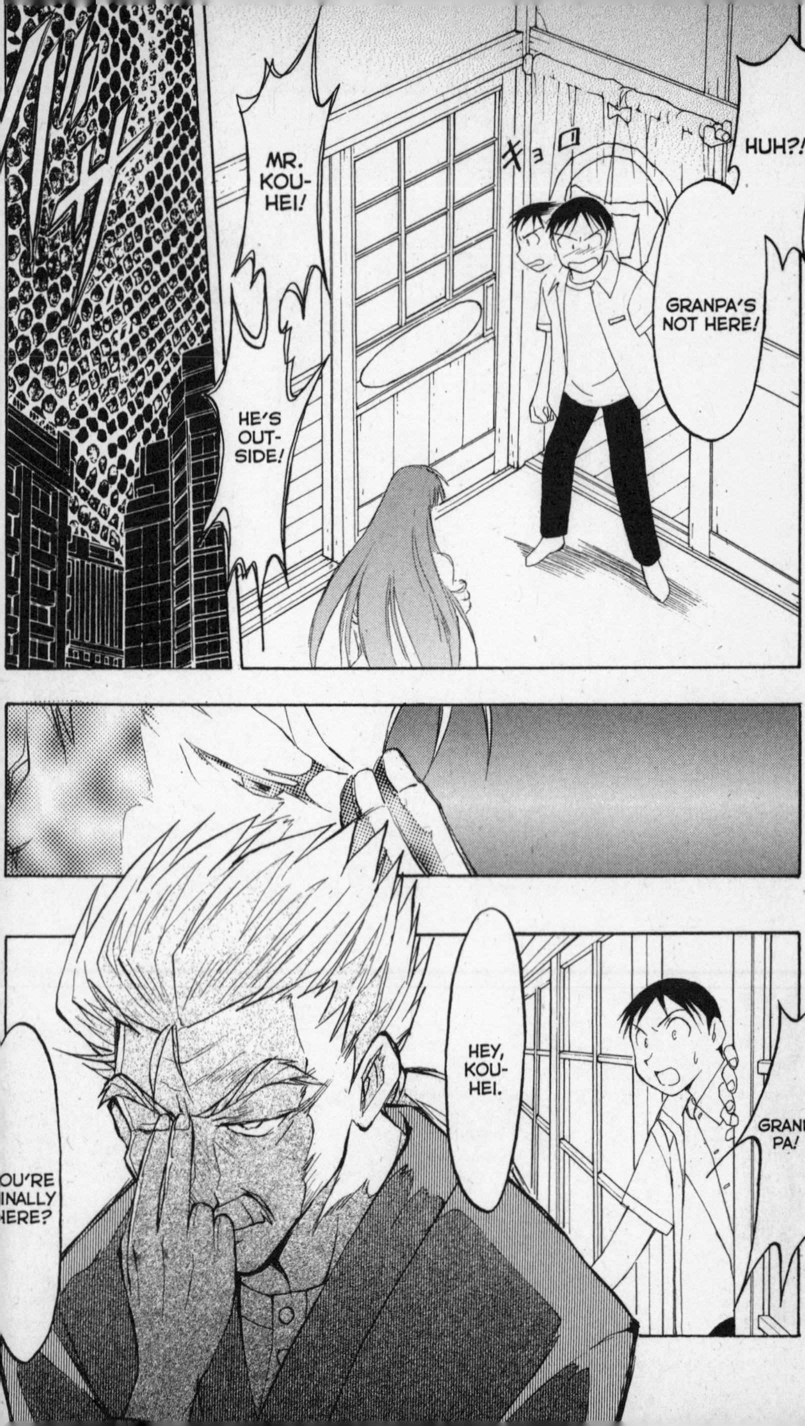
HUH?!
GRANPA'S NOT HERE!
キョロ
MR. KOU-HEI!
HE'S OUT-SIDE!
GRAND PA!
HEY, KOU-HEI.
OU'RE INALLY HERE?

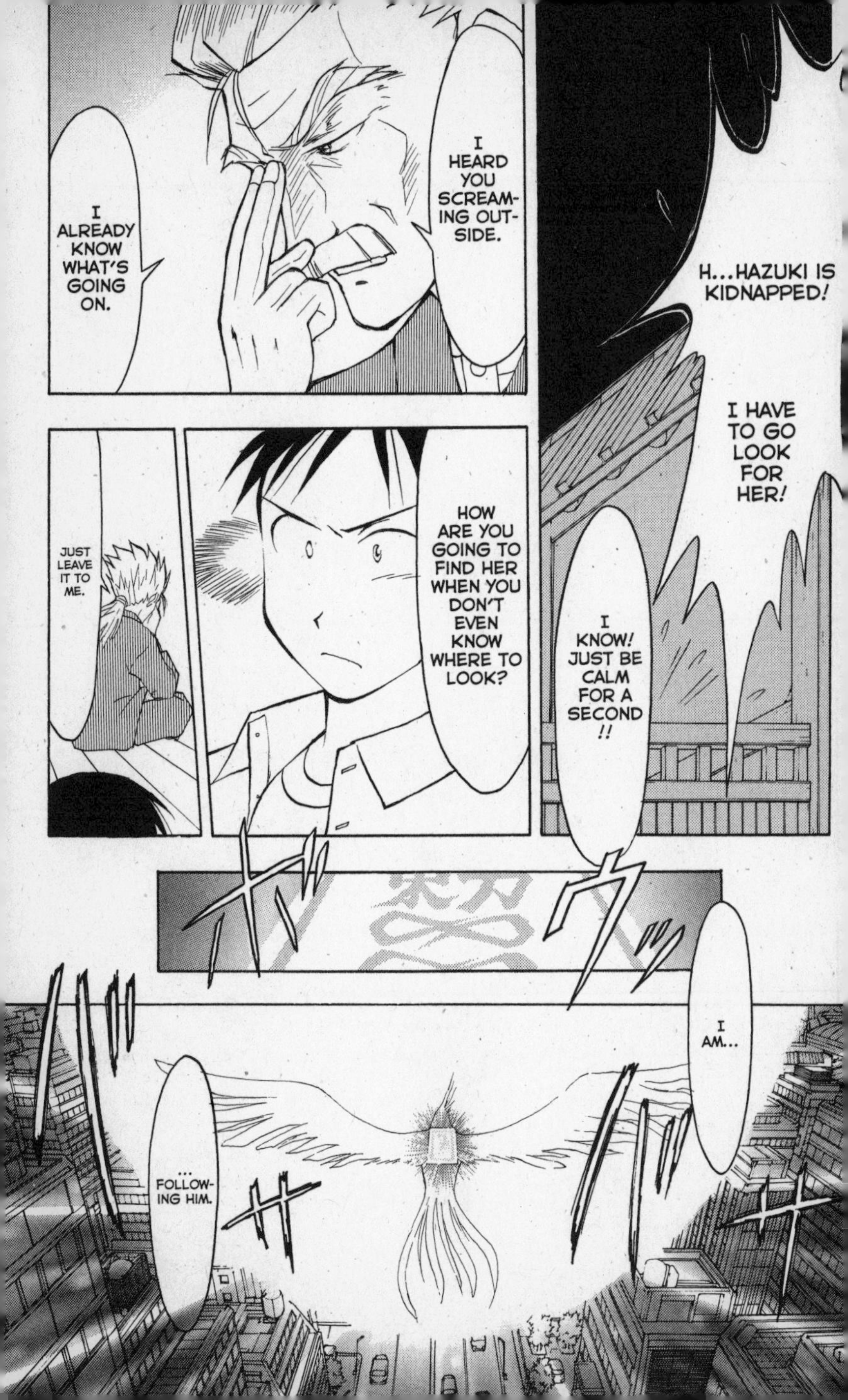
H...HAZUKI IS KIDNAPPED!
I HAVE TO GO LOOK FOR HER!
I KNOW! JUST BE CALM FOR A SECOND!!
I HEARD YOU SCREAMING OUTSIDE.
I ALREADY KNOW WHAT'S GOING ON.
HOW ARE YOU GOING TO FIND HER WHEN YOU DON'T EVEN KNOW WHERE TO LOOK?
JUST LEAVE IT TO ME.
I AM...
...FOLLOWING HIM.

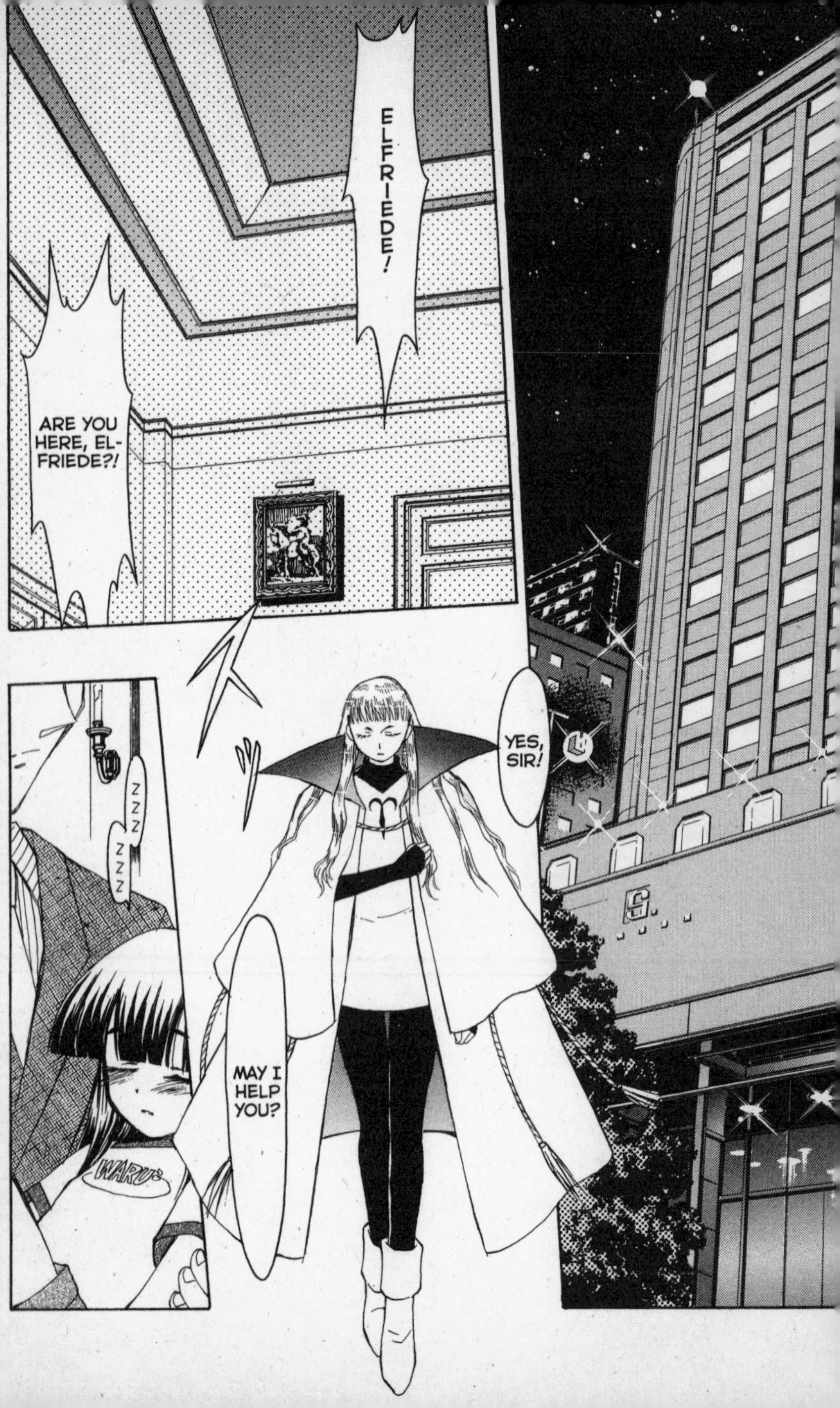
ELFRIEDE!
ARE YOU HERE, EL-FRIEDE?!
YES, SIR!
MAY I HELP YOU?
ZZZ ZZZ
WARU

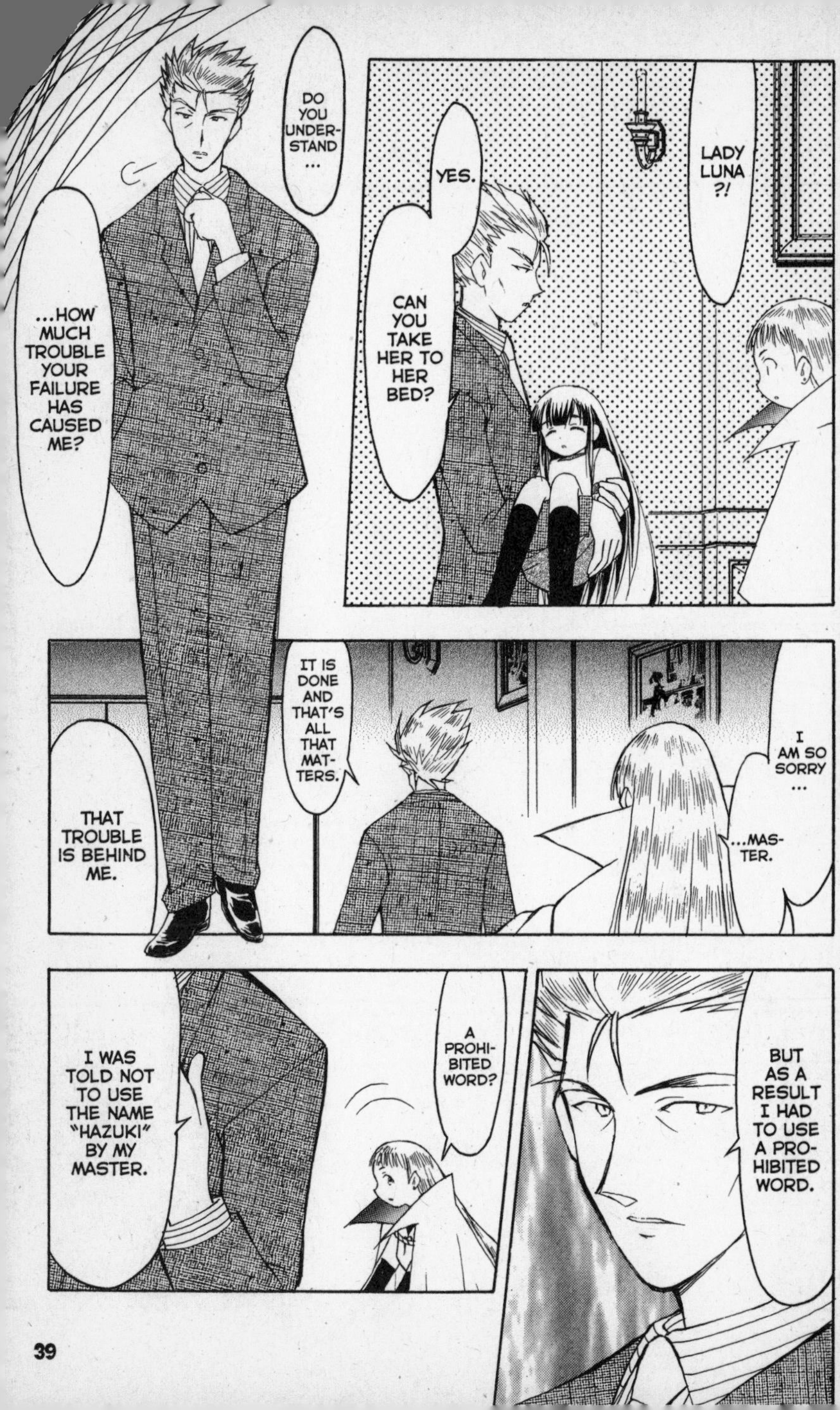
LADY LUNA ?!
YES.
CAN YOU TAKE HER TO HER BED?
DO YOU UNDERSTAND ...
...HOW MUCH TROUBLE YOUR FAILURE HAS CAUSED ME?
I AM SO SORRY ...
...MASTER.
IT IS DONE AND THAT'S ALL THAT MATTERS.
THAT TROUBLE IS BEHIND ME.
BUT AS A RESULT I HAD TO USE A PROHIBITED WORD.
A PROHIBITED WORD?
I WAS TOLD NOT TO USE THE NAME "HAZUKI" BY MY MASTER.

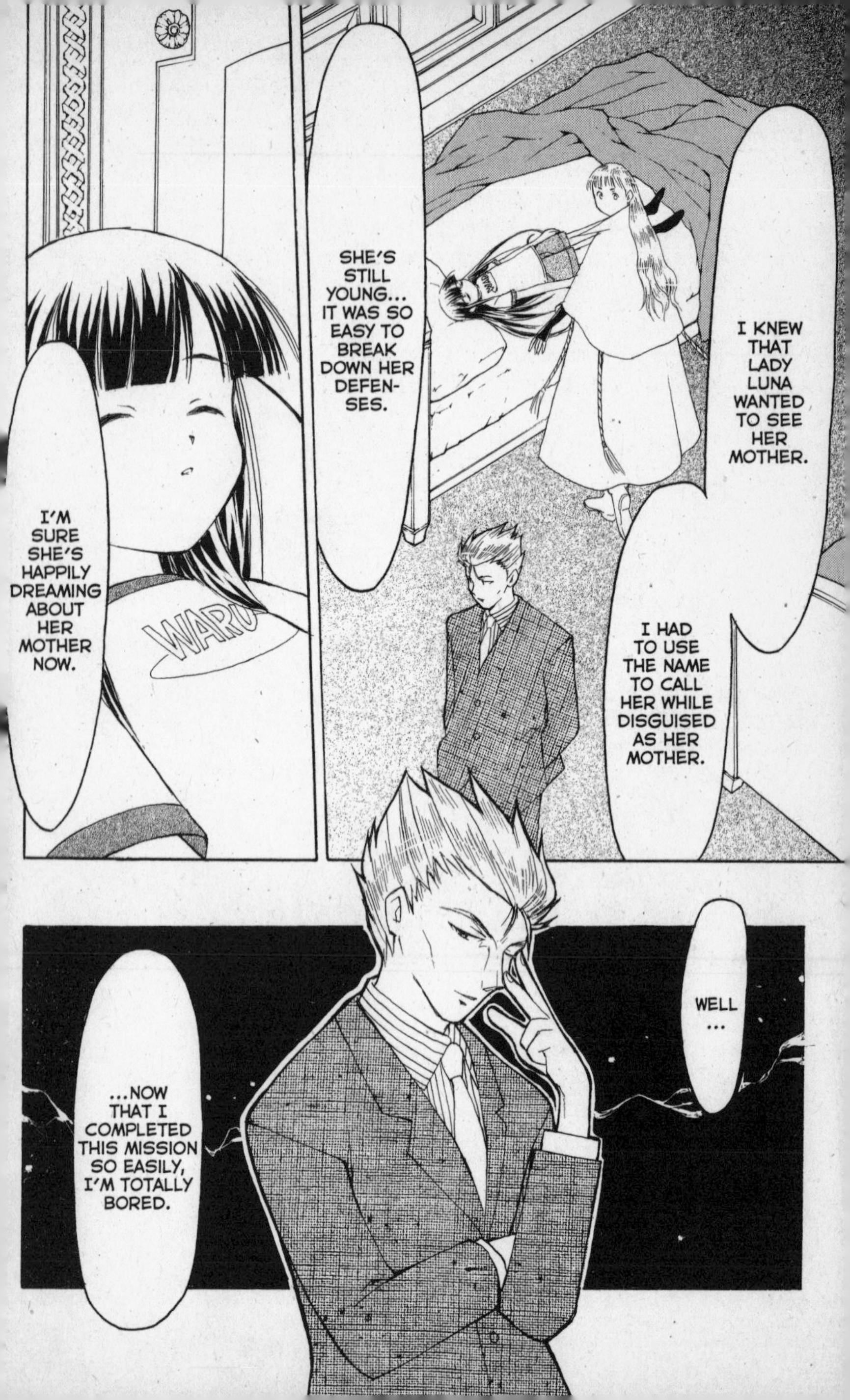
I KNEW THAT LADY LUNA WANTED TO SEE HER MOTHER.
I HAD TO USE THE NAME TO CALL HER WHILE DISGUISED AS HER MOTHER.
SHE'S STILL YOUNG... IT WAS SO EASY TO BREAK DOWN HER DEFEN-SES.
I'M SURE SHE'S HAPPILY DREAMING ABOUT HER MOTHER NOW.
WARU
WELL...
...NOW THAT I COMPLETED THIS MISSION SO EASILY, I'M TOTALLY BORED.

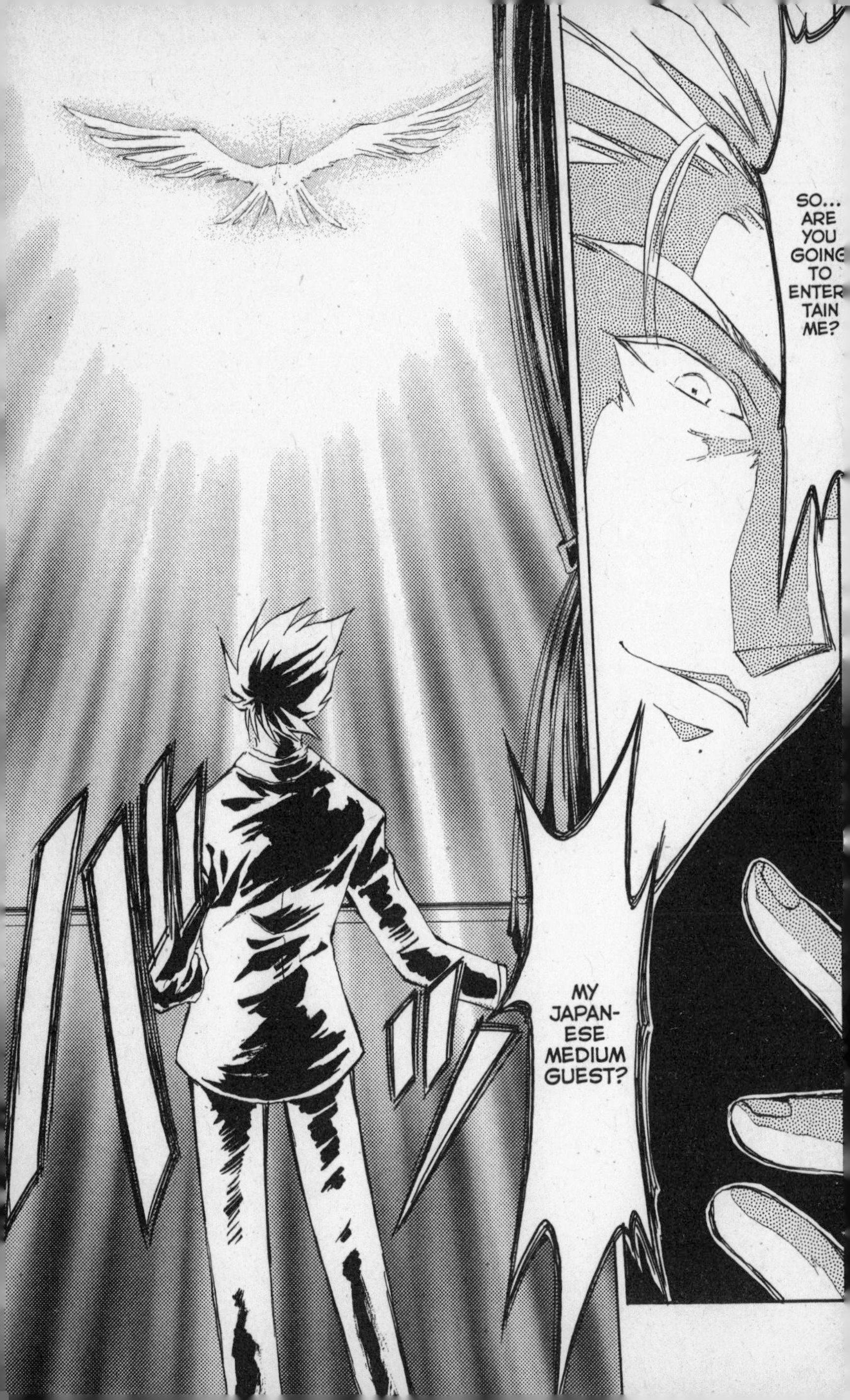
SO... ARE YOU GOING TO ENTERTAIN ME?
MY JAPANESE MEDIUM GUEST?

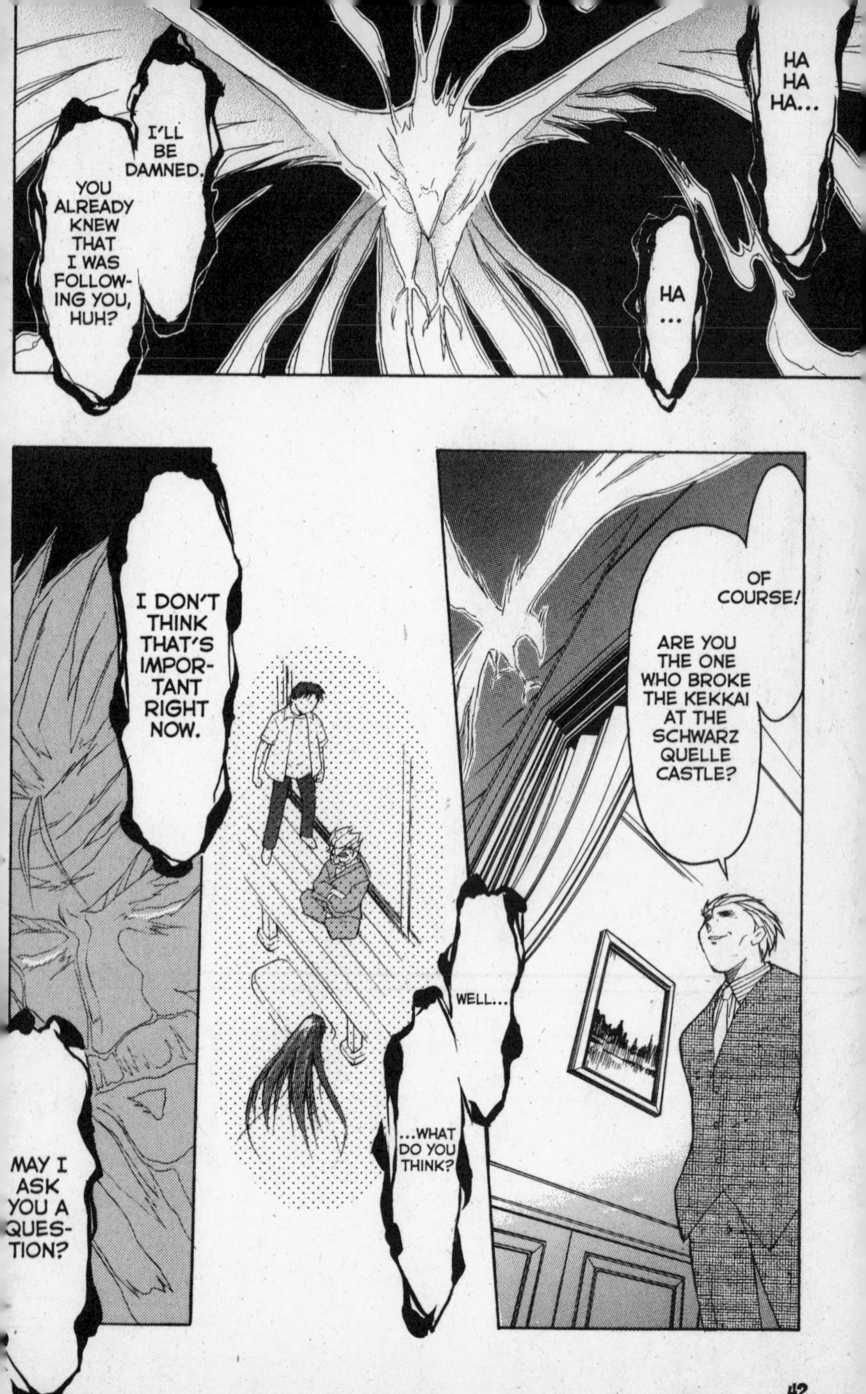
HA HA HA...
HA ...
I'LL BE DAMNED.
YOU ALREADY KNEW THAT I WAS FOLLOWING YOU, HUH?
OF COURSE!
ARE YOU THE ONE WHO BROKE THE KEKKAI AT THE SCHWARZ QUELLE CASTLE?
WELL...
...WHAT DO YOU THINK?
I DON'T THINK THAT'S IMPORTANT RIGHT NOW.
MAY I ASK YOU A QUESTION?

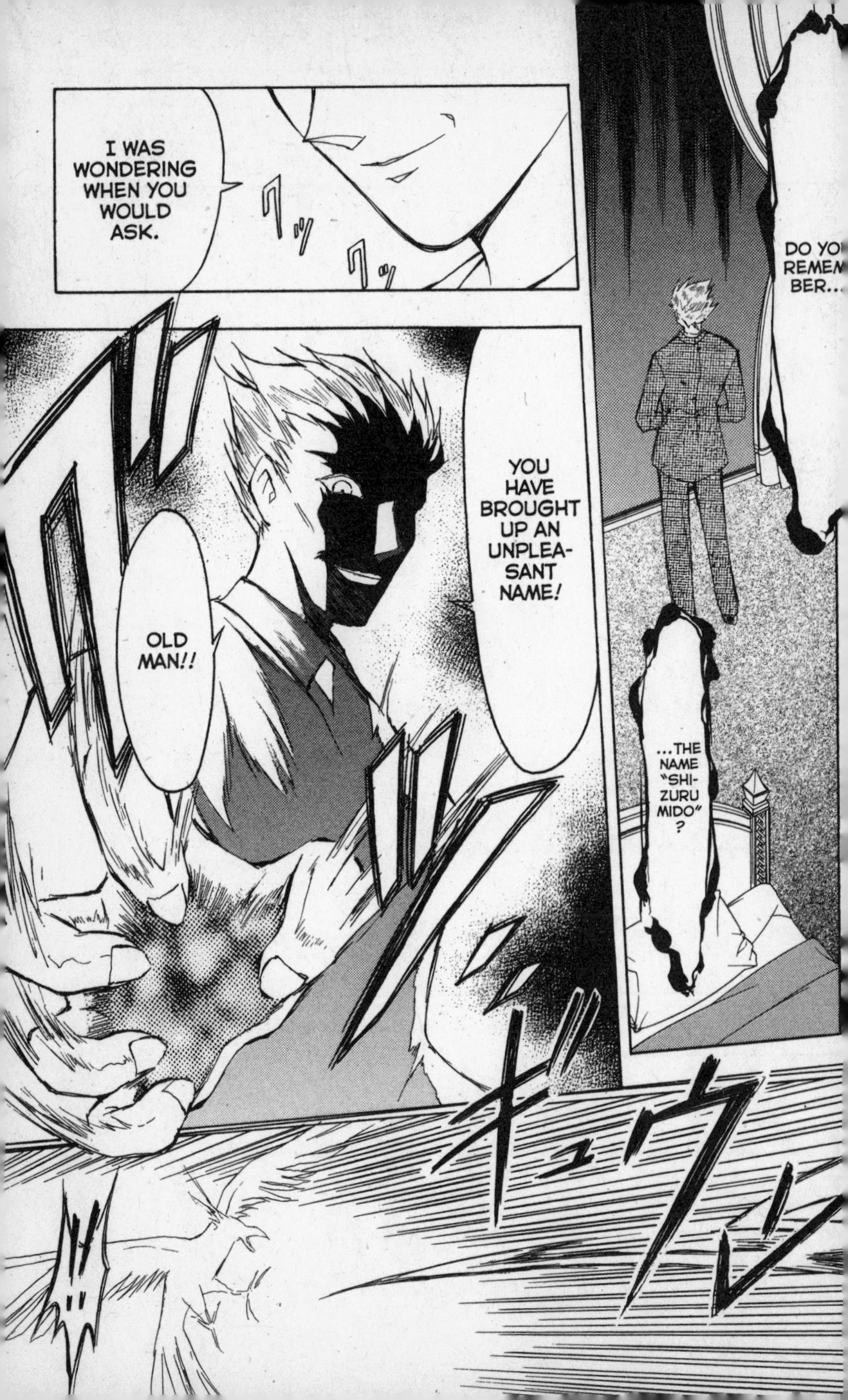
DO YOU REMEMBER...
...THE NAME "SHIZURU MIDO"?
I WAS WONDERING WHEN YOU WOULD ASK.
YOU HAVE BROUGHT UP AN UNPLEASANT NAME!
OLD MAN!!

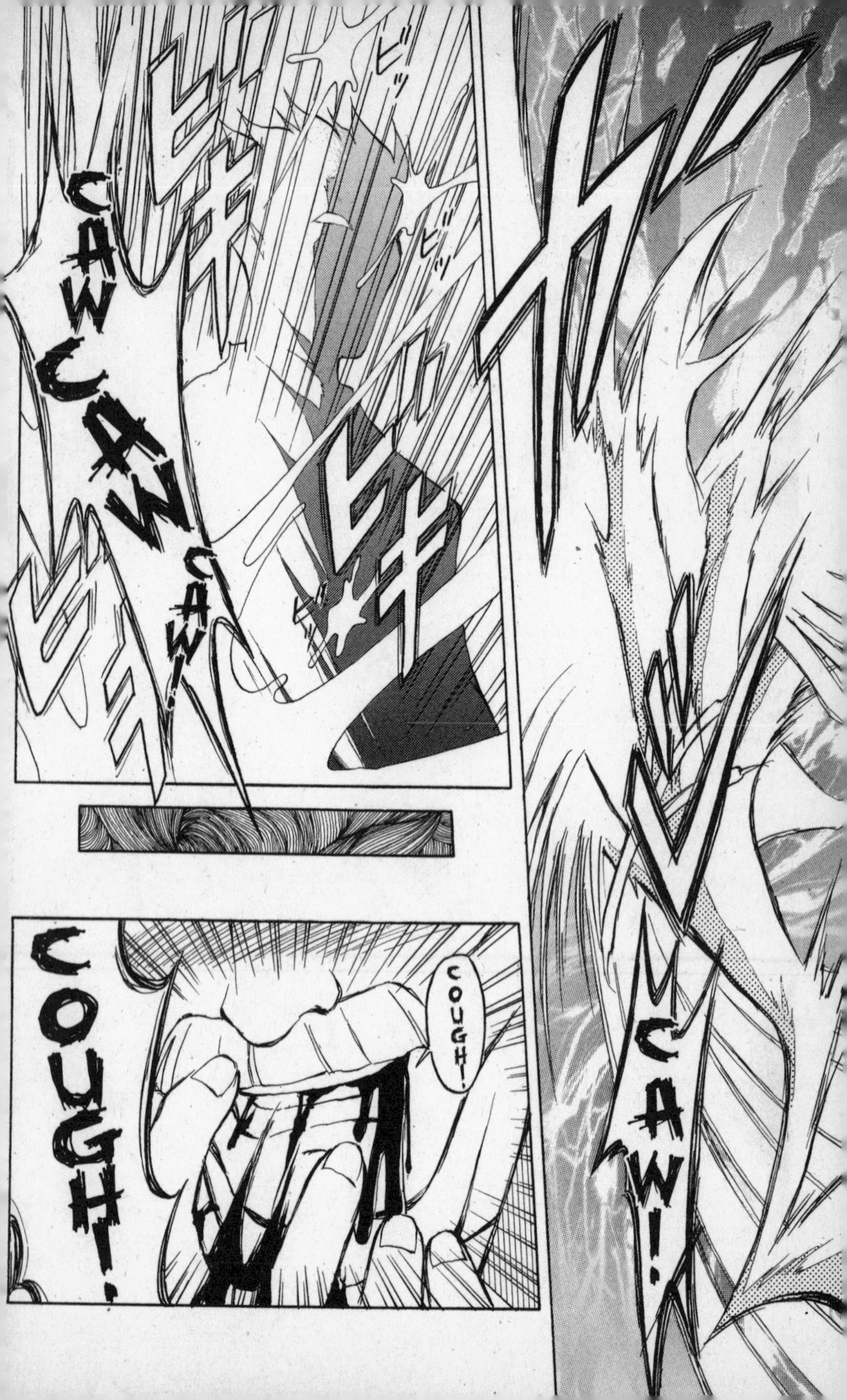
CAW!
ビッ
ビッ
CAW CAW
CAW CAW!
COUGH!
COUGH COUGH!

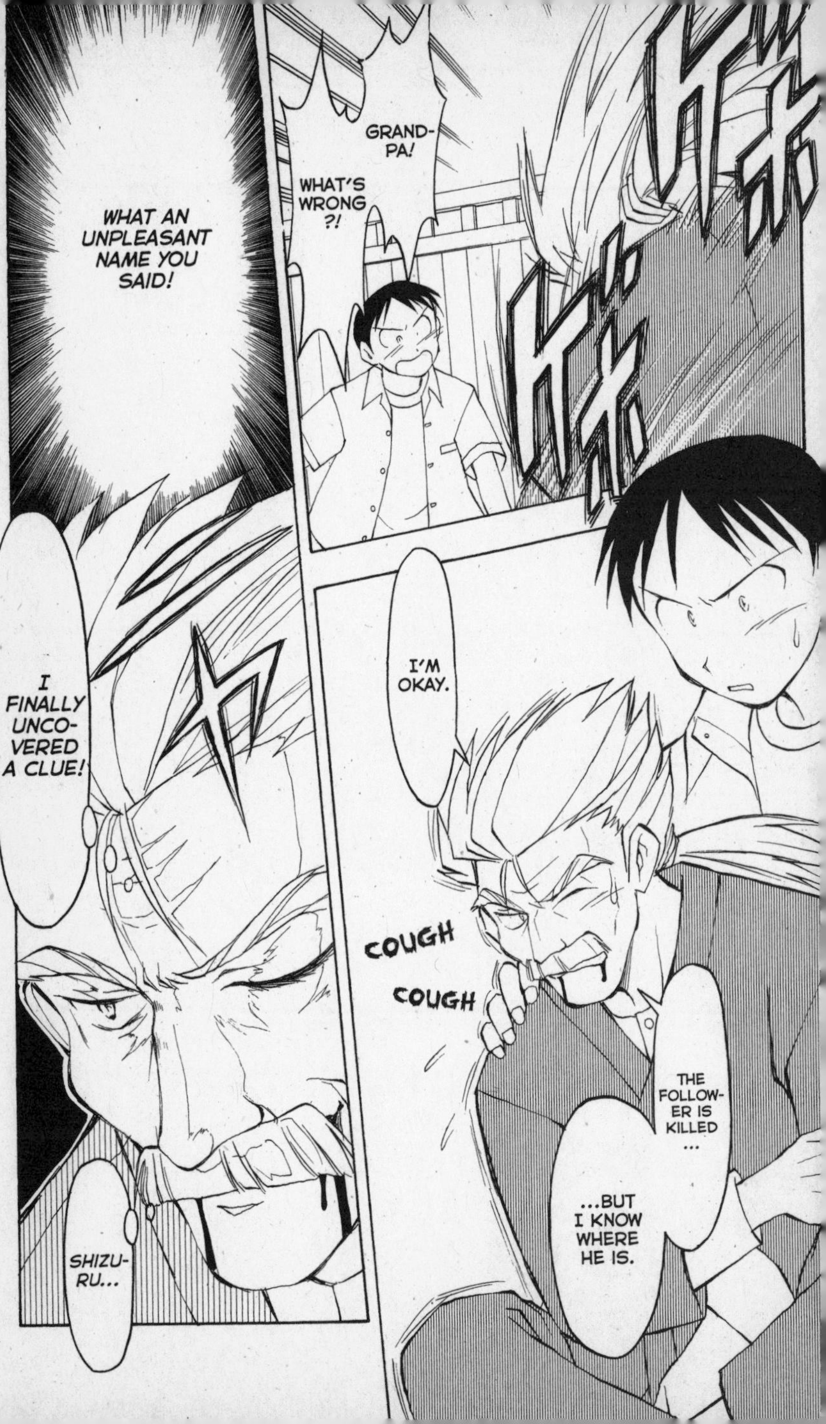
GRAND-PA!
WHAT'S WRONG ?!
I'M OKAY.
COUGH
COUGH
THE FOLLOWER IS KILLED ...
...BUT I KNOW WHERE HE IS.
WHAT AN UNPLEASANT NAME YOU SAID!
I FINALLY UNCOVERED A CLUE!
SHIZURU...

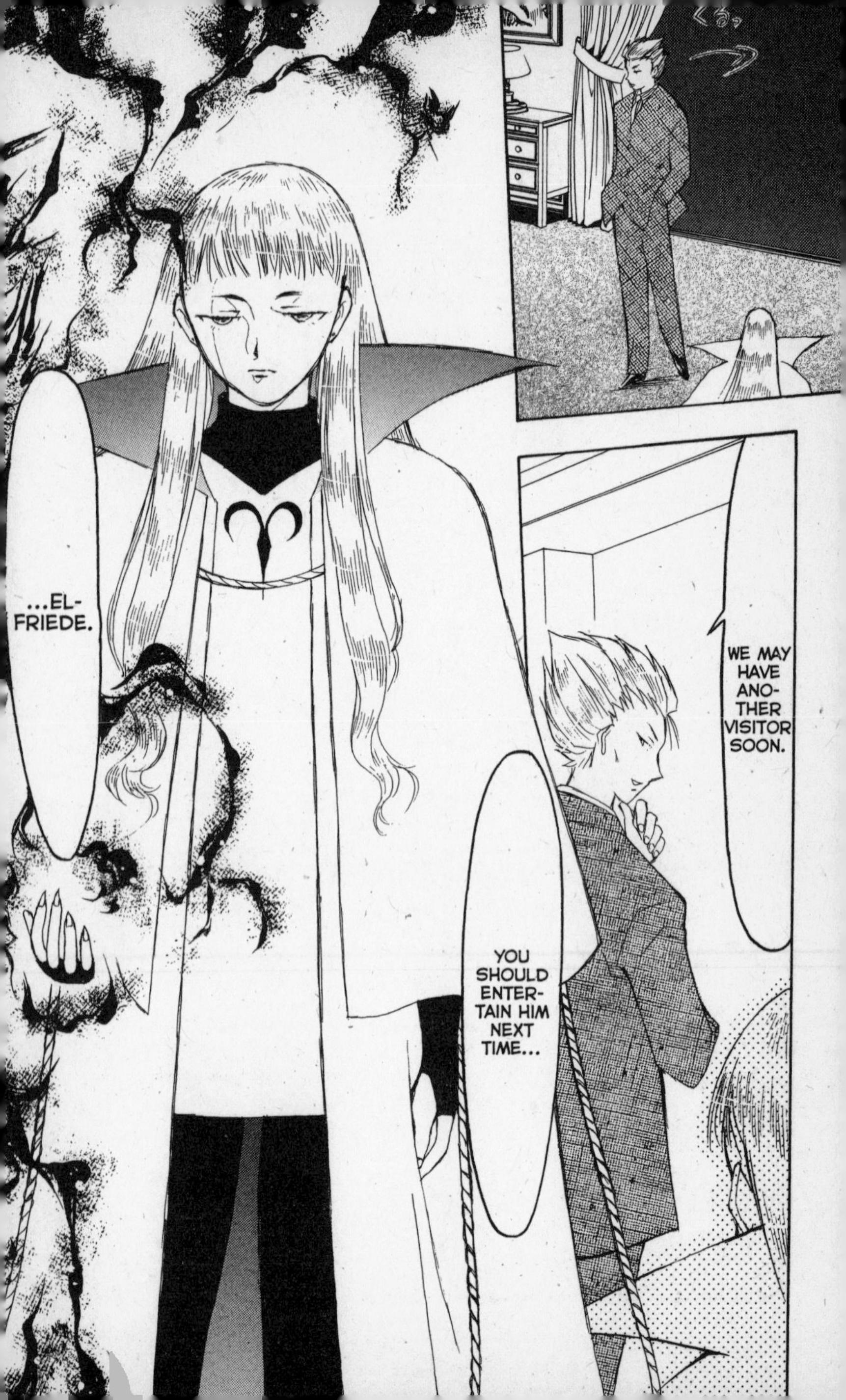
くるっ
WE MAY HAVE ANOTHER VISITOR SOON.
YOU SHOULD ENTERTAIN HIM NEXT TIME...
...ELFRIEDE.

JUST BECAUSE HAZUKI IS A
VAMPIRE DOESN'T MEAN SHE'S
100 YEARS OLD.

SHE'S A REGULAR JUNIOR
HIGH SCHOOL GIRL, ABOUT 12
OR 13 YEARS OLD.

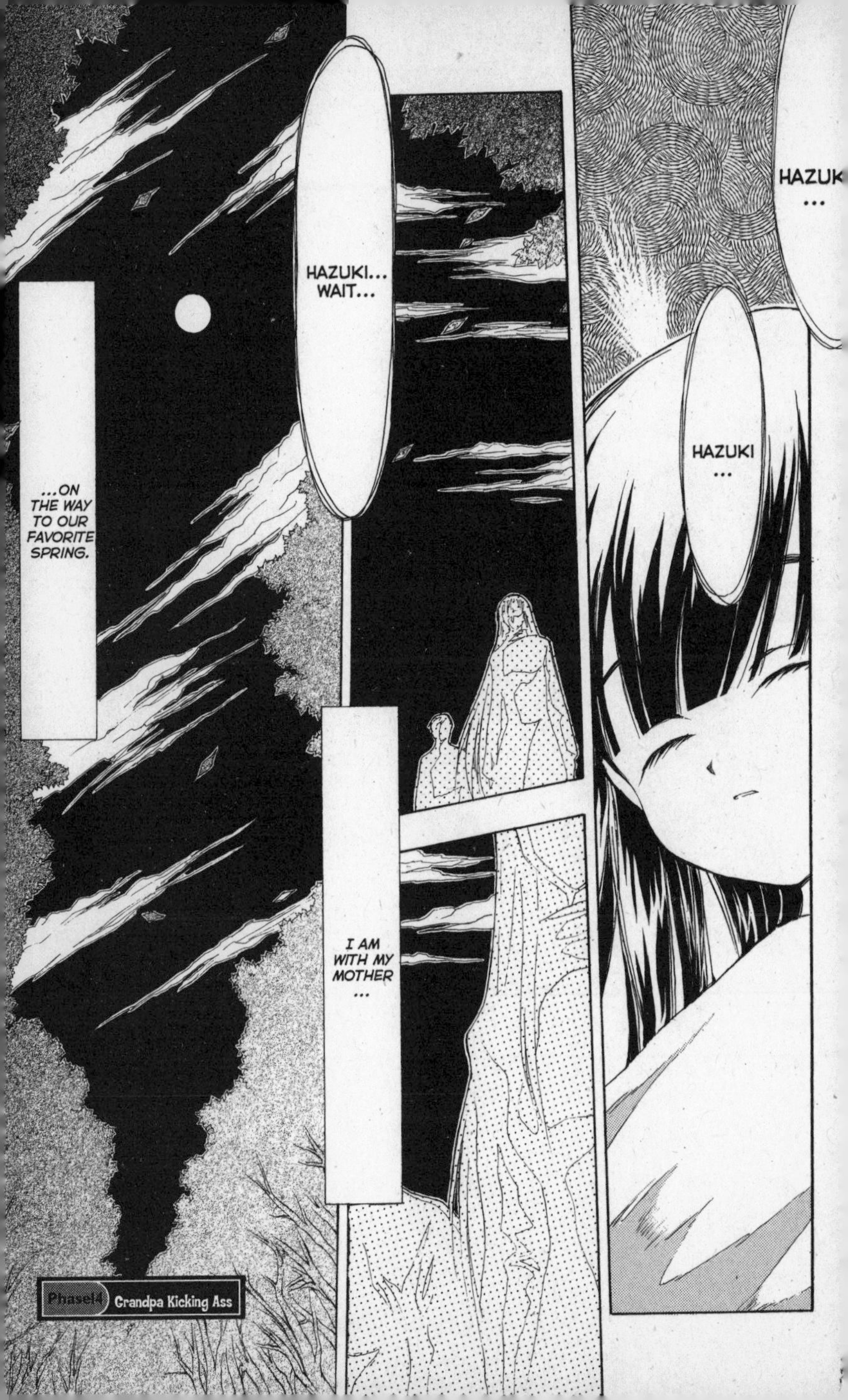
HAZUK ...
HAZUKI ...
HAZUKI... WAIT...
I AM WITH MY MOTHER ...
...ON THE WAY TO OUR FAVORITE SPRING.
Phase14 Grandpa Kicking Ass

Phase14 Grandpa Kicking Ass

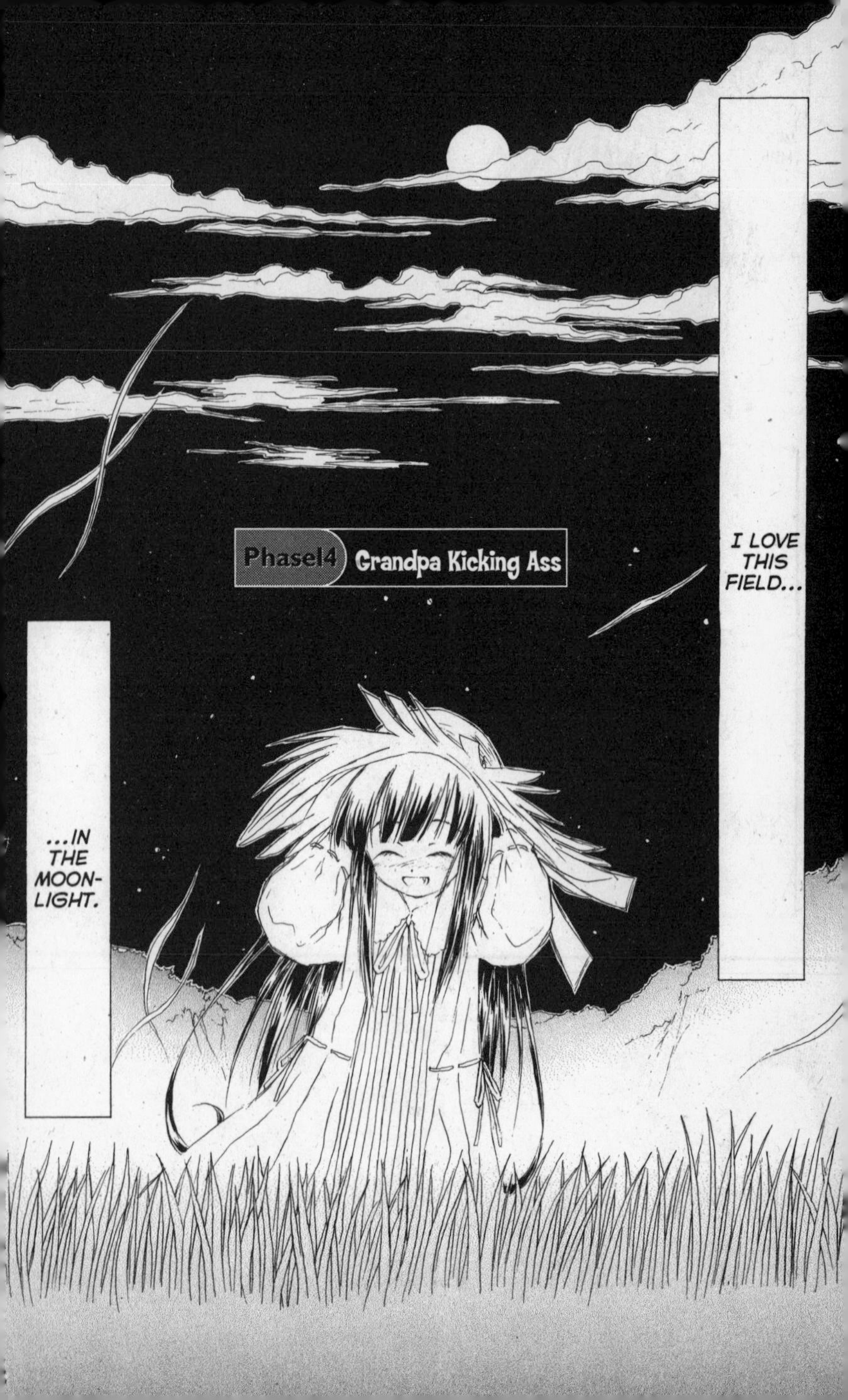

I LOVE THIS FIELD...
...IN THE MOON-LIGHT.

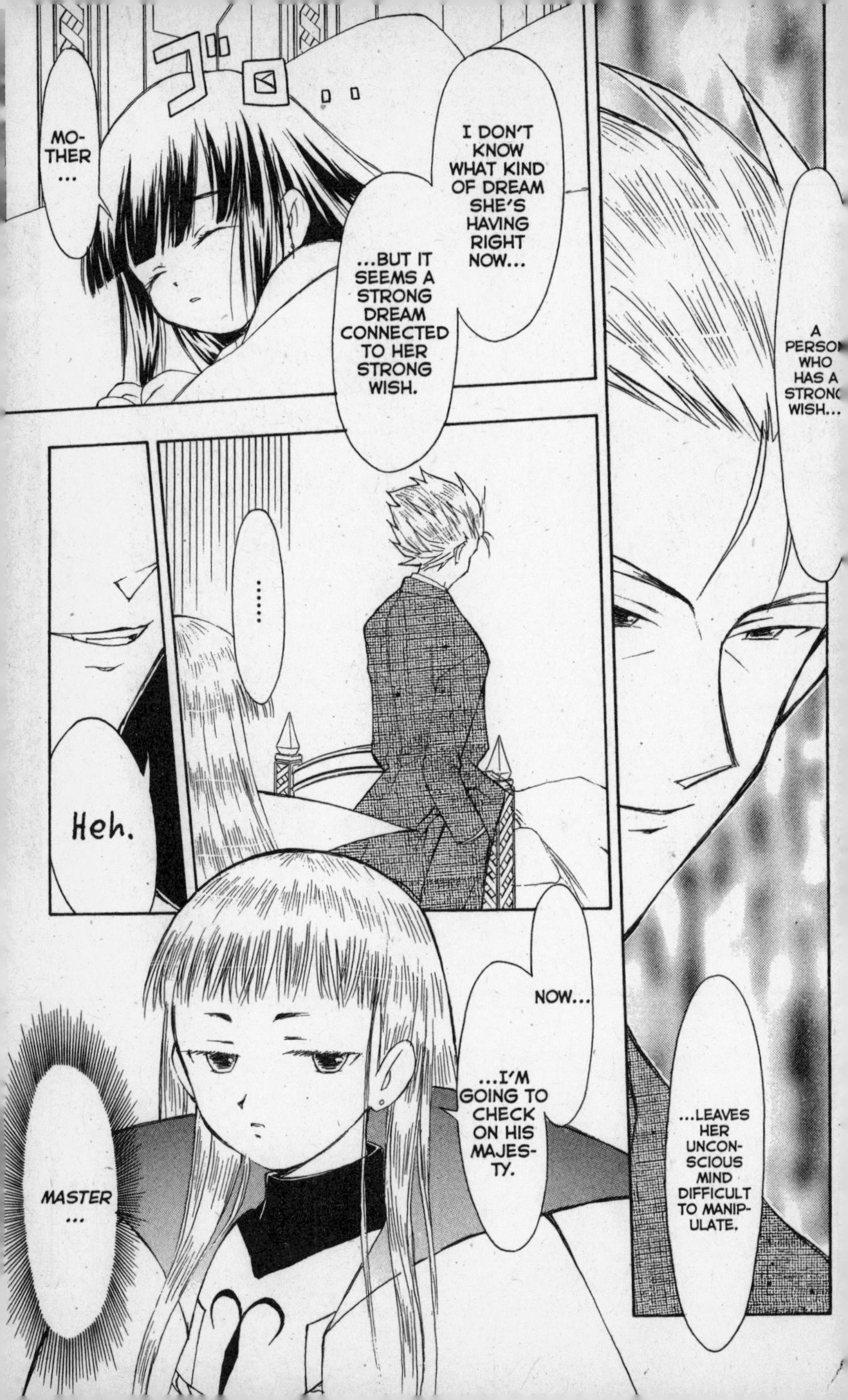
ゴロ
MO-THER...
I DON'T KNOW WHAT KIND OF DREAM SHE'S HAVING RIGHT NOW...
...BUT IT SEEMS A STRONG DREAM CONNECTED TO HER STRONG WISH.
A PERSON WHO HAS A STRONG WISH...
...LEAVES HER UNCON-SCIOUS MIND DIFFICULT TO MANIP-ULATE.
......
Heh.
NOW...
...I'M GOING TO CHECK ON HIS MAJES-TY.
MASTER...

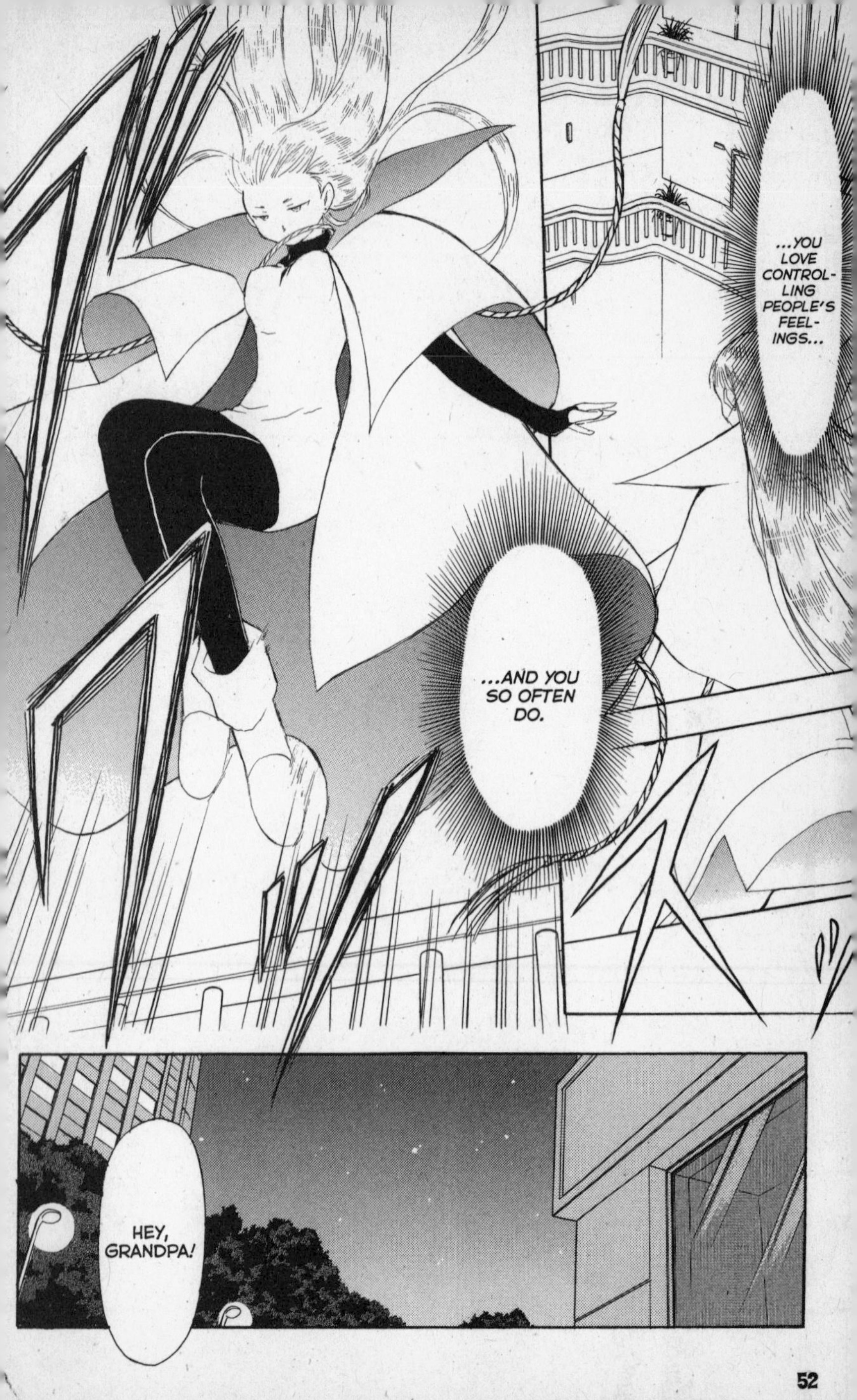
...YOU LOVE CONTROLLING PEOPLE'S FEELINGS...
...AND YOU SO OFTEN DO.
HEY, GRANDPA!

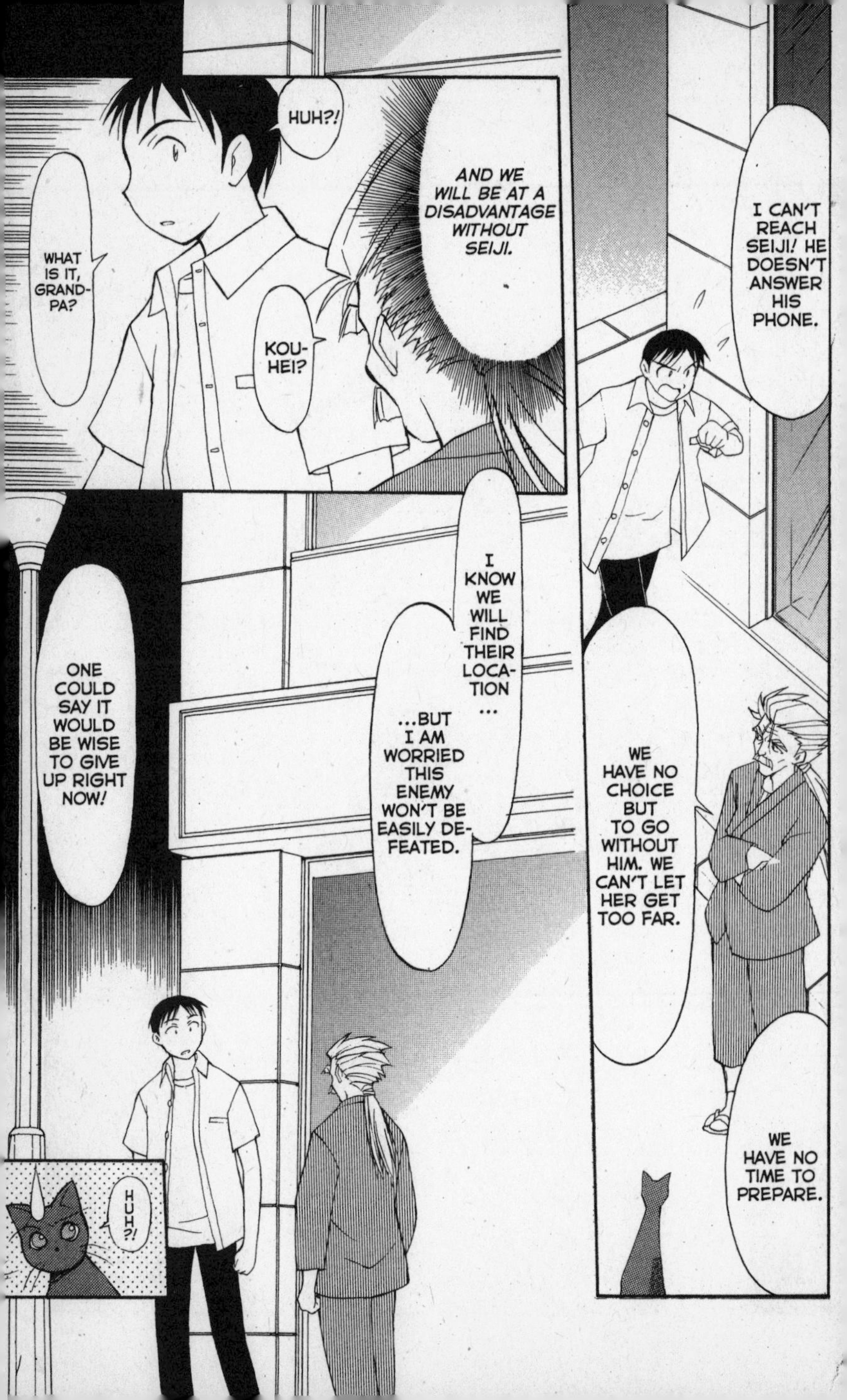
I CAN'T REACH SEIJI! HE DOESN'T ANSWER HIS PHONE.
WE HAVE NO CHOICE BUT TO GO WITHOUT HIM. WE CAN'T LET HER GET TOO FAR.
WE HAVE NO TIME TO PREPARE.
AND WE WILL BE AT A DISADVANTAGE WITHOUT SEIJI.
HUH?!
KOU-HEI?
WHAT IS IT, GRAND-PA?
I KNOW WE WILL FIND THEIR LOCA-TION ...
...BUT I AM WORRIED THIS ENEMY WON'T BE EASILY DE-FEATED.
ONE COULD SAY IT WOULD BE WISE TO GIVE UP RIGHT NOW!
HUH?!

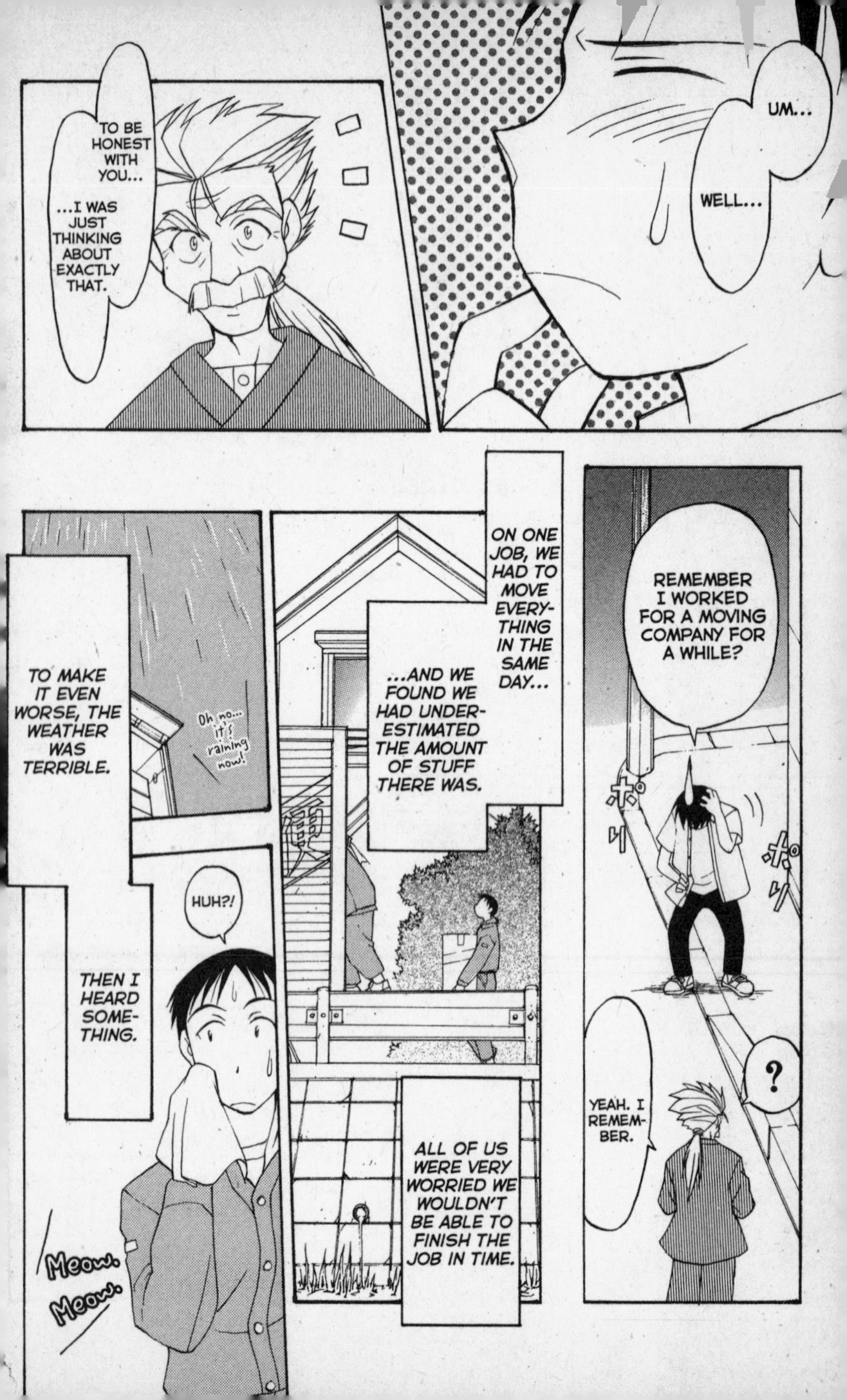
UM...
WELL...
TO BE HONEST WITH YOU...
...I WAS JUST THINKING ABOUT EXACTLY THAT.
REMEMBER I WORKED FOR A MOVING COMPANY FOR A WHILE?
?
YEAH. I REMEMBER.
ON ONE JOB, WE HAD TO MOVE EVERYTHING IN THE SAME DAY...
...AND WE FOUND WE HAD UNDER-ESTIMATED THE AMOUNT OF STUFF THERE WAS.
ALL OF US WERE VERY WORRIED WE WOULDN'T BE ABLE TO FINISH THE JOB IN TIME.
TO MAKE IT EVEN WORSE, THE WEATHER WAS TERRIBLE.
Oh no... it's raining now!
HUH?!
THEN I HEARD SOMETHING.
Meow.
Meow.

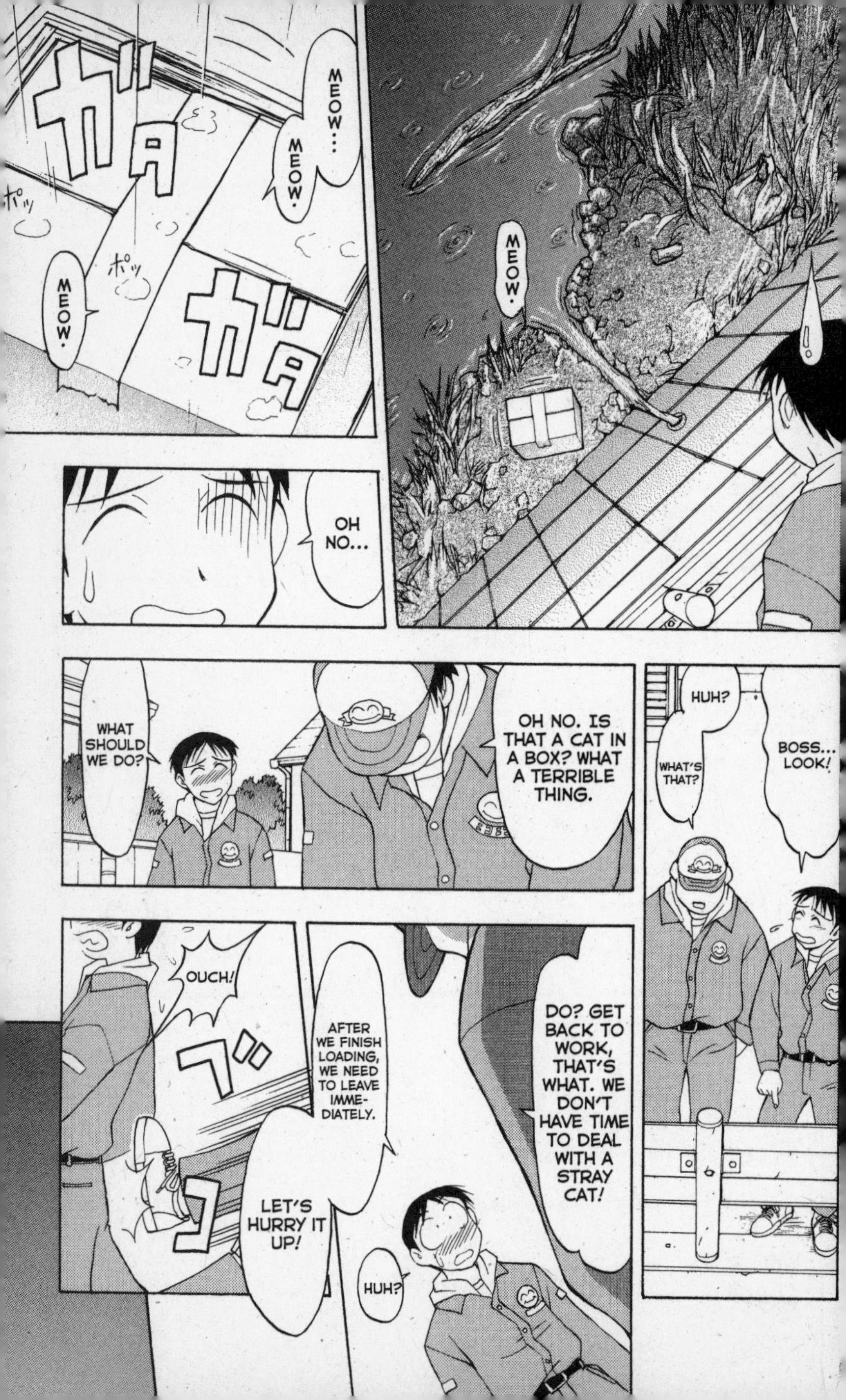
MEOW.
MEOW...
MEOW.
ガタ
ガタ
ポッ
ポッ
MEOW.
OH NO...
BOSS... LOOK!
HUH?
WHAT'S THAT?
OH NO. IS THAT A CAT IN A BOX? WHAT A TERRIBLE THING.
WHAT SHOULD WE DO?
DO? GET BACK TO WORK, THAT'S WHAT. WE DON'T HAVE TIME TO DEAL WITH A STRAY CAT!
AFTER WE FINISH LOADING, WE NEED TO LEAVE IMME-DIATELY.
LET'S HURRY IT UP!
HUH?
OUCH!
ベコ

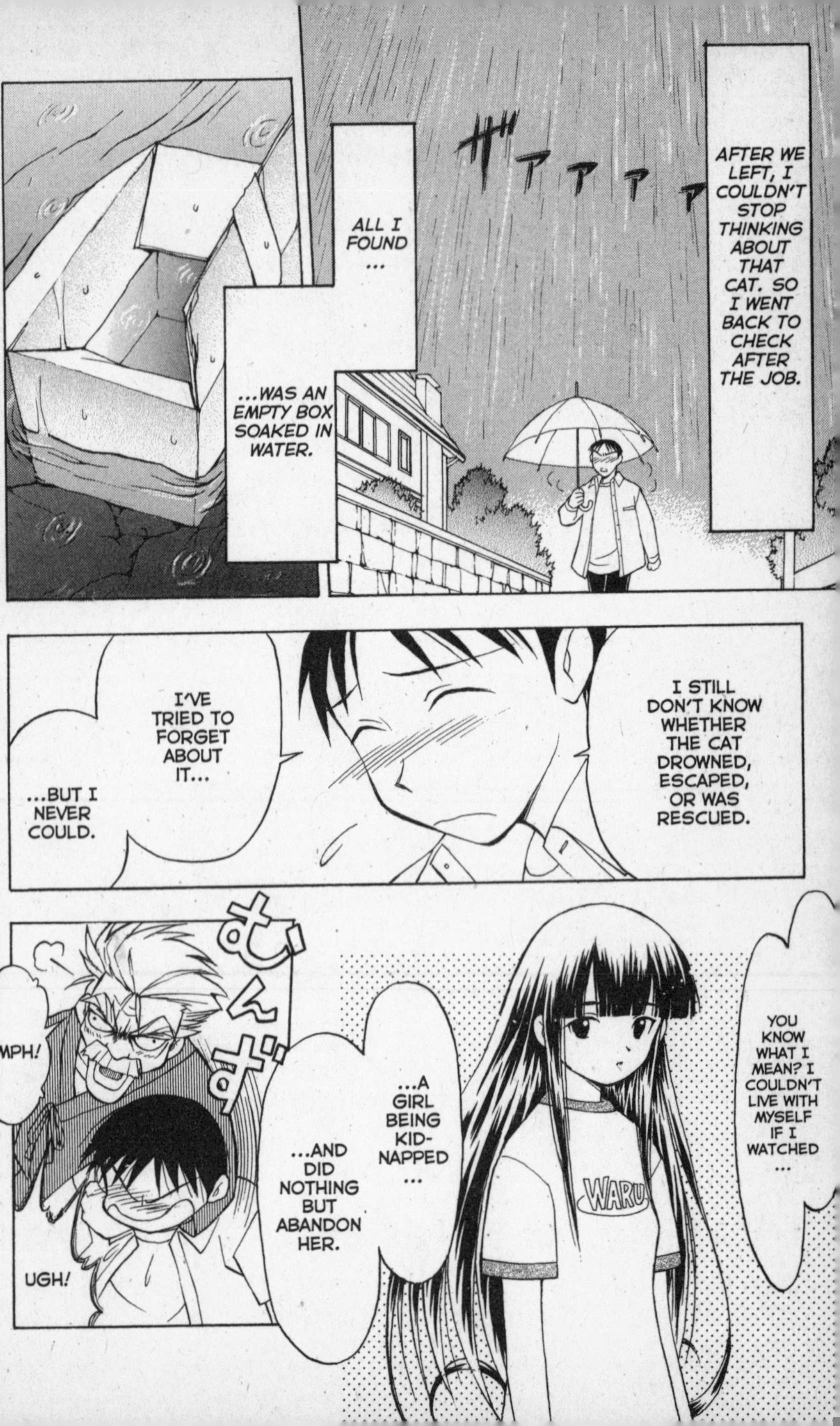

AFTER WE LEFT, I COULDN'T STOP THINKING ABOUT THAT CAT. SO I WENT BACK TO CHECK AFTER THE JOB.
ザアアアア
ALL I FOUND ...
...WAS AN EMPTY BOX SOAKED IN WATER.
I STILL DON'T KNOW WHETHER THE CAT DROWNED, ESCAPED, OR WAS RESCUED.
I'VE TRIED TO FORGET ABOUT IT...
...BUT I NEVER COULD.
YOU KNOW WHAT I MEAN? I COULDN'T LIVE WITH MYSELF IF I WATCHED ...
...A GIRL BEING KID-NAPPED ...
...AND DID NOTHING BUT ABANDON HER.
WARU
むんず
HMPH!
UGH!

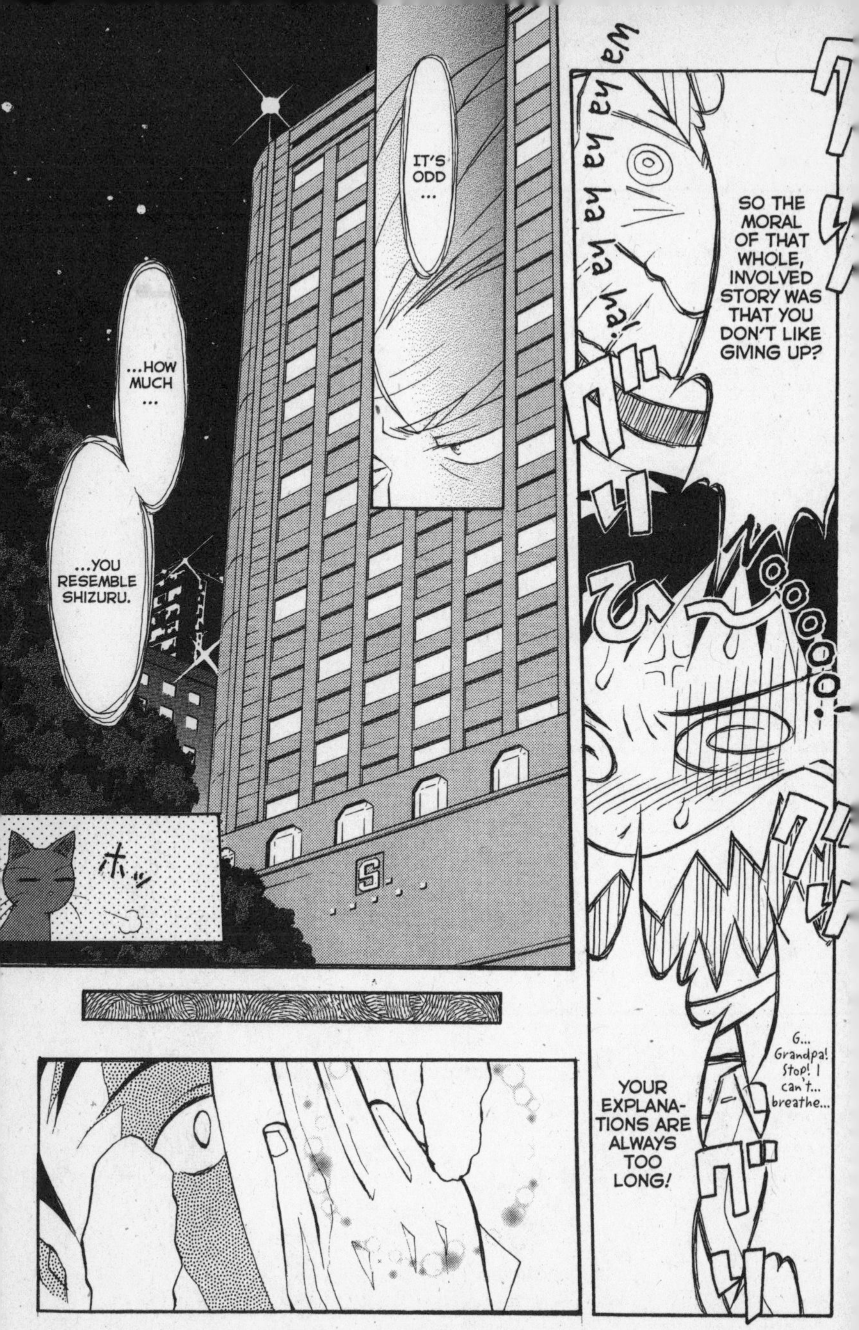
SO THE MORAL OF THAT WHOLE, INVOLVED STORY WAS THAT YOU DON'T LIKE GIVING UP?
Wa ha ha ha ha!
NOOOOOO...
YOUR EXPLANATIONS ARE ALWAYS TOO LONG!
G... Grandpa! Stop! I can't... breathe...
IT'S ODD...
...HOW MUCH...
...YOU RESEMBLE SHIZURU.
ホッ

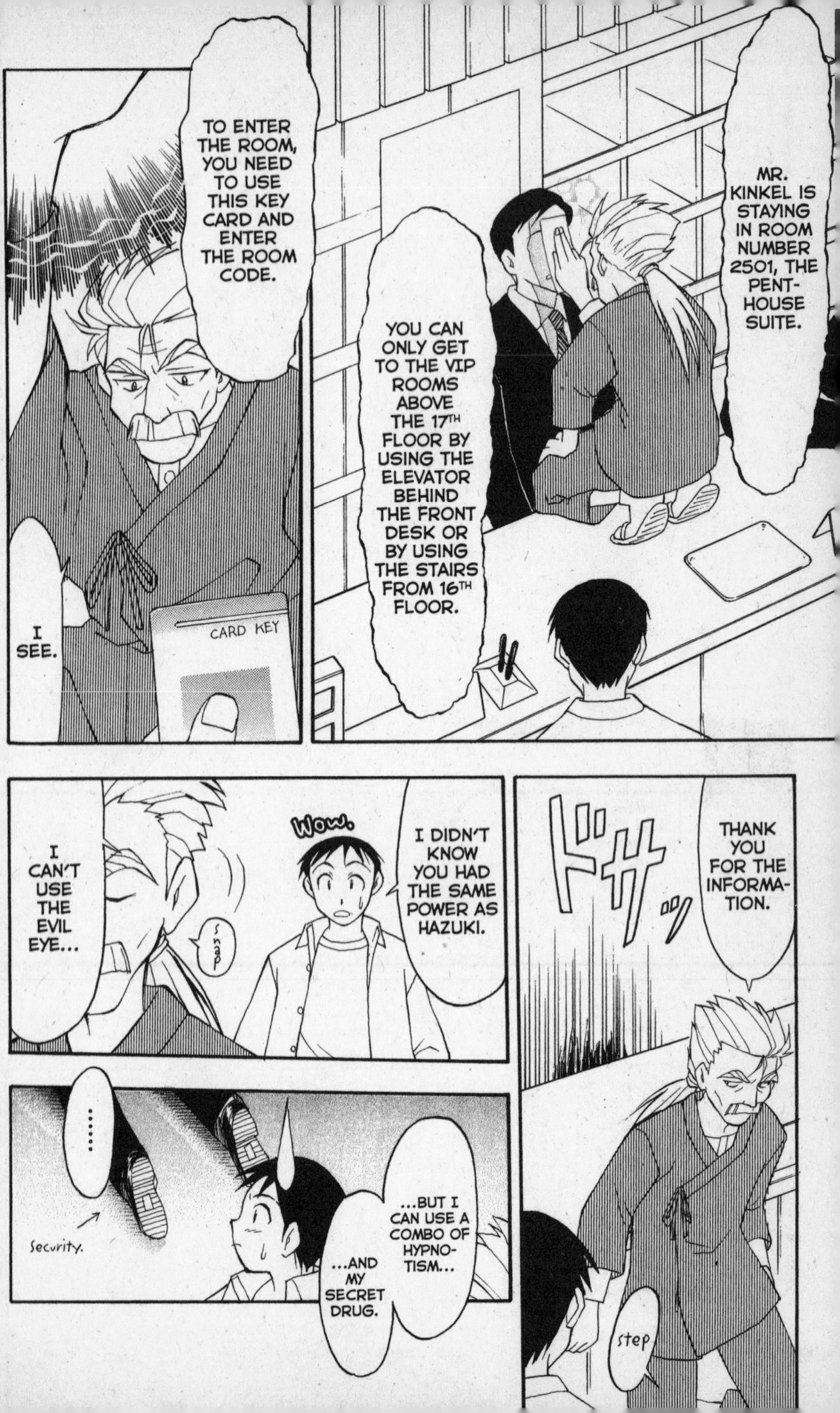
MR. KINKEL IS STAYING IN ROOM NUMBER 2501, THE PENT-HOUSE SUITE.
YOU CAN ONLY GET TO THE VIP ROOMS ABOVE THE 17TH FLOOR BY USING THE ELEVATOR BEHIND THE FRONT DESK OR BY USING THE STAIRS FROM 16TH FLOOR.
TO ENTER THE ROOM, YOU NEED TO USE THIS KEY CARD AND ENTER THE ROOM CODE.
CARD KEY
I SEE.
THANK YOU FOR THE INFORMATION.
ドサッ
step
Wow.
I DIDN'T KNOW YOU HAD THE SAME POWER AS HAZUKI.
snap
I CAN'T USE THE EVIL EYE...
......
...BUT I CAN USE A COMBO OF HYPNOTISM...
...AND MY SECRET DRUG.
Security.

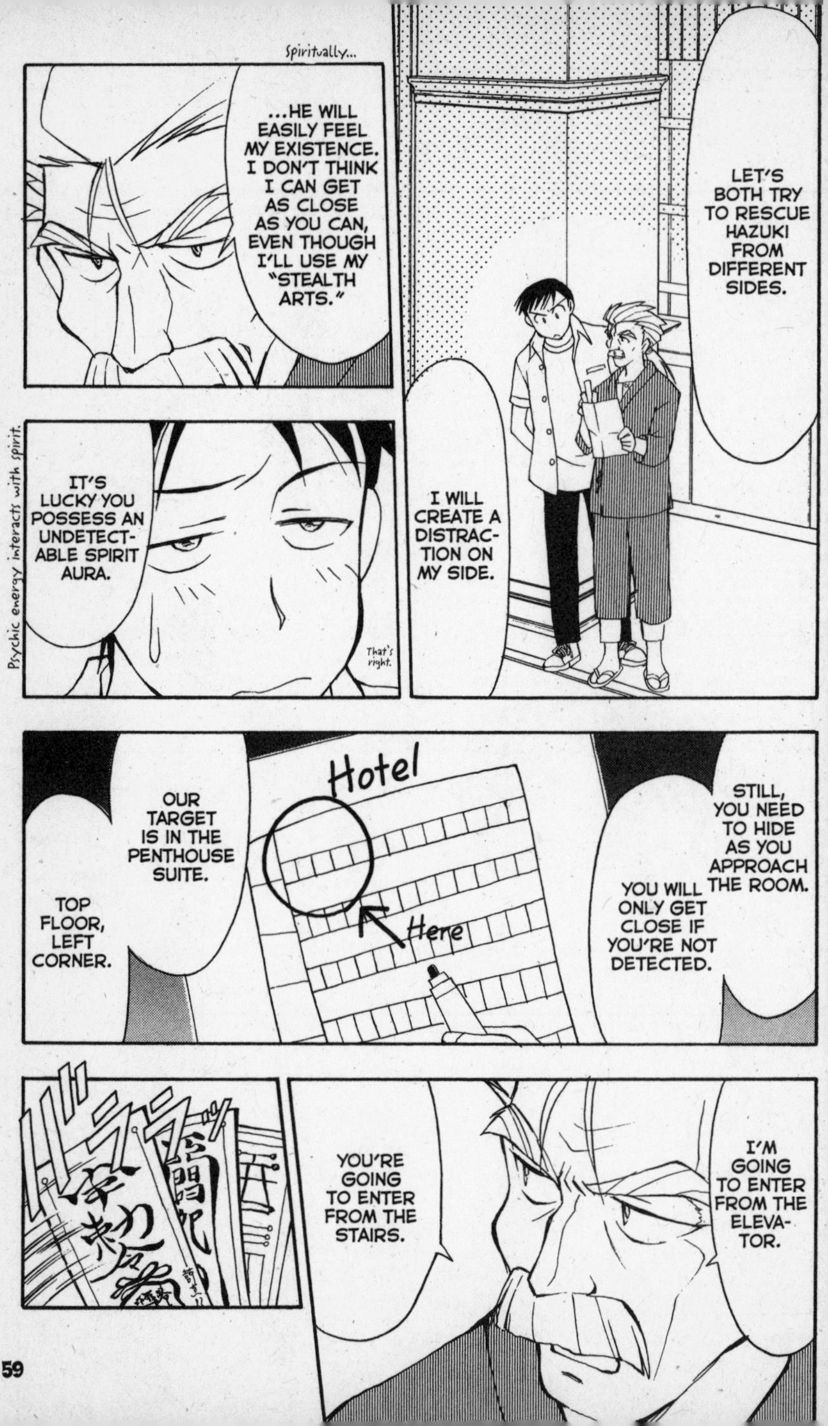
LET'S BOTH TRY TO RESCUE HAZUKI FROM DIFFERENT SIDES.
I WILL CREATE A DISTRACTION ON MY SIDE.
Spiritually...
...HE WILL EASILY FEEL MY EXISTENCE. I DON'T THINK I CAN GET AS CLOSE AS YOU CAN, EVEN THOUGH I'LL USE MY "STEALTH ARTS."
IT'S LUCKY YOU POSSESS AN UNDETECTABLE SPIRIT AURA.
That's right.
Psychic energy interacts with spirit.
STILL, YOU NEED TO HIDE AS YOU APPROACH THE ROOM.
YOU WILL ONLY GET CLOSE IF YOU'RE NOT DETECTED.
Hotel
Here
OUR TARGET IS IN THE PENTHOUSE SUITE.
TOP FLOOR, LEFT CORNER.
I'M GOING TO ENTER FROM THE ELEVATOR.
YOU'RE GOING TO ENTER FROM THE STAIRS.

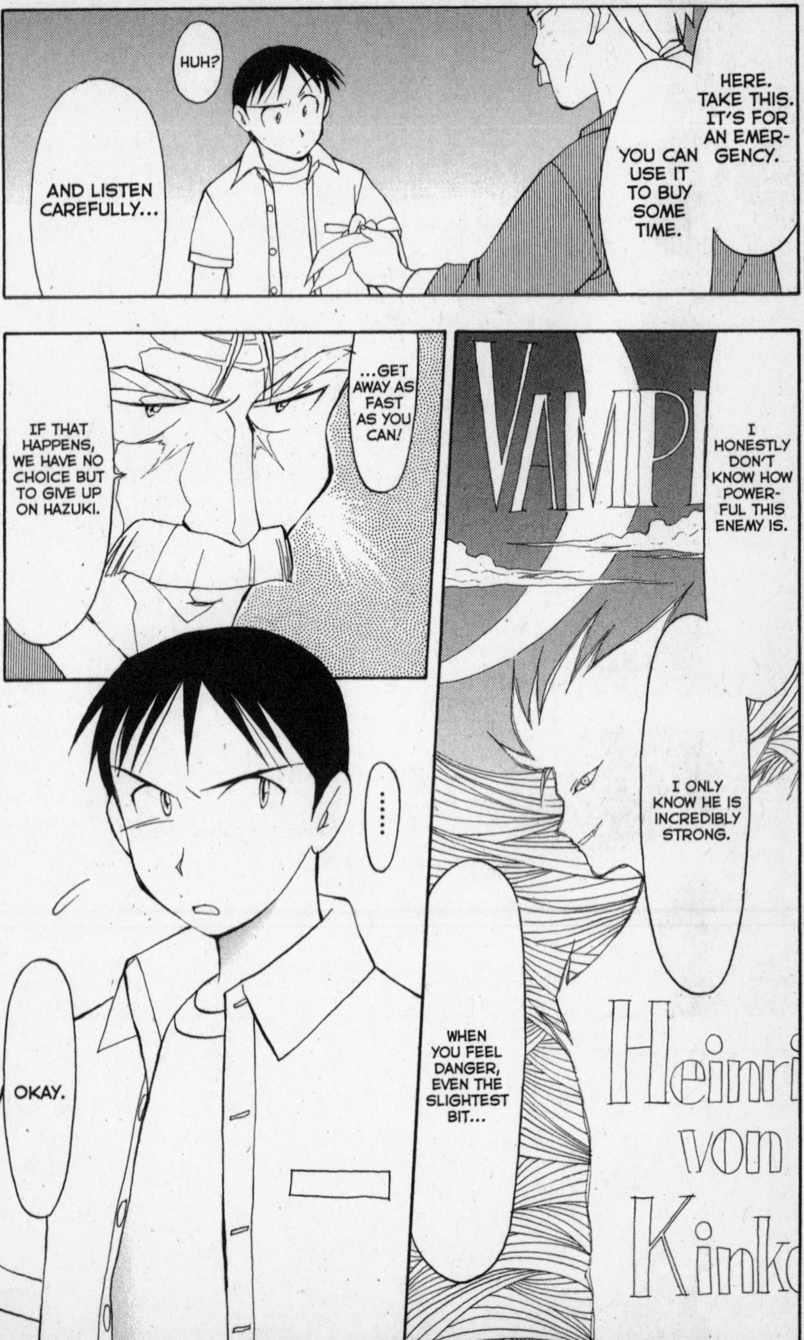
HERE. TAKE THIS. IT'S FOR AN EMERGENCY.
YOU CAN USE IT TO BUY SOME TIME.
HUH?
AND LISTEN CAREFULLY...
VAMPI
I HONESTLY DON'T KNOW HOW POWERFUL THIS ENEMY IS.
I ONLY KNOW HE IS INCREDIBLY STRONG.
Heinri von Kink
WHEN YOU FEEL DANGER, EVEN THE SLIGHTEST BIT...
...GET AWAY AS FAST AS YOU CAN!
IF THAT HAPPENS, WE HAVE NO CHOICE BUT TO GIVE UP ON HAZUKI.
......
OKAY.

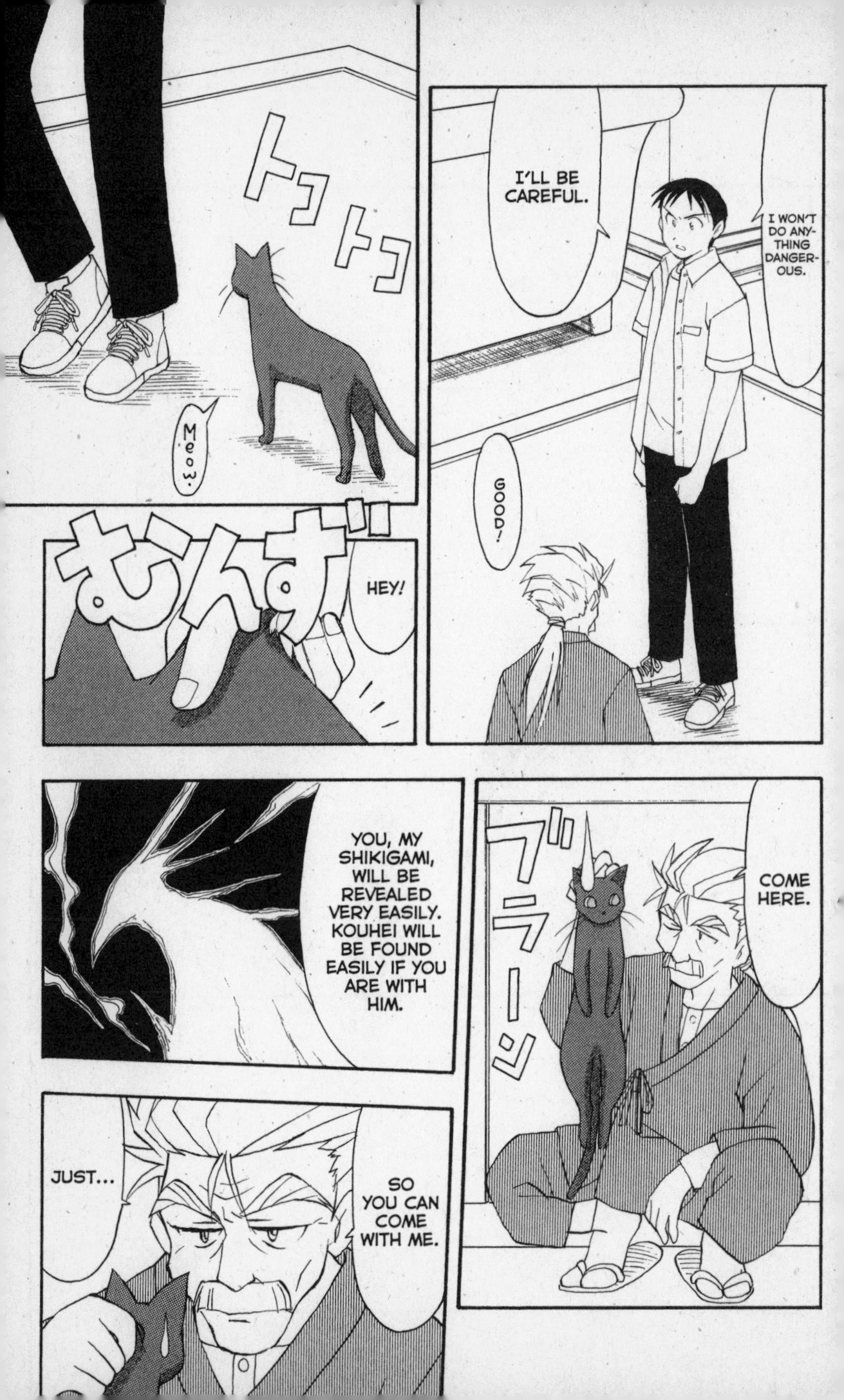
I WON'T DO ANY-THING DANGER-OUS.
I'LL BE CAREFUL.
GOOD!
トコトコ
Meow.
むんず
HEY!
COME HERE.
ブラーン
YOU, MY SHIKIGAMI, WILL BE REVEALED VERY EASILY. KOUHEI WILL BE FOUND EASILY IF YOU ARE WITH HIM.
SO YOU CAN COME WITH ME.
JUST...

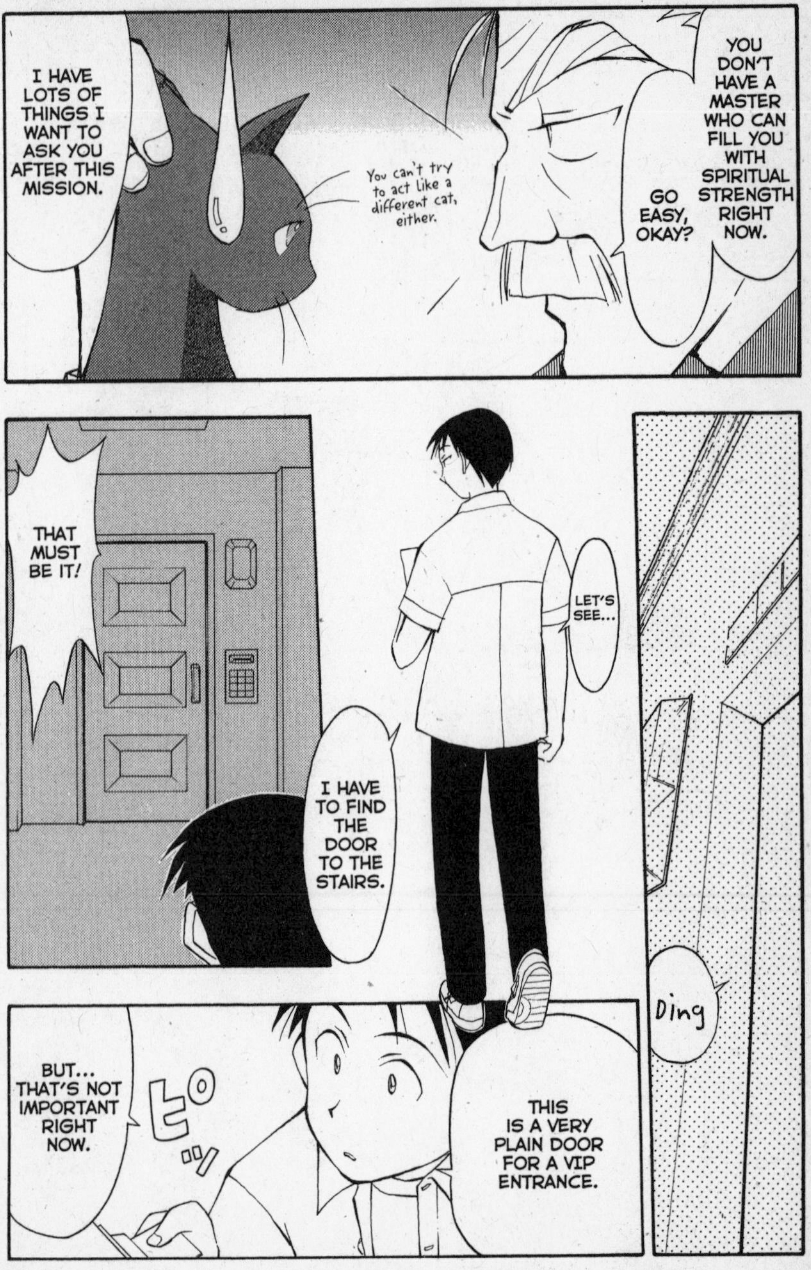
YOU DON'T HAVE A MASTER WHO CAN FILL YOU WITH SPIRITUAL STRENGTH RIGHT NOW.
GO EASY, OKAY?
You can't try to act like a different cat, either.
I HAVE LOTS OF THINGS I WANT TO ASK YOU AFTER THIS MISSION.
Ding
LET'S SEE...
I HAVE TO FIND THE DOOR TO THE STAIRS.
THAT MUST BE IT!
THIS IS A VERY PLAIN DOOR FOR A VIP ENTRANCE.
BUT... THAT'S NOT IMPORTANT RIGHT NOW.

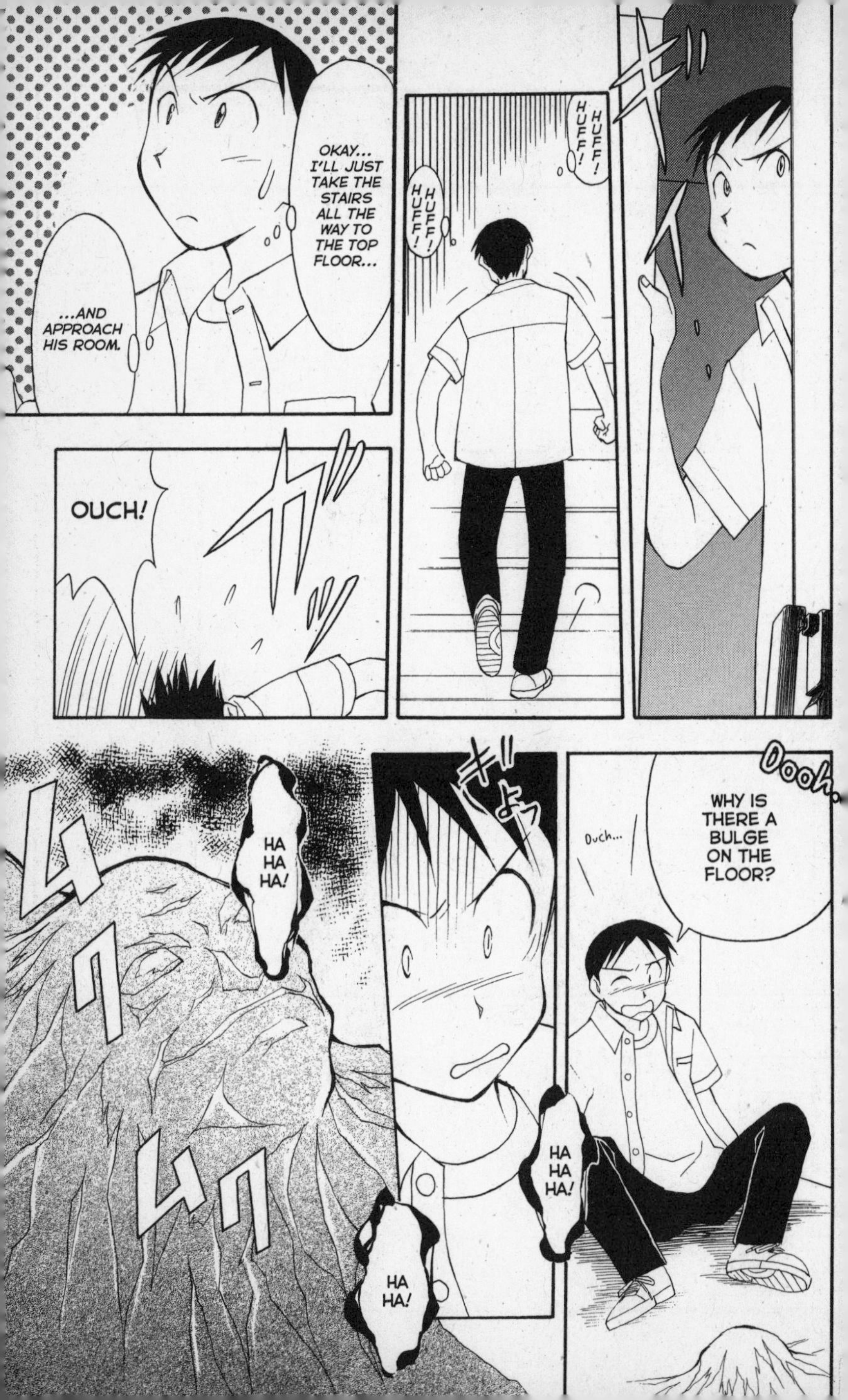
ギィ
HUFF! HUFF!
HUFF! HUFF!
OKAY... I'LL JUST TAKE THE STAIRS ALL THE WAY TO THE TOP FLOOR...
...AND APPROACH HIS ROOM.
OUCH!
Oooh..
Ouch...
WHY IS THERE A BULGE ON THE FLOOR?
ぎょっ
HA HA HA!
HA HA!
HA HA HA!
ムク ムク

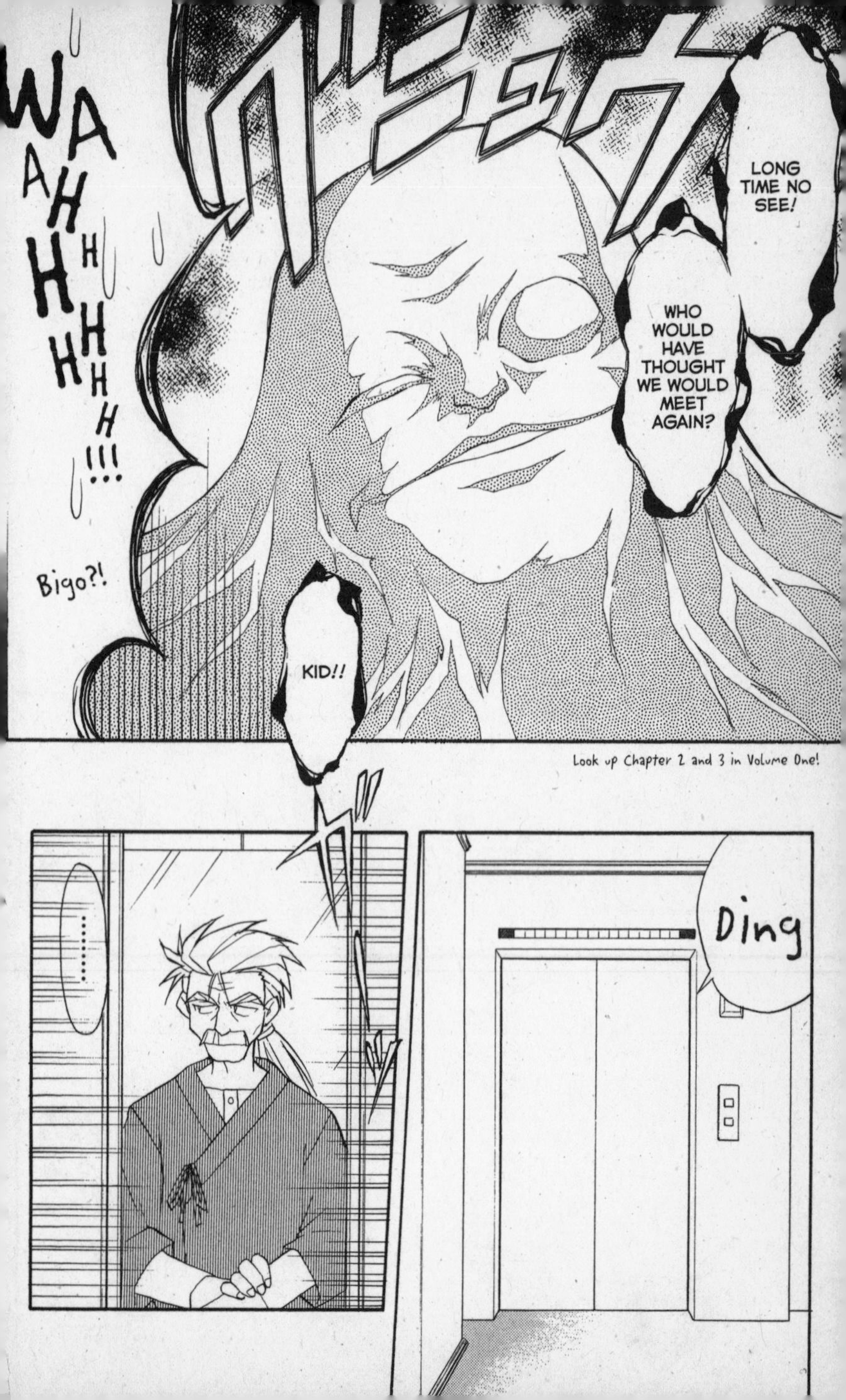
LONG TIME NO SEE!
WHO WOULD HAVE THOUGHT WE WOULD MEET AGAIN?
KID!!
WAHHHHHHHH!!!
Bigo?!
Look up Chapter 2 and 3 in Volume One!
Ding
......

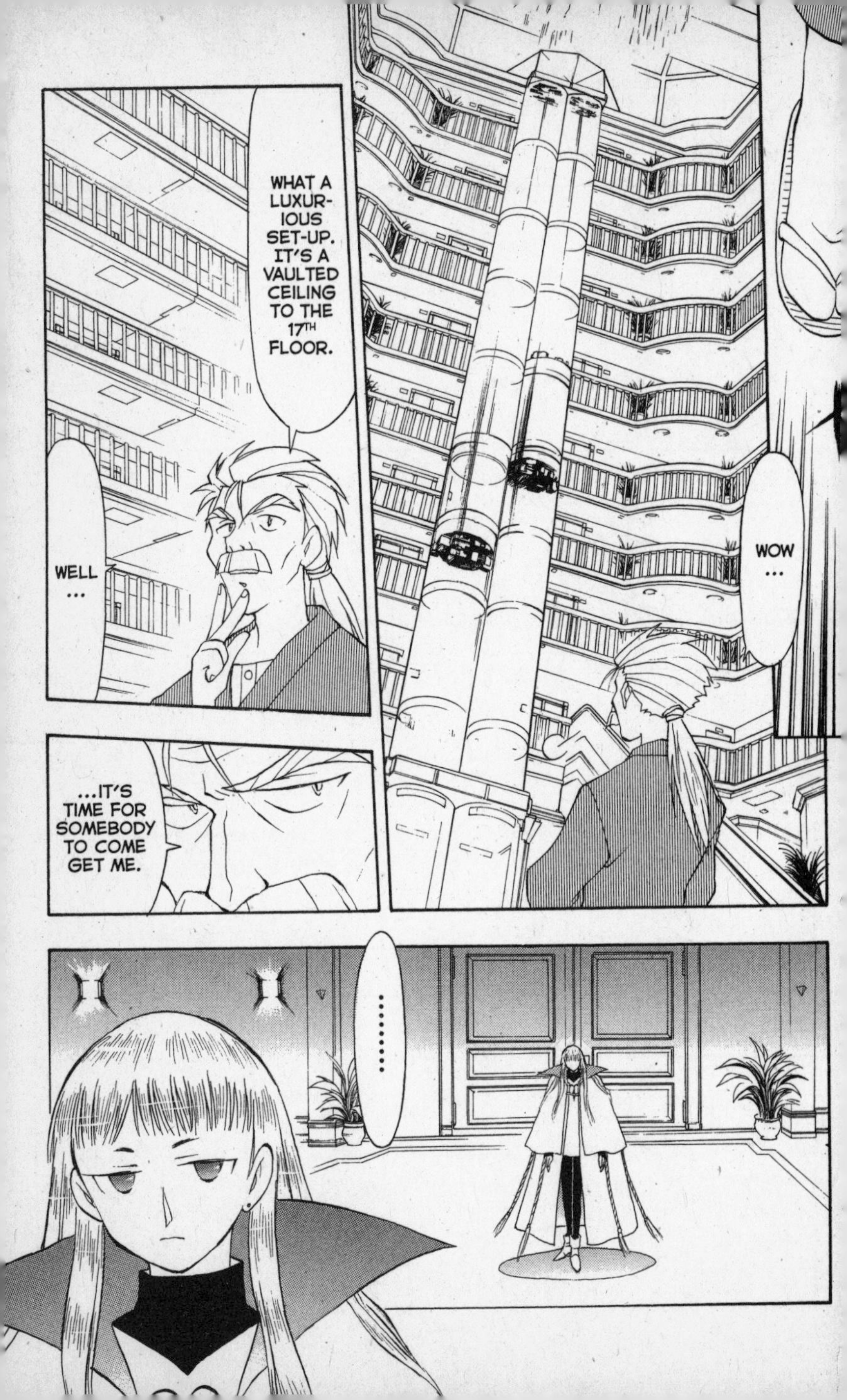
WOW ...
WHAT A LUXURIOUS SET-UP. IT'S A VAULTED CEILING TO THE 17TH FLOOR.
WELL ...
...IT'S TIME FOR SOMEBODY TO COME GET ME.
....

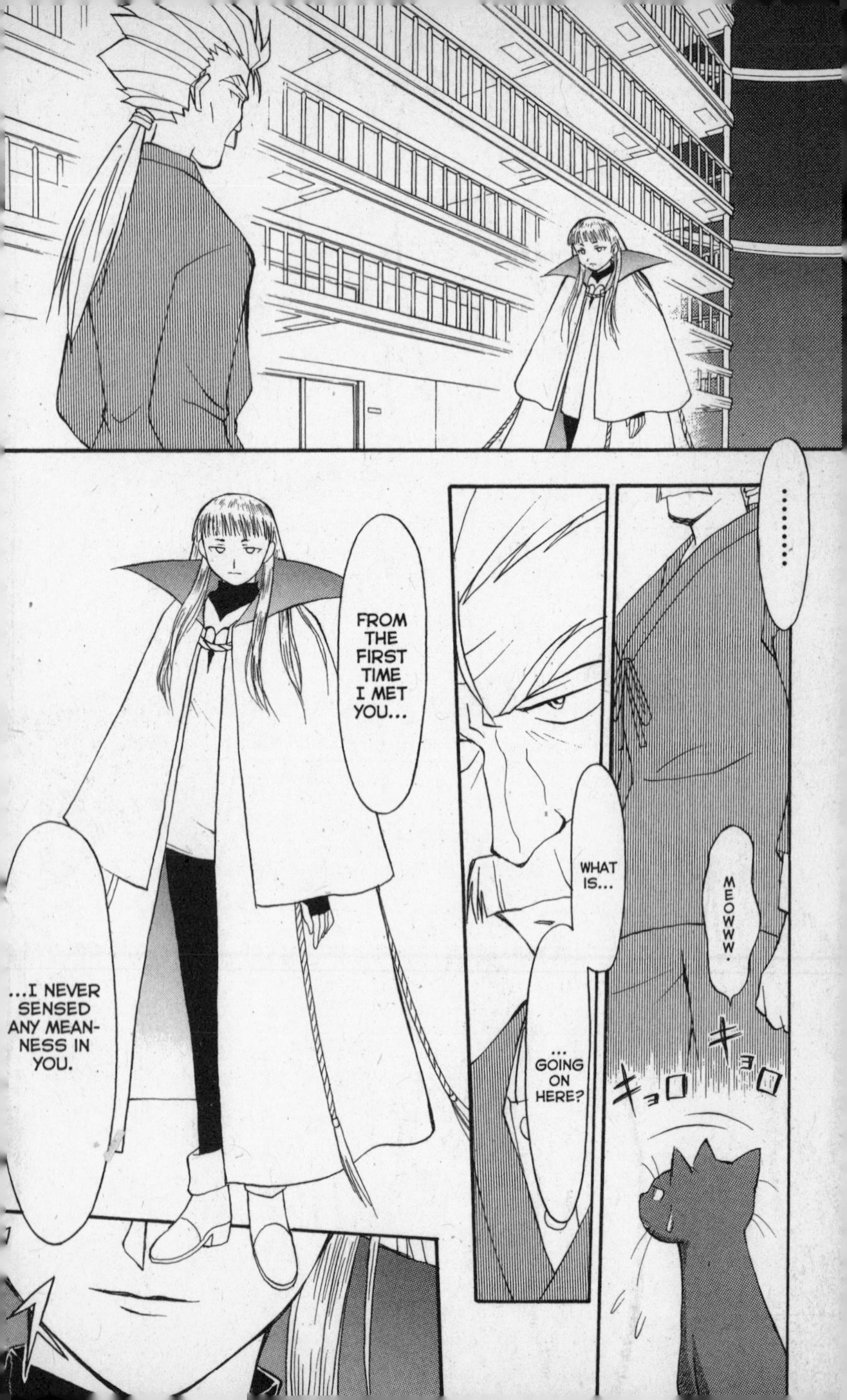
......
MEOWWW.
キョロキョロ
WHAT IS...
...GOING ON HERE?
FROM THE FIRST TIME I MET YOU...
...I NEVER SENSED ANY MEANNESS IN YOU.

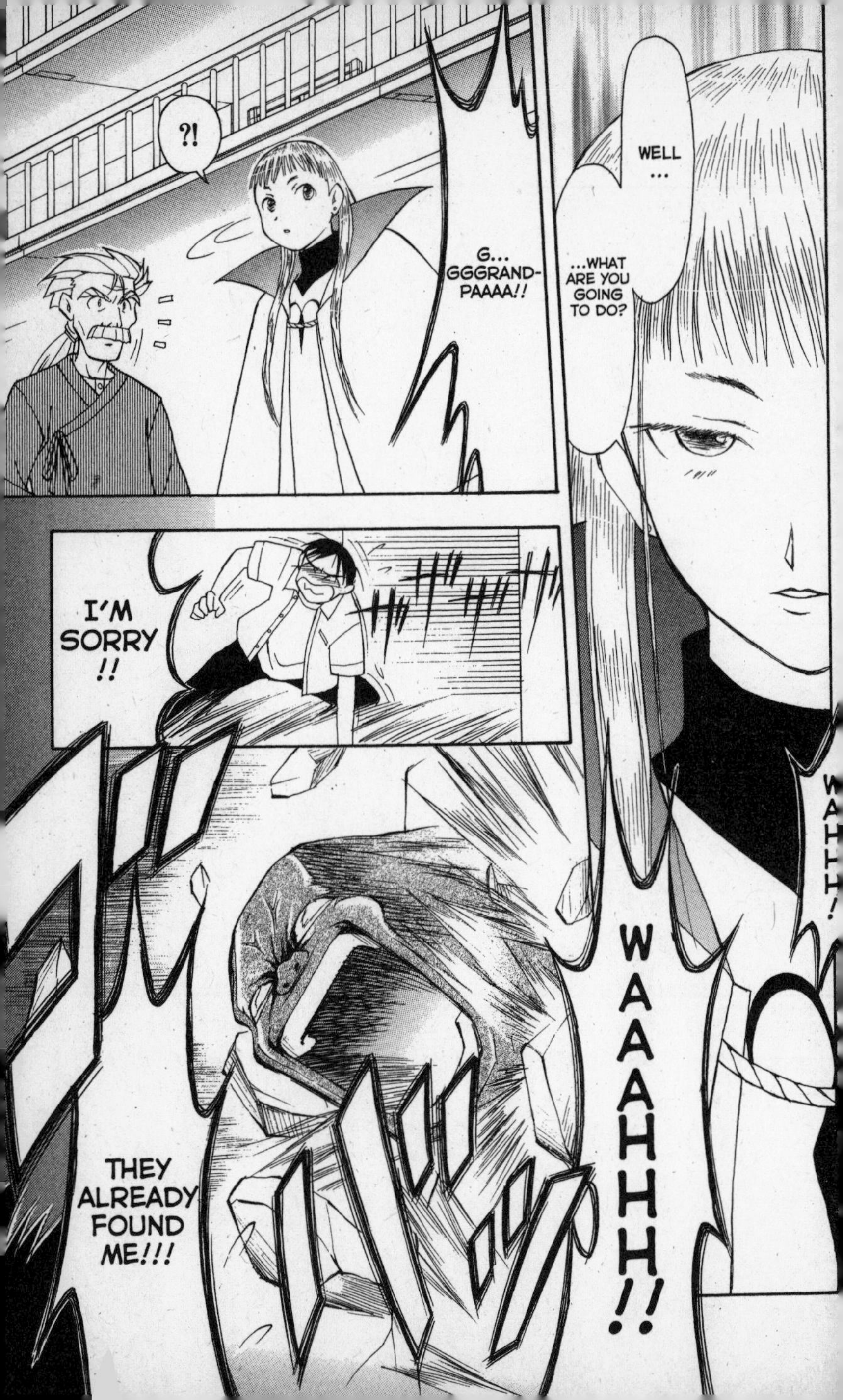
WELL...
...WHAT ARE YOU GOING TO DO?
G... GGGRAND-PAAAA!!
?!
I'M SORRY!!
WAHHH!
WAAAHHH!!
THEY ALREADY FOUND ME!!!

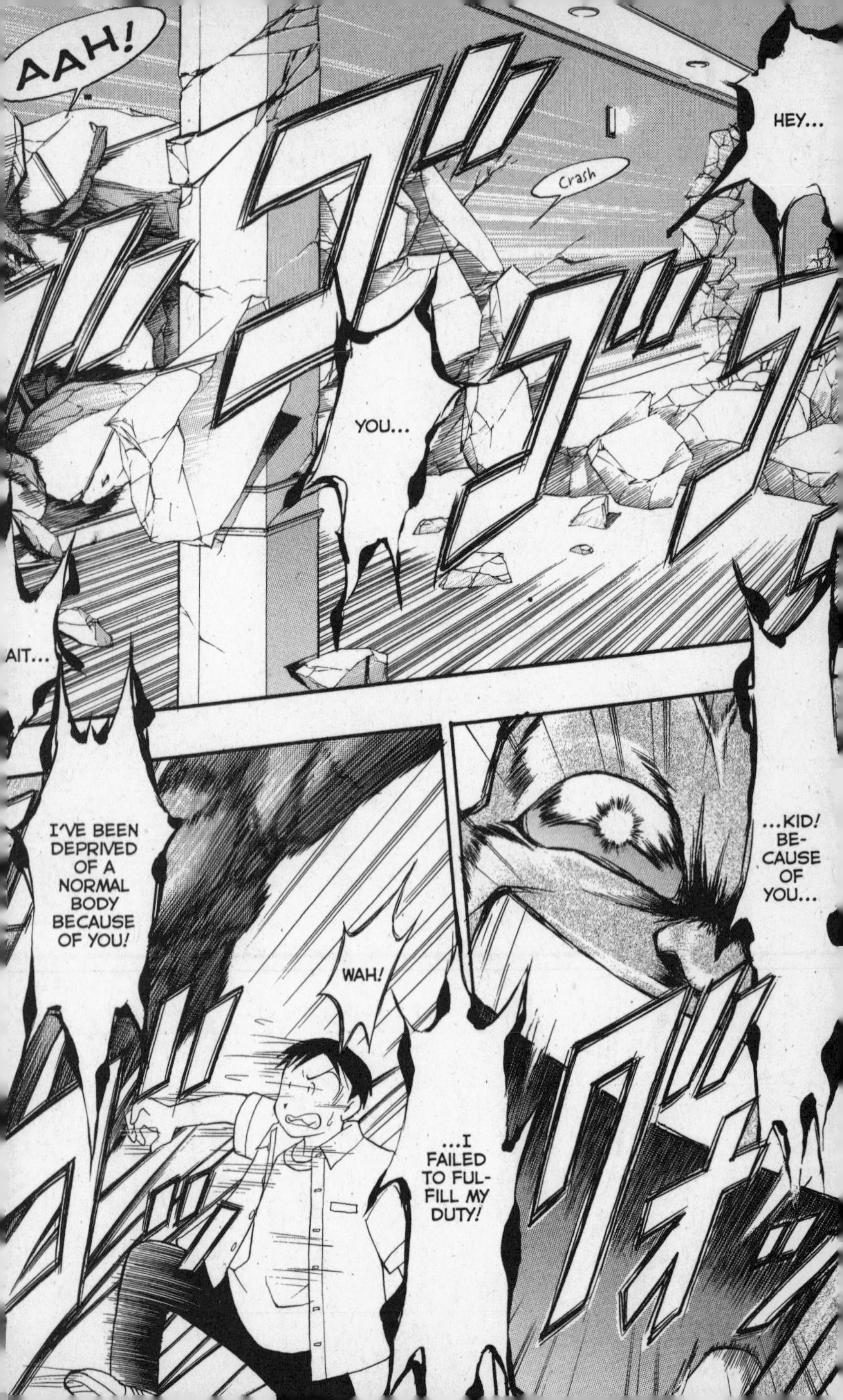
HEY...
Crash
YOU...
AAH!
AIT...
...KID! BE-CAUSE OF YOU...
...I FAILED TO FUL-FILL MY DUTY!
I'VE BEEN DEPRIVED OF A NORMAL BODY BECAUSE OF YOU!
WAH!

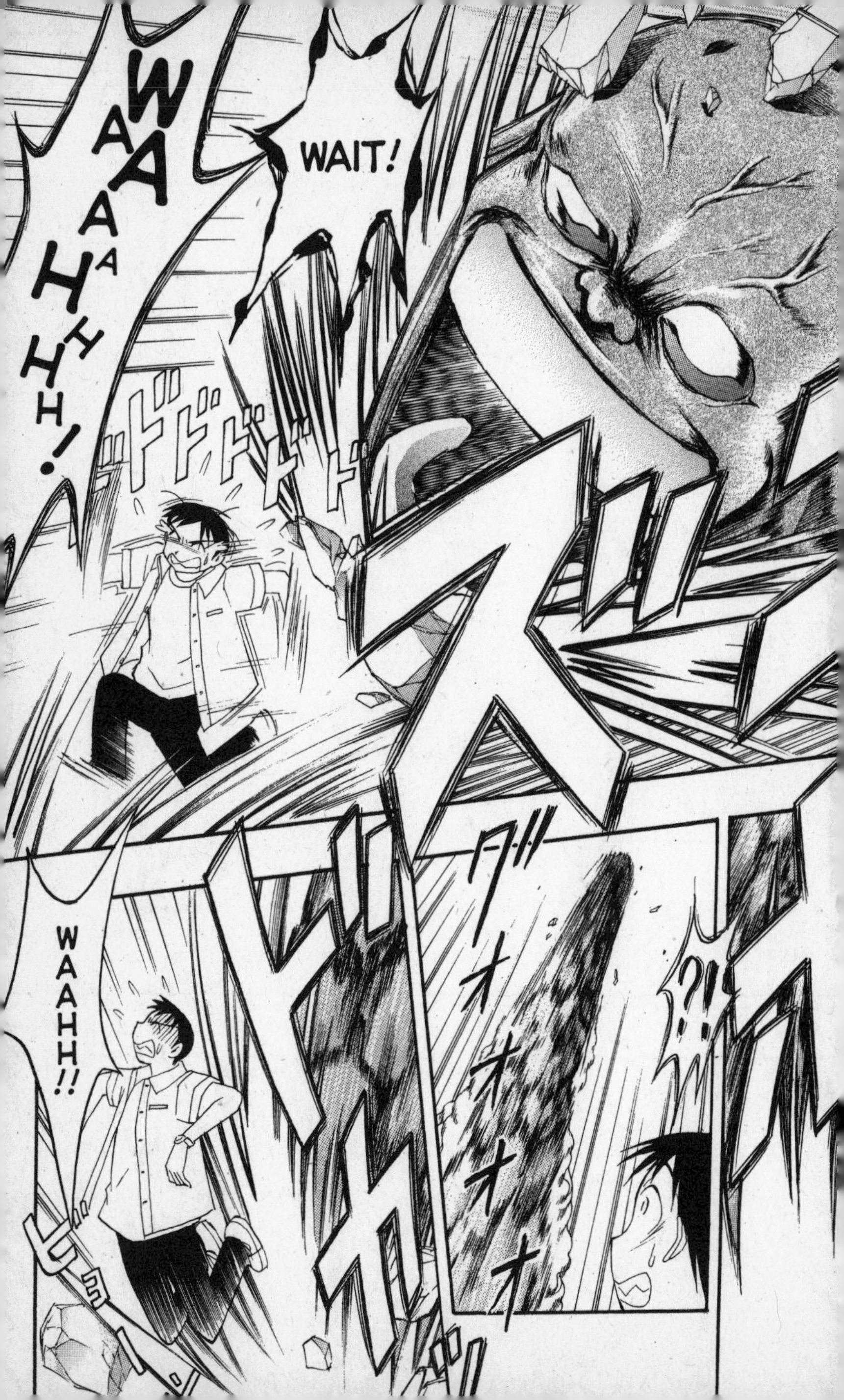
WAIT!
WAAAAHHHH!
?!
WAAAHH!!

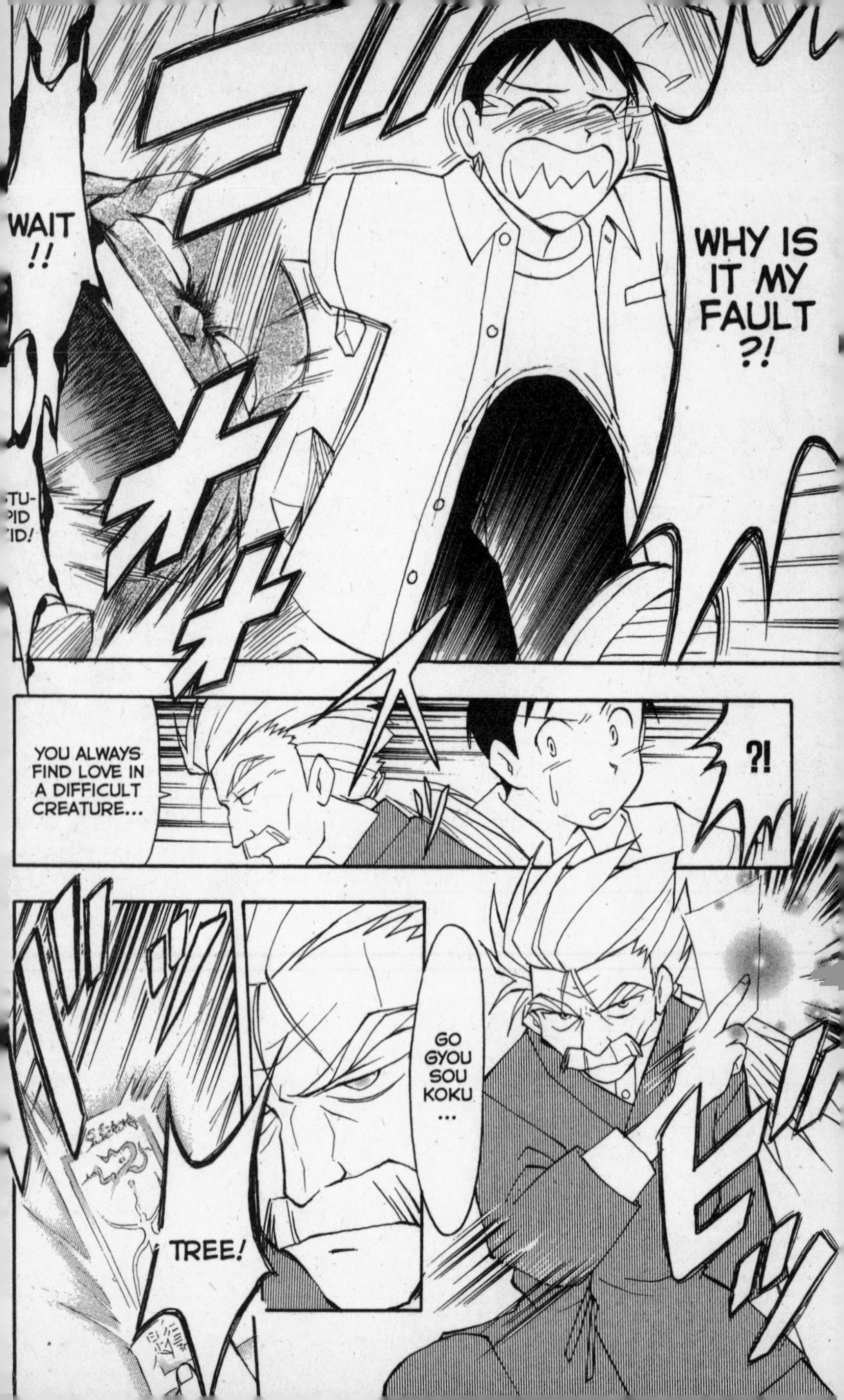
WHY IS IT MY FAULT ?!
WAIT !!
TU- PID ID!
?!
YOU ALWAYS FIND LOVE IN A DIFFICULT CREATURE...
GO GYOU SOU KOKU ...
TREE!

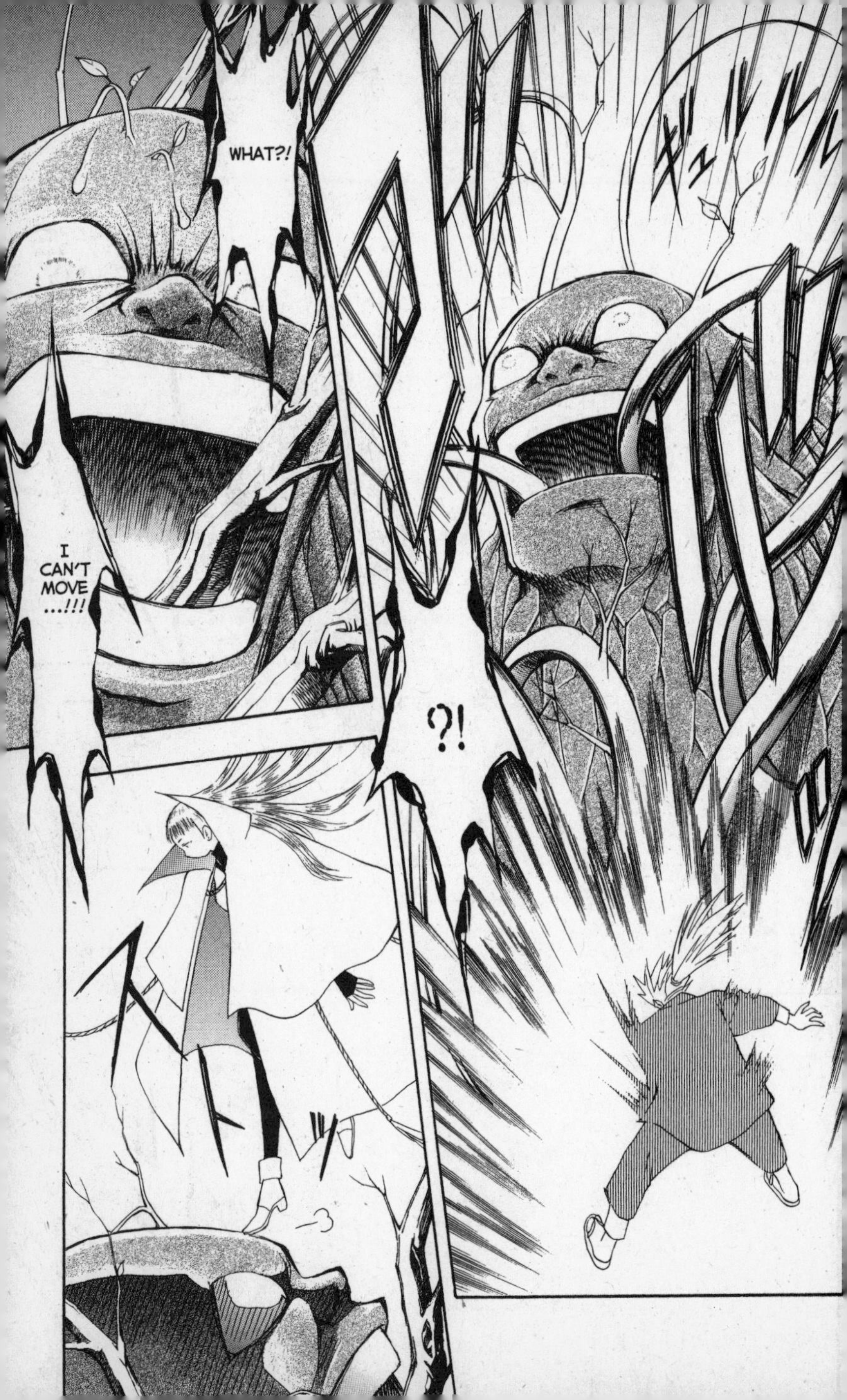
WHAT?!
I CAN'T MOVE ...!!!
?!

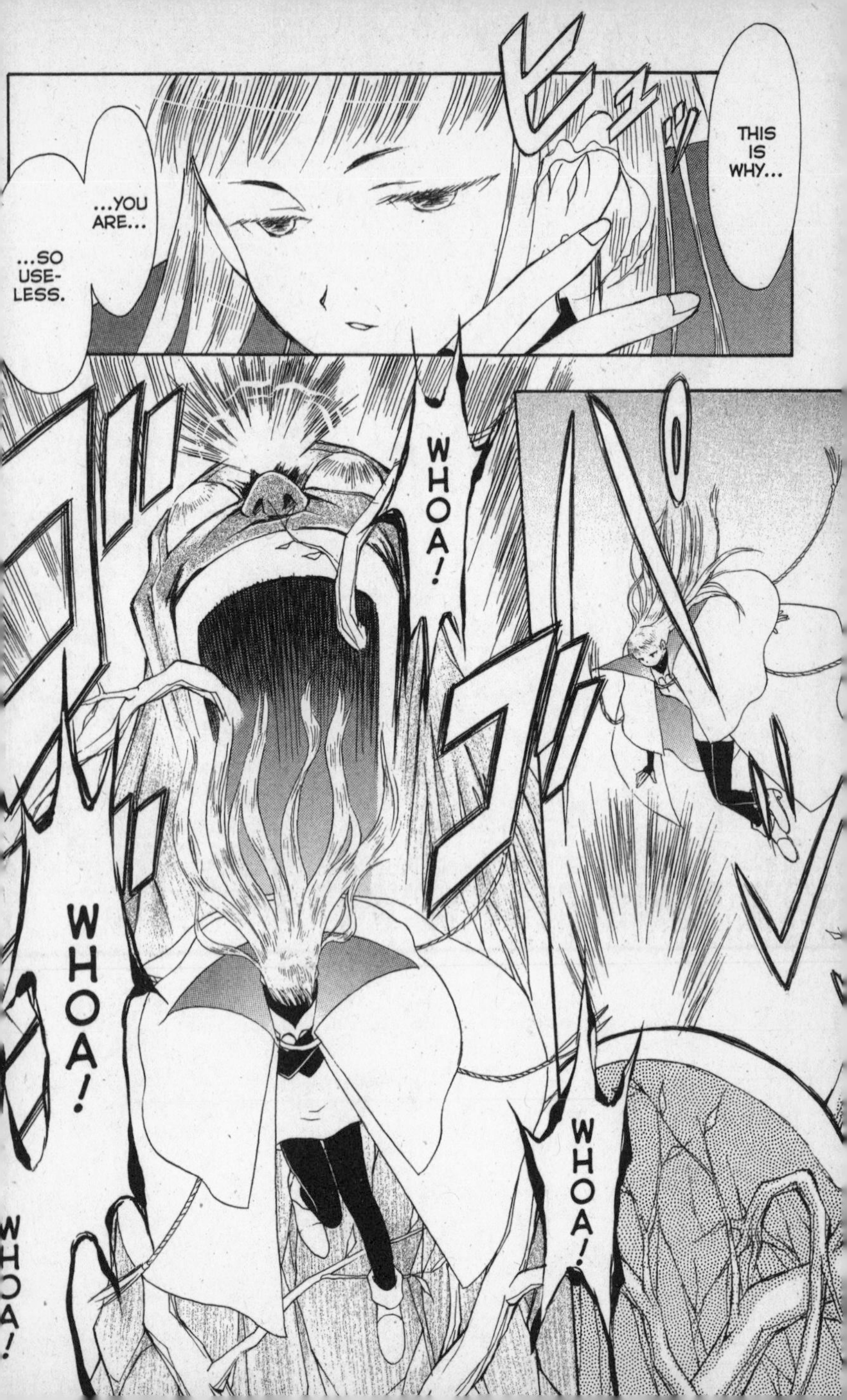
THIS IS WHY...
...YOU ARE...
...SO USE-LESS.
WHOA!
WHOA!
WHOA!
WHOA!

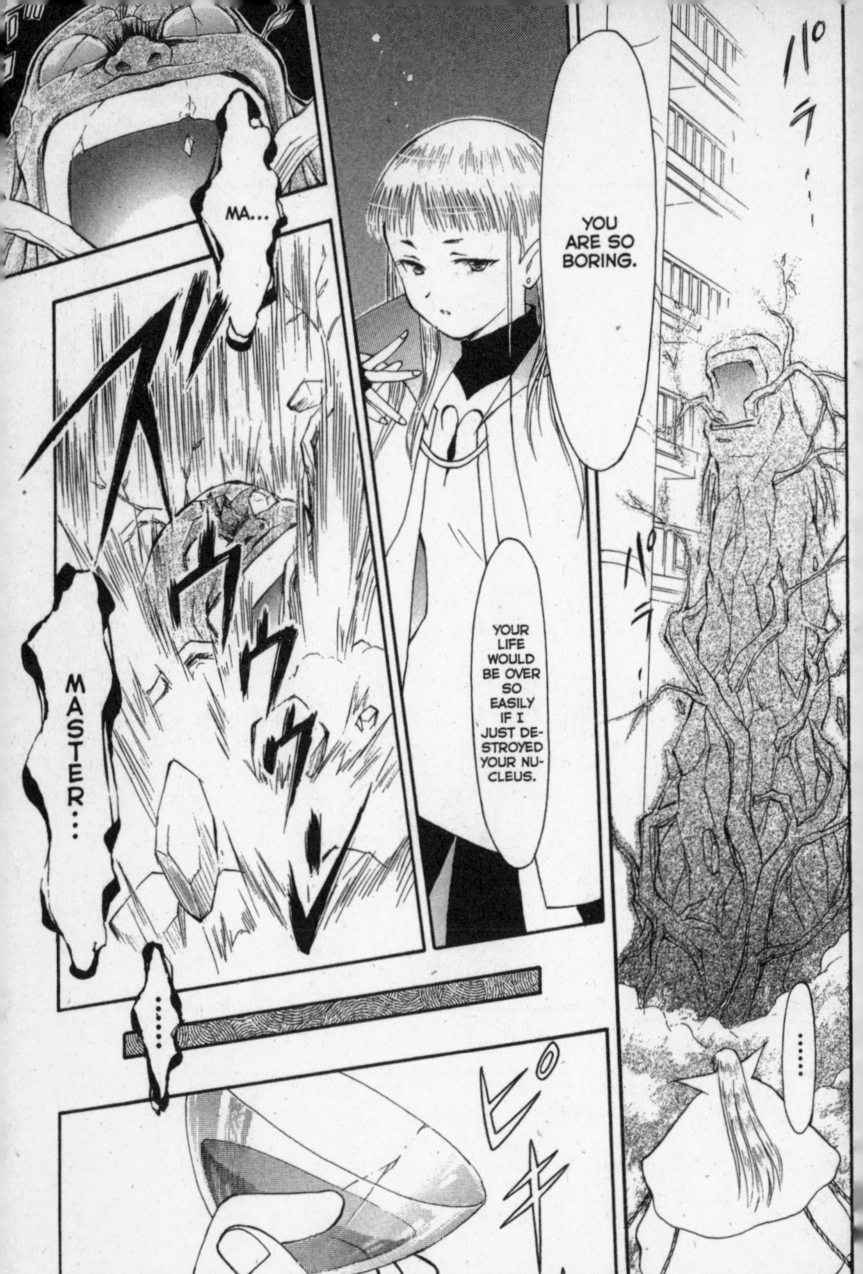
パラ…
YOU ARE SO BORING.
YOUR LIFE WOULD BE OVER SO EASILY IF I JUST DE-STROYED YOUR NU-CLEUS.
パラ…
……
MA…
MASTER…
……
ピキ

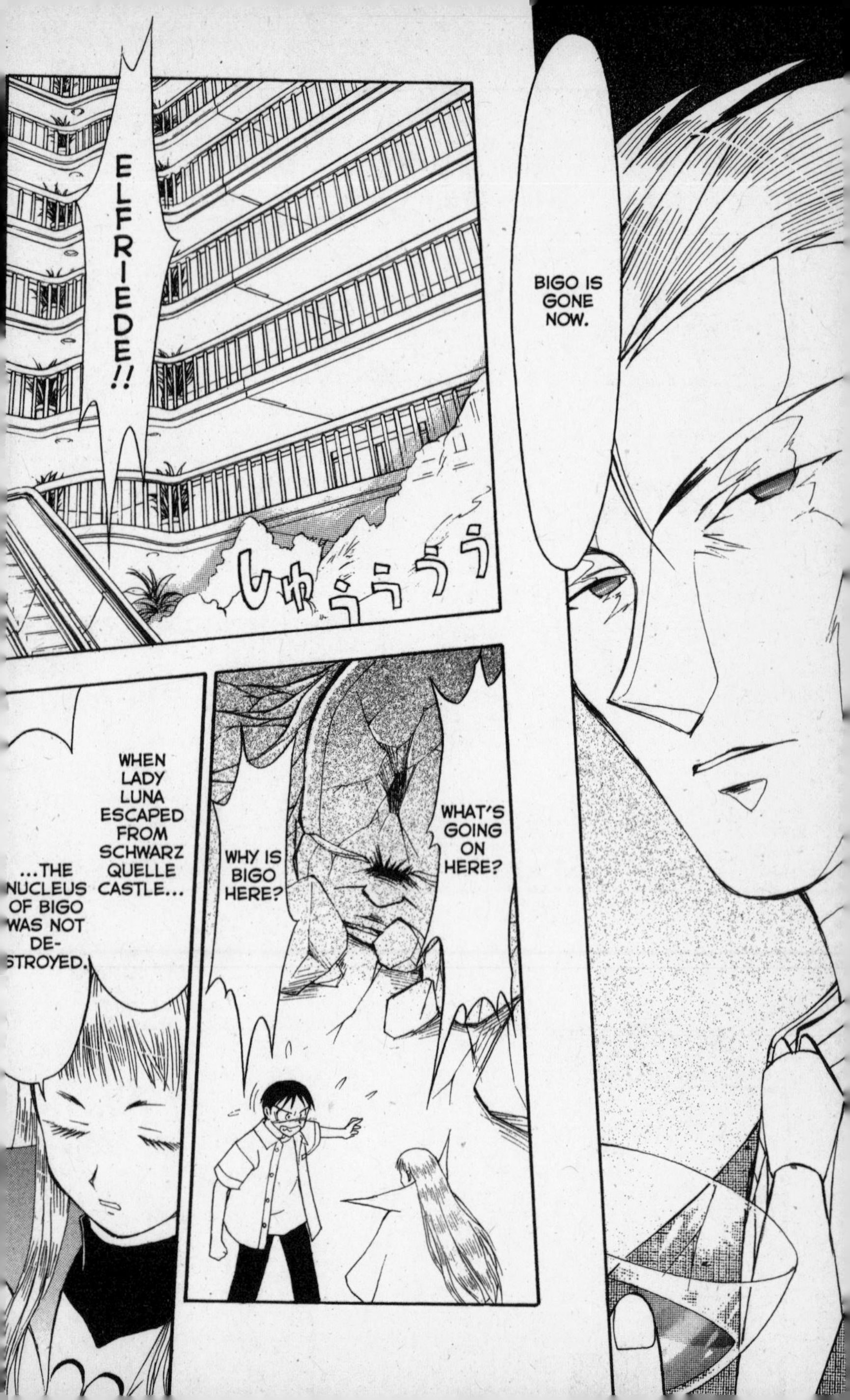
BIGO IS GONE NOW.
ELFRIEDE!!
しゅううう
WHAT'S GOING ON HERE?
WHY IS BIGO HERE?
WHEN LADY LUNA ESCAPED FROM SCHWARZ QUELLE CASTLE...
...THE NUCLEUS OF BIGO WAS NOT DE-STROYED.

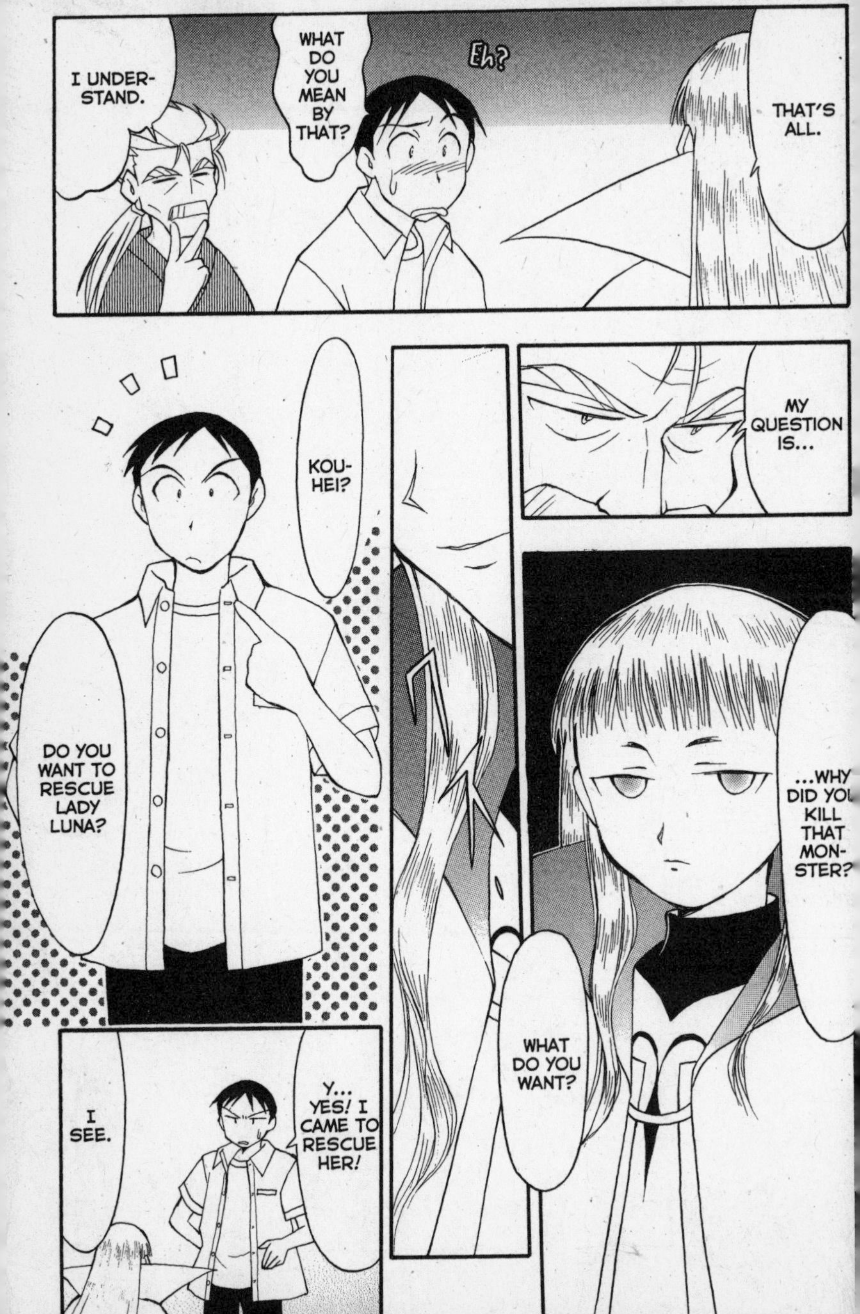
THAT'S ALL.
Eh?
WHAT DO YOU MEAN BY THAT?
I UNDER-STAND.
MY QUESTION IS...
...WHY DID YOU KILL THAT MON-STER?
WHAT DO YOU WANT?
KOU-HEI?
DO YOU WANT TO RESCUE LADY LUNA?
Y... YES! I CAME TO RESCUE HER!
I SEE.

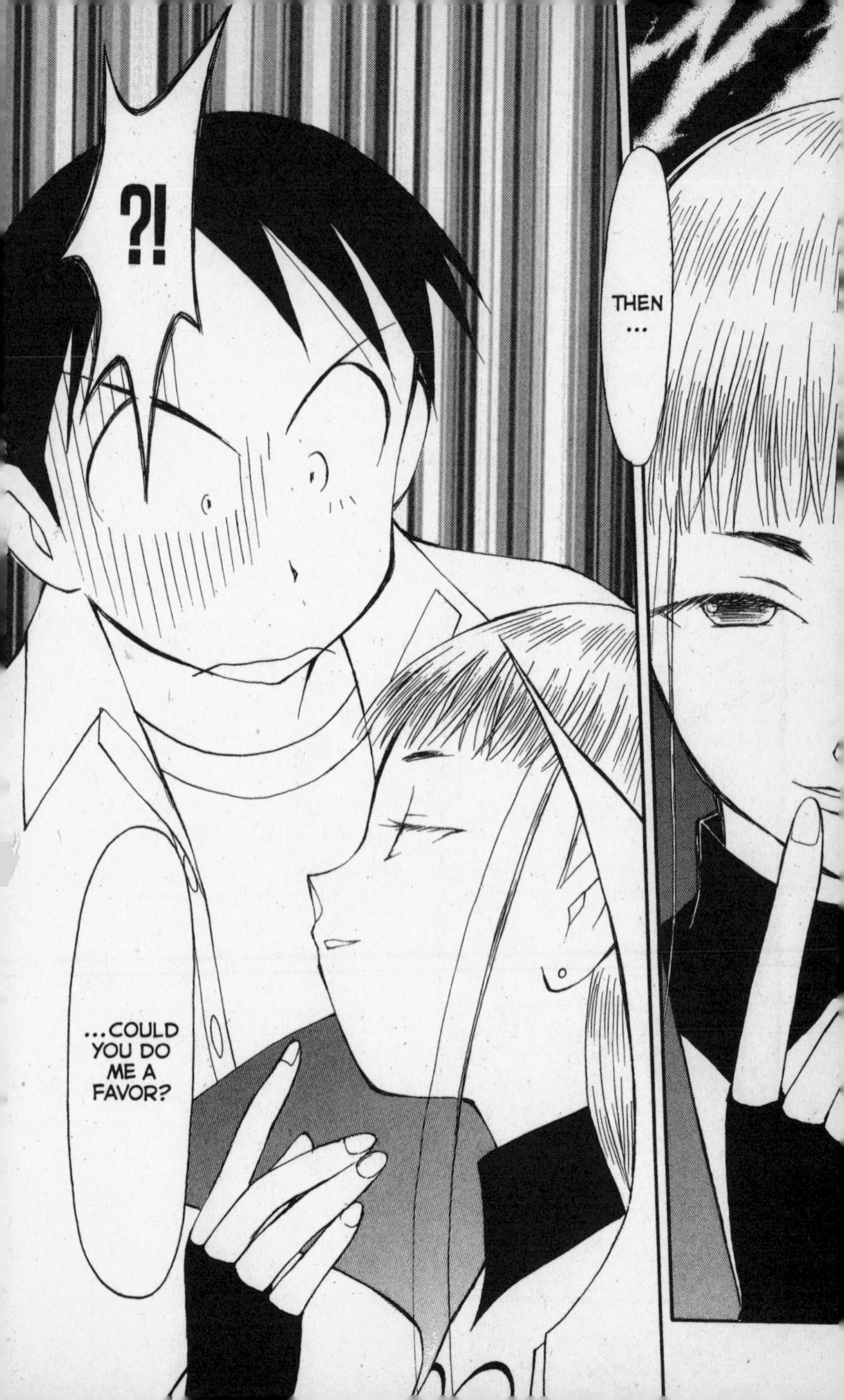
THEN...
?!
...COULD YOU DO ME A FAVOR?

UNLIKE HAZUKI, ELFRIEDE IS OVER A HUNDRED YEARS OLD. COUNT KINKEL IS SEVERAL HUNDRED YEARS OLD.

HE MAY BE MORE THAN A THOUSAND YEARS OLD. HE'S A DIRTY PERVERT.

I'LL TELL YOU MORE ABOUT THE STORY BETWEEN THESE TWO LATER.

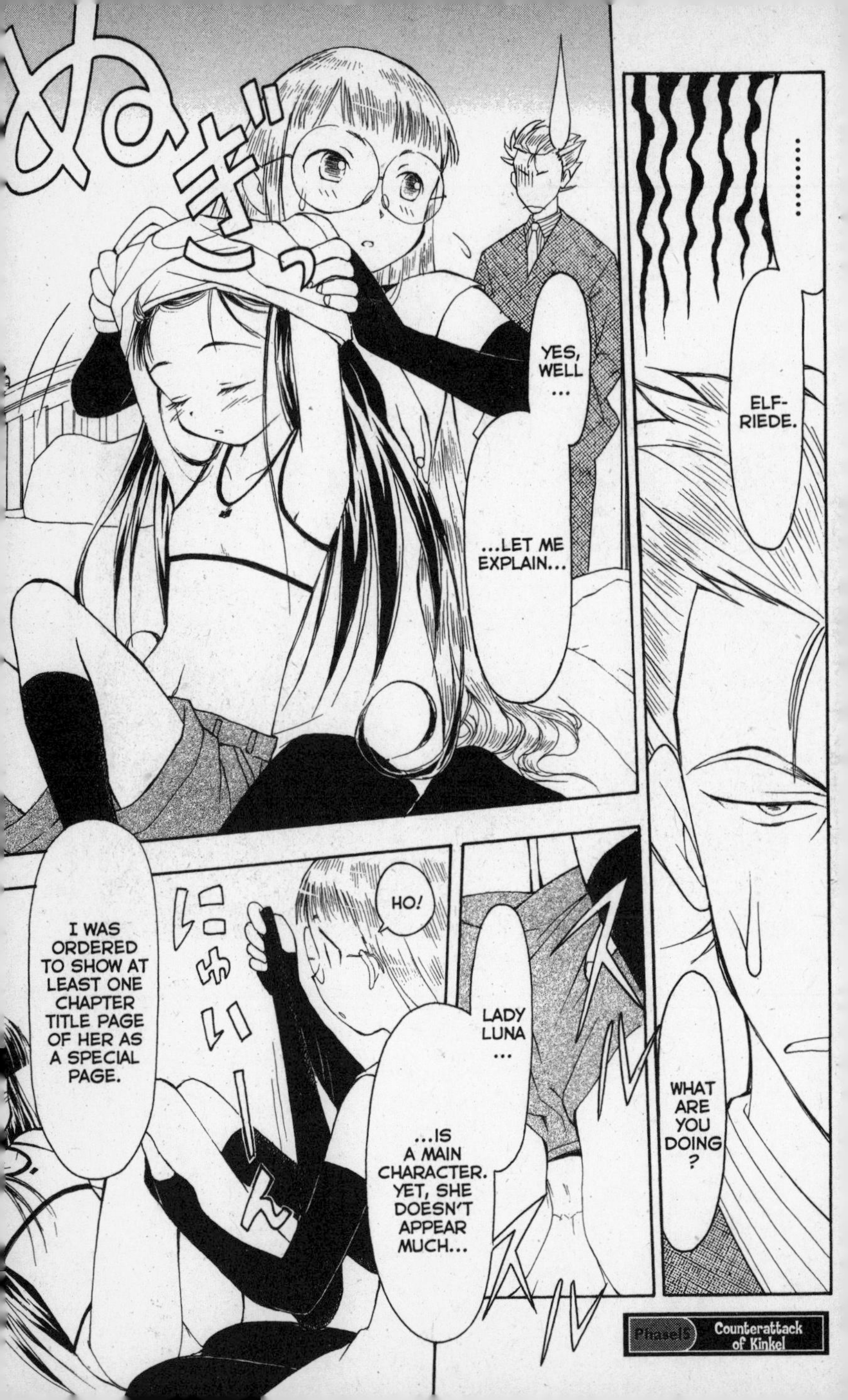
......
ELF-RIEDE.
WHAT ARE YOU DOING?
ぬぎっ
YES, WELL...
...LET ME EXPLAIN...
HO!
LADY LUNA...
...IS A MAIN CHARACTER. YET, SHE DOESN'T APPEAR MUCH...
にゅいーん
I WAS ORDERED TO SHOW AT LEAST ONE CHAPTER TITLE PAGE OF HER AS A SPECIAL PAGE.

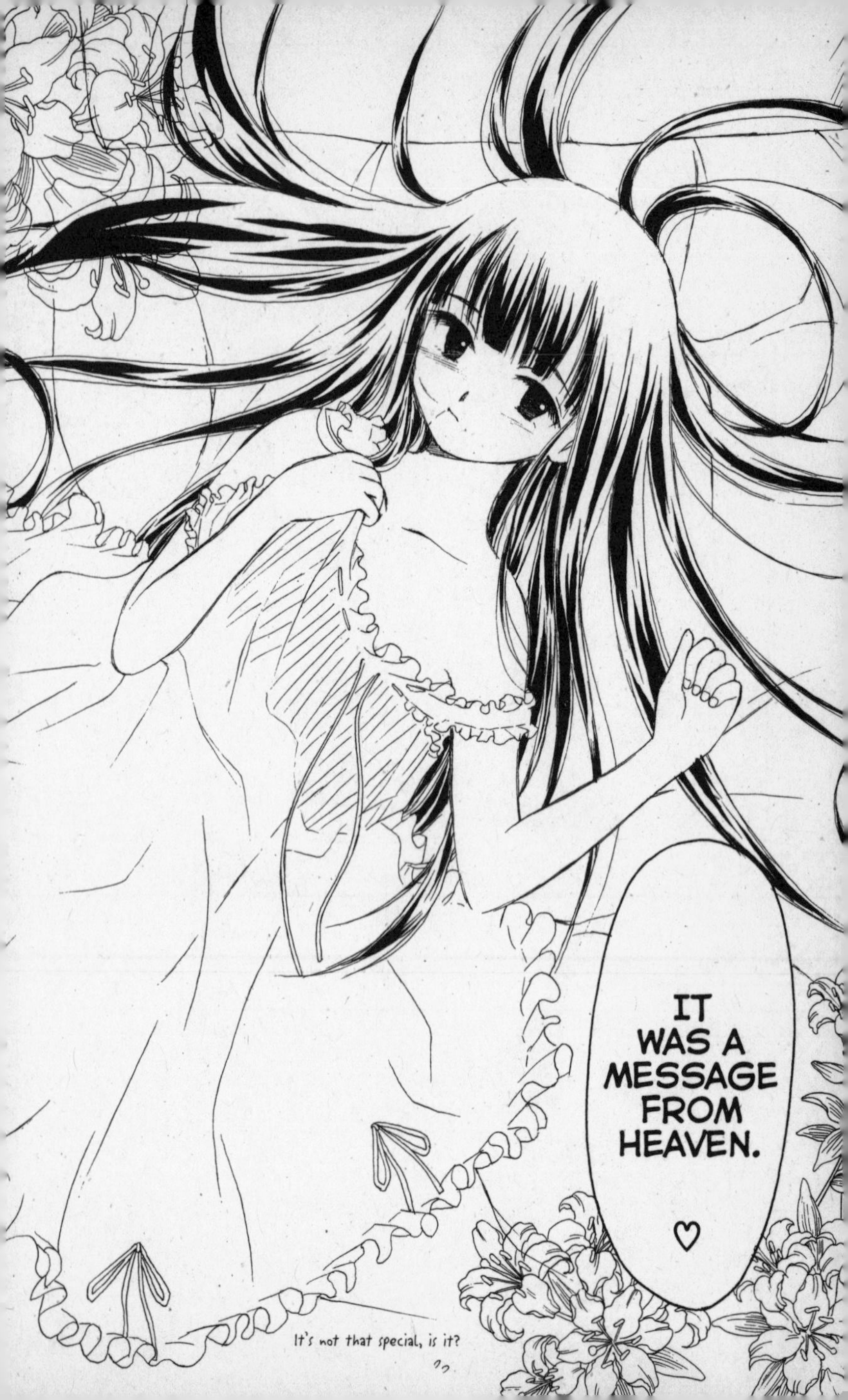
IT WAS A MESSAGE FROM HEAVEN. ♡
It's not that special, is it?

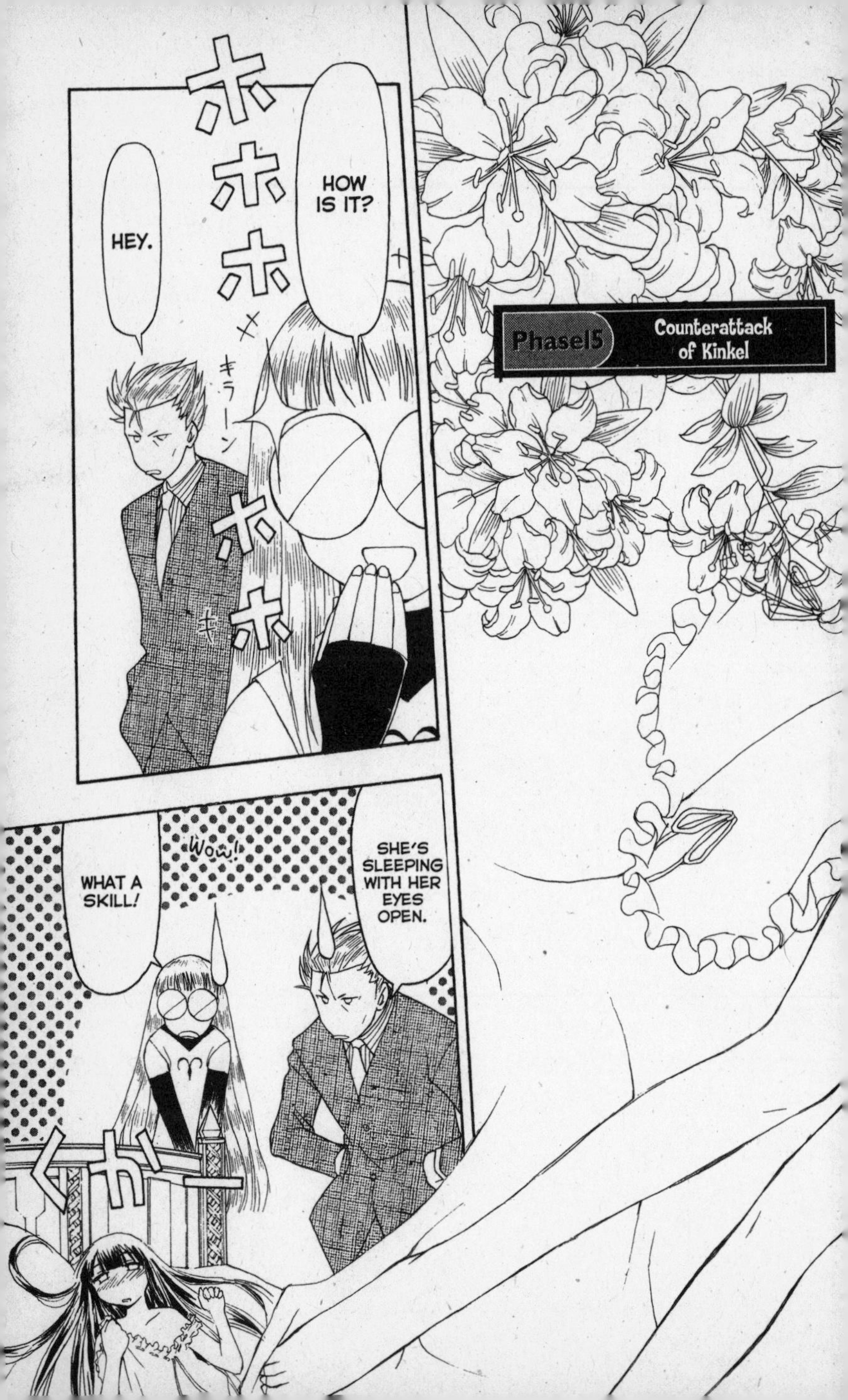
Phase15
Counterattack of Kinkel
HOW IS IT?
ホホホ
キラーン
ホホ
HEY.
SHE'S SLEEPING WITH HER EYES OPEN.
WOW!
WHAT A SKILL!
くかー

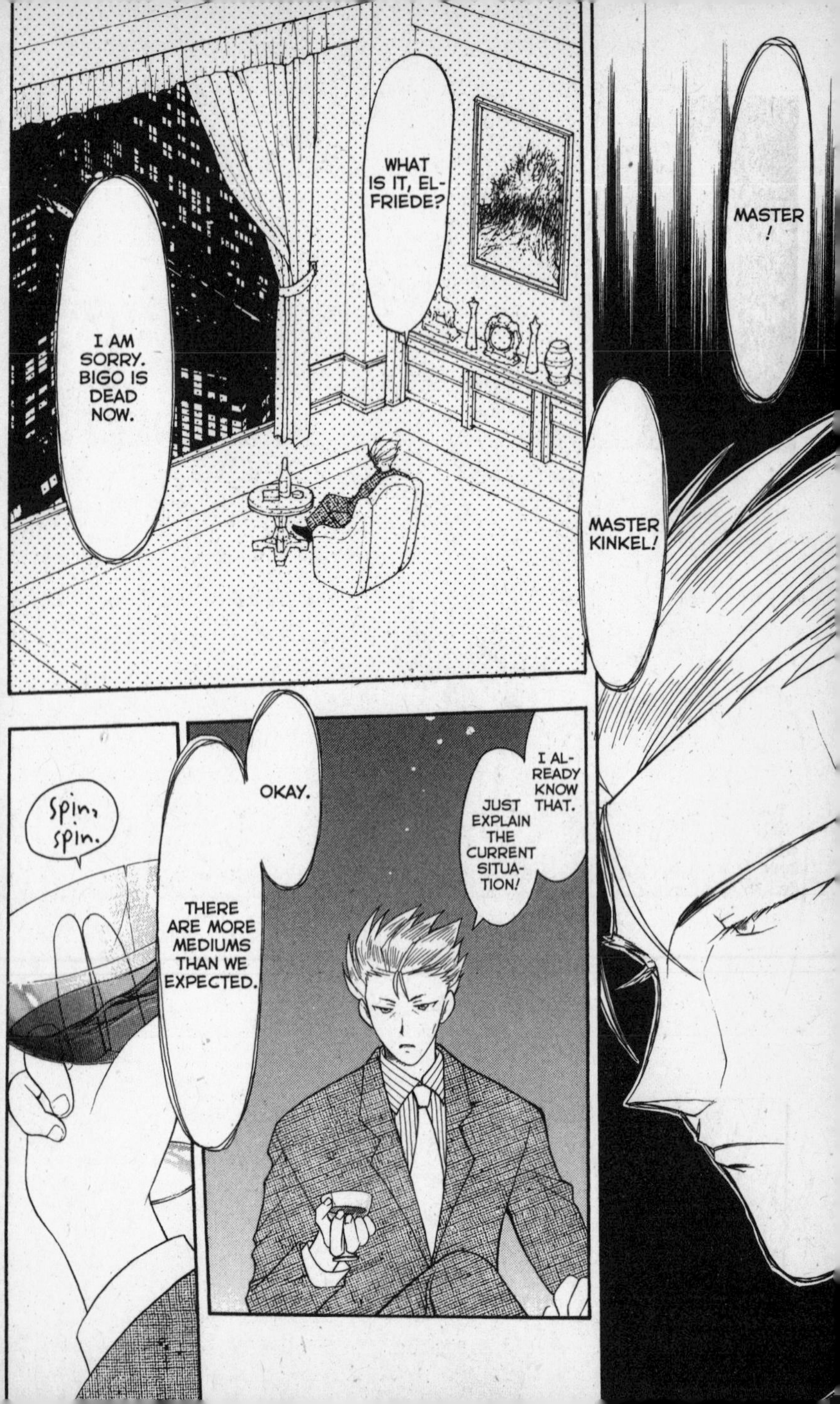
MASTER!
MASTER KINKEL!
WHAT IS IT, EL-FRIEDE?
I AM SORRY. BIGO IS DEAD NOW.
I ALREADY KNOW THAT. JUST EXPLAIN THE CURRENT SITUATION!
OKAY. THERE ARE MORE MEDIUMS THAN WE EXPECTED.
Spin, spin.

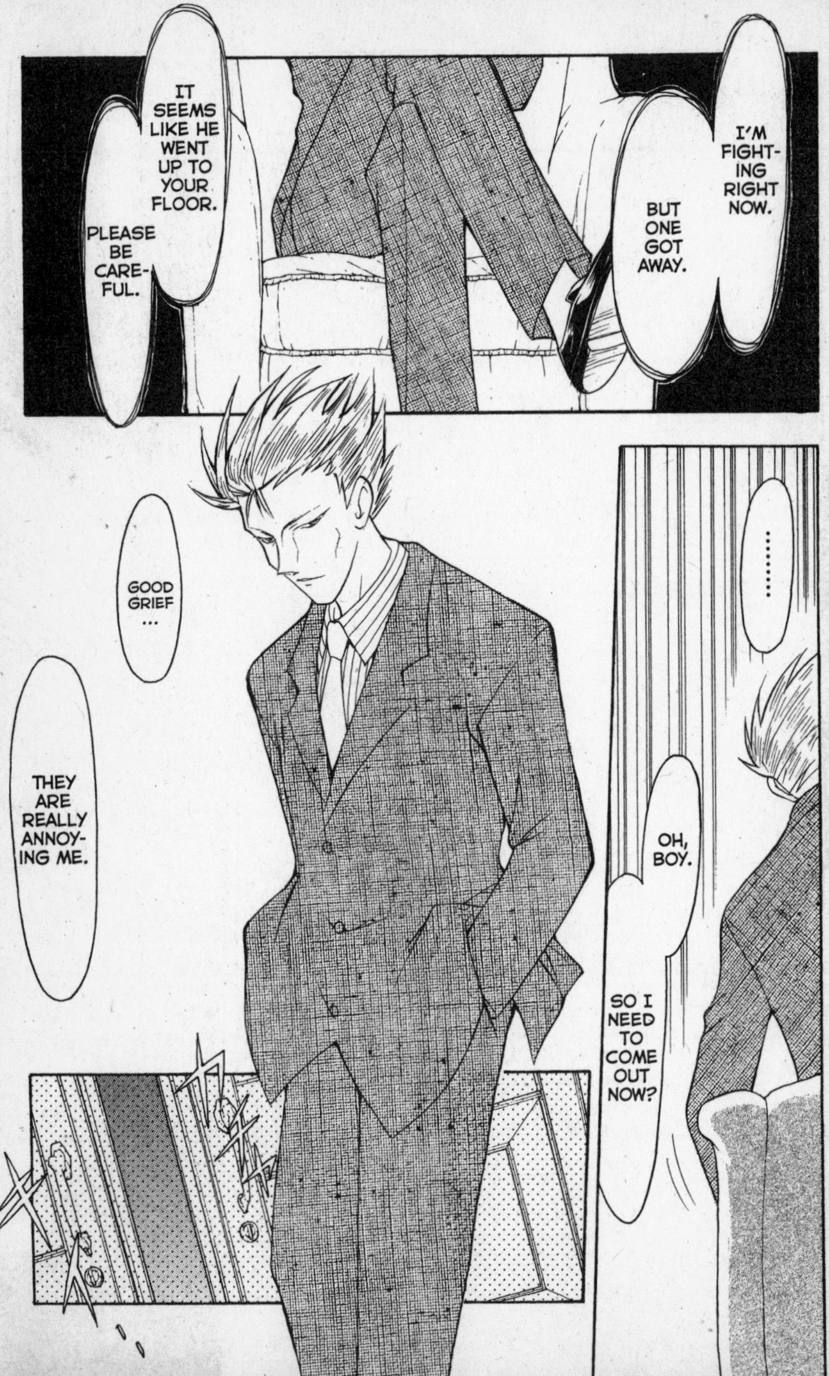
I'M FIGHTING RIGHT NOW.
BUT ONE GOT AWAY.
IT SEEMS LIKE HE WENT UP TO YOUR FLOOR.
PLEASE BE CAREFUL.
....
OH, BOY.
SO I NEED TO COME OUT NOW?
GOOD GRIEF...
THEY ARE REALLY ANNOYING ME.

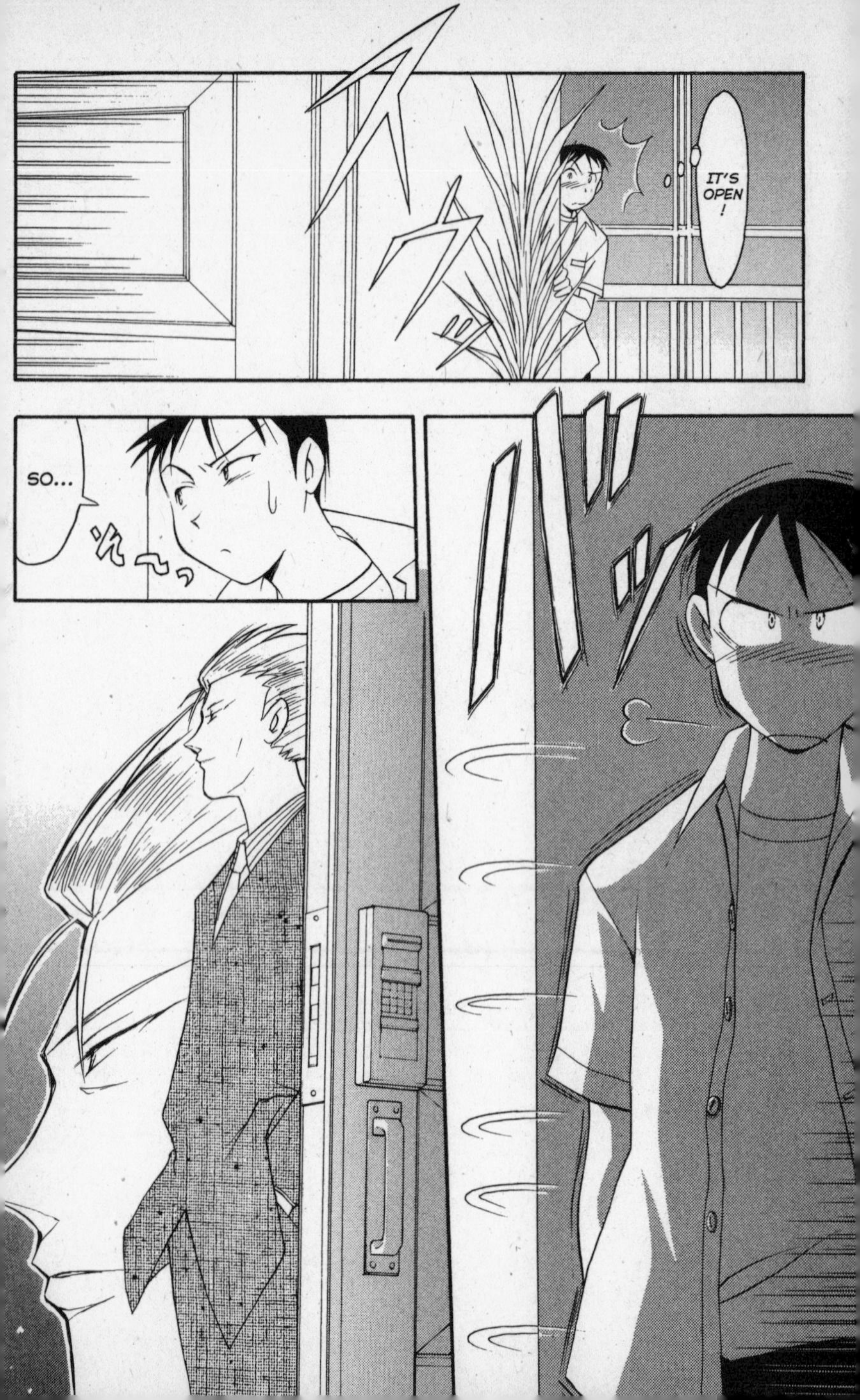
IT'S OPEN !
SO...

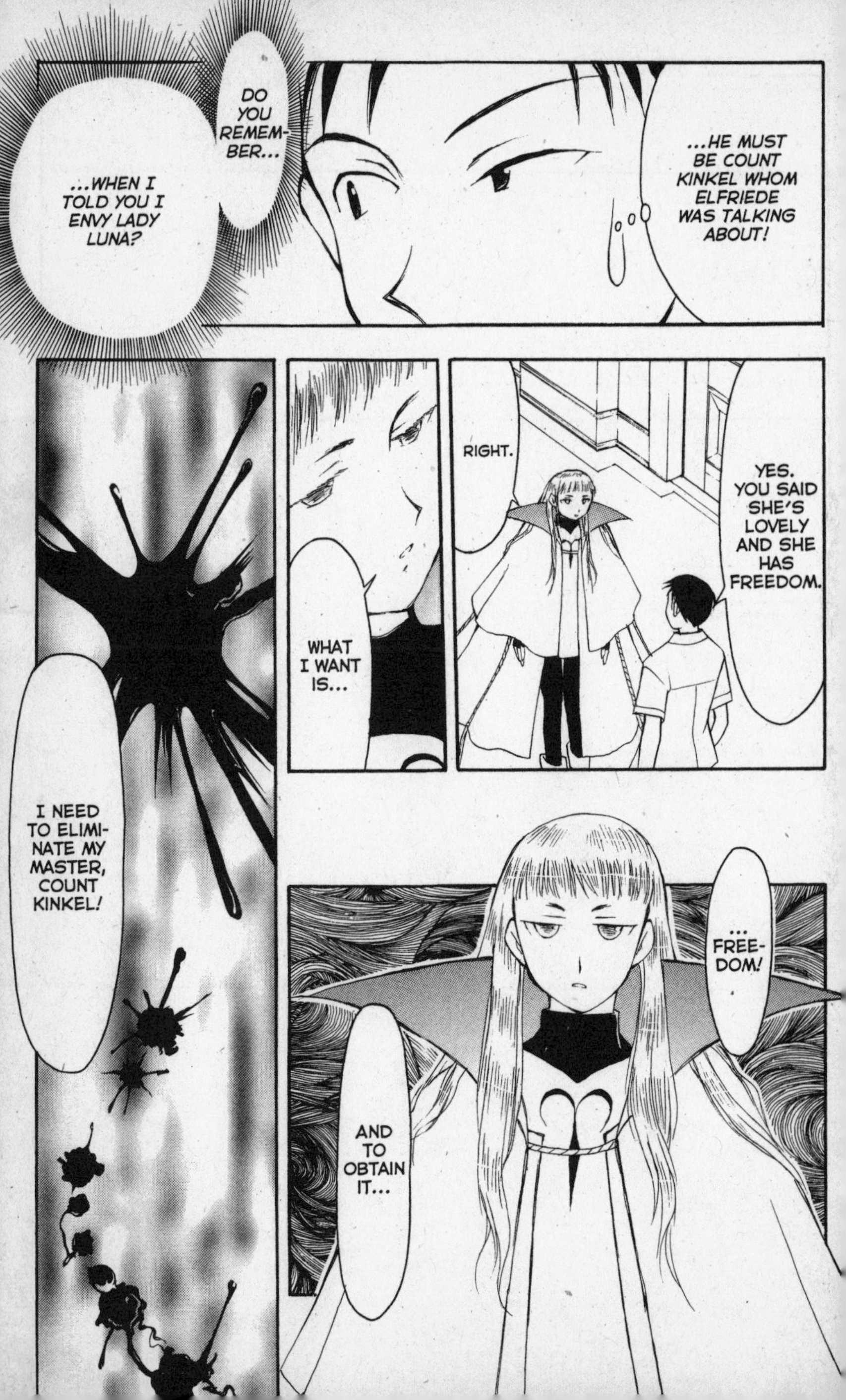
...HE MUST BE COUNT KINKEL WHOM ELFRIEDE WAS TALKING ABOUT!
DO YOU REMEMBER...
...WHEN I TOLD YOU I ENVY LADY LUNA?
YES. YOU SAID SHE'S LOVELY AND SHE HAS FREEDOM.
RIGHT.
WHAT I WANT IS...
...FREEDOM!
AND TO OBTAIN IT...
I NEED TO ELIMINATE MY MASTER, COUNT KINKEL!

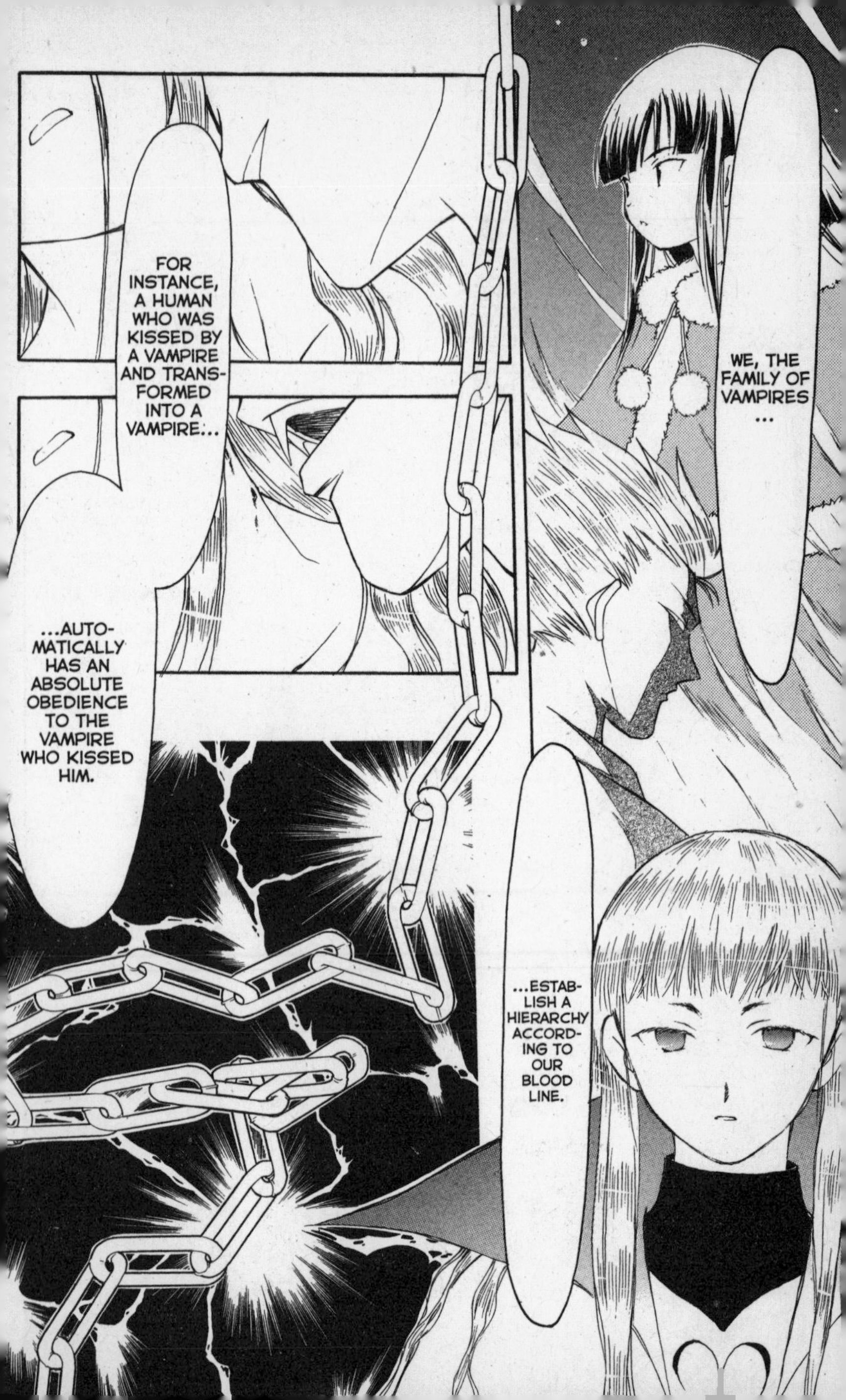
WE, THE FAMILY OF VAMPIRES...
...ESTAB-LISH A HIERARCHY ACCORD-ING TO OUR BLOOD LINE.
FOR INSTANCE, A HUMAN WHO WAS KISSED BY A VAMPIRE AND TRANS-FORMED INTO A VAMPIRE...
...AUTO-MATICALLY HAS AN ABSOLUTE OBEDIENCE TO THE VAMPIRE WHO KISSED HIM.

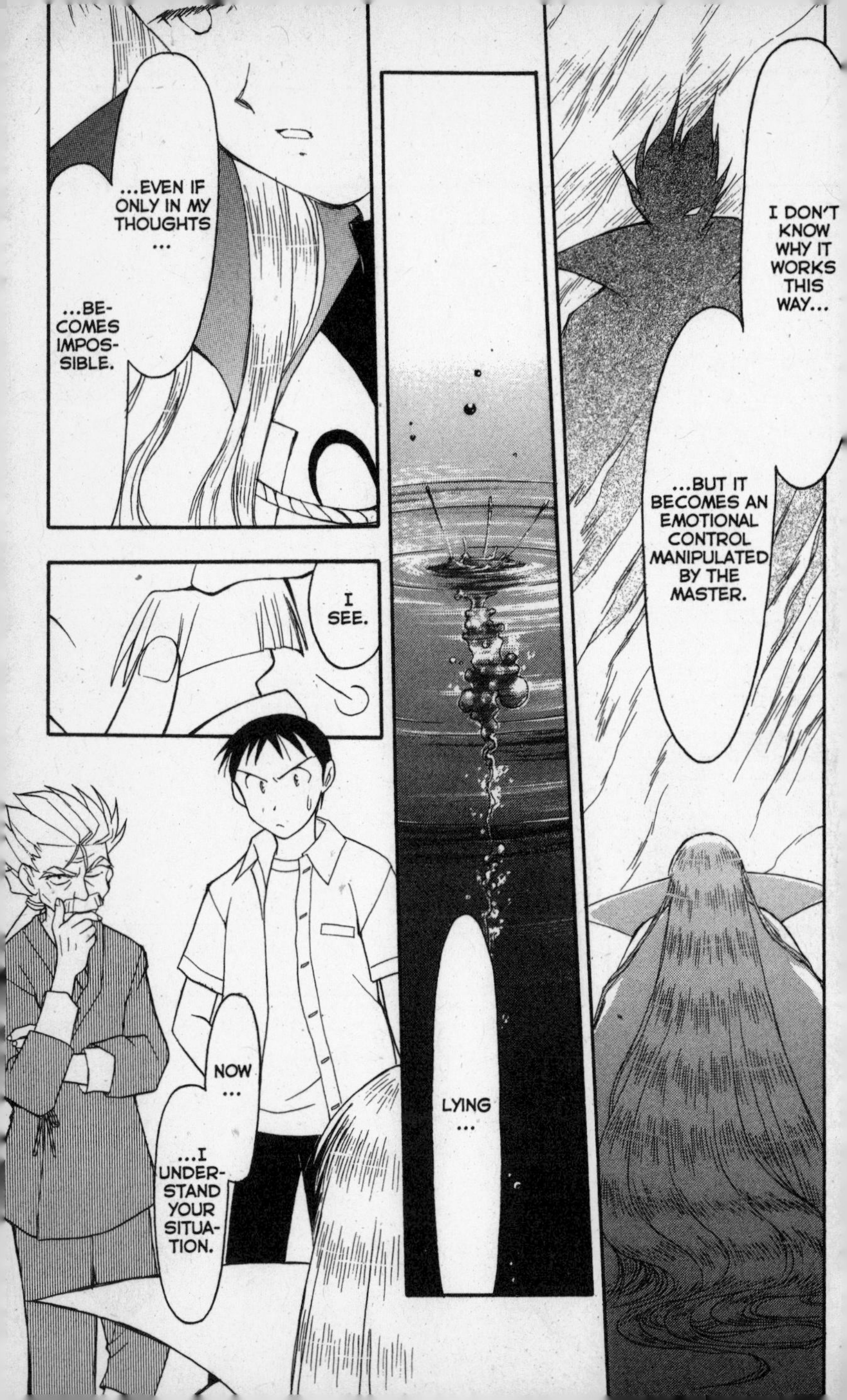
I DON'T KNOW WHY IT WORKS THIS WAY...
...BUT IT BECOMES AN EMOTIONAL CONTROL MANIPULATED BY THE MASTER.
LYING...
...EVEN IF ONLY IN MY THOUGHTS...
...BE-COMES IMPOS-SIBLE.
I SEE.
NOW...
...I UNDER-STAND YOUR SITUA-TION.

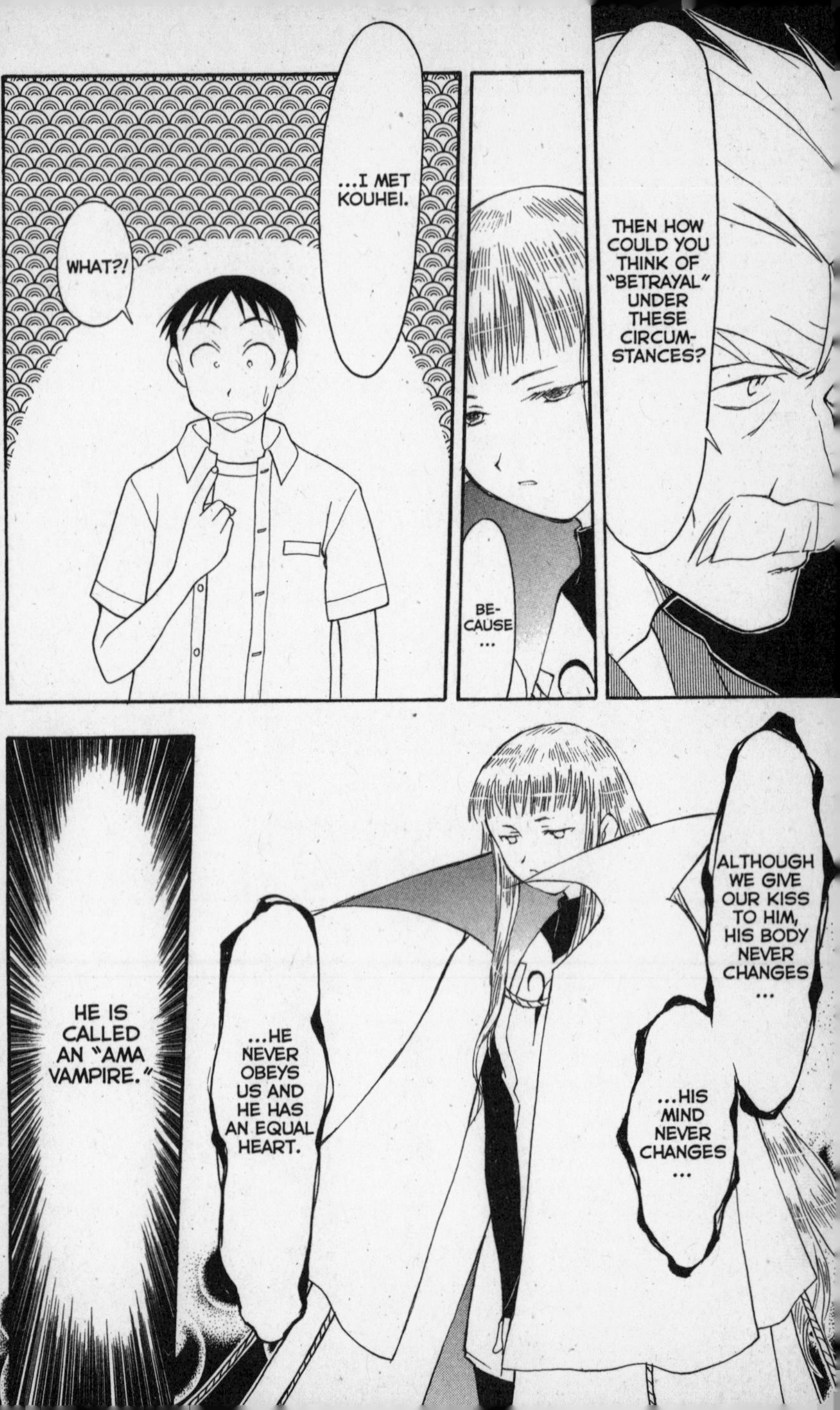
THEN HOW COULD YOU THINK OF "BETRAYAL" UNDER THESE CIRCUM-STANCES?
BE-CAUSE...
...I MET KOUHEI.
WHAT?!
ALTHOUGH WE GIVE OUR KISS TO HIM, HIS BODY NEVER CHANGES...
...HIS MIND NEVER CHANGES...
...HE NEVER OBEYS US AND HE HAS AN EQUAL HEART.
HE IS CALLED AN "AMA VAMPIRE."

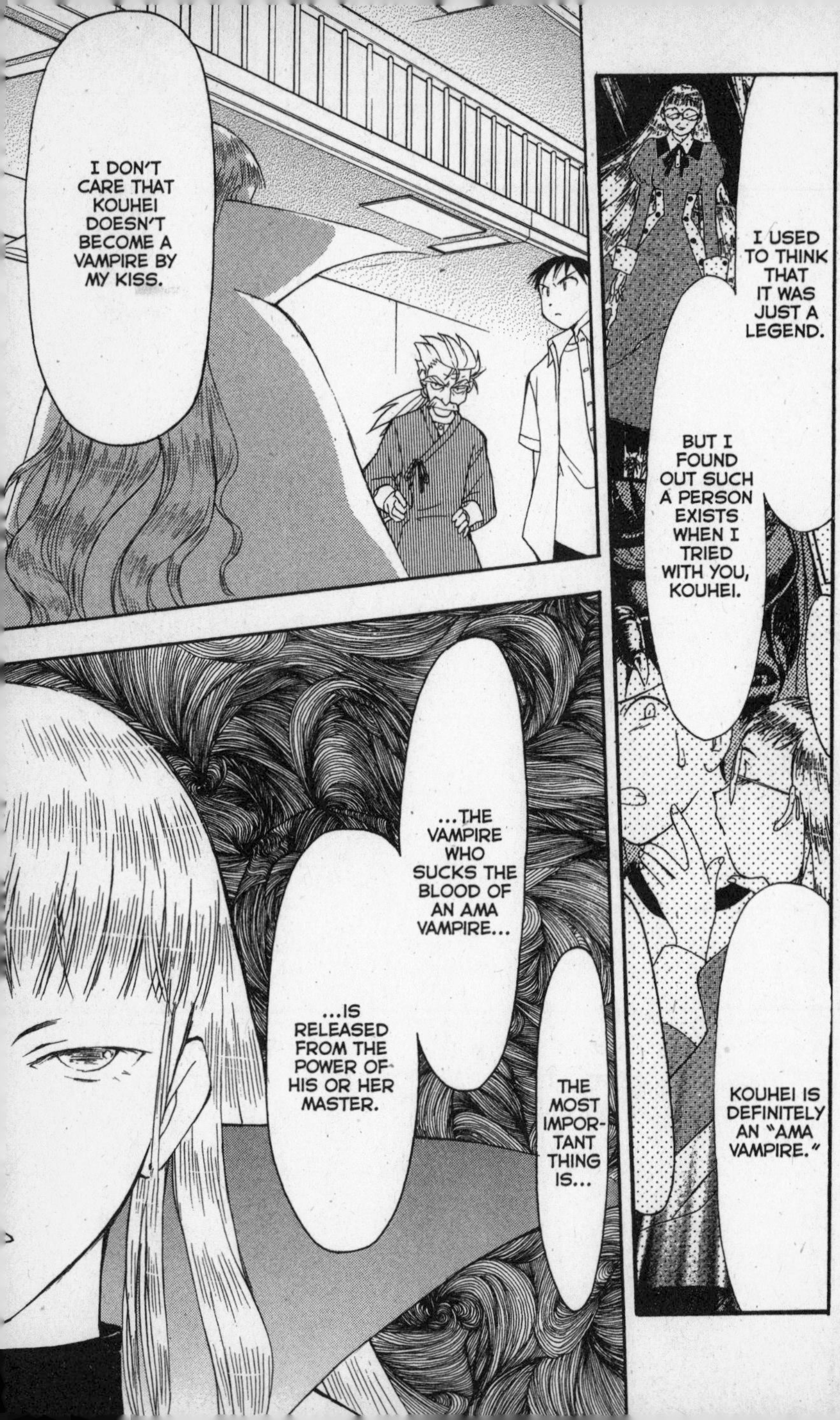
I USED TO THINK THAT IT WAS JUST A LEGEND.
BUT I FOUND OUT SUCH A PERSON EXISTS WHEN I TRIED WITH YOU, KOUHEI.
KOUHEI IS DEFINITELY AN "AMA VAMPIRE."
I DON'T CARE THAT KOUHEI DOESN'T BECOME A VAMPIRE BY MY KISS.
THE MOST IMPORTANT THING IS...
...THE VAMPIRE WHO SUCKS THE BLOOD OF AN AMA VAMPIRE...
...IS RELEASED FROM THE POWER OF HIS OR HER MASTER.

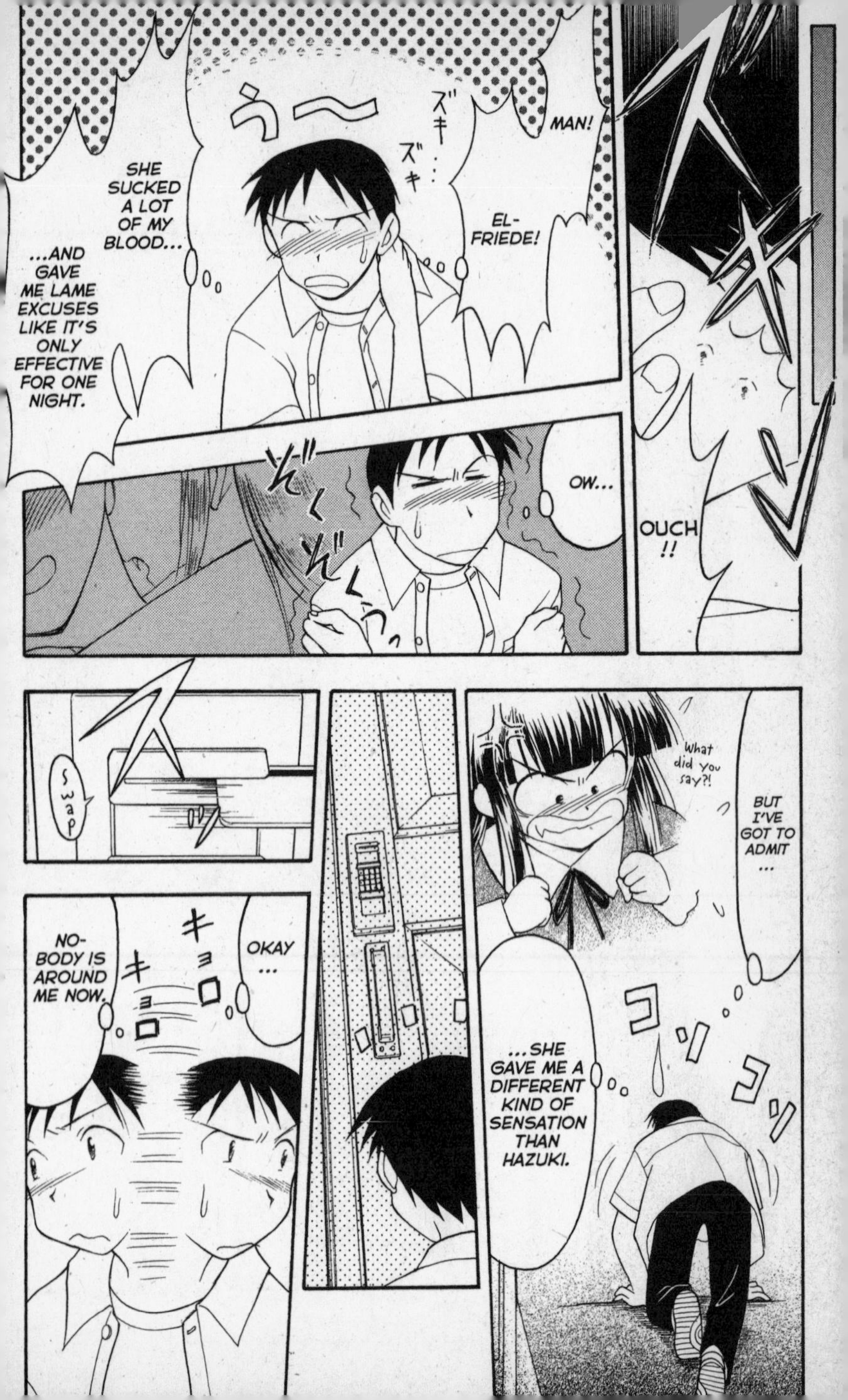
OUCH !!
ズキ‥ズキ
MAN! EL-FRIEDE!
う〜
SHE SUCKED A LOT OF MY BLOOD...
...AND GAVE ME LAME EXCUSES LIKE IT'S ONLY EFFECTIVE FOR ONE NIGHT.
OW...
BUT I'VE GOT TO ADMIT ...
What did you say?!
...SHE GAVE ME A DIFFERENT KIND OF SENSATION THAN HAZUKI.
swap
OKAY ...
NO-BODY IS AROUND ME NOW.
キョロキョロ

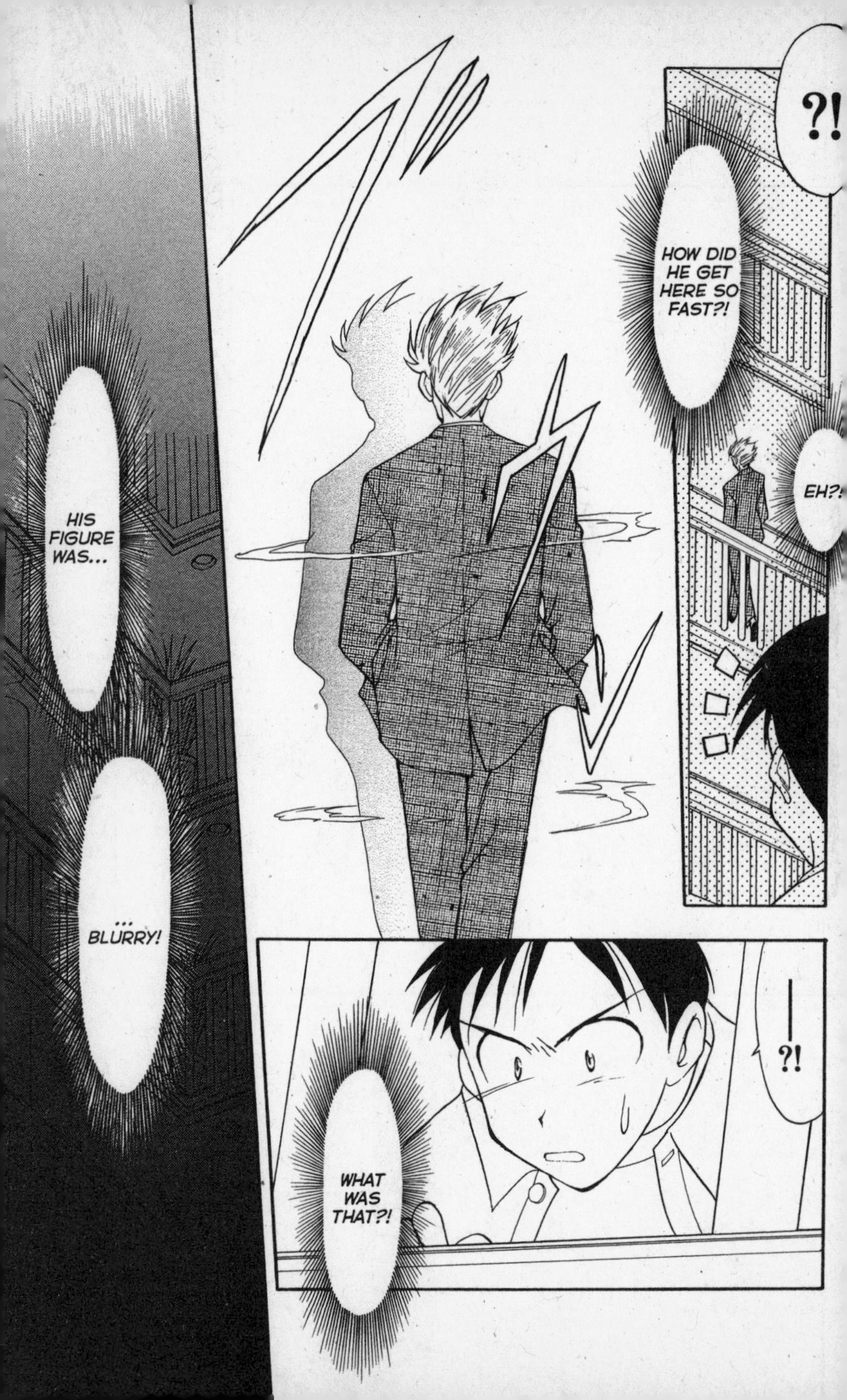
?!
EH?!
HOW DID HE GET HERE SO FAST?!
—?!
WHAT WAS THAT?!
HIS FIGURE WAS...
...BLURRY!

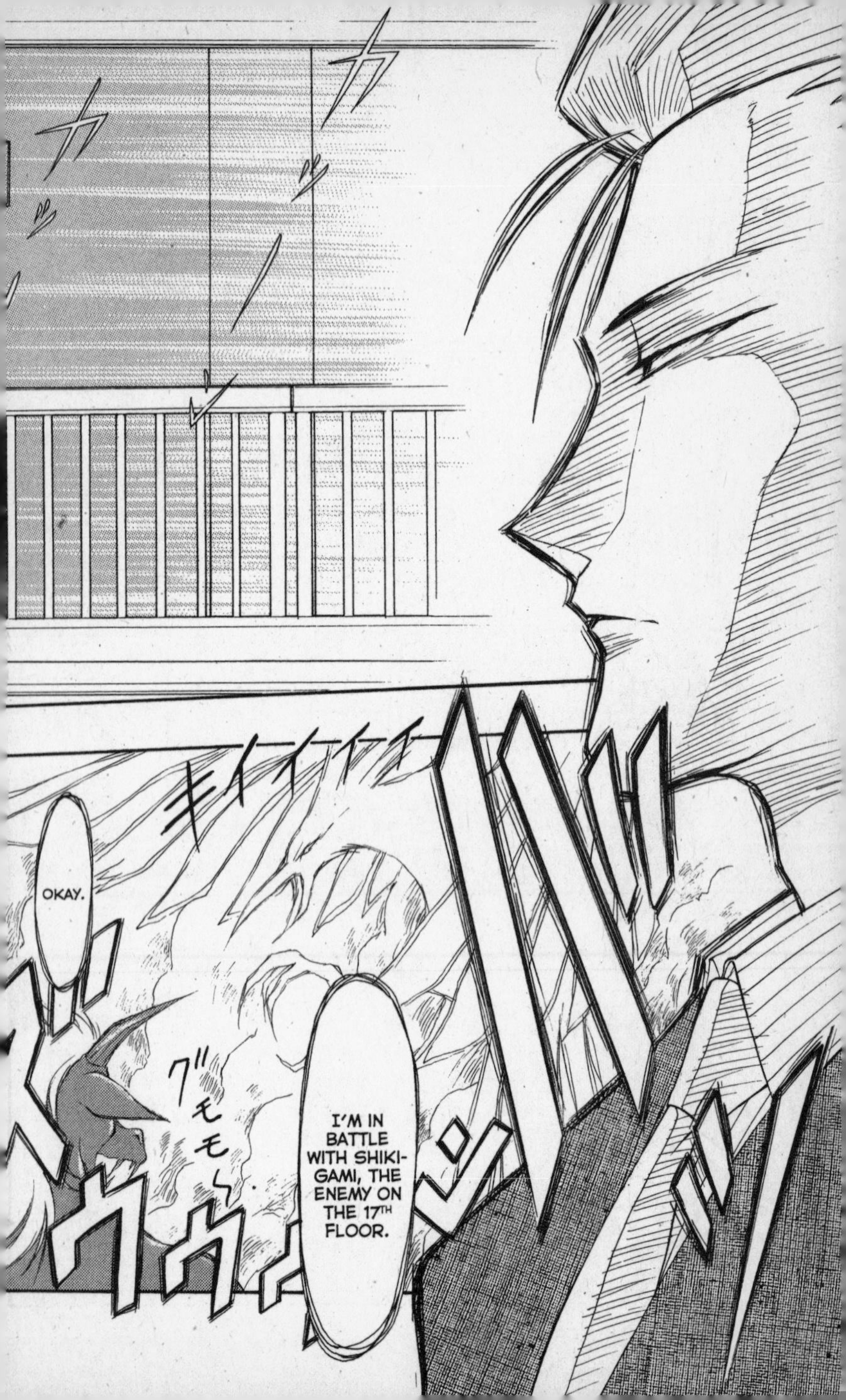
I'M IN BATTLE WITH SHIKI-GAMI, THE ENEMY ON THE 17TH FLOOR.
OKAY.

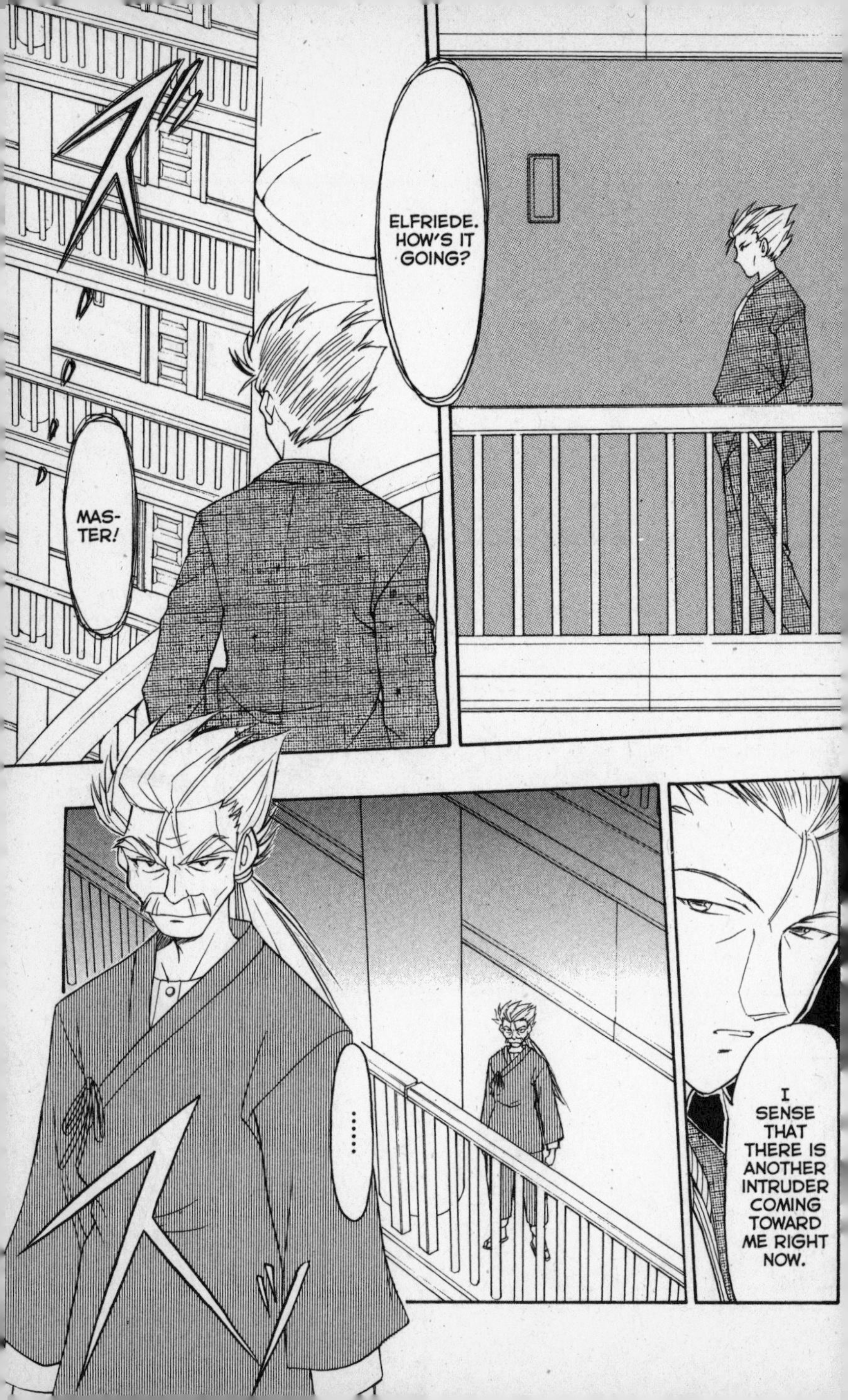
ELFRIEDE. HOW'S IT GOING?
MAS-TER!
I SENSE THAT THERE IS ANOTHER INTRUDER COMING TOWARD ME RIGHT NOW.
......

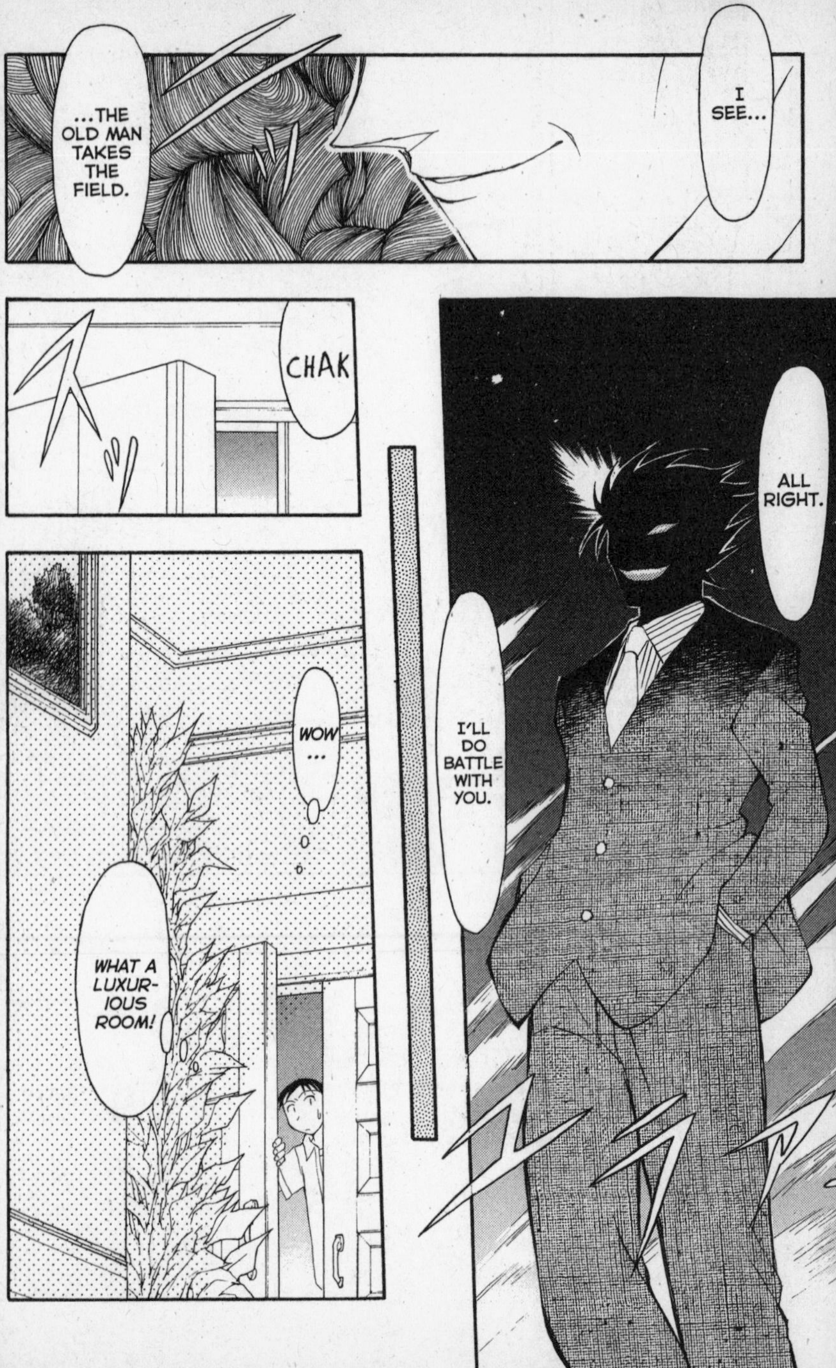
I SEE...
...THE OLD MAN TAKES THE FIELD.
ALL RIGHT.
I'LL DO BATTLE WITH YOU.
CHAK
WOW...
WHAT A LUXURIOUS ROOM!

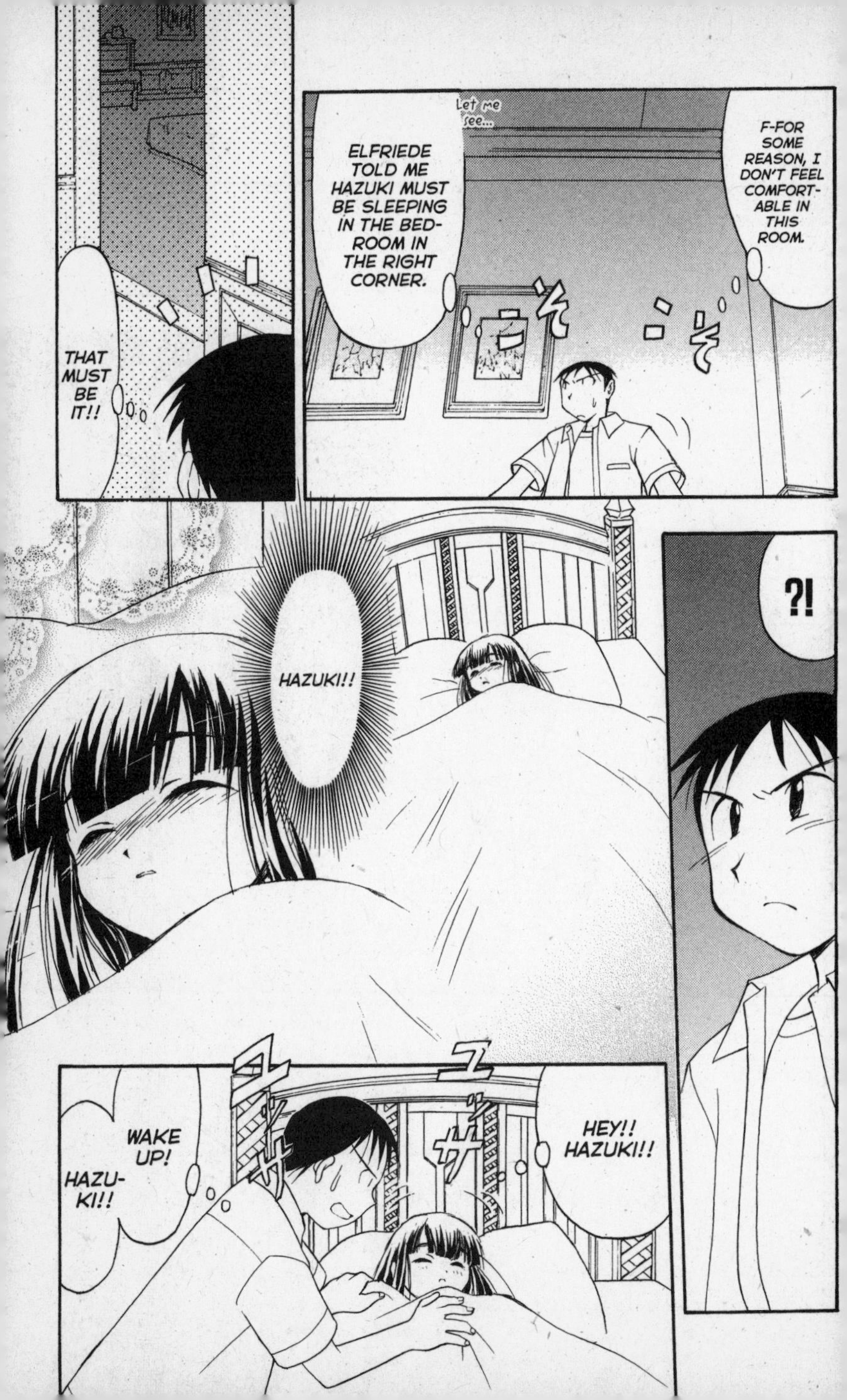
F-FOR SOME REASON, I DON'T FEEL COMFORTABLE IN THIS ROOM.
Let me see...
ELFRIEDE TOLD ME HAZUKI MUST BE SLEEPING IN THE BED-ROOM IN THE RIGHT CORNER.
THAT MUST BE IT!!
?!
HAZUKI!!
HEY!! HAZUKI!!
WAKE UP! HAZU-KI!!

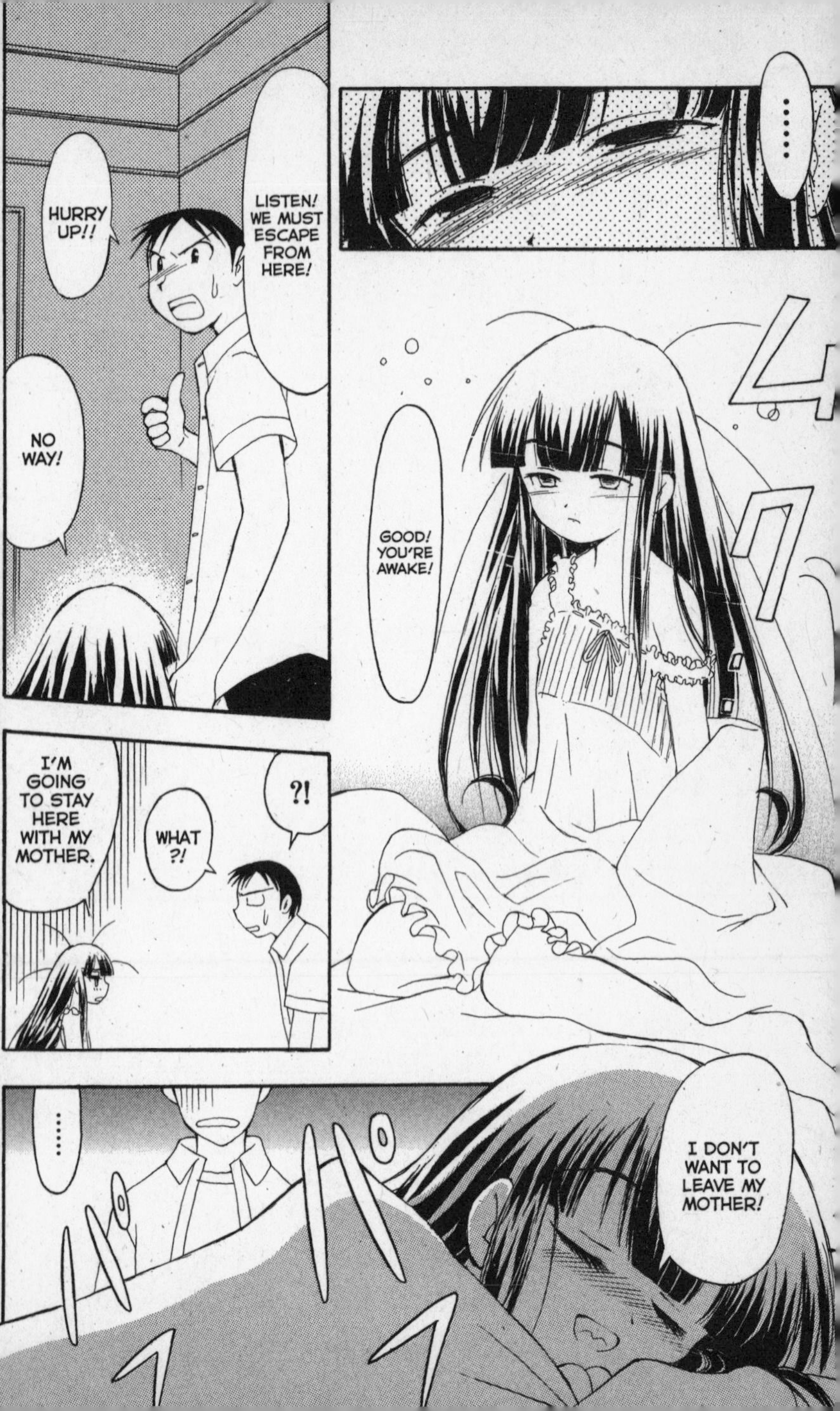
......
GOOD! YOU'RE AWAKE!
LISTEN! WE MUST ESCAPE FROM HERE!
HURRY UP!!
NO WAY!
?!
WHAT ?!
I'M GOING TO STAY HERE WITH MY MOTHER.
I DON'T WANT TO LEAVE MY MOTHER!
......

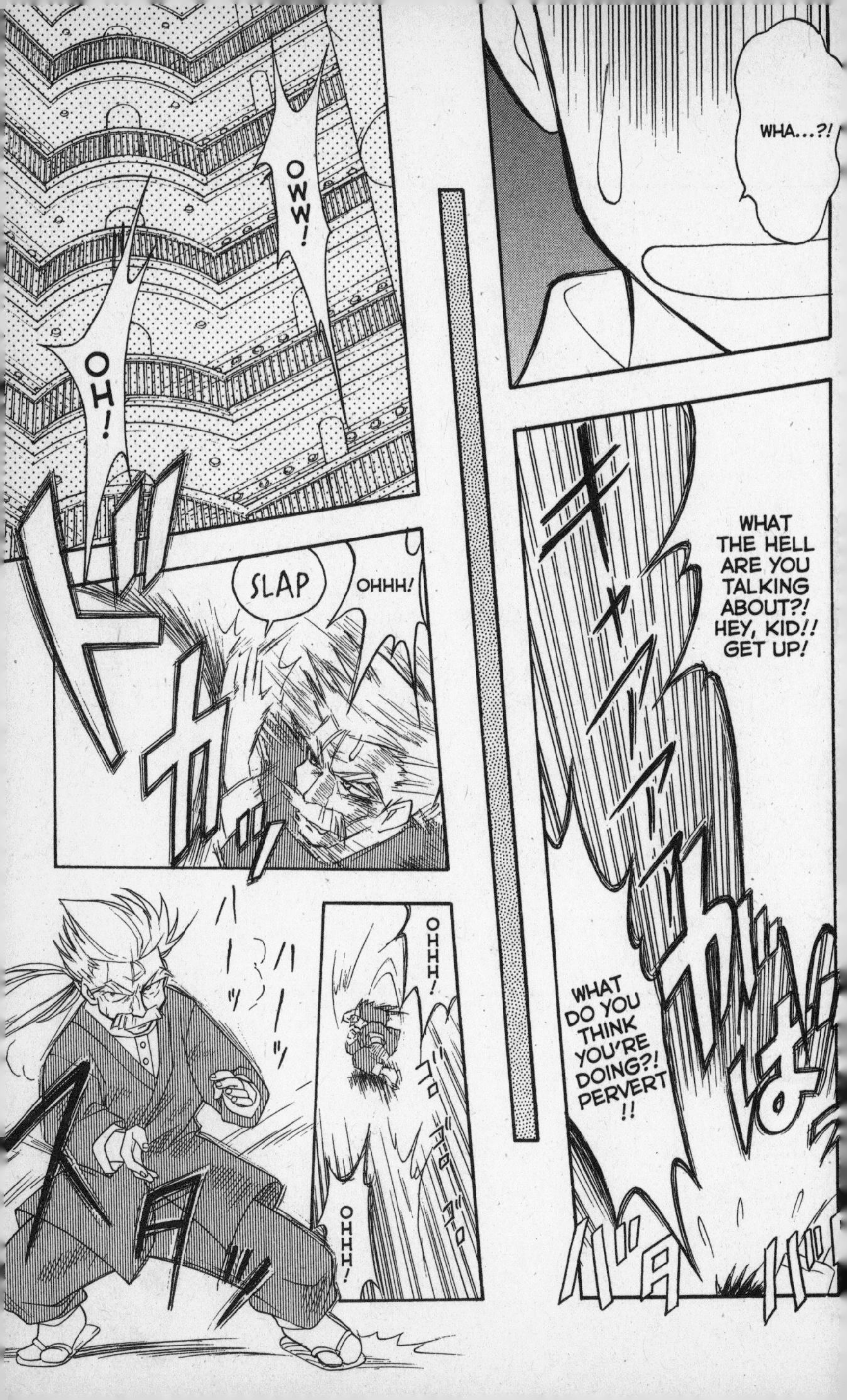

WHA...?!
WHAT THE HELL ARE YOU TALKING ABOUT?! HEY, KID!! GET UP!
WHAT DO YOU THINK YOU'RE DOING?! PERVERT!!
OWW!
OH!
OHHH!
SLAP
OHHH!
OHHH!

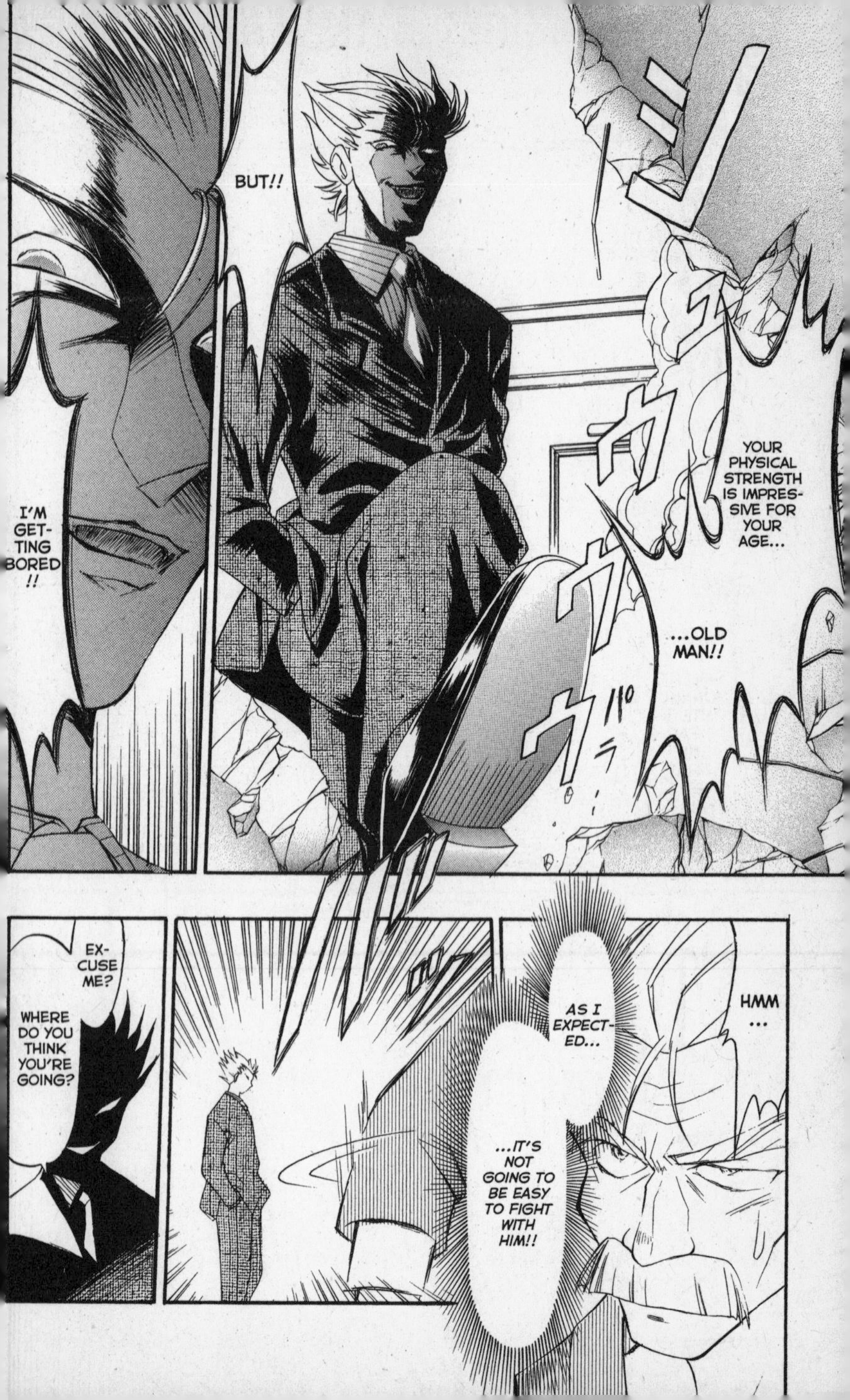
YOUR PHYSICAL STRENGTH IS IMPRESSIVE FOR YOUR AGE...
...OLD MAN!!
BUT!!
I'M GETTING BORED!!
HMM...
AS I EXPECTED...
...IT'S NOT GOING TO BE EASY TO FIGHT WITH HIM!!
EXCUSE ME?
WHERE DO YOU THINK YOU'RE GOING?

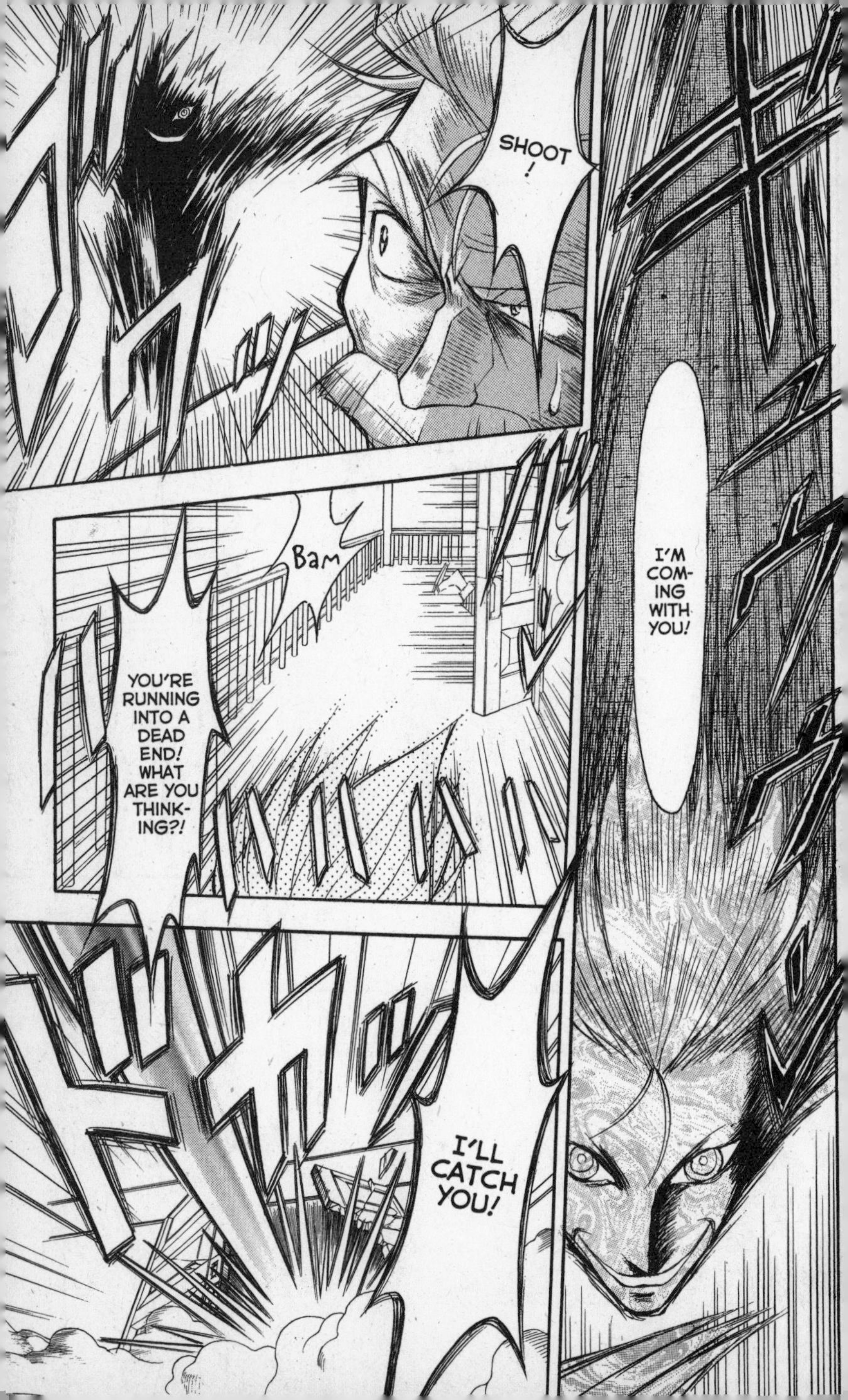
I'M COMING WITH YOU!
SHOOT!
Bam
YOU'RE RUNNING INTO A DEAD END! WHAT ARE YOU THINKING?!
I'LL CATCH YOU!

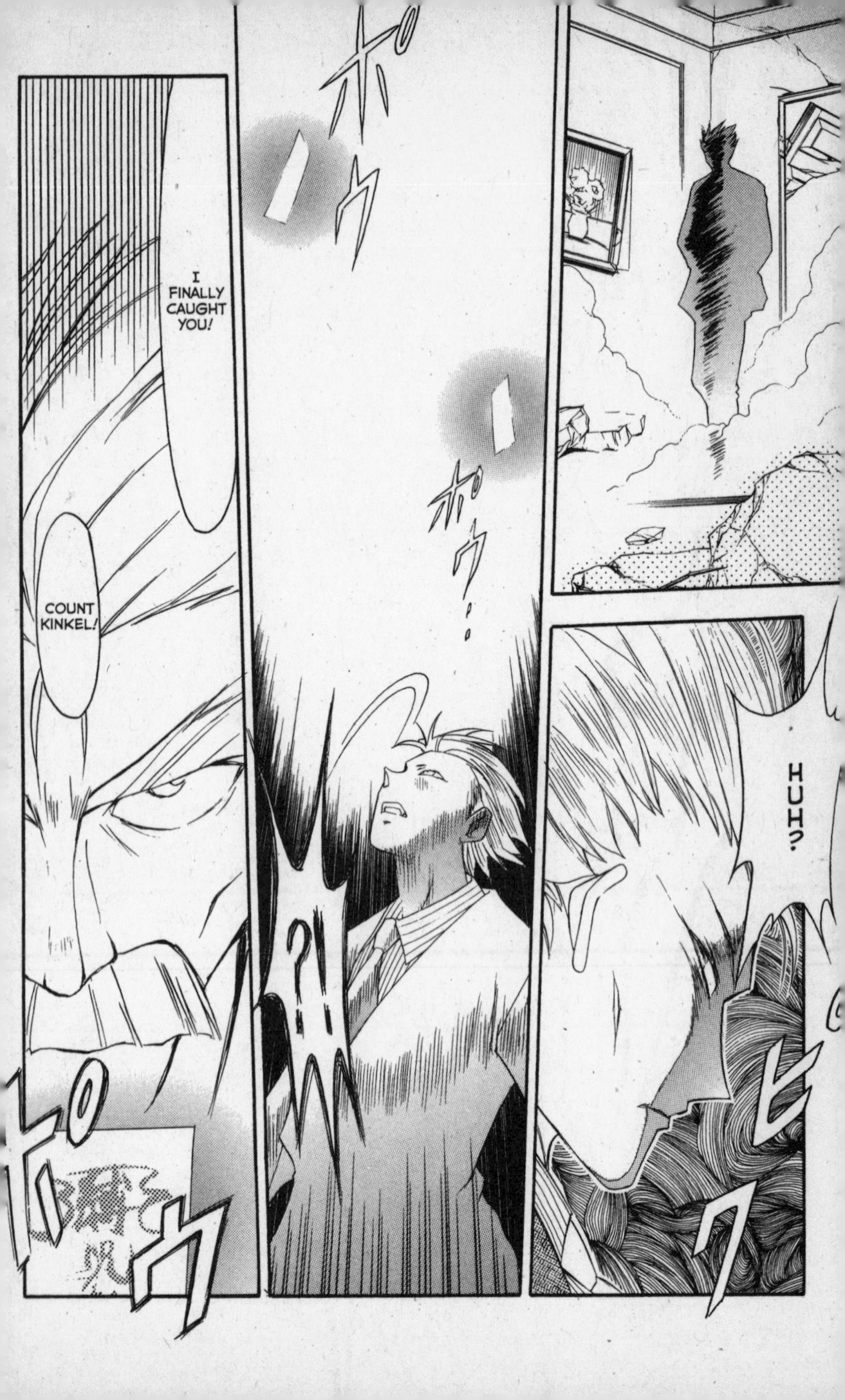
HUH?
?!!
I FINALLY CAUGHT YOU!
COUNT KINKEL!

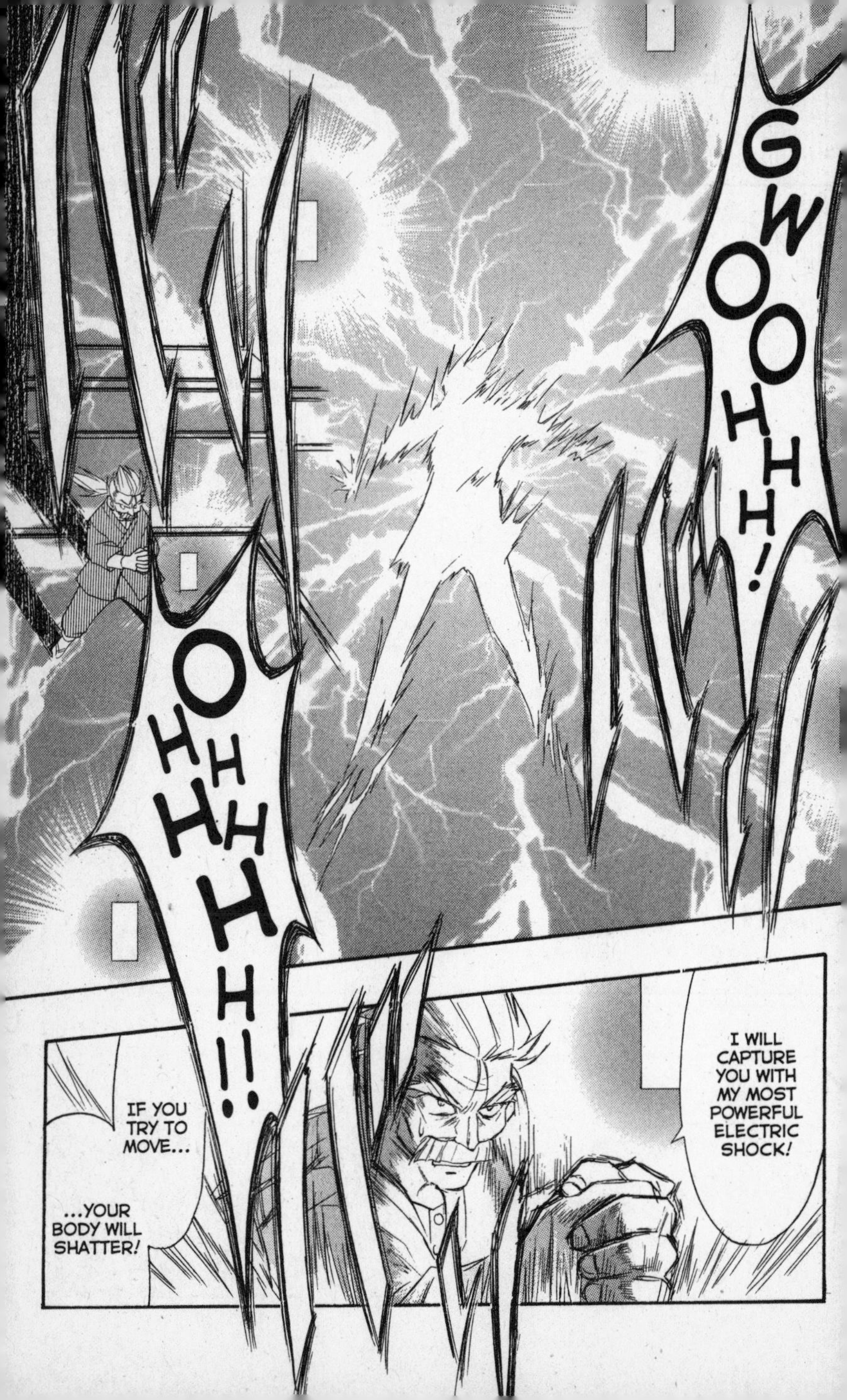
GWOOHHH!
OHHHHHH!!
I WILL CAPTURE YOU WITH MY MOST POWERFUL ELECTRIC SHOCK!
IF YOU TRY TO MOVE...
...YOUR BODY WILL SHATTER!

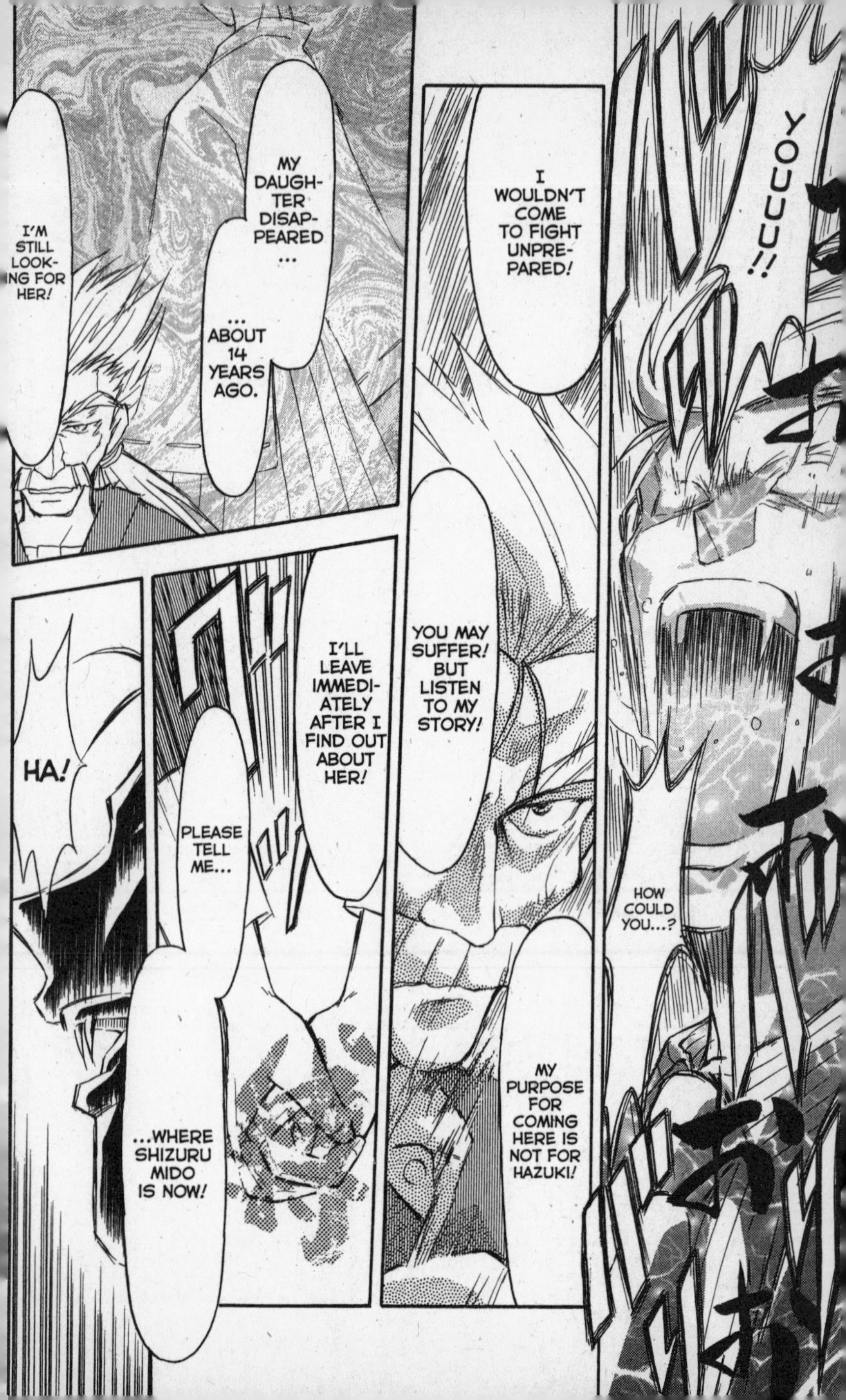

YOUUUU!!
HOW COULD YOU...?
I WOULDN'T COME TO FIGHT UNPREPARED!
YOU MAY SUFFER! BUT LISTEN TO MY STORY!
MY PURPOSE FOR COMING HERE IS NOT FOR HAZUKI!
MY DAUGHTER DISAPPEARED...
...ABOUT 14 YEARS AGO.
I'M STILL LOOKING FOR HER!
I'LL LEAVE IMMEDIATELY AFTER I FIND OUT ABOUT HER!
PLEASE TELL ME...
...WHERE SHIZURU MIDO IS NOW!
HA!

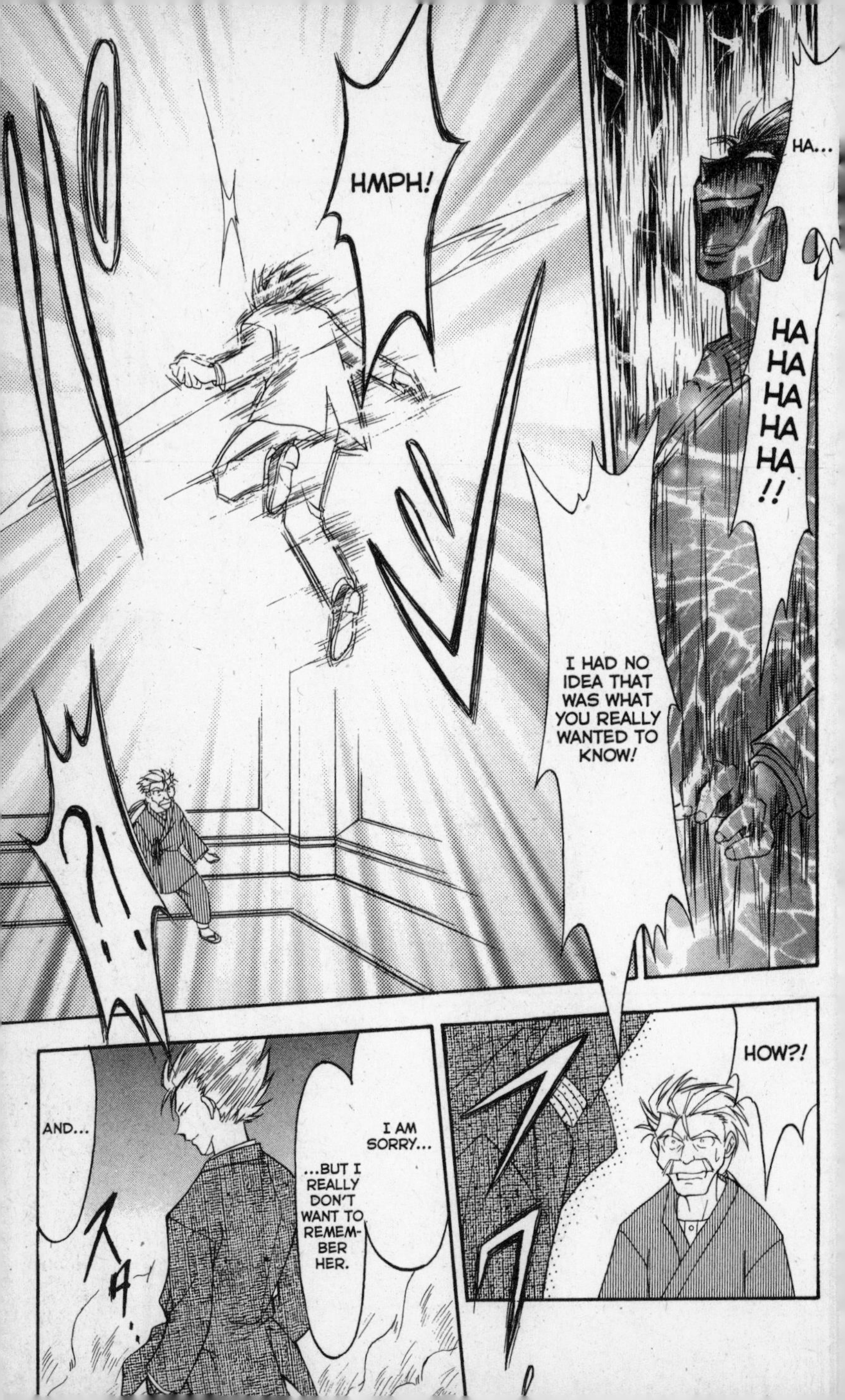
HA...
HA HA HA HA HA!!
I HAD NO IDEA THAT WAS WHAT YOU REALLY WANTED TO KNOW!
HMPH!
HOW?!
I AM SORRY...
...BUT I REALLY DON'T WANT TO REMEMBER HER.
AND...

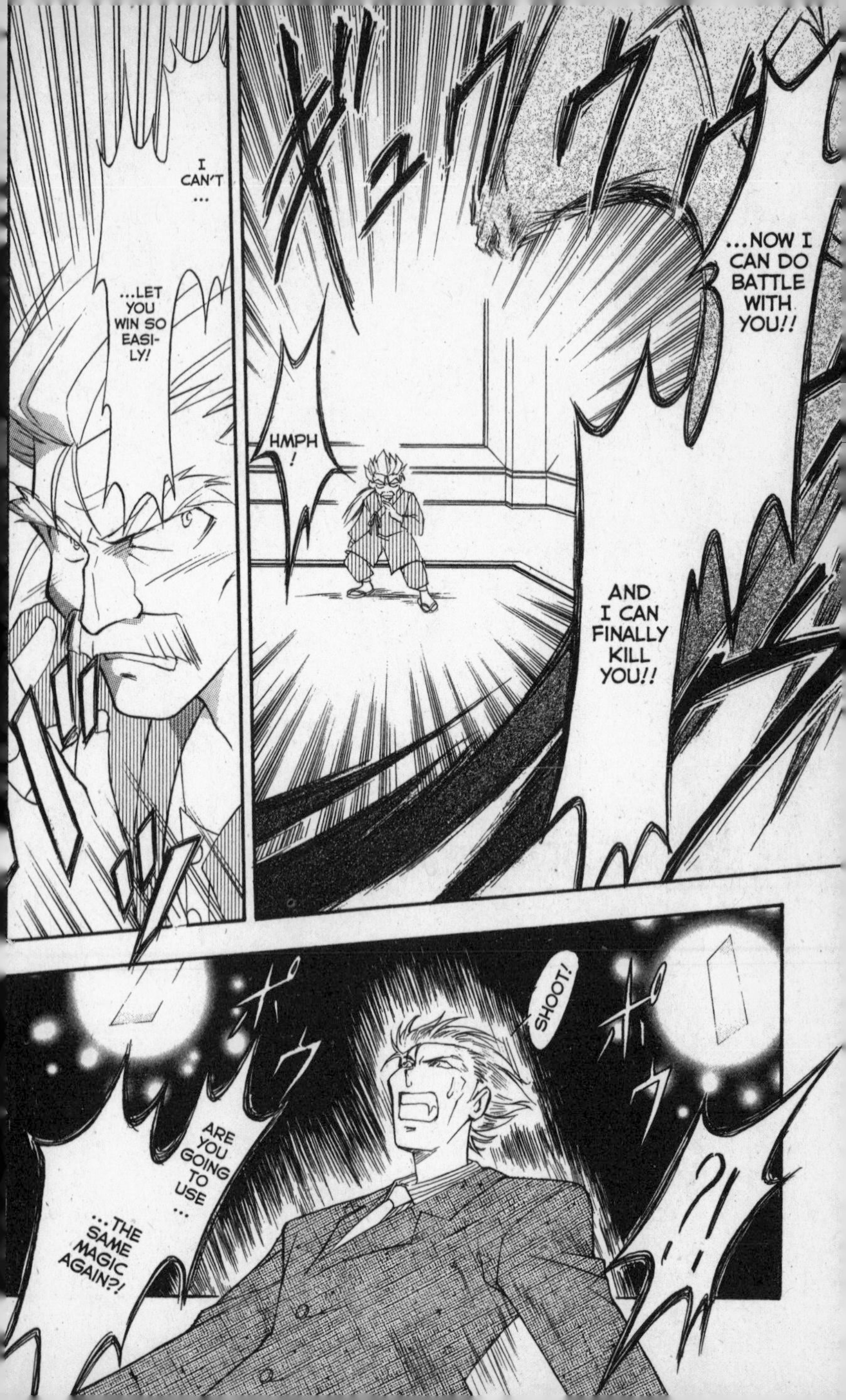
...NOW I CAN DO BATTLE WITH YOU!!
AND I CAN FINALLY KILL YOU!!
HMPH!
I CAN'T ...
...LET YOU WIN SO EASILY!
SHOOT!
?!
ARE YOU GOING TO USE ...
...THE SAME MAGIC AGAIN?!

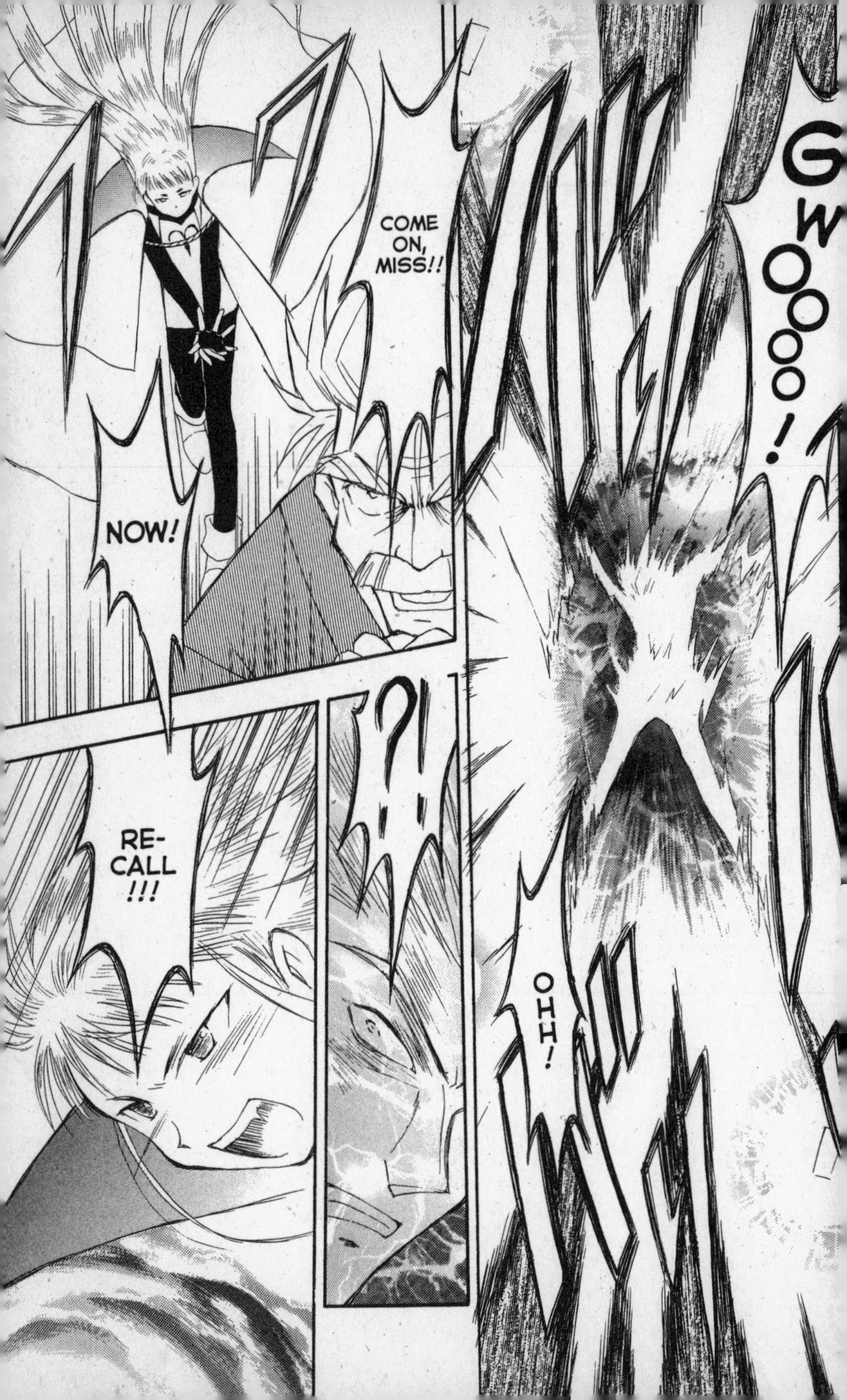
GWOOOO!
OHH!
COME ON, MISS!!
NOW!
?!
RE-CALL!!!

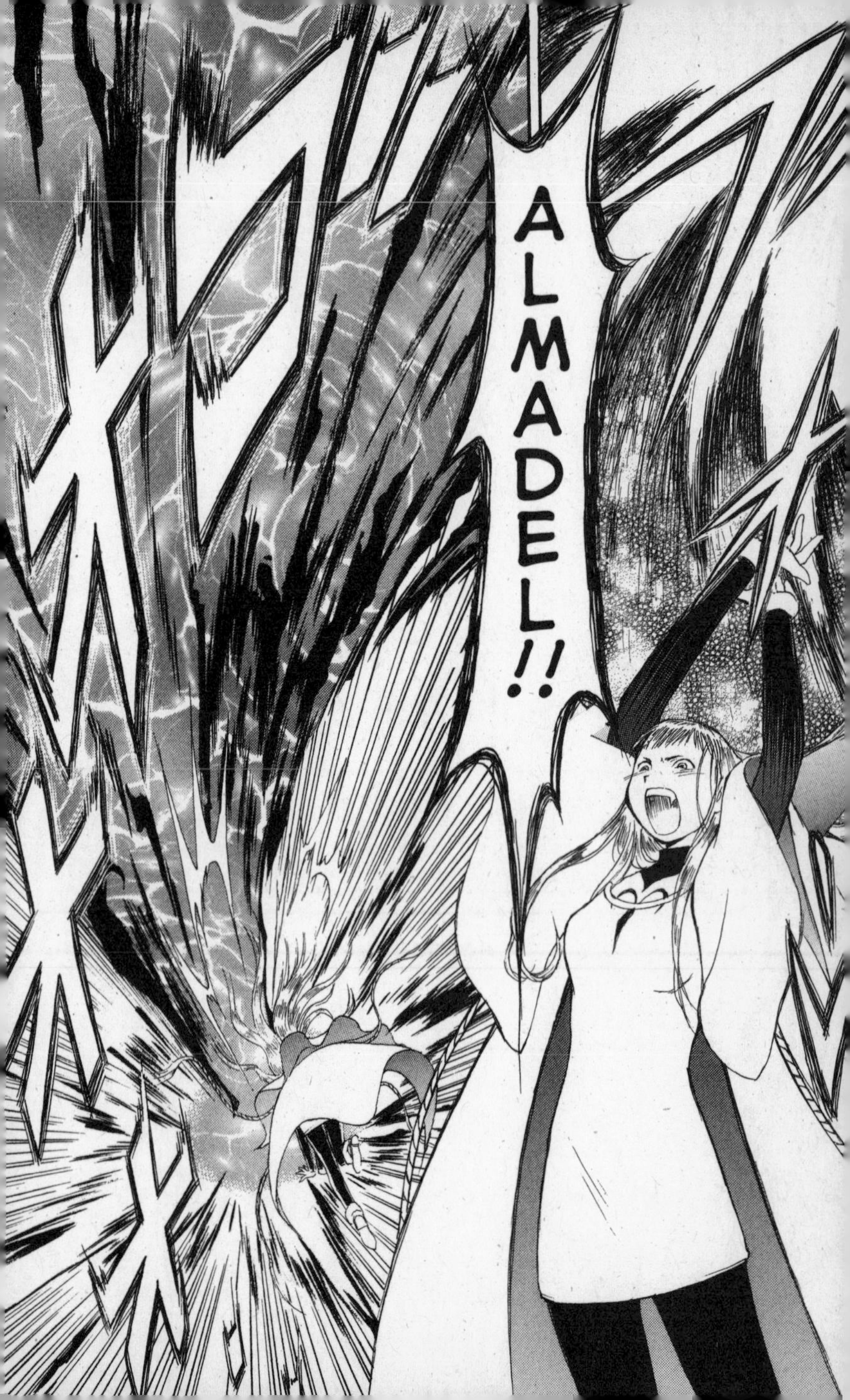
ALMADEL!!

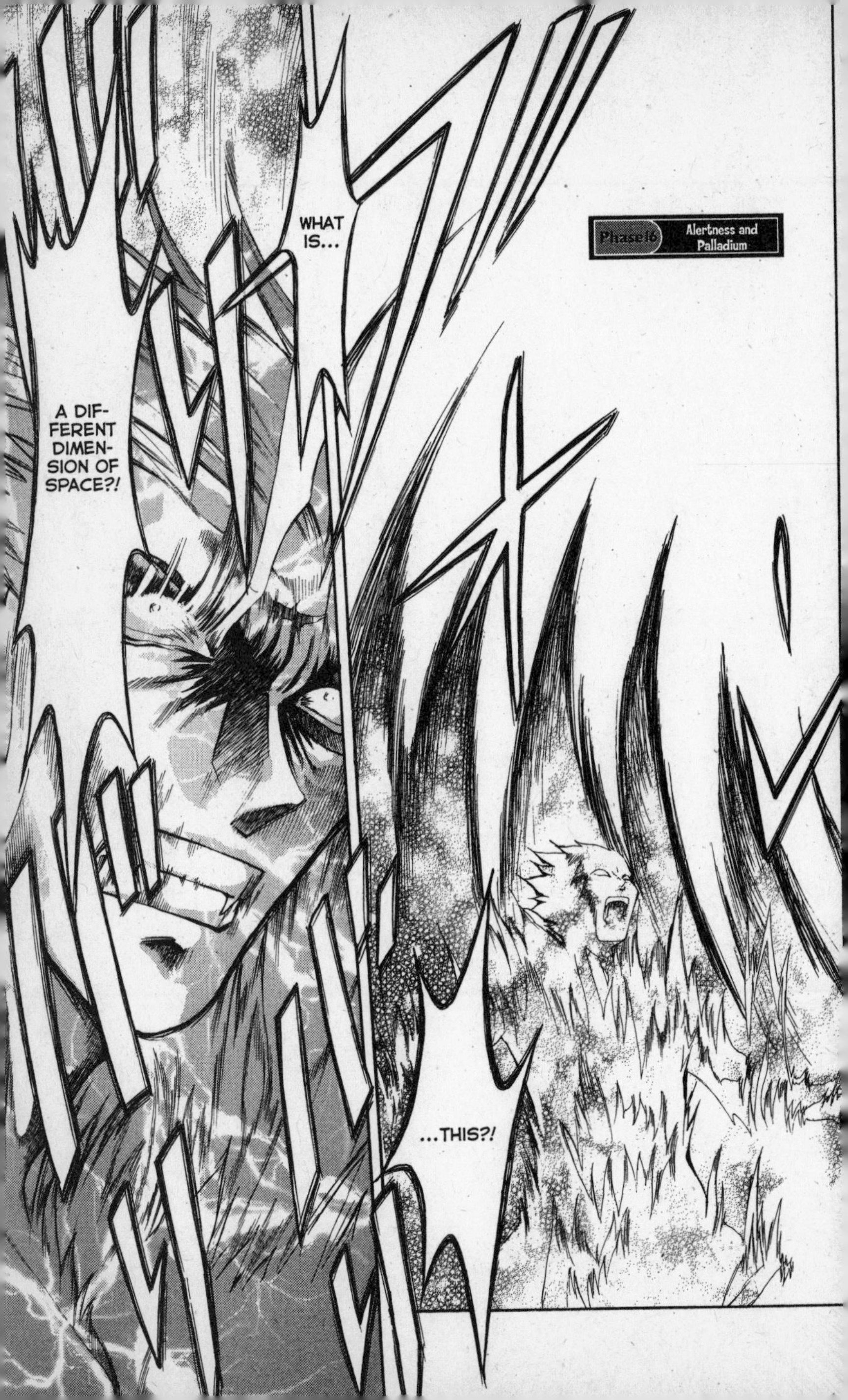
Phase16 Alertness and Palladium
WHAT IS...
A DIFFERENT DIMENSION OF SPACE?!
...THIS?!

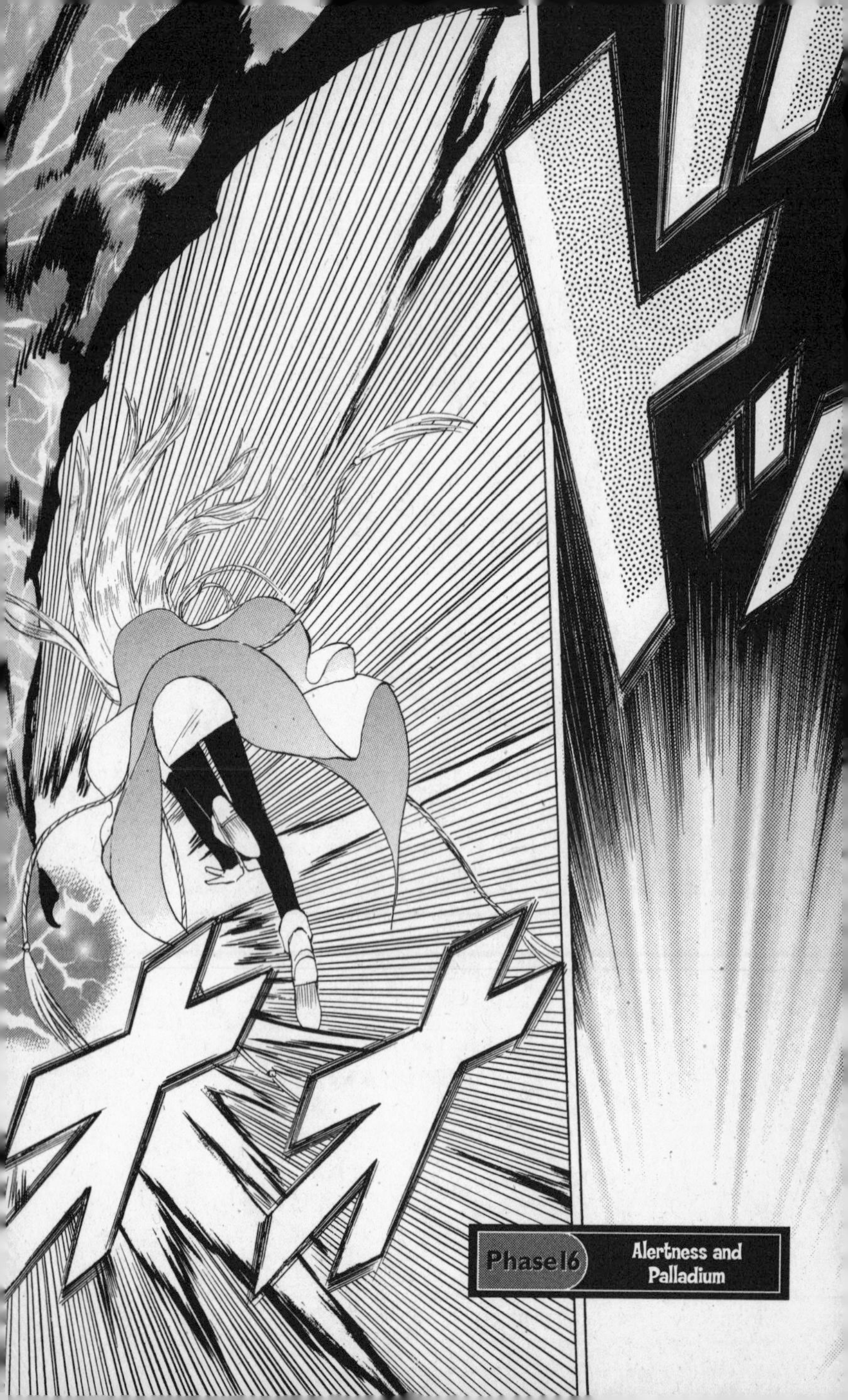
Phase 16
Alertness and Palladium

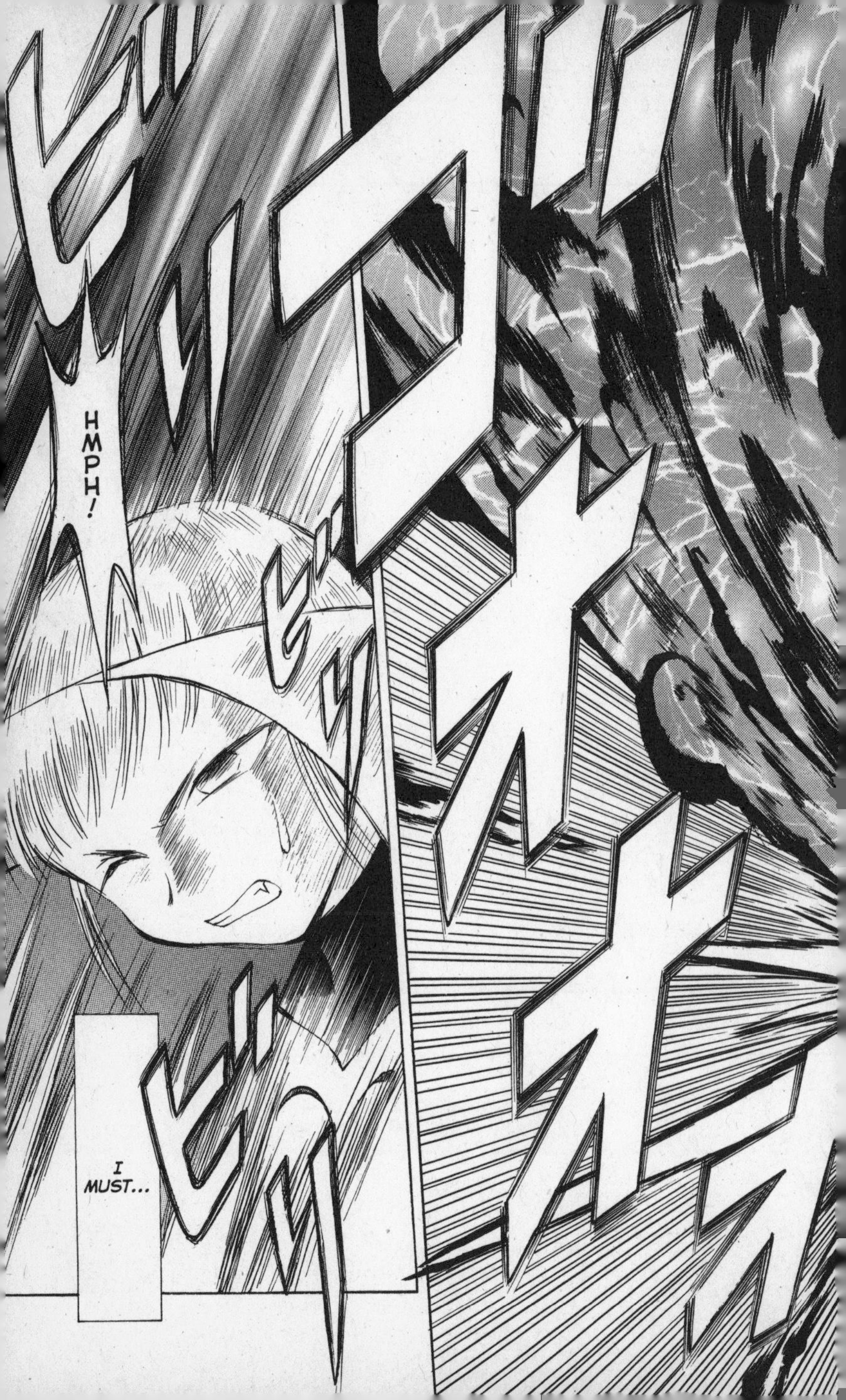
HMPH!
I MUST...

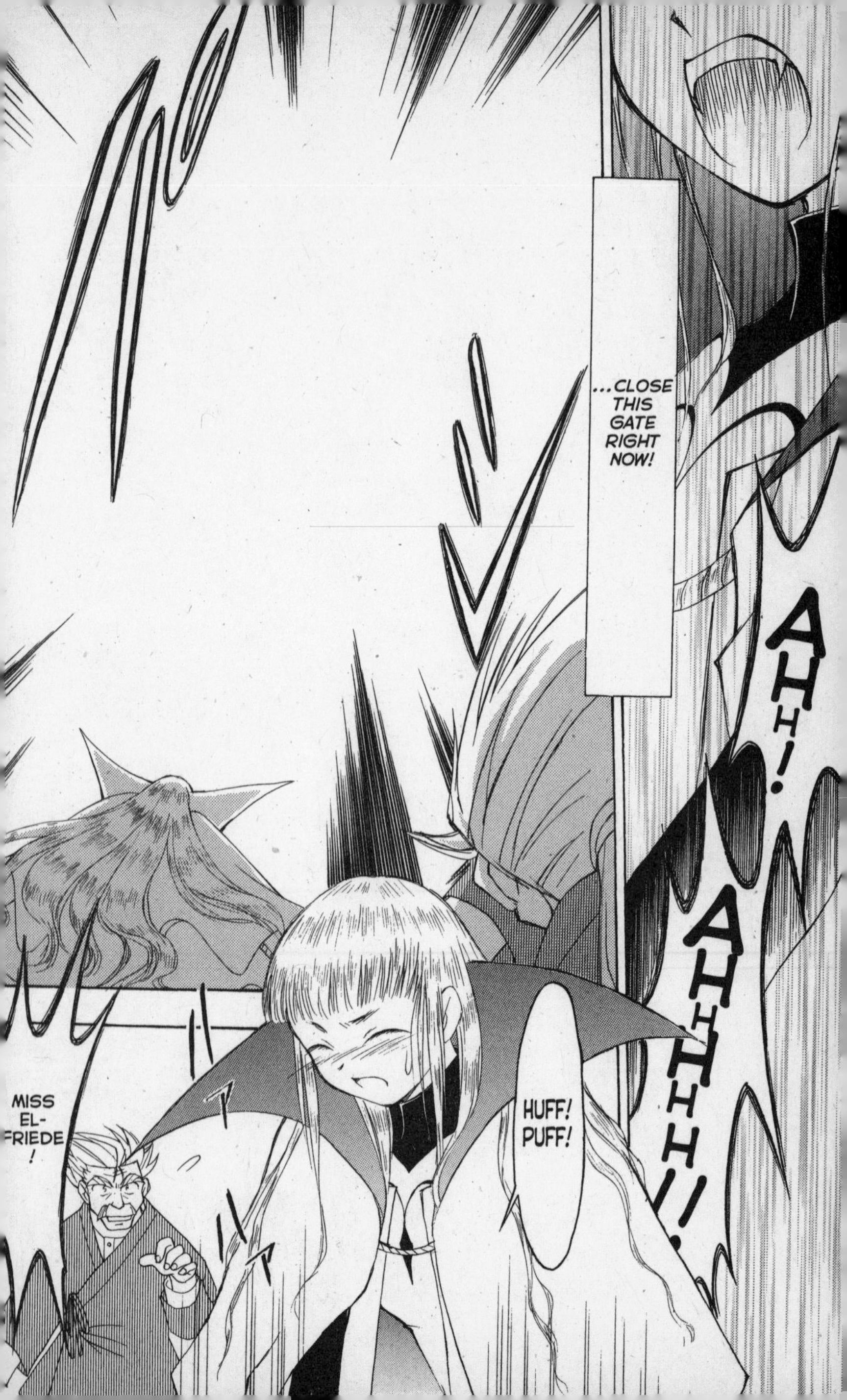
...CLOSE THIS GATE RIGHT NOW!
AHH! AHHHHHH!!
HUFF! PUFF!
MISS EL-FRIEDE!

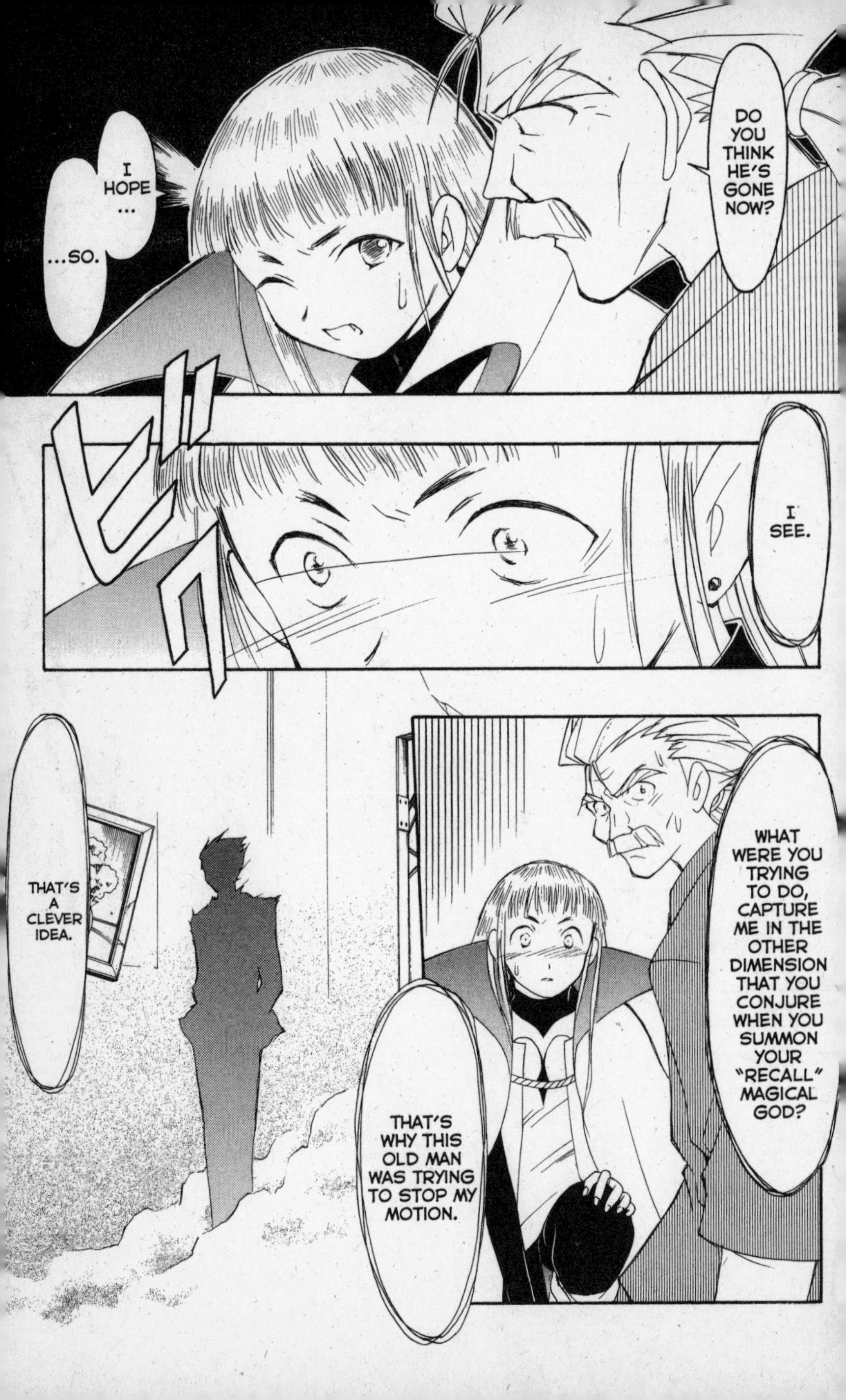
DO YOU THINK HE'S GONE NOW?
I HOPE...
...SO.
I SEE.
WHAT WERE YOU TRYING TO DO, CAPTURE ME IN THE OTHER DIMENSION THAT YOU CONJURE WHEN YOU SUMMON YOUR "RECALL" MAGICAL GOD?
THAT'S WHY THIS OLD MAN WAS TRYING TO STOP MY MOTION.
THAT'S A CLEVER IDEA.

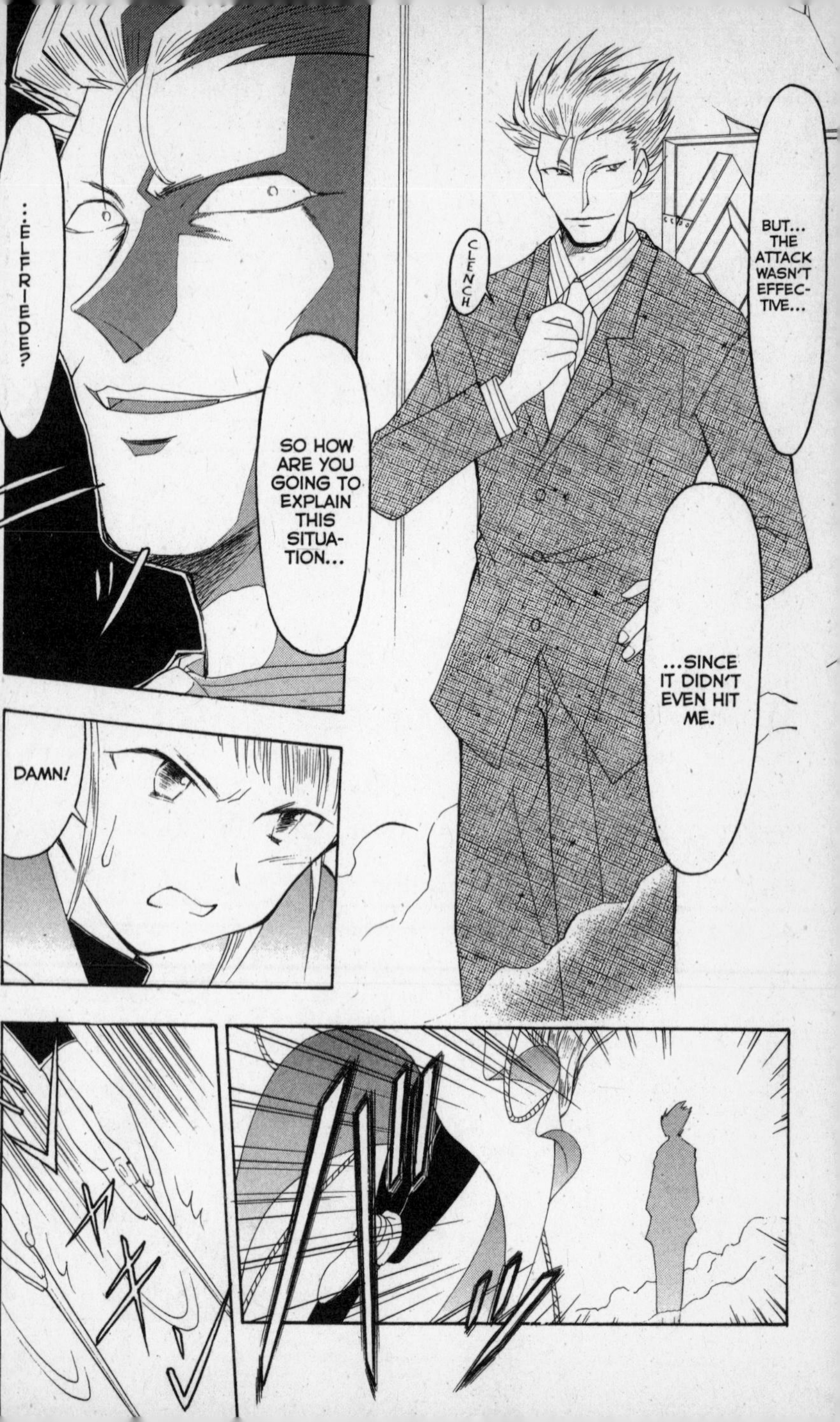
BUT... THE ATTACK WASN'T EFFEC-TIVE...
CLENCH
...SINCE IT DIDN'T EVEN HIT ME.
...ELFRIEDE?
SO HOW ARE YOU GOING TO EXPLAIN THIS SITUA-TION...
DAMN!

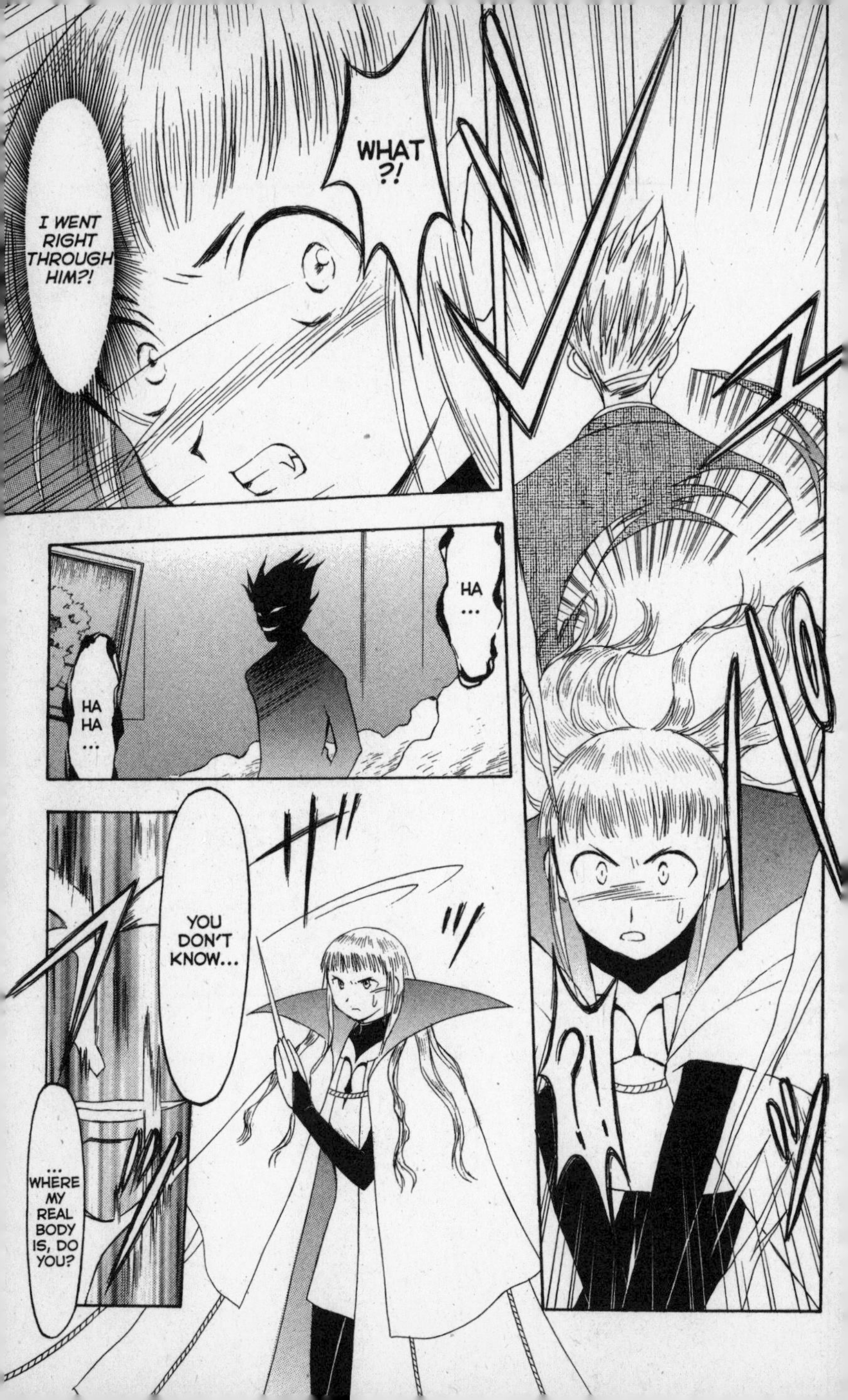
?!
WHAT ?!
I WENT RIGHT THROUGH HIM?!
HA ...
HA HA ...
YOU DON'T KNOW...
... WHERE MY REAL BODY IS, DO YOU?

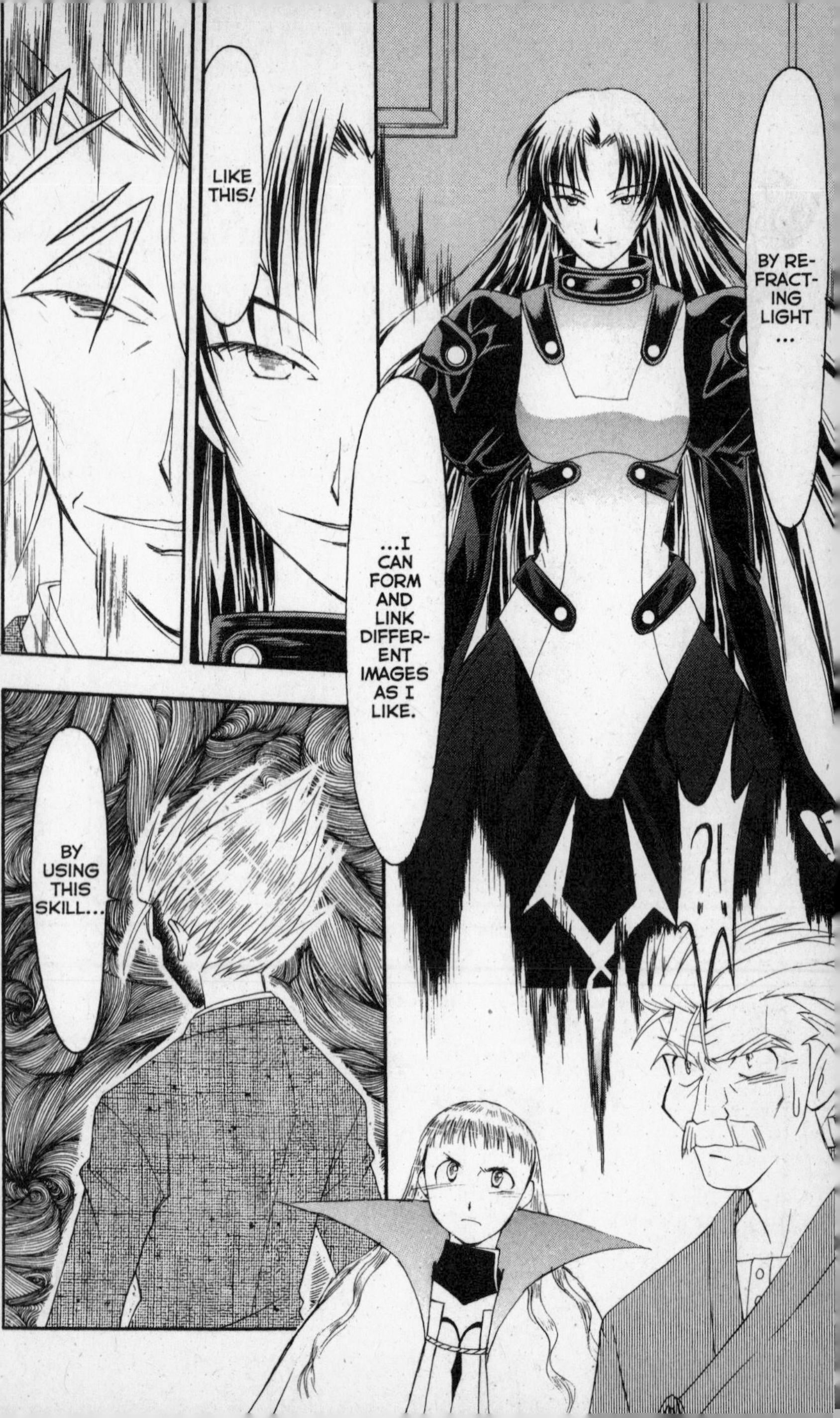

BY RE-FRACT-ING LIGHT...
...I CAN FORM AND LINK DIFFER-ENT IMAGES AS I LIKE.
?!
LIKE THIS!
BY USING THIS SKILL...

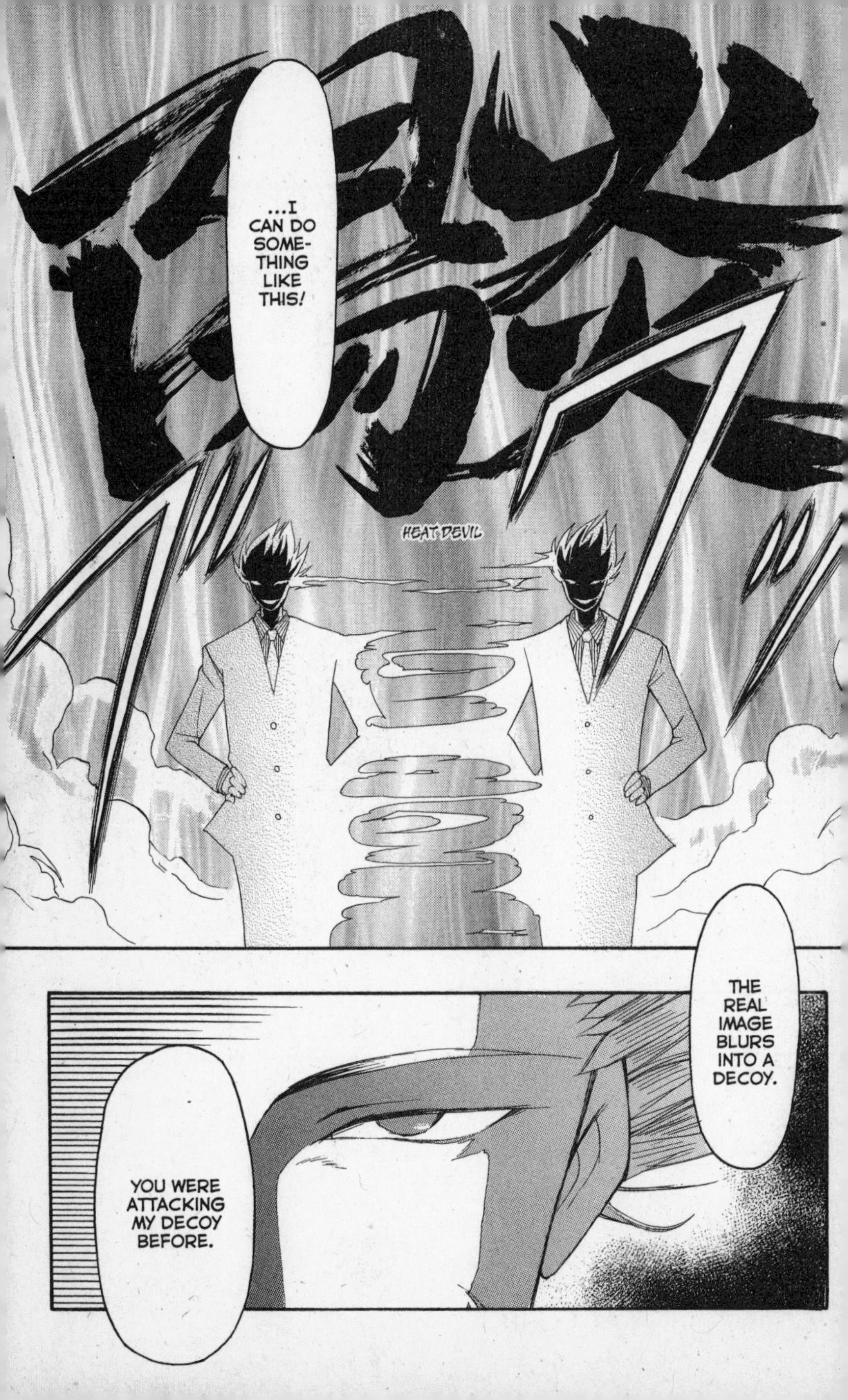
...I CAN DO SOME-THING LIKE THIS!
HEAT DEVIL
THE REAL IMAGE BLURS INTO A DECOY.
YOU WERE ATTACKING MY DECOY BEFORE.

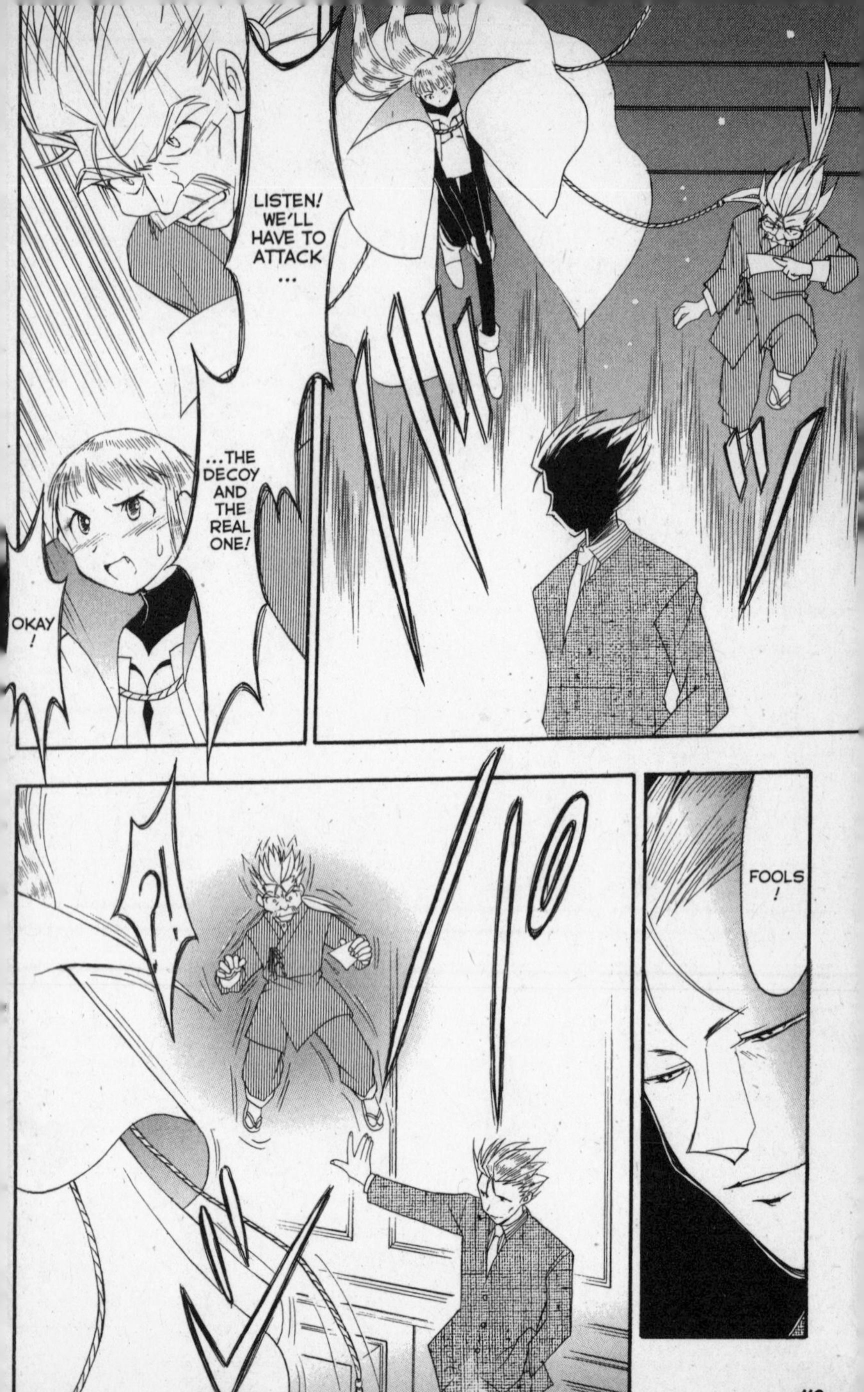
LISTEN! WE'LL HAVE TO ATTACK ...
...THE DECOY AND THE REAL ONE!
OKAY!
FOOLS!
?!

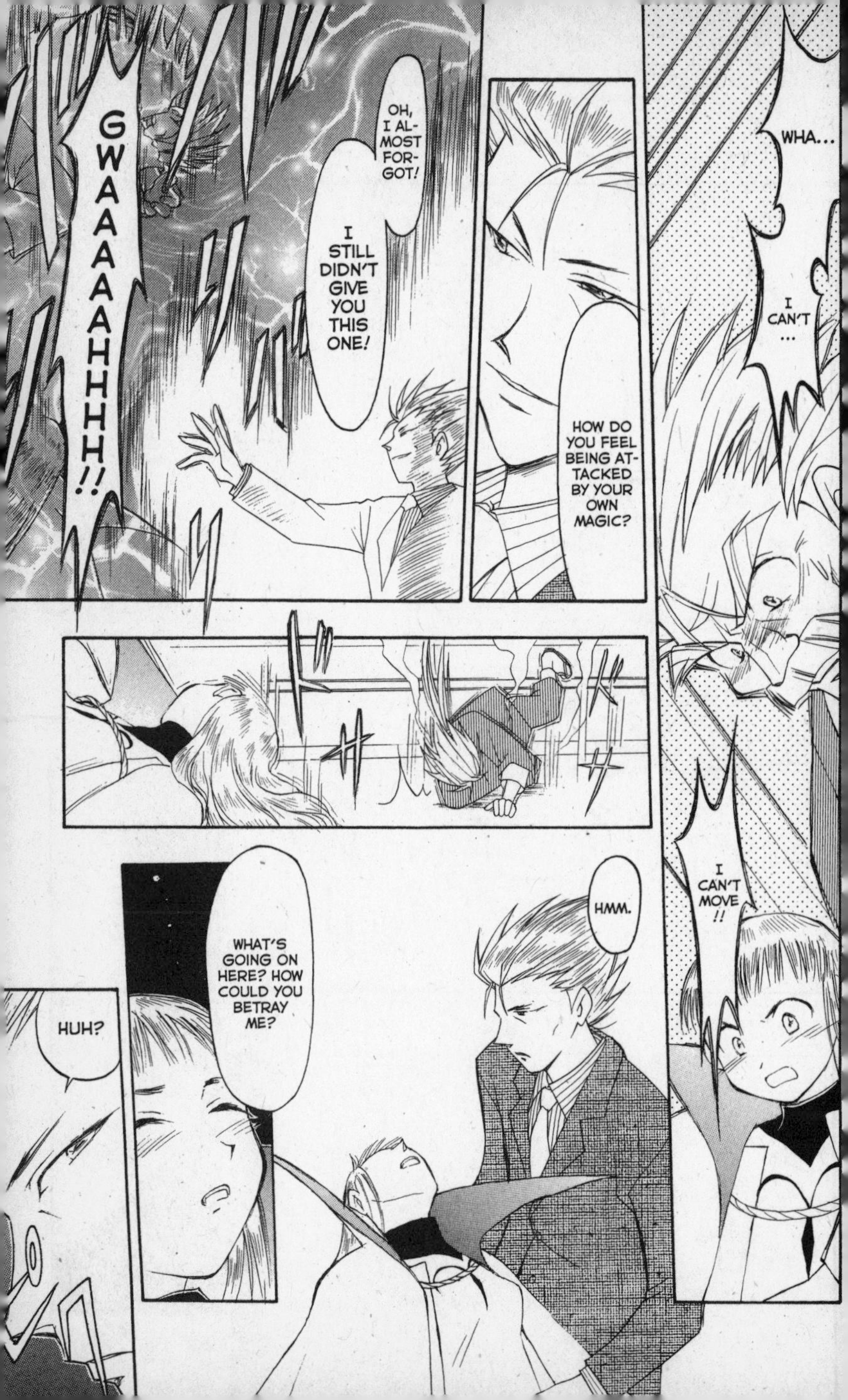
WHA...
I CAN'T ...
I CAN'T MOVE !!
HOW DO YOU FEEL BEING ATTACKED BY YOUR OWN MAGIC?
OH, I ALMOST FORGOT!
I STILL DIDN'T GIVE YOU THIS ONE!
GWAAAAAAAHHHHH!!
HMM.
WHAT'S GOING ON HERE? HOW COULD YOU BETRAY ME?
HUH?

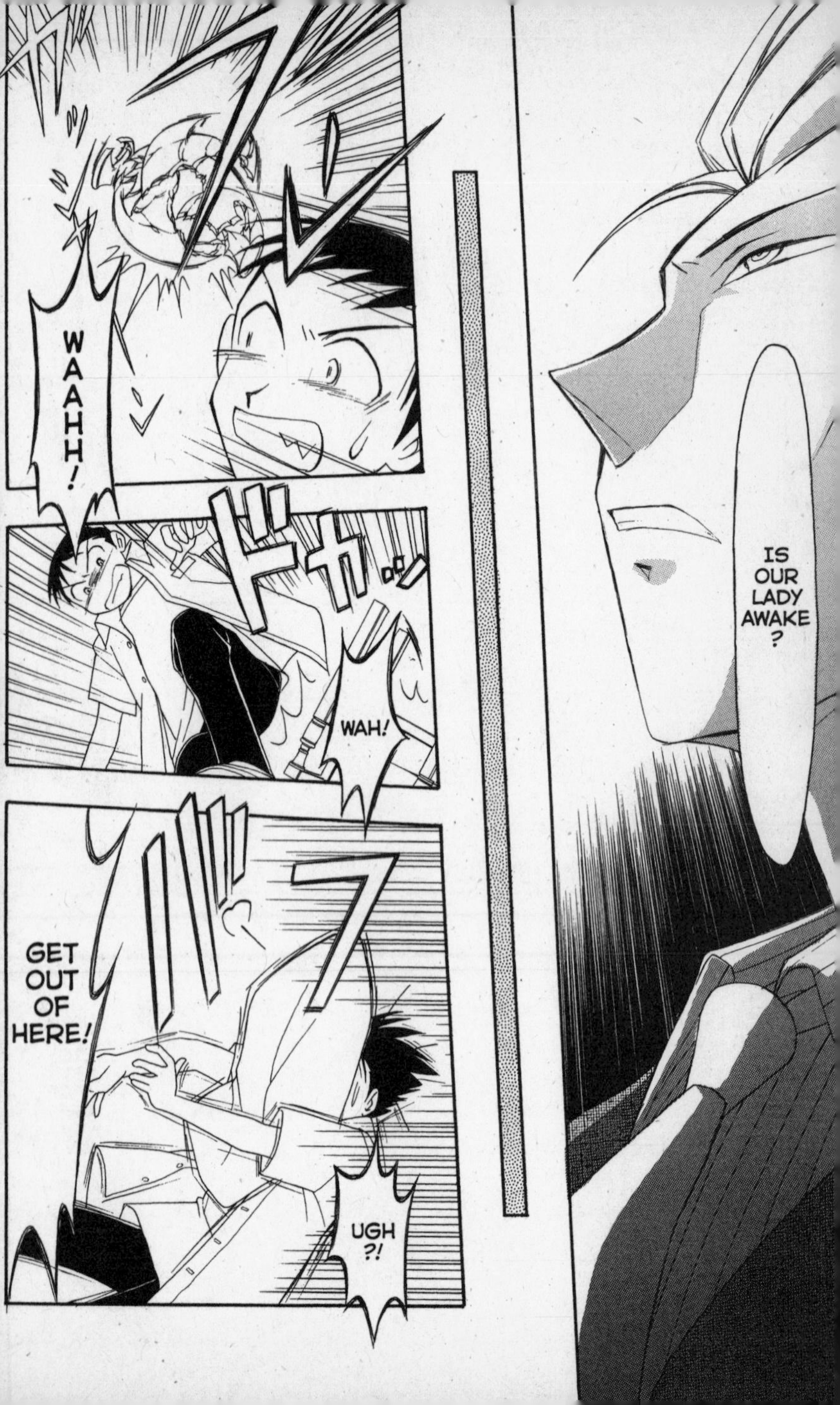
IS OUR LADY AWAKE?
WAAHH!
WAH!
GET OUT OF HERE!
UGH?!

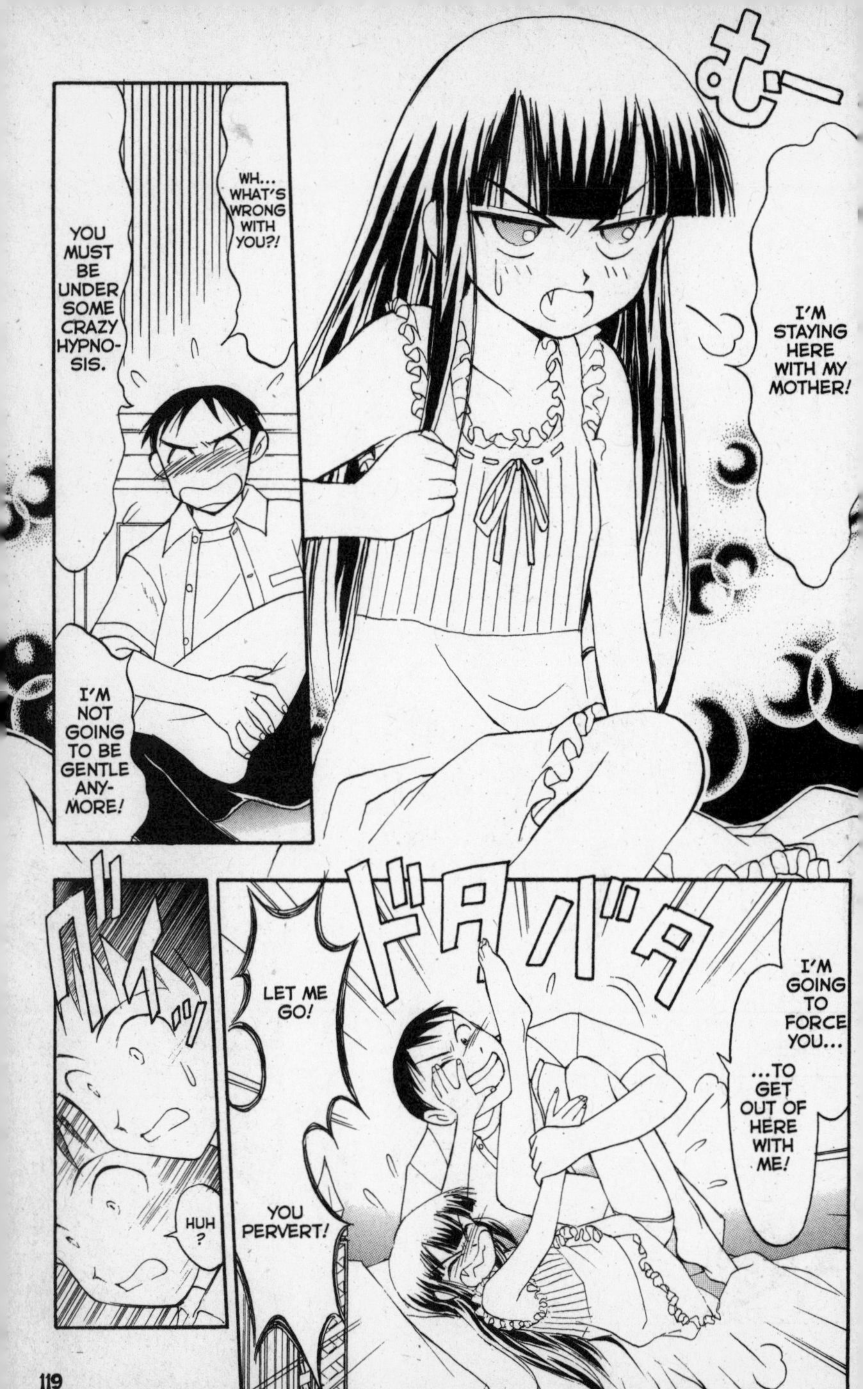
むー
I'M STAYING HERE WITH MY MOTHER!
WH... WHAT'S WRONG WITH YOU?!
YOU MUST BE UNDER SOME CRAZY HYPNO-SIS.
I'M NOT GOING TO BE GENTLE ANY-MORE!
ドタバタ
I'M GOING TO FORCE YOU...
...TO GET OUT OF HERE WITH ME!
LET ME GO!
YOU PERVERT!
グイ
HUH?

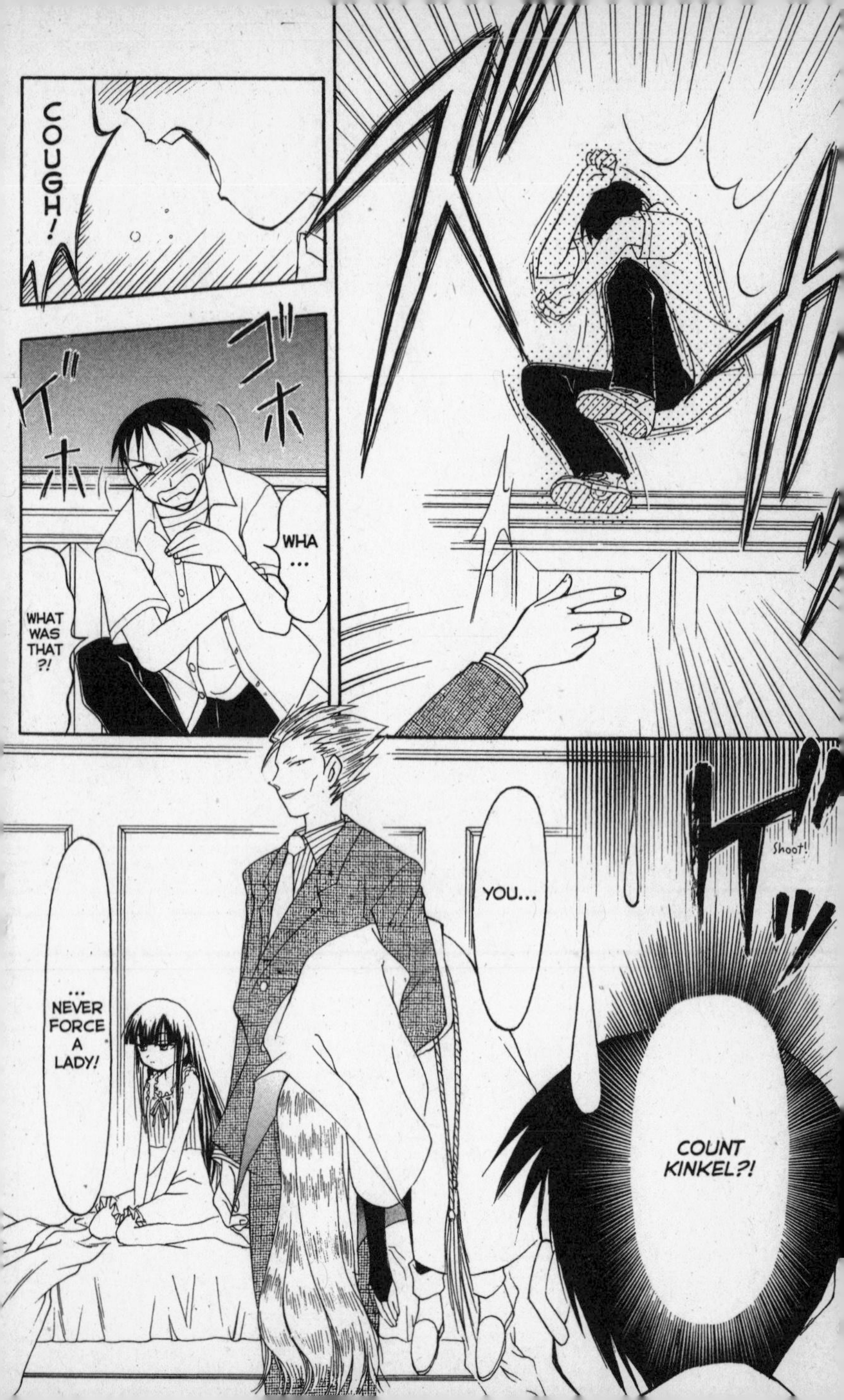
COUGH!
ゴホ
ゲホ
WHA ...
WHAT WAS THAT ?!
Shoot!
COUNT KINKEL?!
YOU...
... NEVER FORCE A LADY!

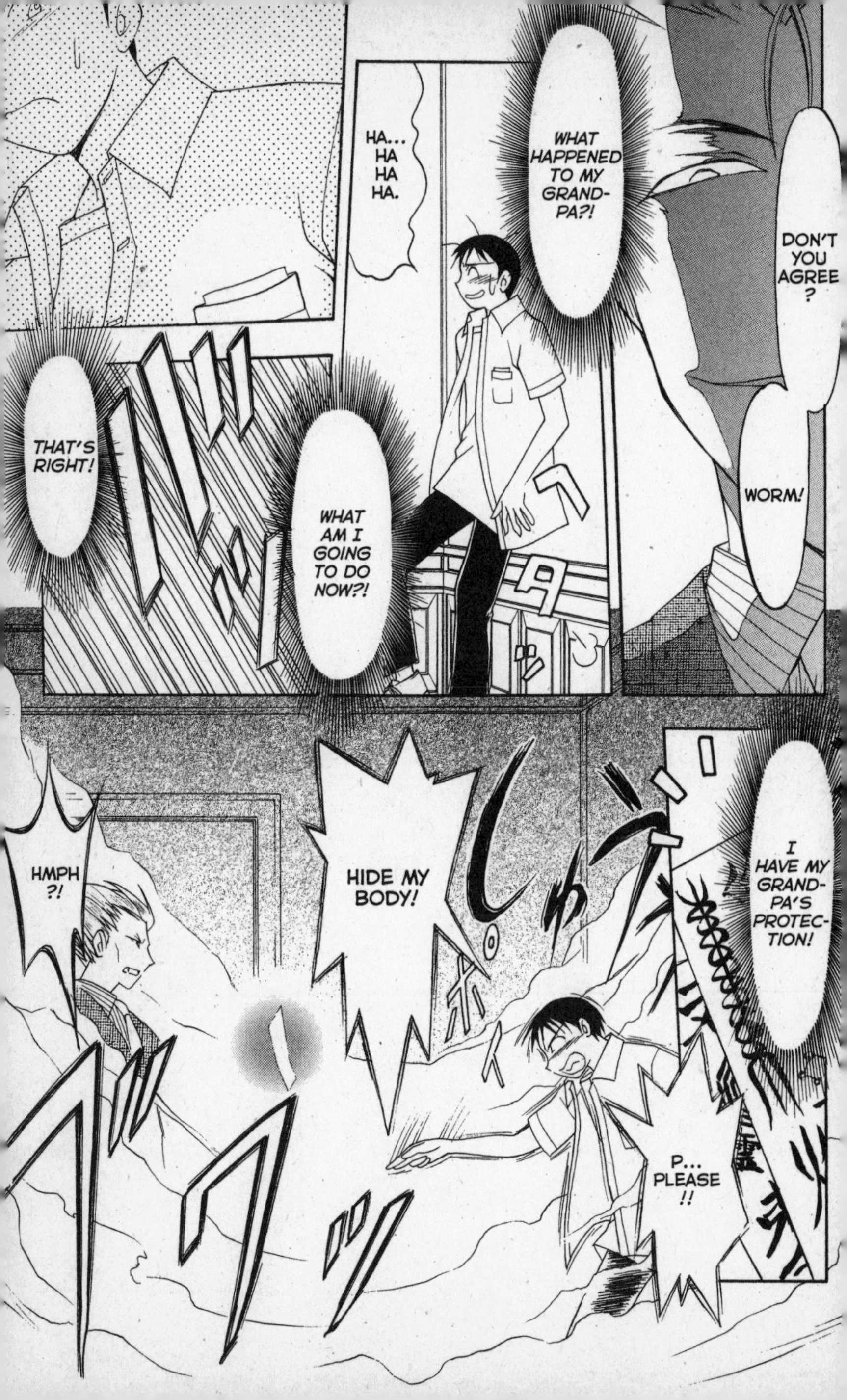
DON'T YOU AGREE?
WORM!
WHAT HAPPENED TO MY GRANDPA?!
HA... HA HA HA.
WHAT AM I GOING TO DO NOW?!
THAT'S RIGHT!
I HAVE MY GRANDPA'S PROTECTION!
HIDE MY BODY!
HMPH?!
P... PLEASE!!

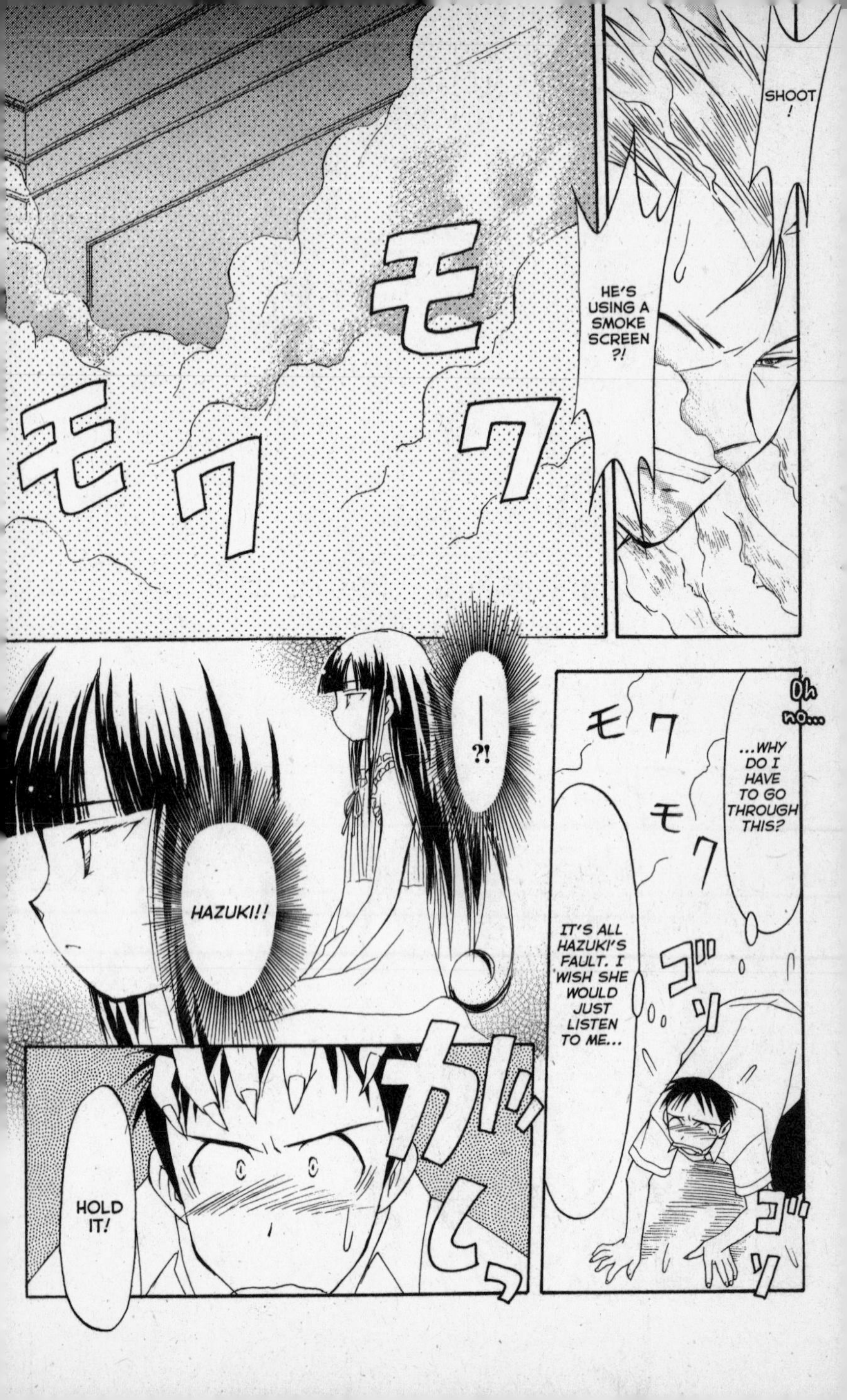
SHOOT!
HE'S USING A SMOKE SCREEN?!
モクモク
Oh no...
...WHY DO I HAVE TO GO THROUGH THIS?
モクモク
IT'S ALL HAZUKI'S FAULT. I WISH SHE WOULD JUST LISTEN TO ME...
ゴッ
ゴッ
—?!
HAZUKI!!
ガしっ
HOLD IT!

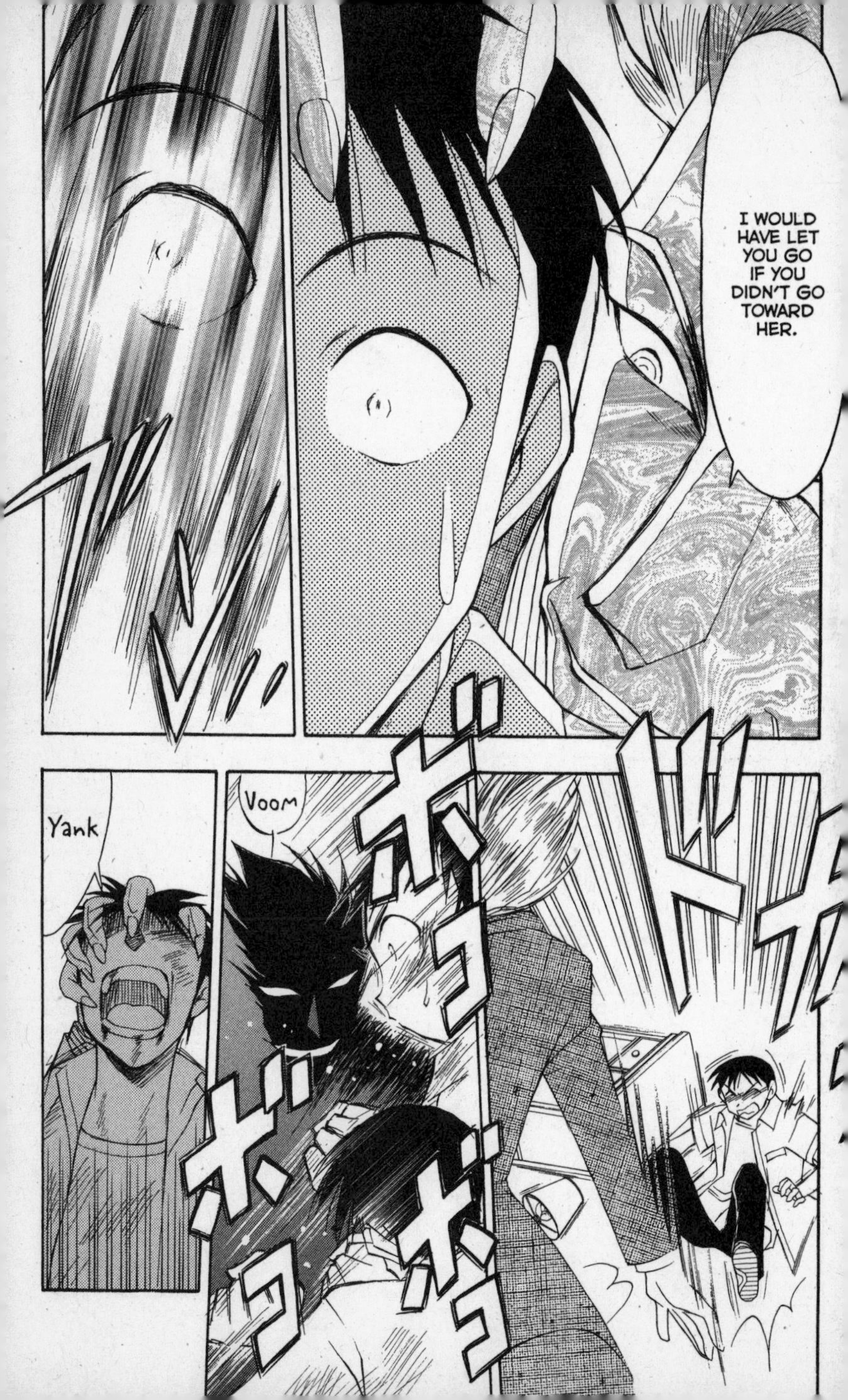
I WOULD HAVE LET YOU GO IF YOU DIDN'T GO TOWARD HER.
Voom
Yank

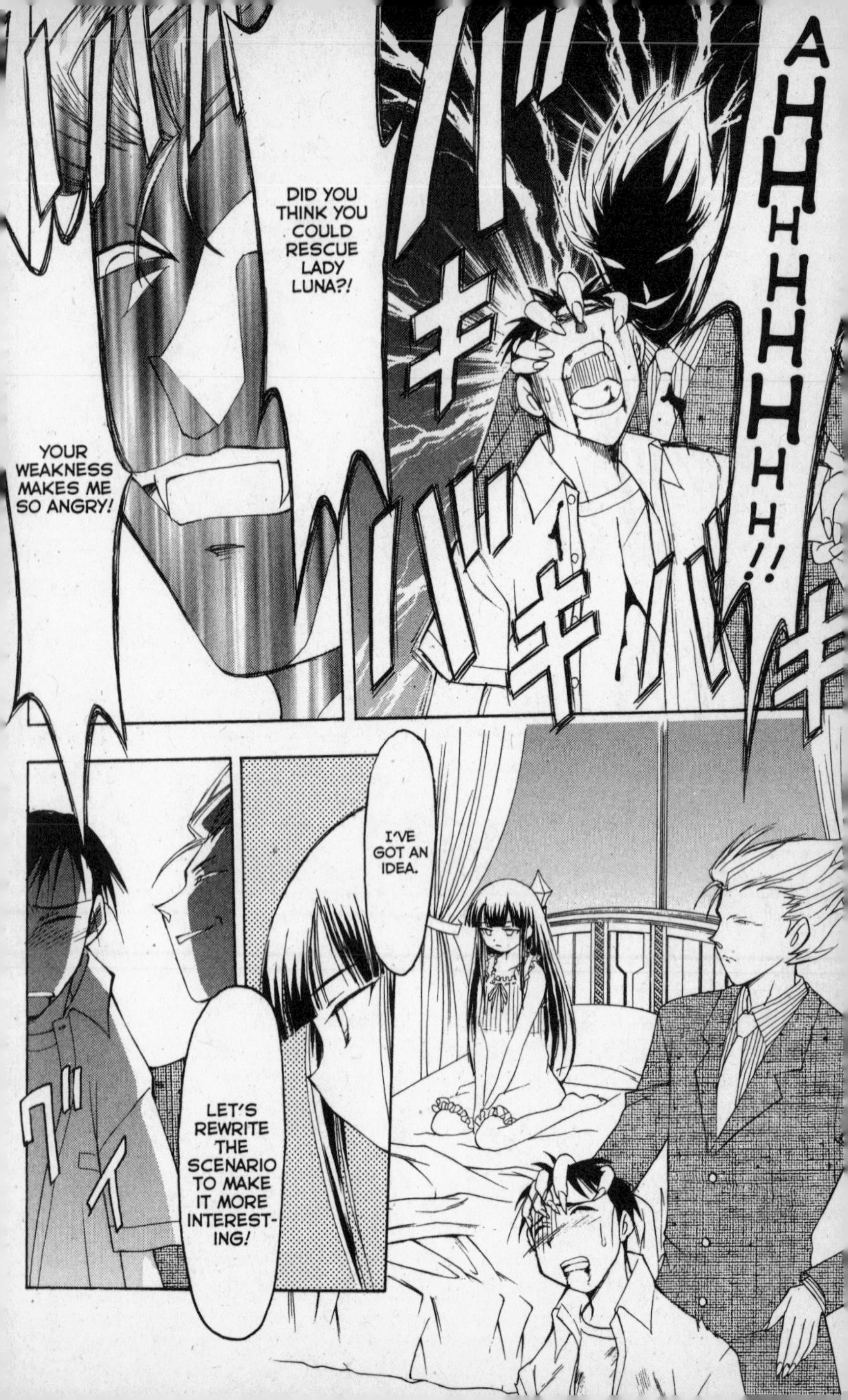
AHHHHHHHH!!
DID YOU THINK YOU COULD RESCUE LADY LUNA?!
YOUR WEAKNESS MAKES ME SO ANGRY!
I'VE GOT AN IDEA.
LET'S REWRITE THE SCENARIO TO MAKE IT MORE INTEREST-ING!

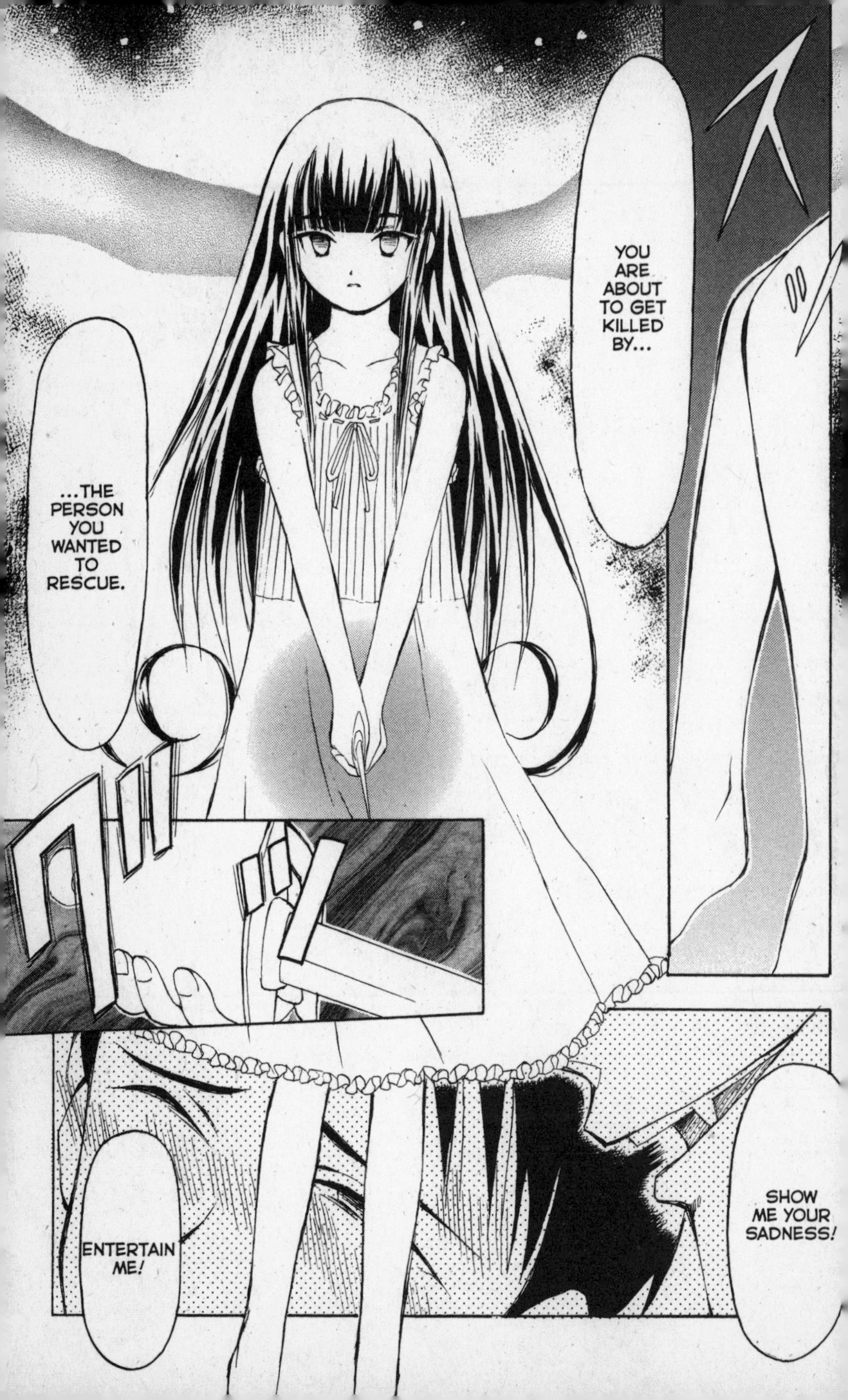
YOU ARE ABOUT TO GET KILLED BY...
...THE PERSON YOU WANTED TO RESCUE.
SHOW ME YOUR SADNESS!
ENTERTAIN ME!

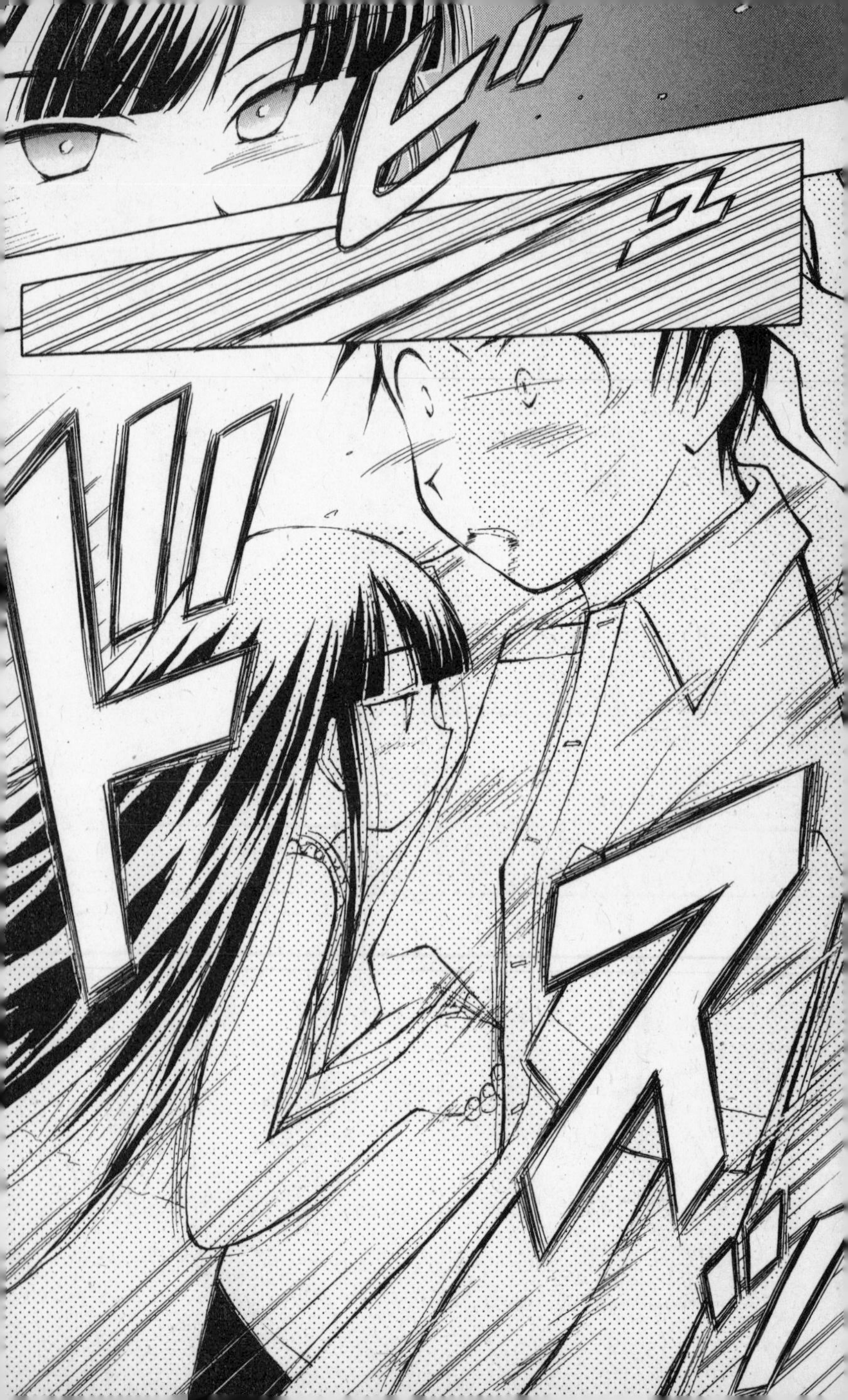

HAZUKI'S MOTHER IS ACTUALLY YOUNGER THAN ELFRIEDE. SHE USED TO BE VERY POPULAR AMONG MEN DURING WORLD WAR I IN THE RUSSIAN EMPIRE.

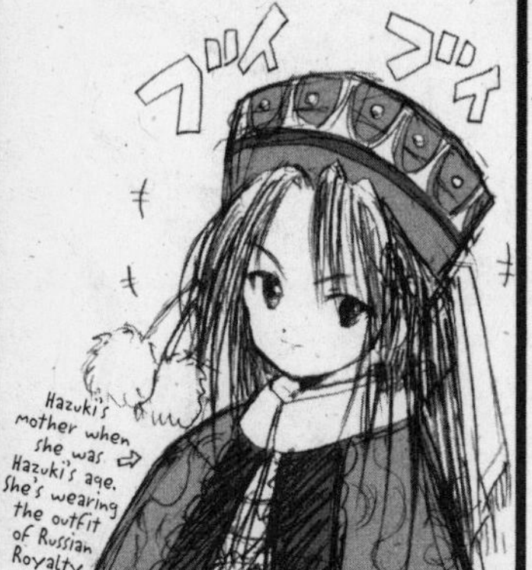
ブイ
ブイ
Hazuki's mother when she was Hazuki's age. She's wearing the outfit of Russian Royalty.

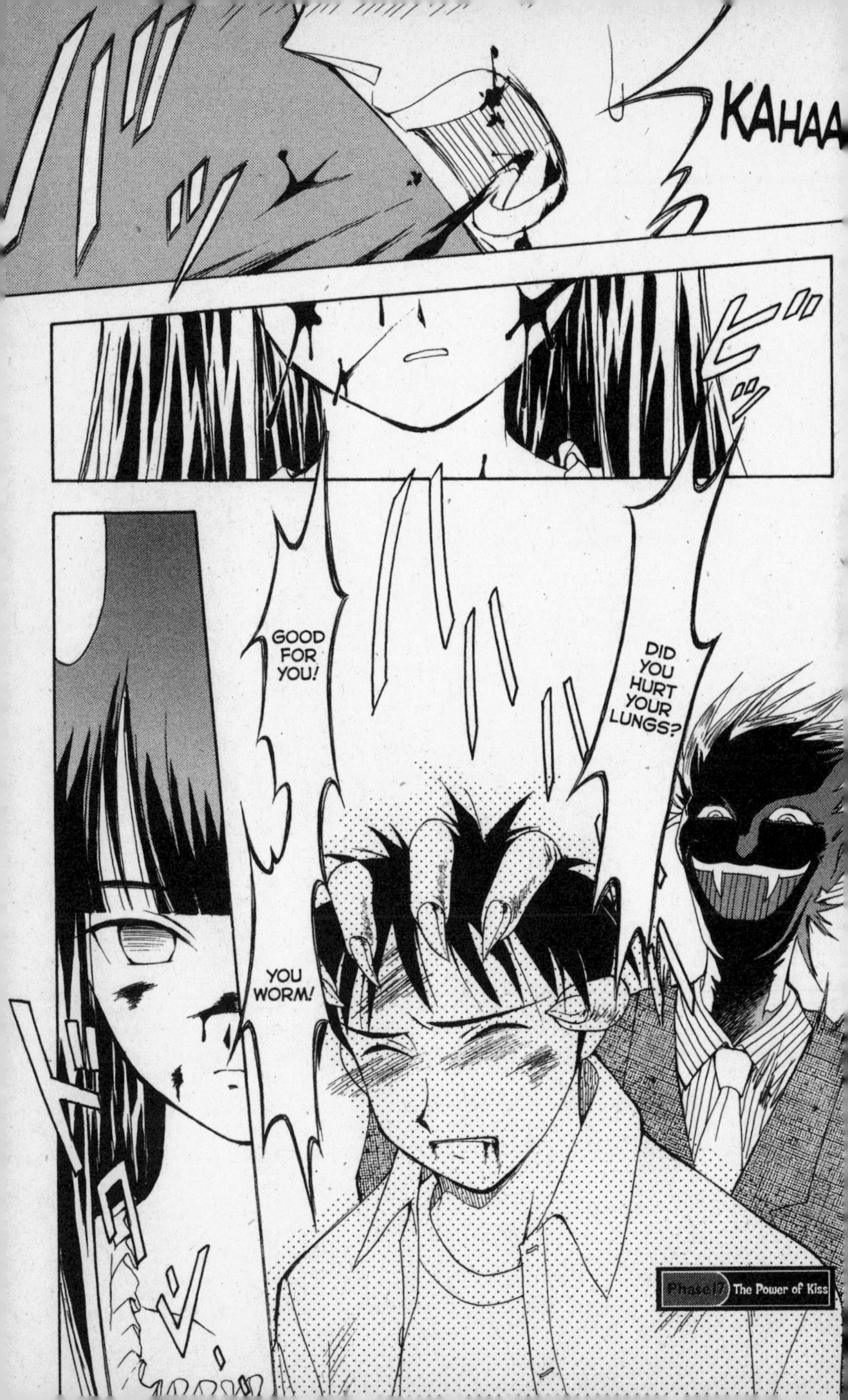
KAHAA
DID YOU HURT YOUR LUNGS?
GOOD FOR YOU!
YOU WORM!
Phase 17 The Power of Kiss

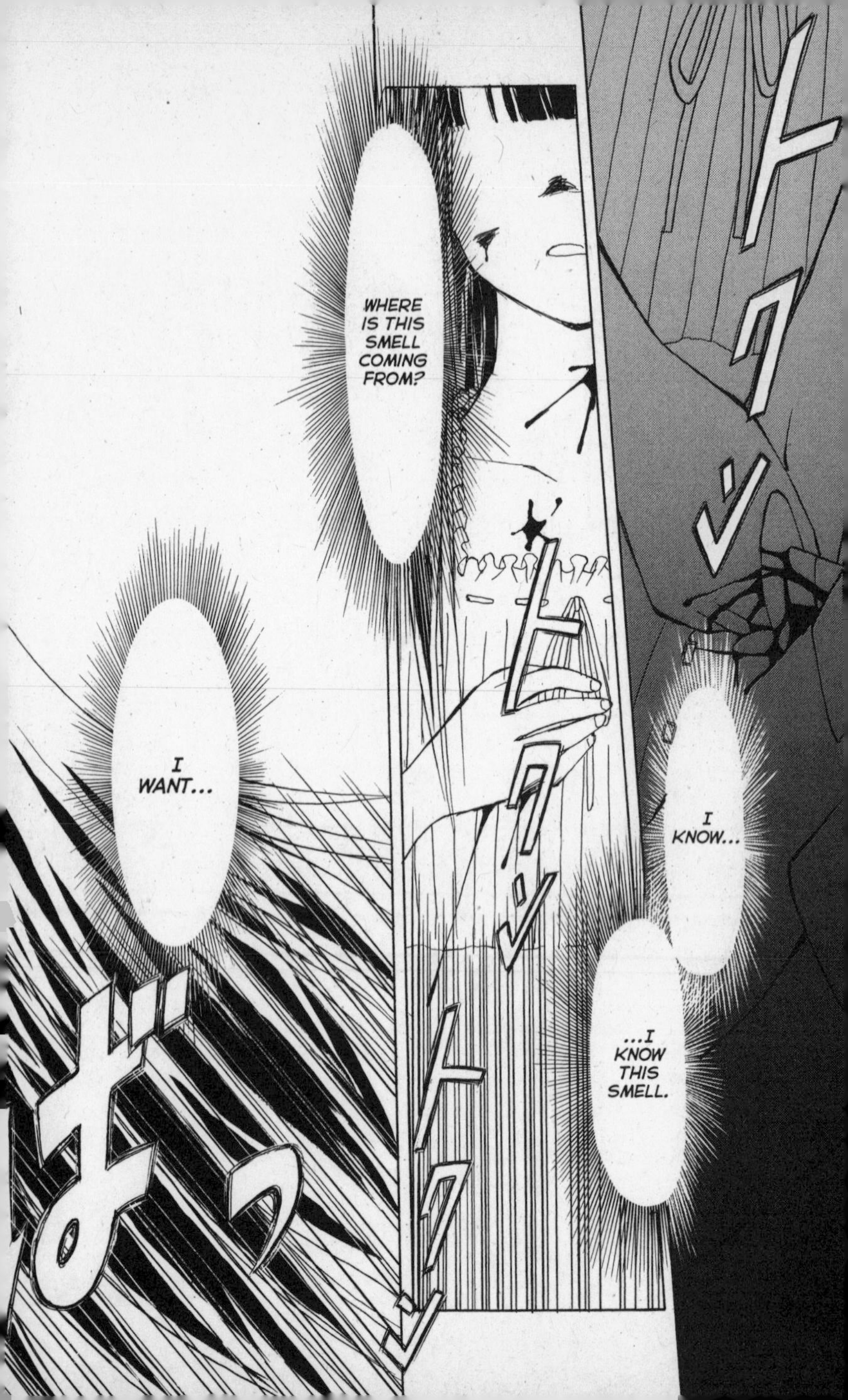
I KNOW...
...I KNOW THIS SMELL.
WHERE IS THIS SMELL COMING FROM?
I WANT...

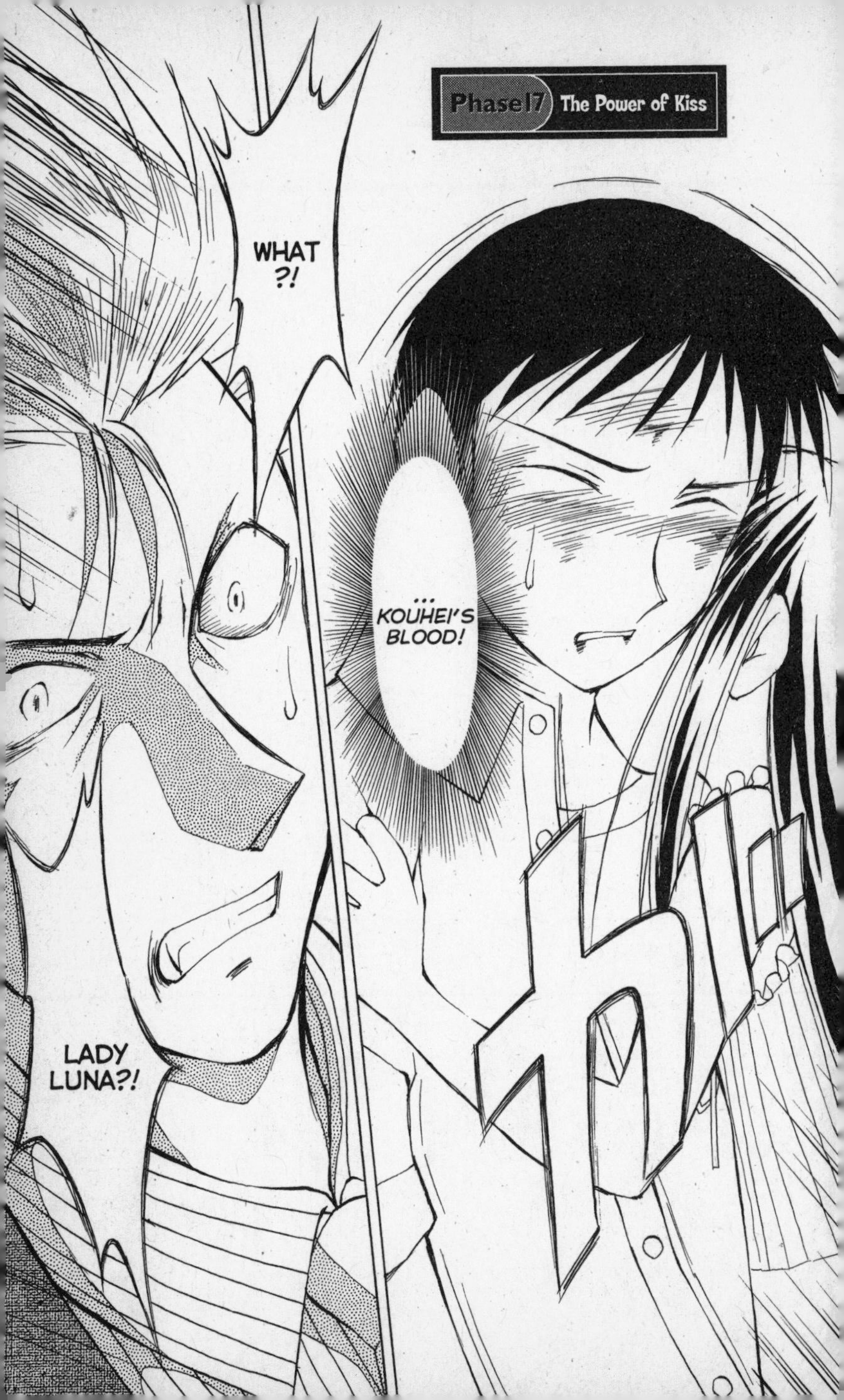
Phase17 The Power of Kiss
... Kouhei's blood!
What?!
Lady Luna?!

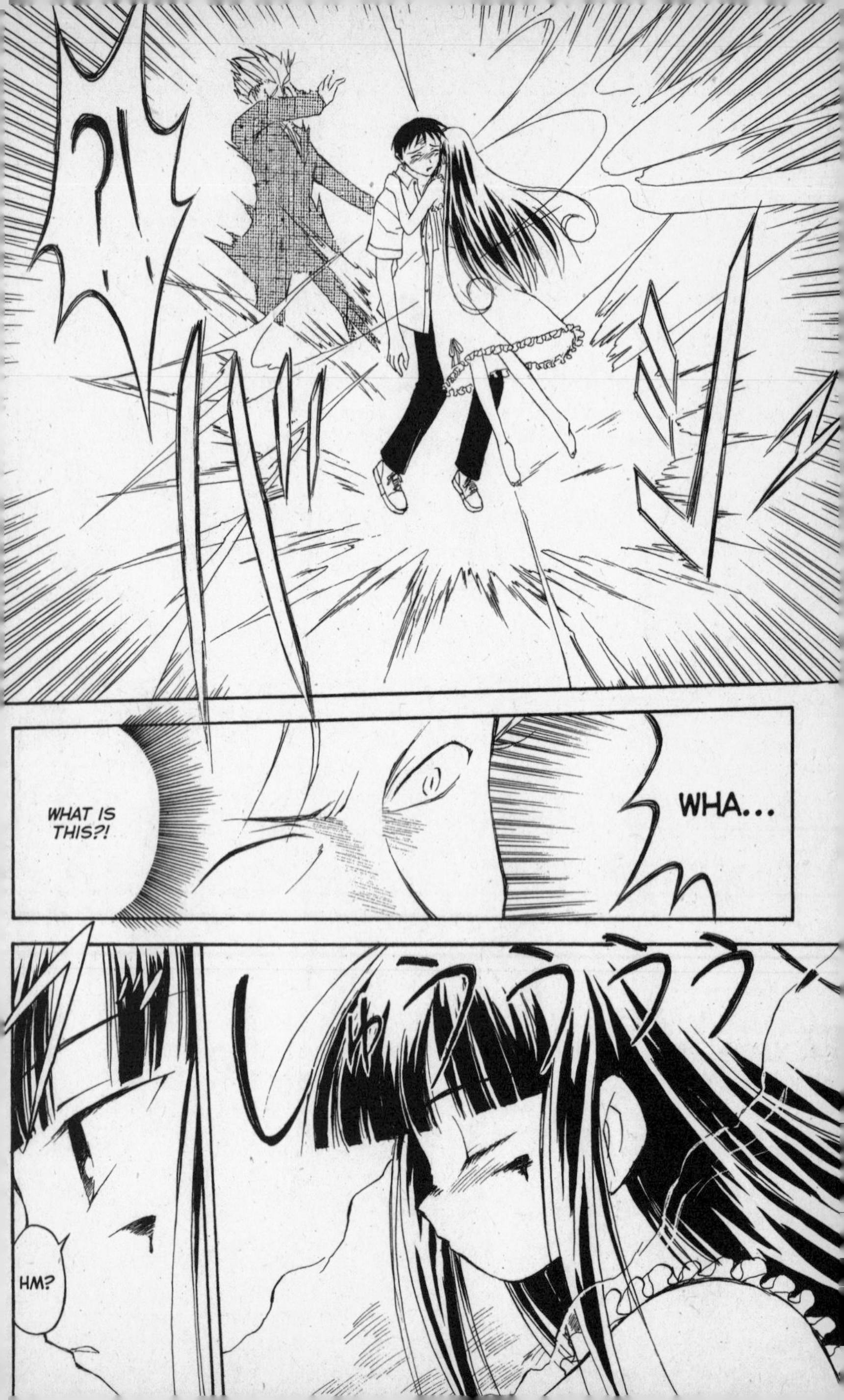
?!
WHA...
WHAT IS THIS?!
HM?

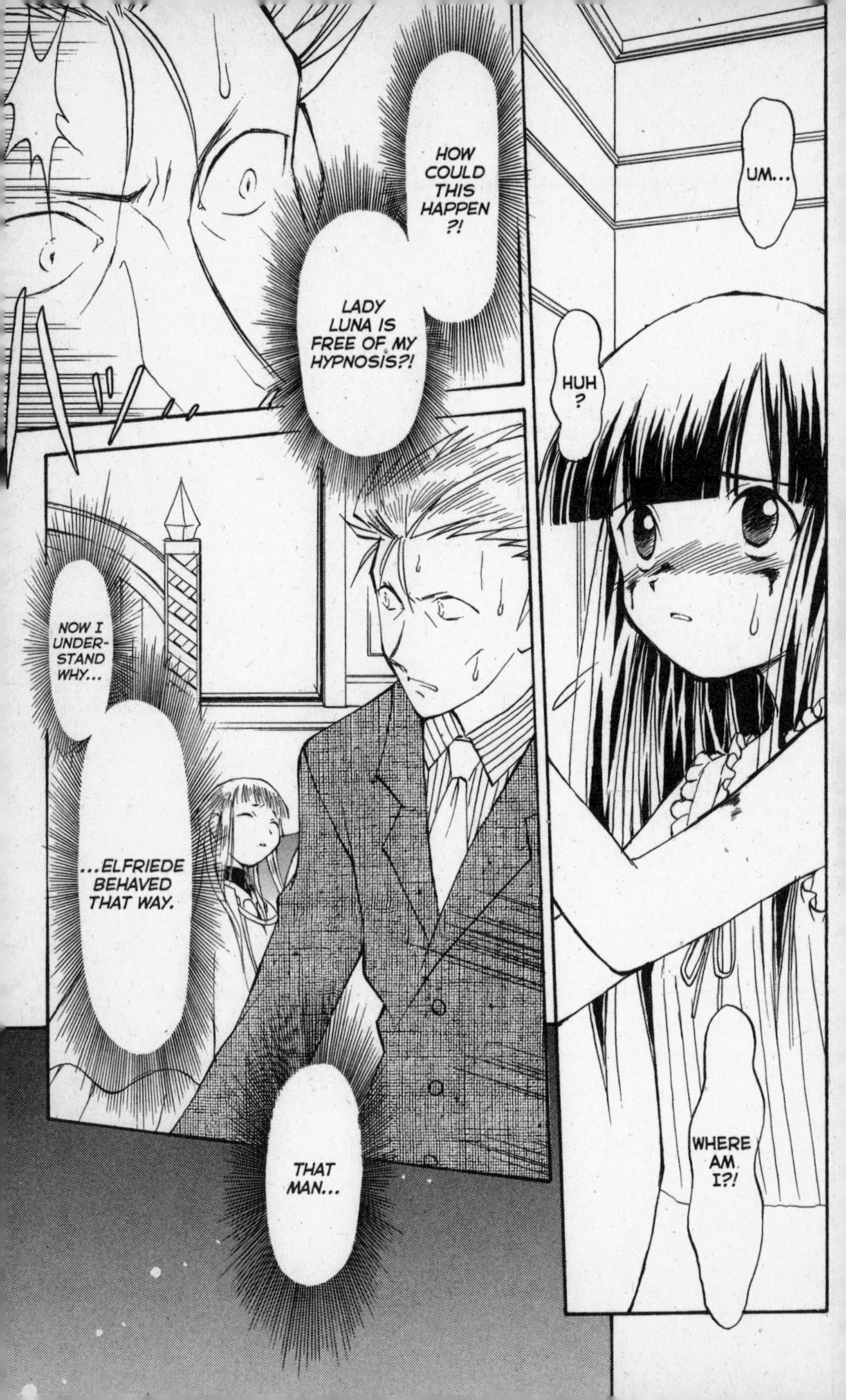
UM...
HUH?
WHERE AM I?!
HOW COULD THIS HAPPEN?!
LADY LUNA IS FREE OF MY HYPNOSIS?!
NOW I UNDER-STAND WHY...
...ELFRIEDE BEHAVED THAT WAY.
THAT MAN...

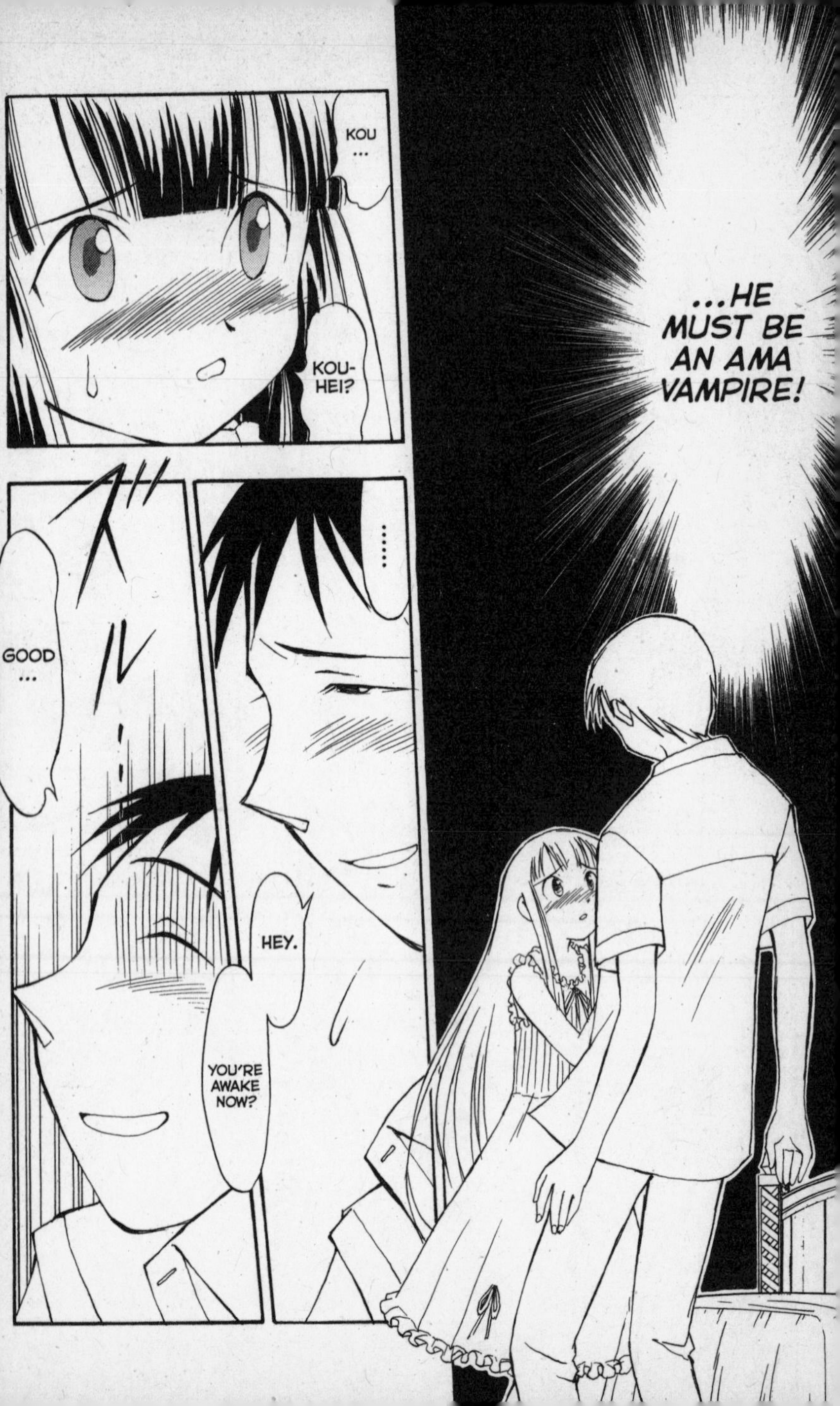
...HE MUST BE AN AMA VAMPIRE!
KOU ...
KOU-HEI?
......
HEY.
YOU'RE AWAKE NOW?
GOOD ...

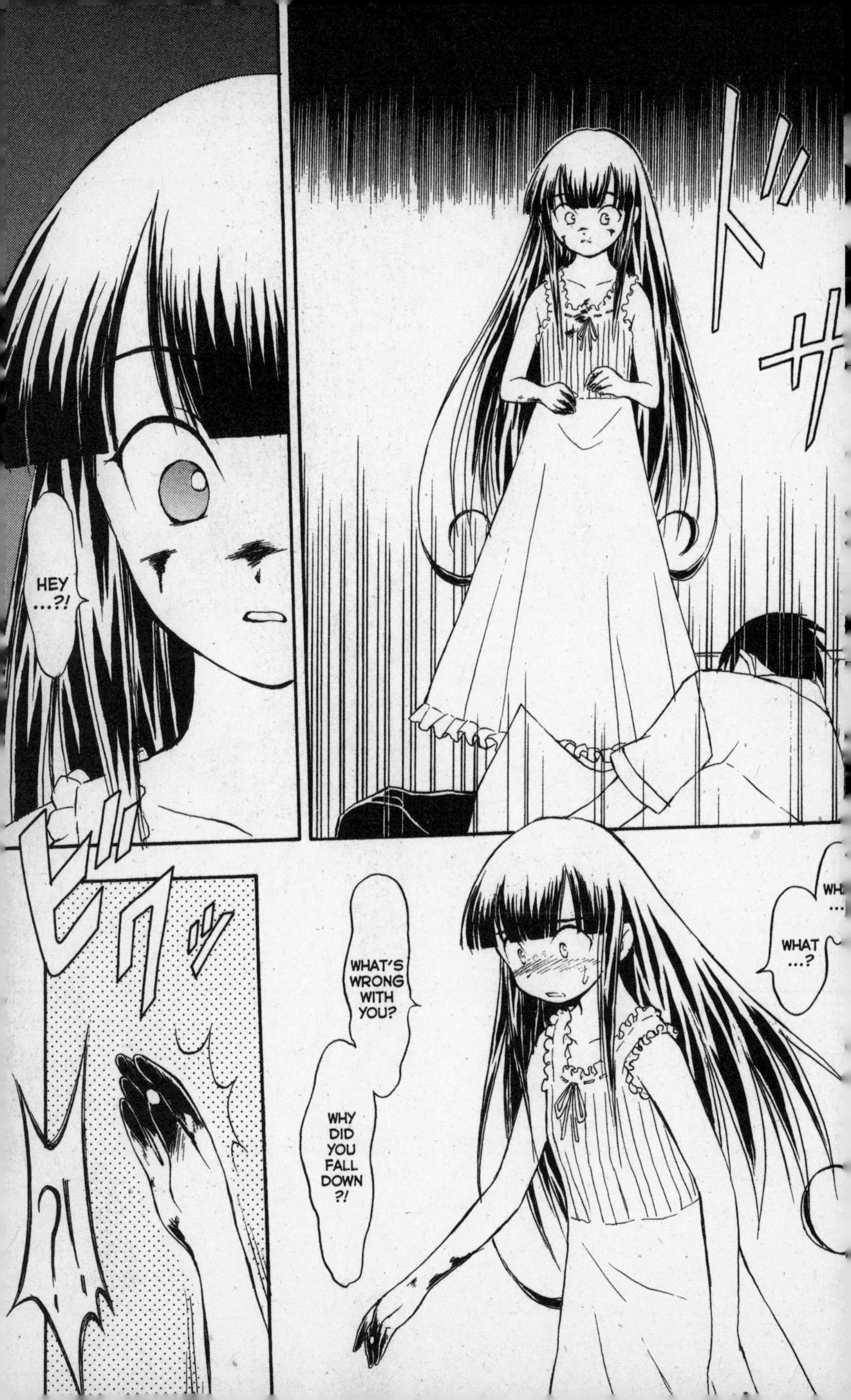
HEY ...?!
WHA ...
WHAT ...?
WHAT'S WRONG WITH YOU?
WHY DID YOU FALL DOWN ?!

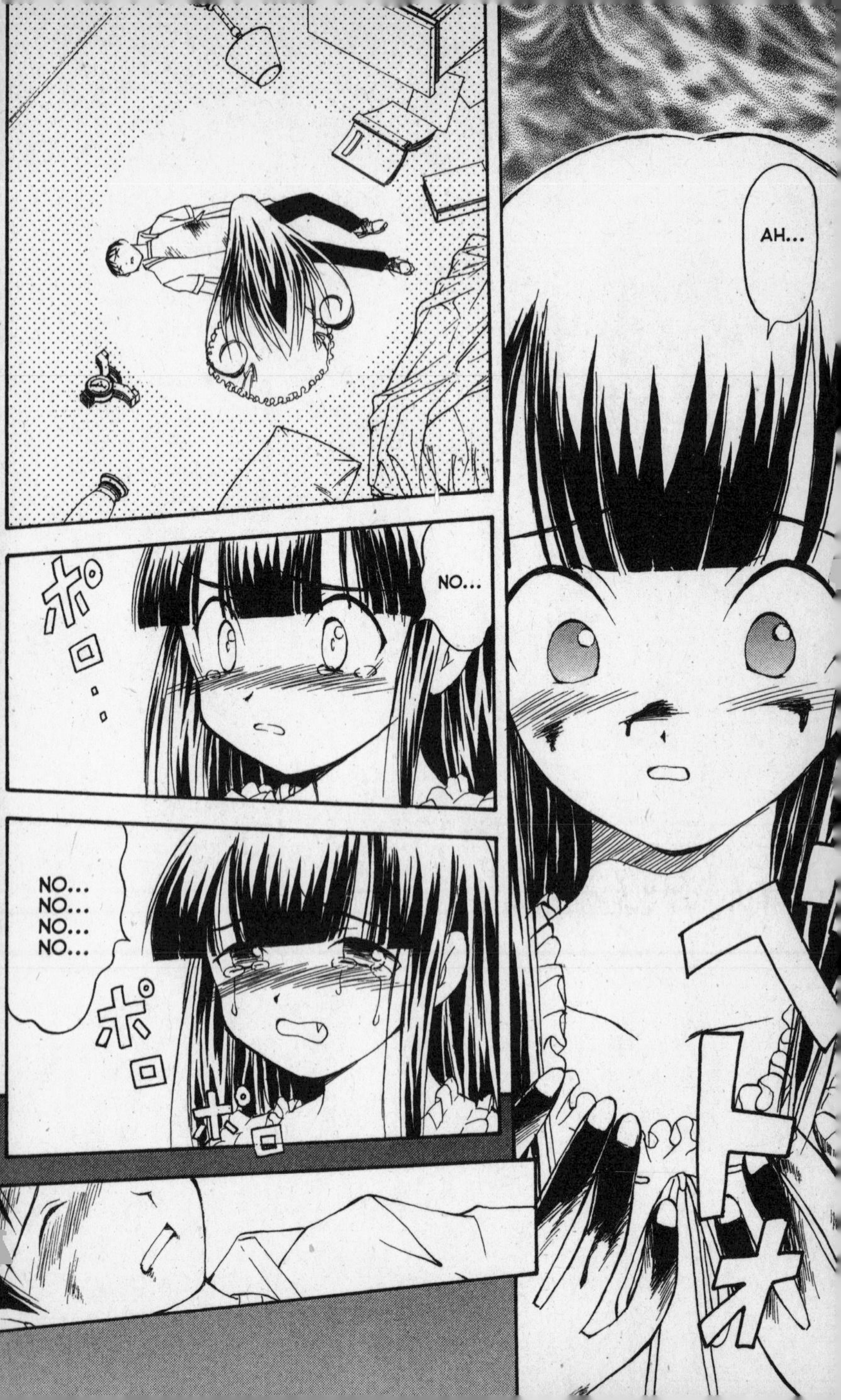
AH...
NO...
ポロ..
NO...
NO...
NO...
NO...
ポロ
ポロ

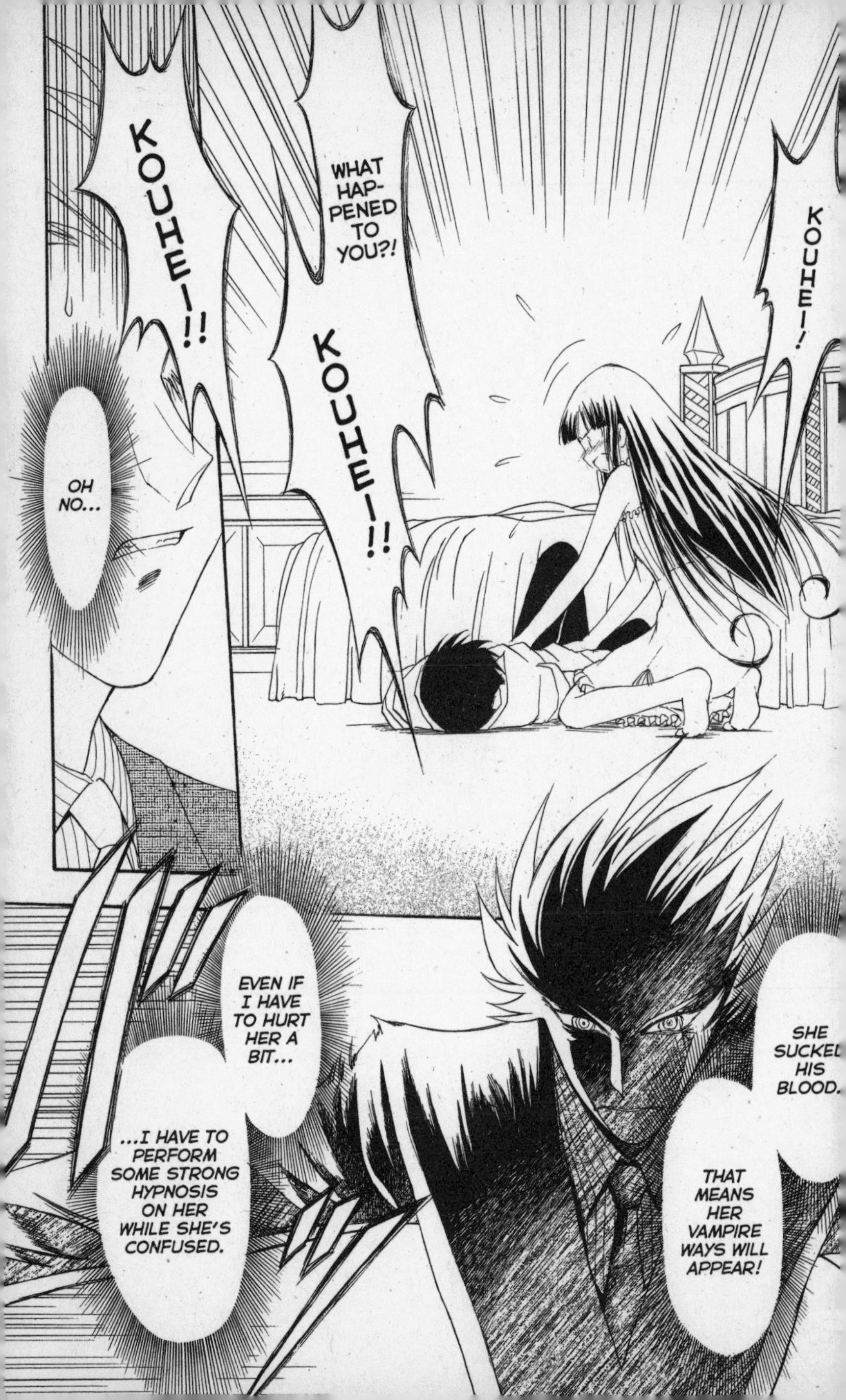
KOUHEI!
WHAT HAP-PENED TO YOU?!
KOUHEI!!
KOUHEI!!
OH NO...
SHE SUCKED HIS BLOOD.
THAT MEANS HER VAMPIRE WAYS WILL APPEAR!
EVEN IF I HAVE TO HURT HER A BIT...
...I HAVE TO PERFORM SOME STRONG HYPNOSIS ON HER WHILE SHE'S CONFUSED.

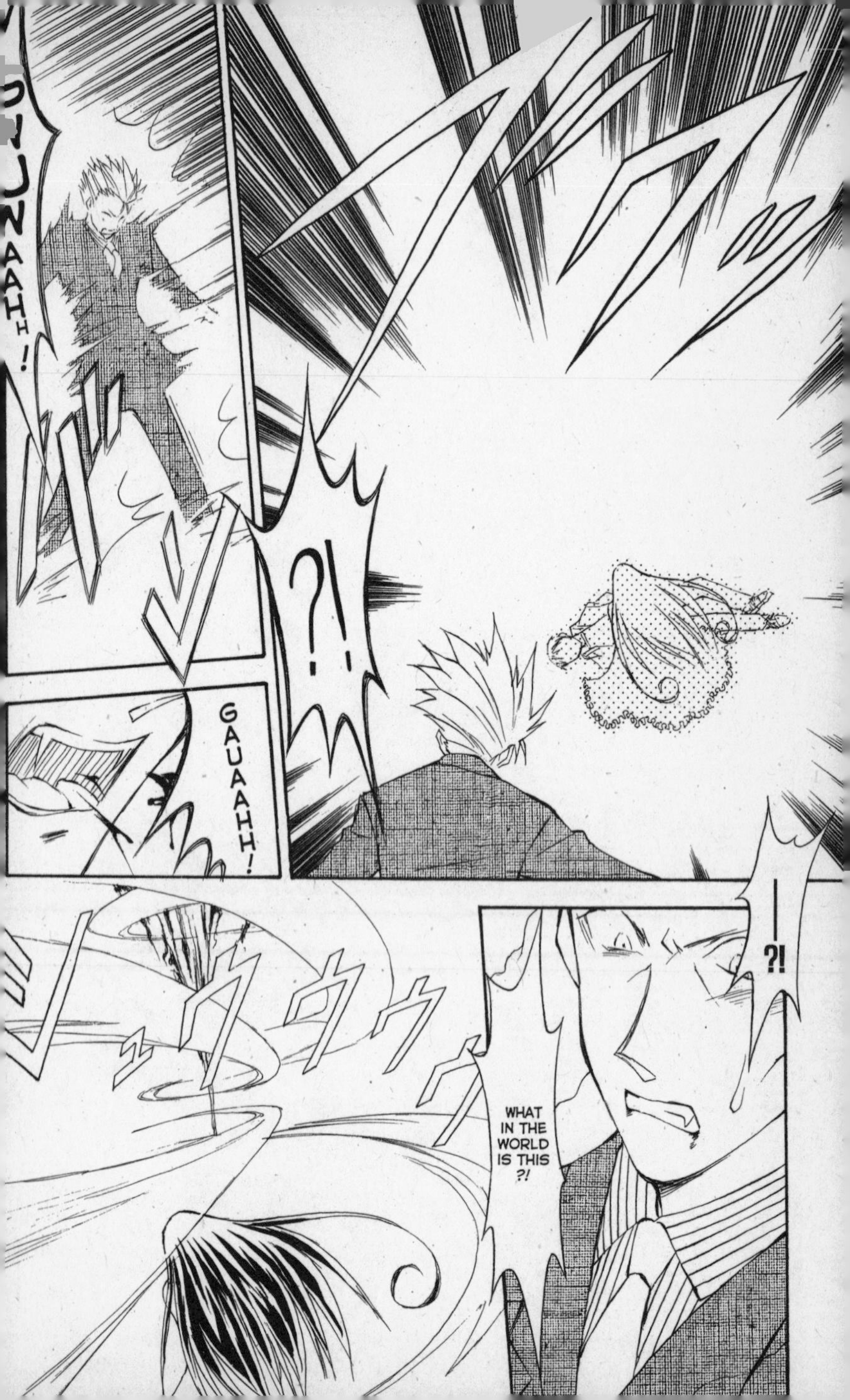
?!
UWAAAHH!
GAUAAAHH!
?!
WHAT IN THE WORLD IS THIS ?!

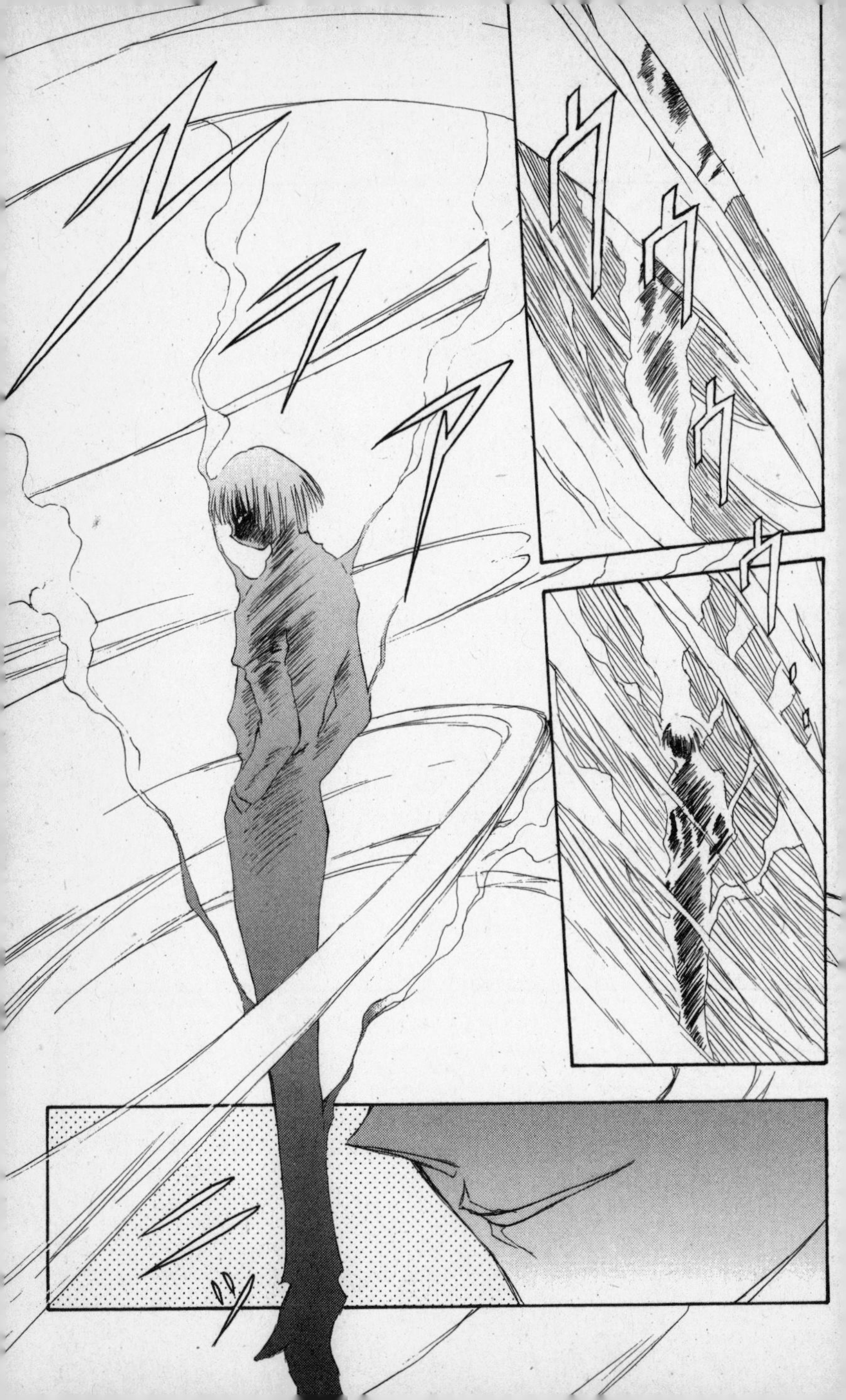

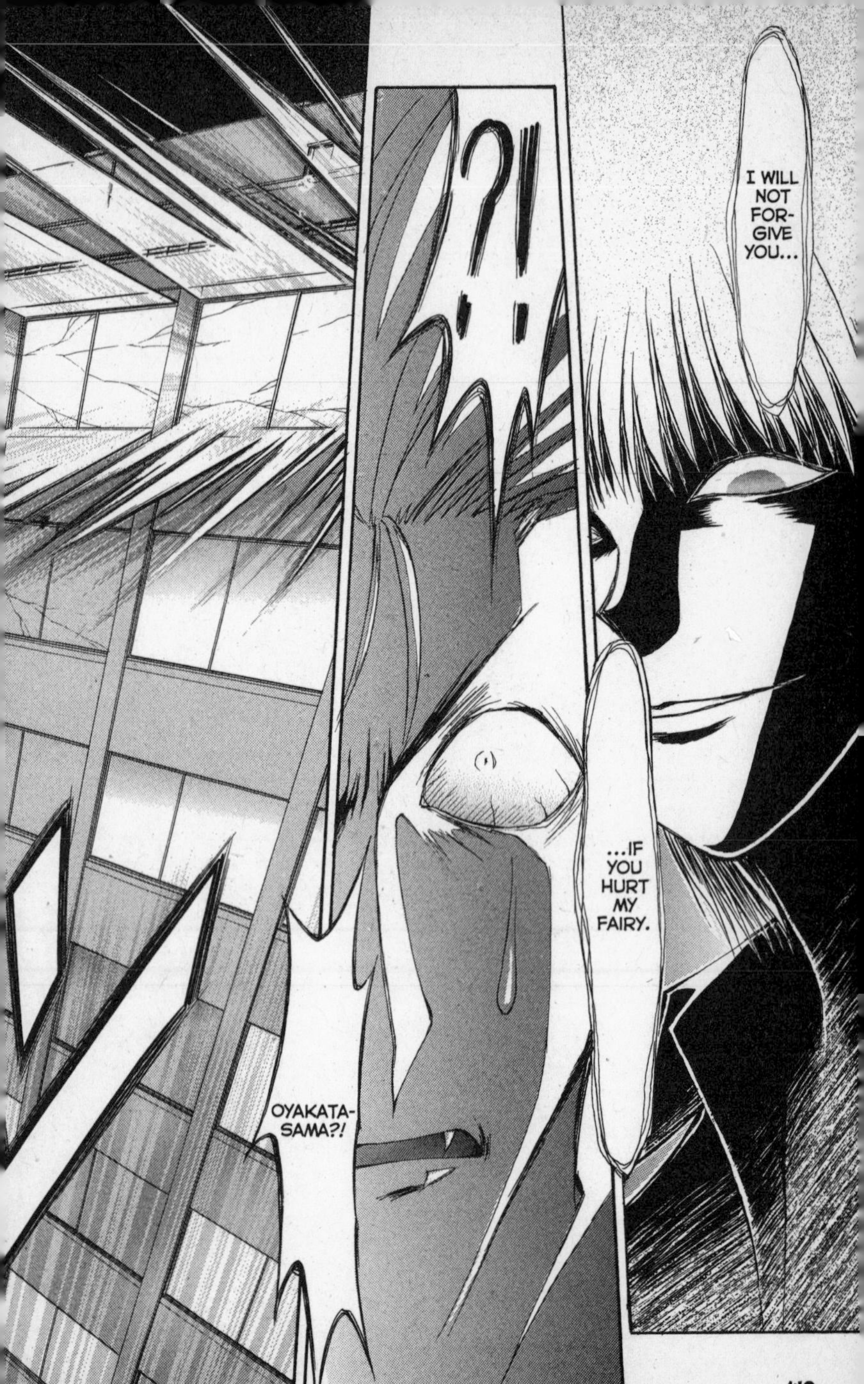
I WILL NOT FOR-GIVE YOU...
...IF YOU HURT MY FAIRY.
?!
OYAKATA-SAMA?!

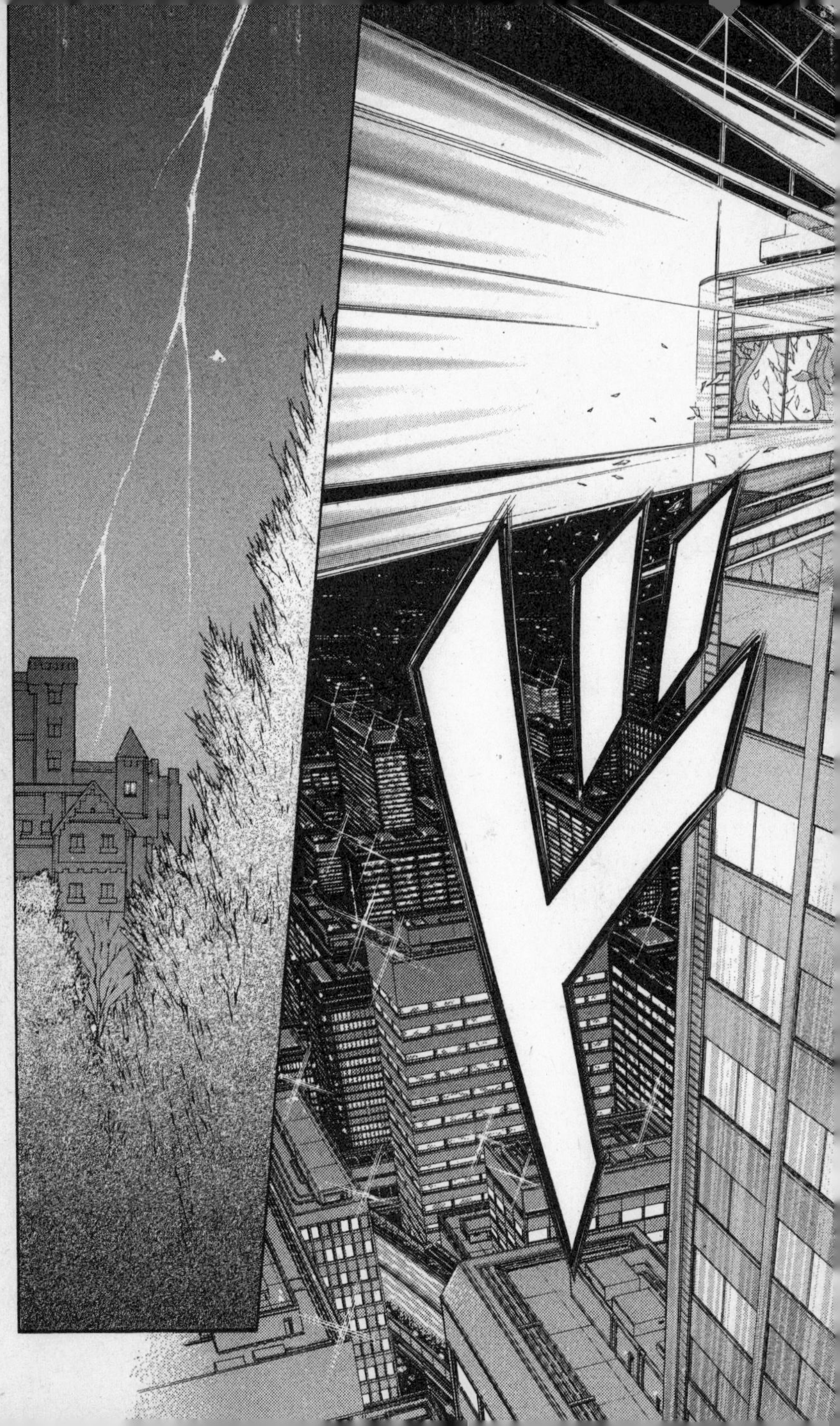

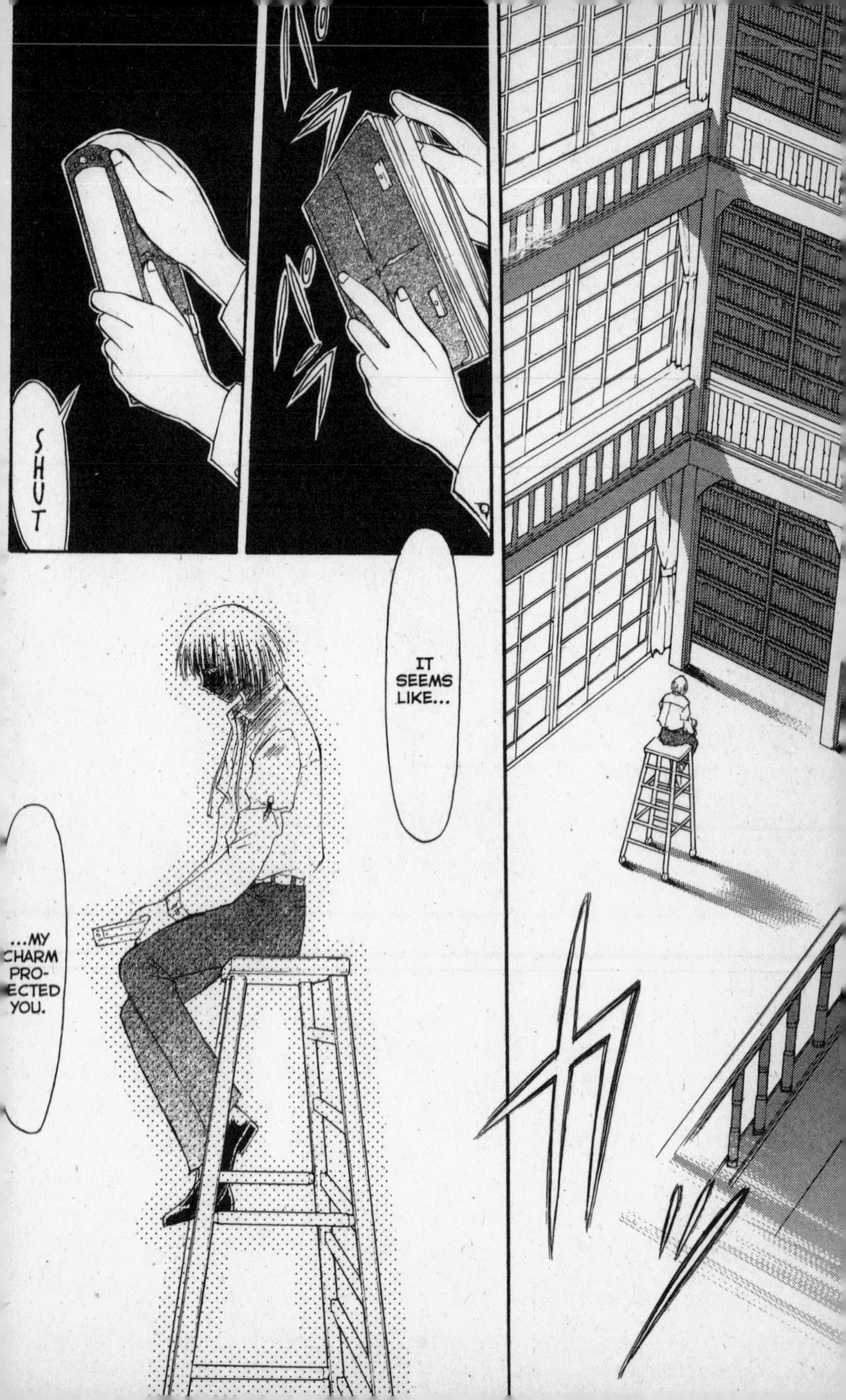
SHUT
IT SEEMS LIKE...
...MY CHARM PRO-TECTED YOU.

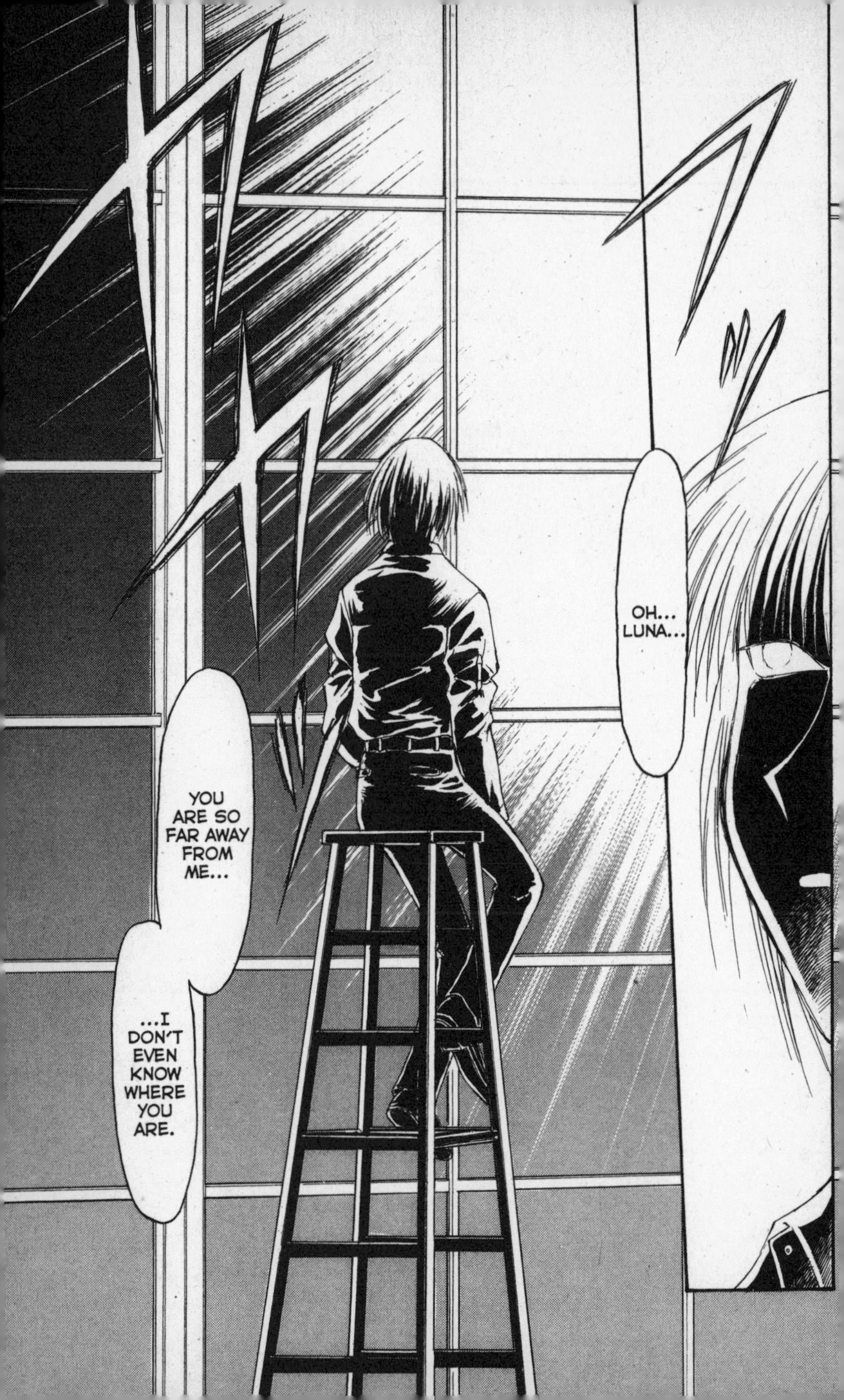
OH... LUNA...
YOU ARE SO FAR AWAY FROM ME...
...I DON'T EVEN KNOW WHERE YOU ARE.

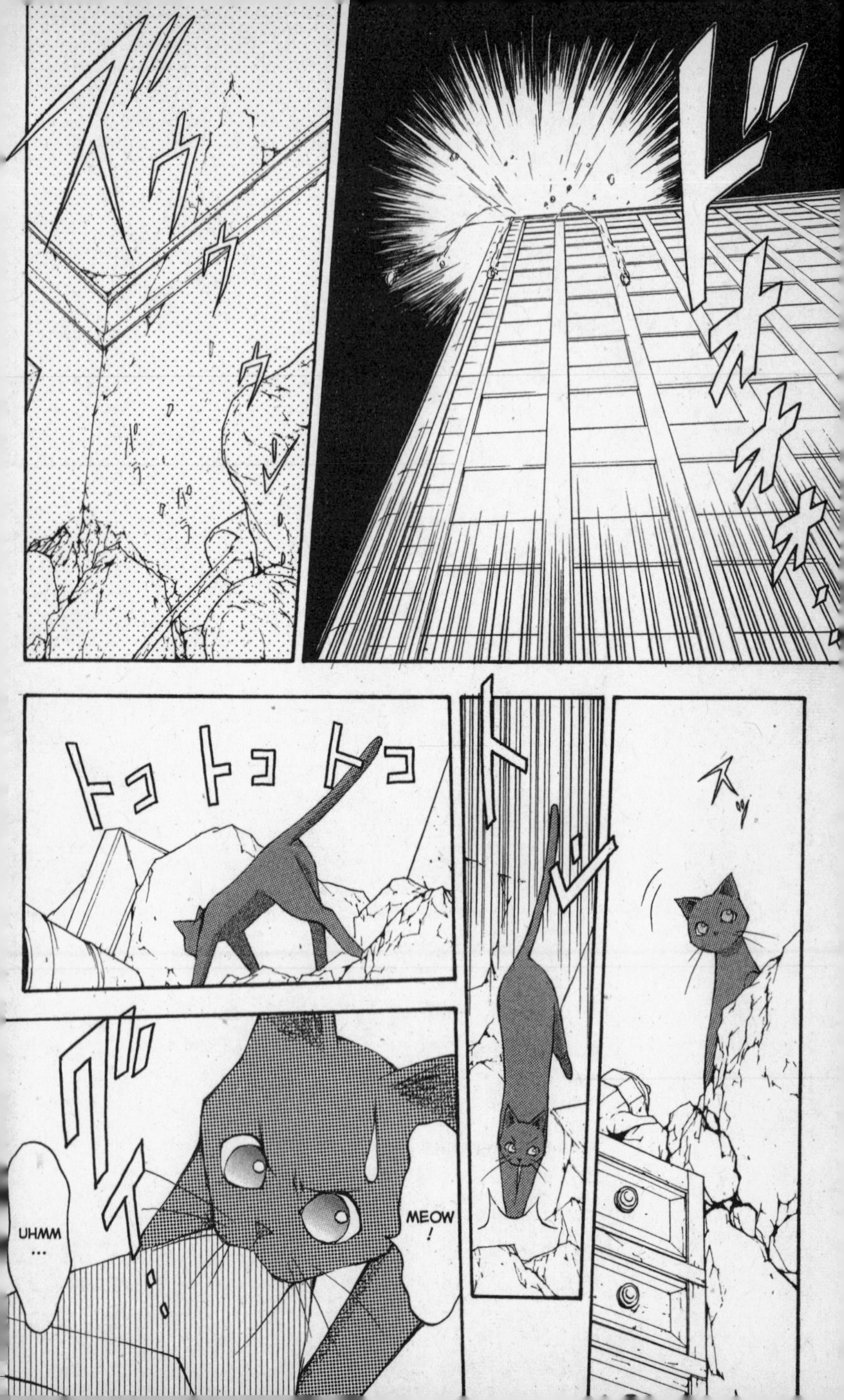
ドオオオオ…
ズウウウン
スッ
トン
トコトコトコ
グイ
MEOW !
UHMM ...

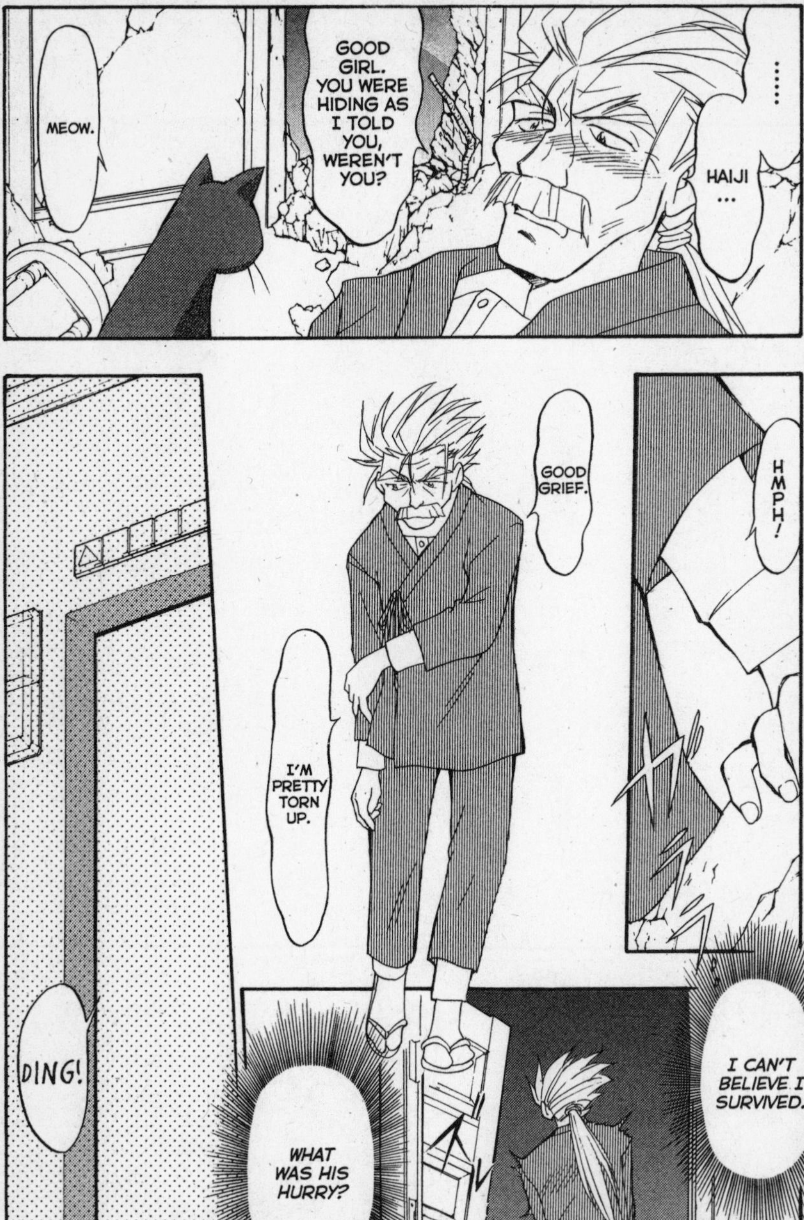
……
HAIJI …
GOOD GIRL. YOU WERE HIDING AS I TOLD YOU, WEREN'T YOU?
MEOW.
HMPH!
GOOD GRIEF.
I'M PRETTY TORN UP.
I CAN'T BELIEVE I SURVIVED.
WHAT WAS HIS HURRY?
DING!

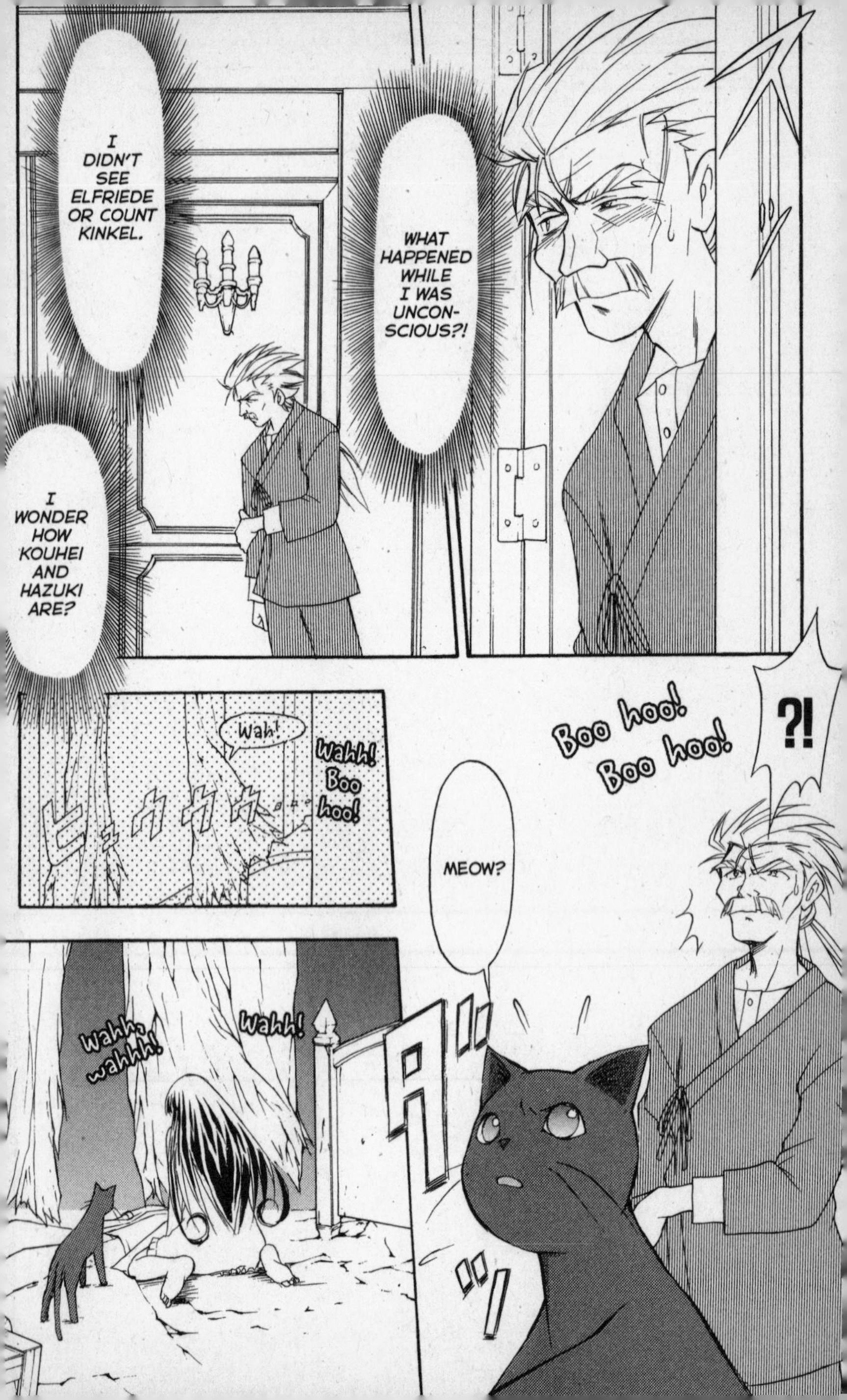
WHAT HAPPENED WHILE I WAS UNCON- SCIOUS?!
I DIDN'T SEE ELFRIEDE OR COUNT KINKEL.
I WONDER HOW KOUHEI AND HAZUKI ARE?
?!
Boo hoo! Boo hoo!
MEOW?
Wahh! Boo hoo!
Wah!
Wahh!
Wahh, wahhh!

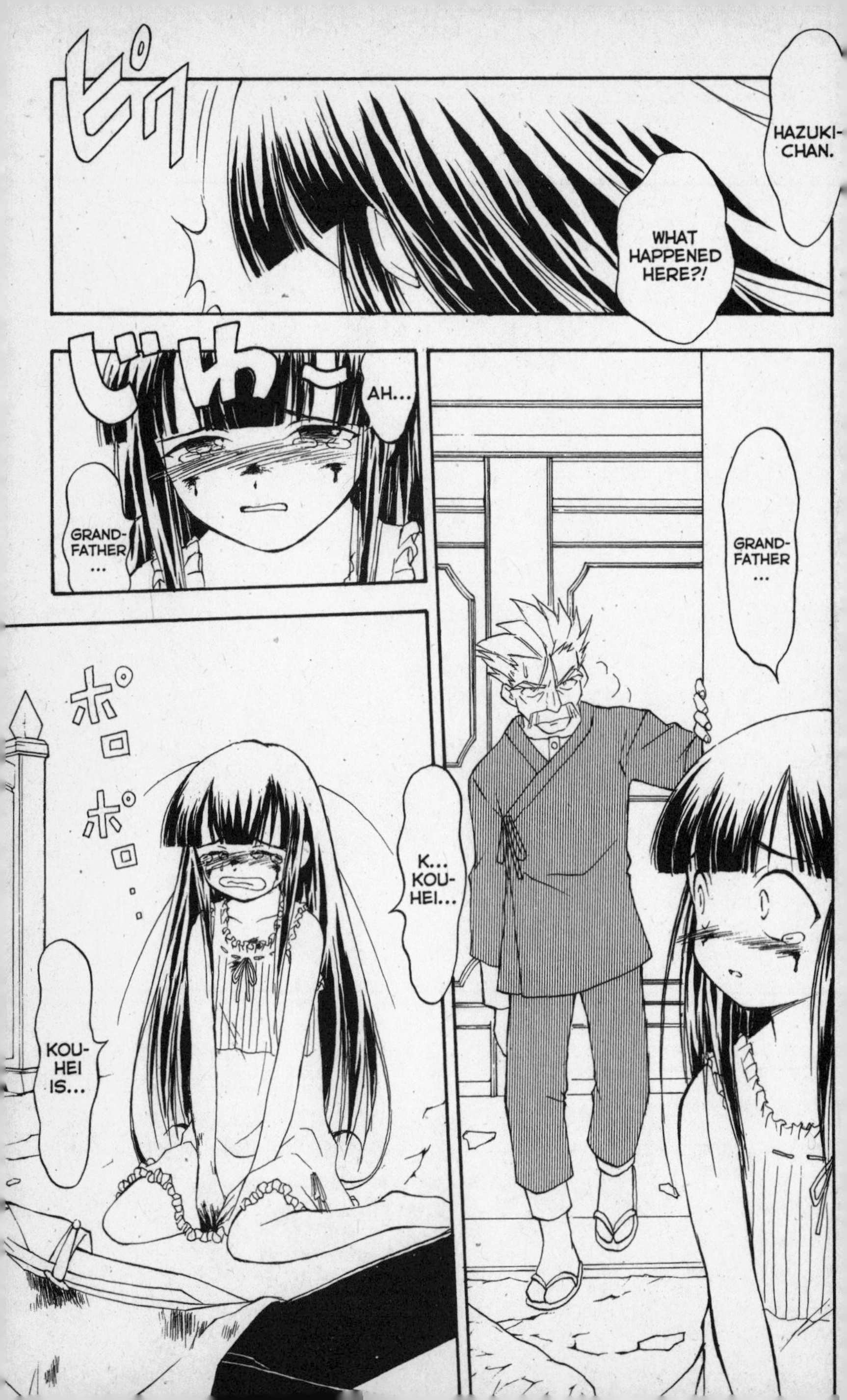

ピク
HAZUKI-CHAN.
WHAT HAPPENED HERE?!
GRAND-FATHER ...
じわ〜
AH...
GRAND-FATHER ...
ポロポロ
K... KOU-HEI...
KOU-HEI IS...

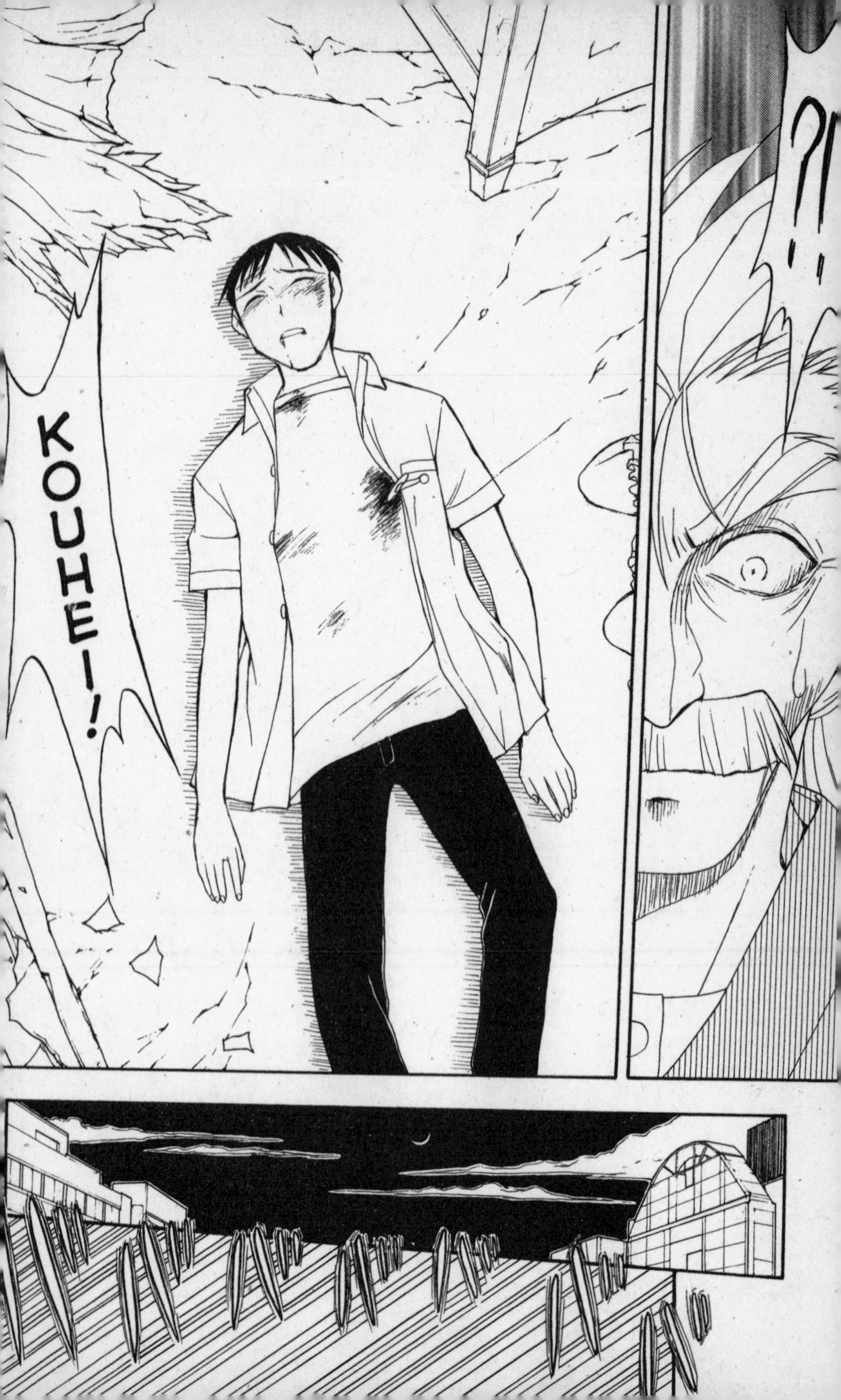
?!!
KOUHEI!!

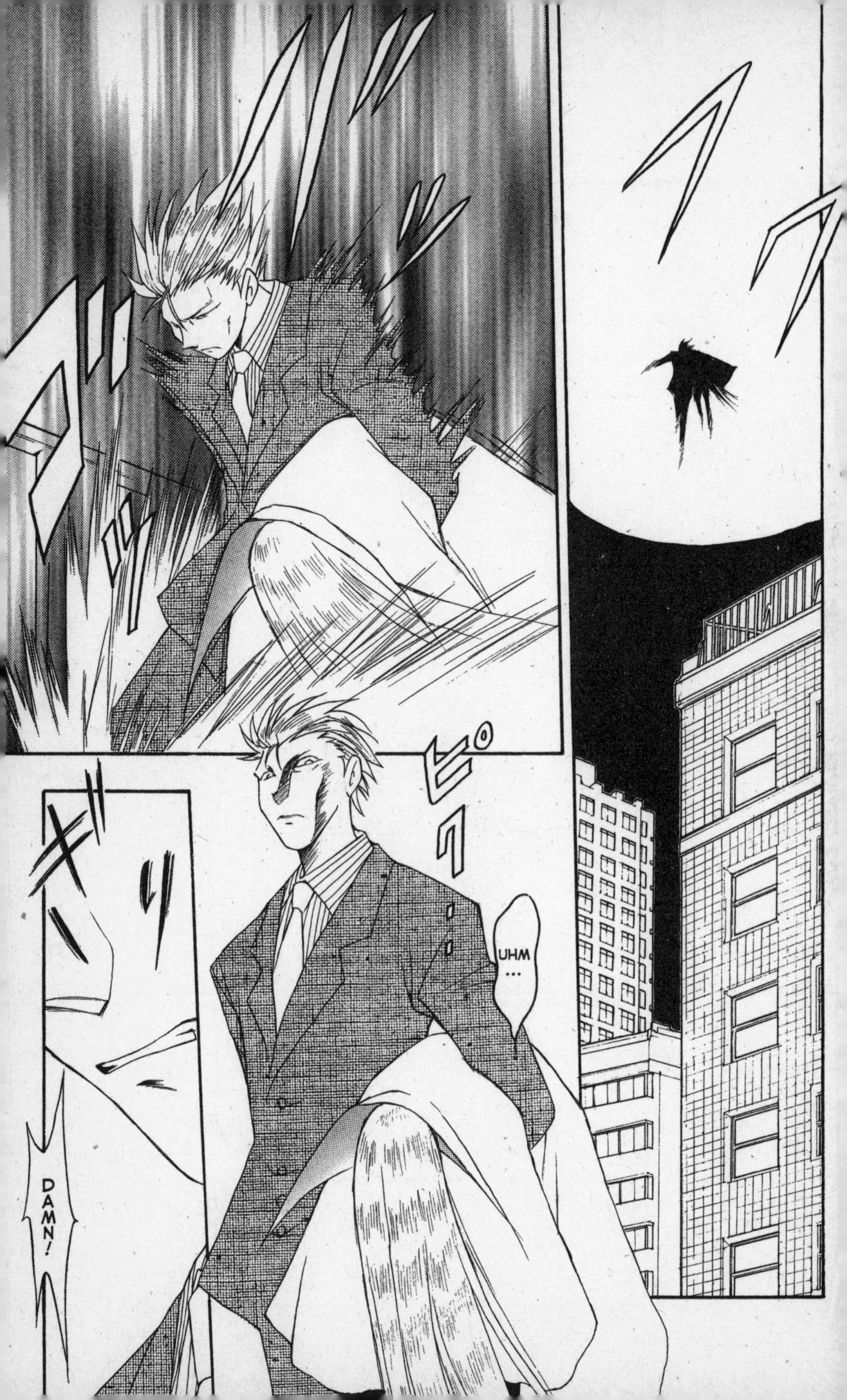
UHM...
DAMN!

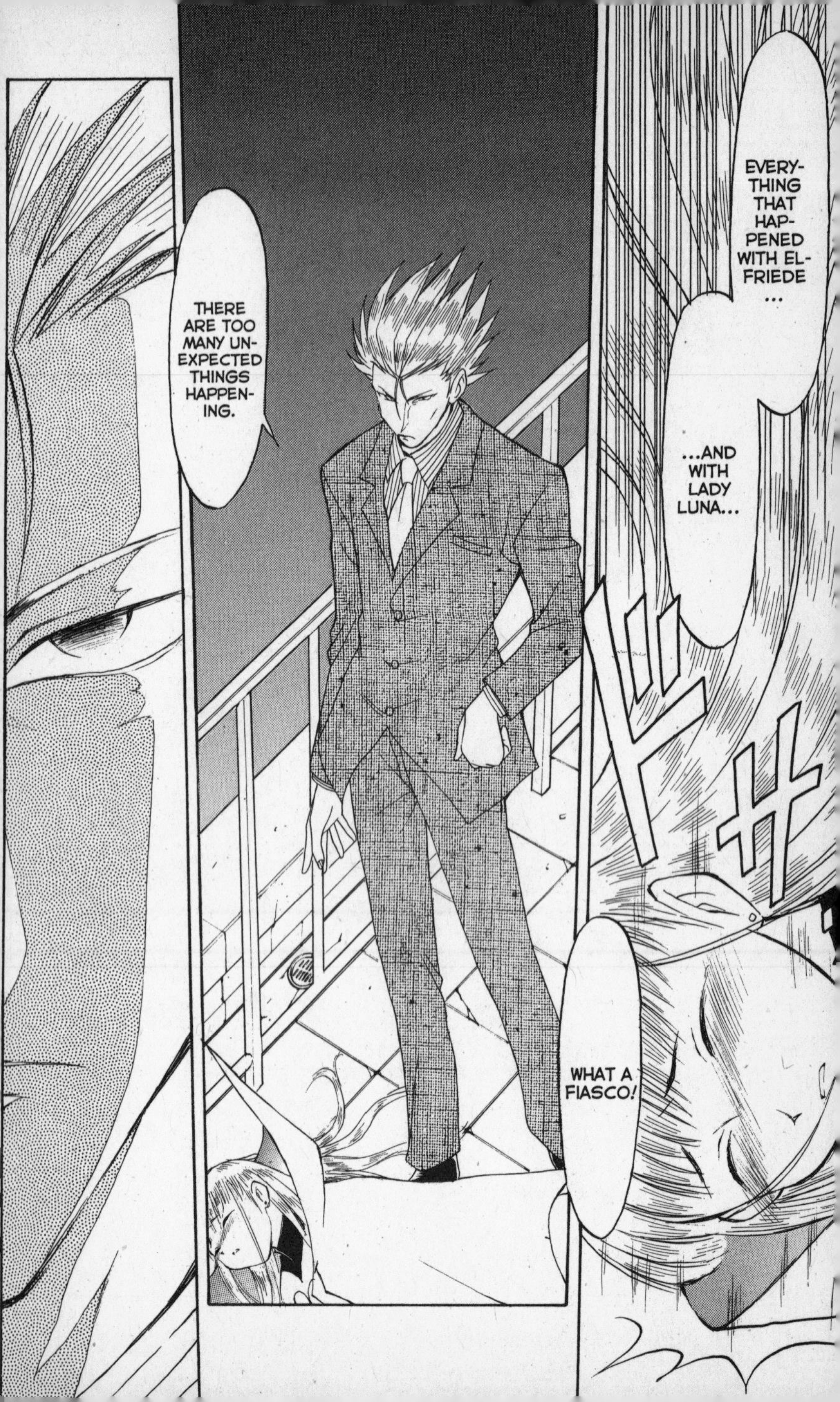
EVERY-THING THAT HAP-PENED WITH EL-FRIEDE ...
...AND WITH LADY LUNA...
ドサ
WHAT A FIASCO!
THERE ARE TOO MANY UN-EXPECTED THINGS HAPPEN-ING.

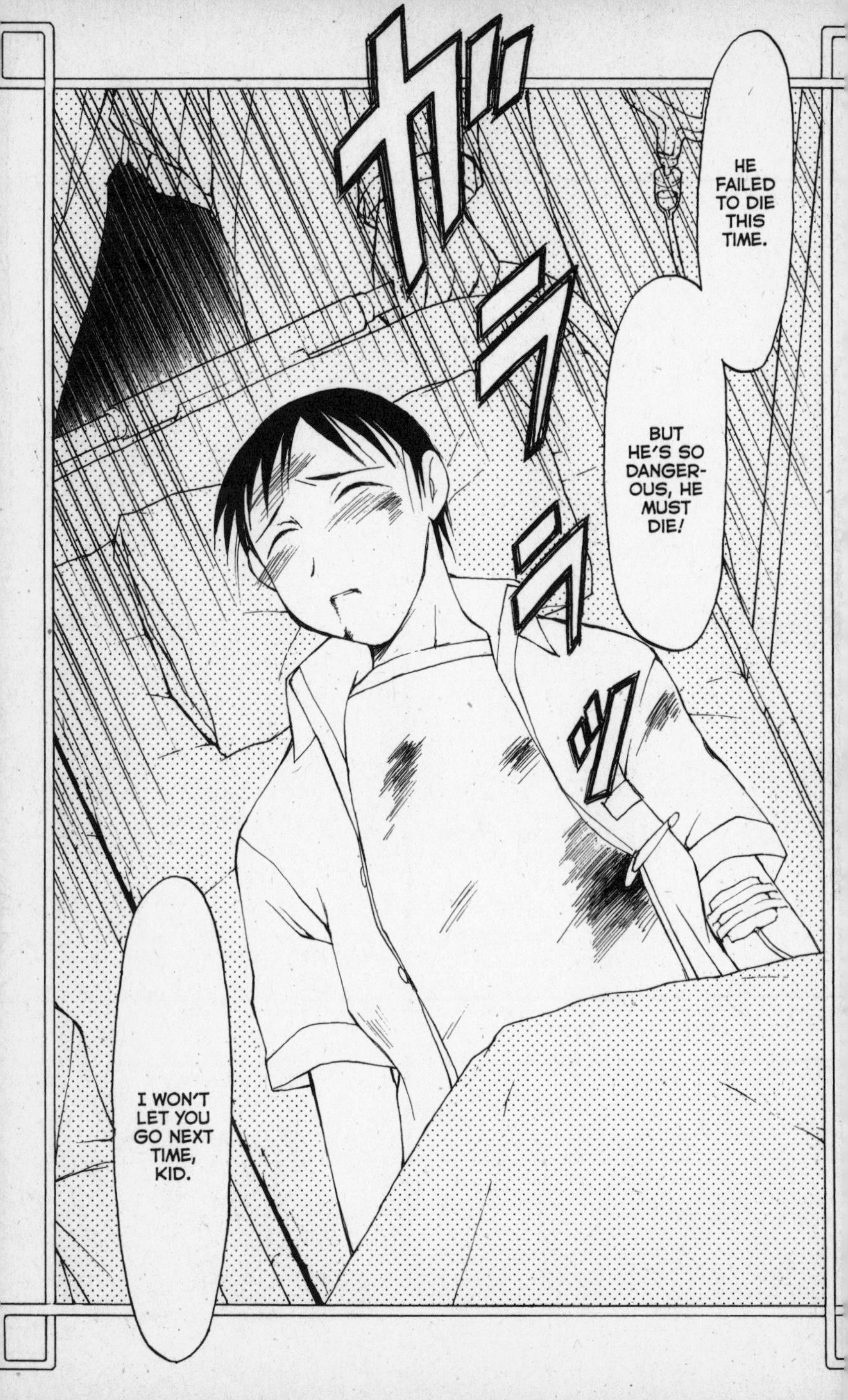
HE FAILED TO DIE THIS TIME.
BUT HE'S SO DANGER-OUS, HE MUST DIE!
I WON'T LET YOU GO NEXT TIME, KID.

LATELY HIS FIGHTING HAS BEEN OUTSTANDING. IT'S LIKE HE BECAME A SUPER-SAIYA-JIN! (HA!)
HIS NAME IS RYUHEI MIDO. (REVEALING THIS FOR THE FIRST TIME...!)
HIS LATE BROTHER IS THE REAL MIDO MEDIUM.

HIS FATHER USED TO BE THE STRONGEST MEDIUM.

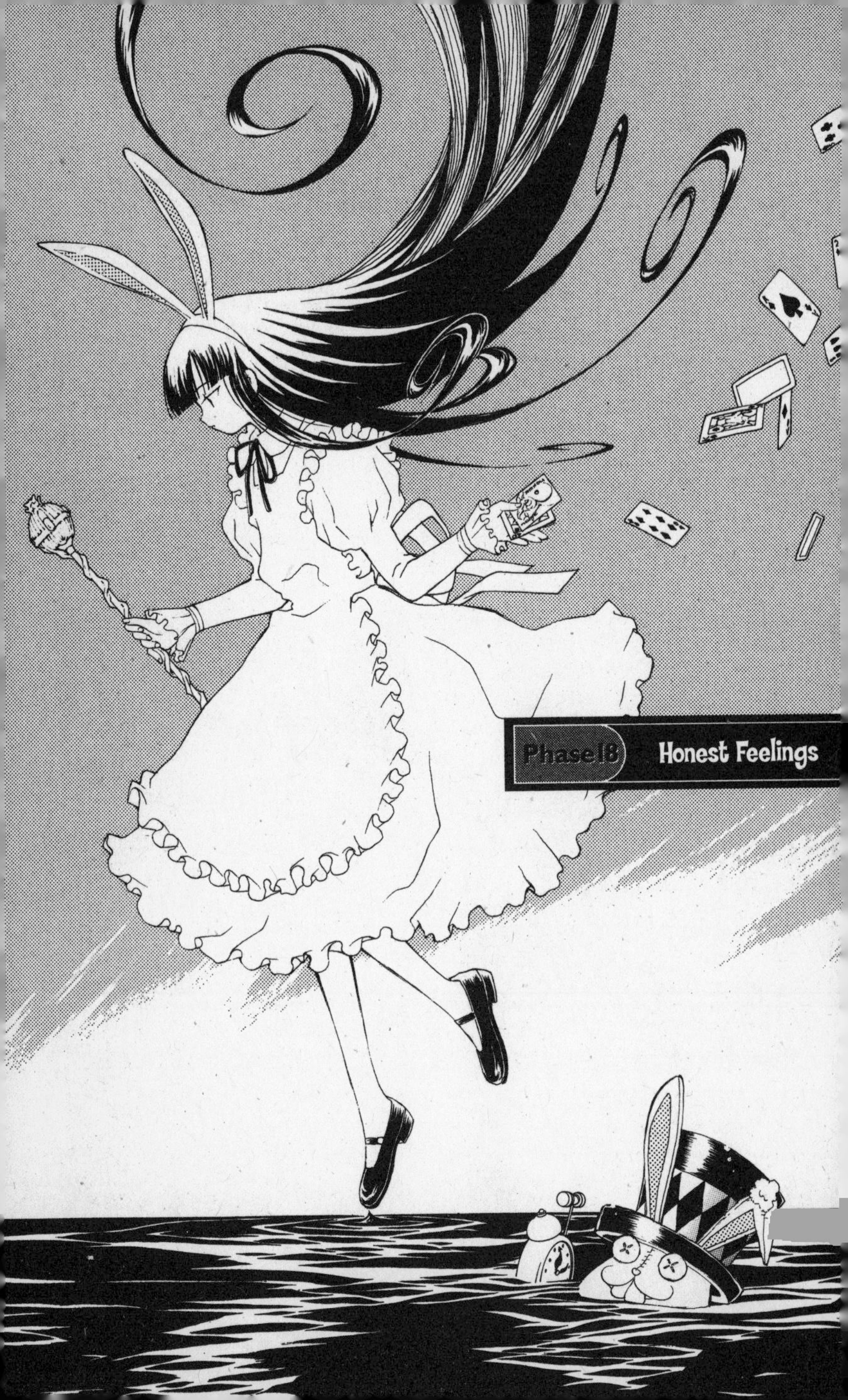
Phase 18
Honest Feelings

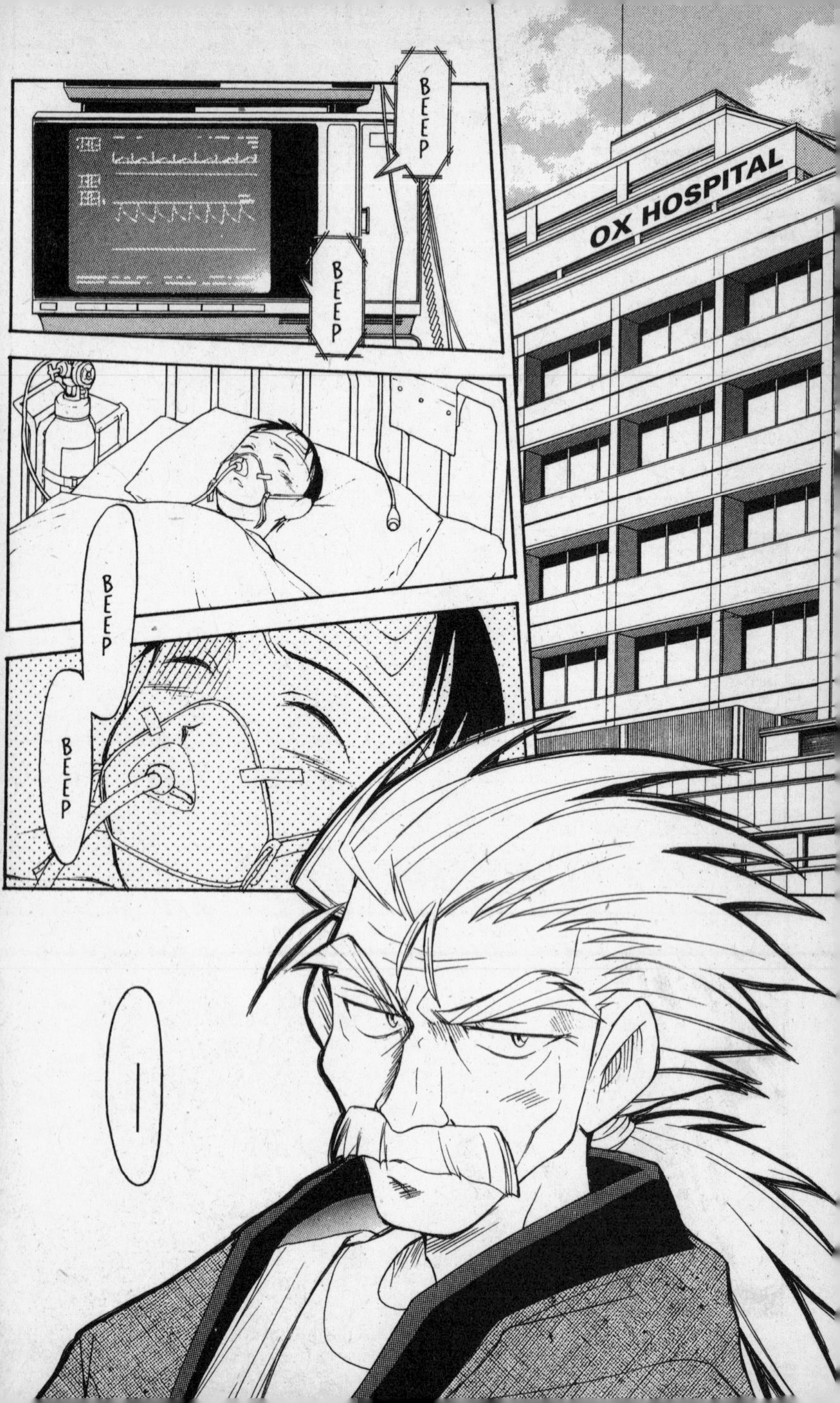
OX HOSPITAL
BEEP
BEEP
BEEP
BEEP
—

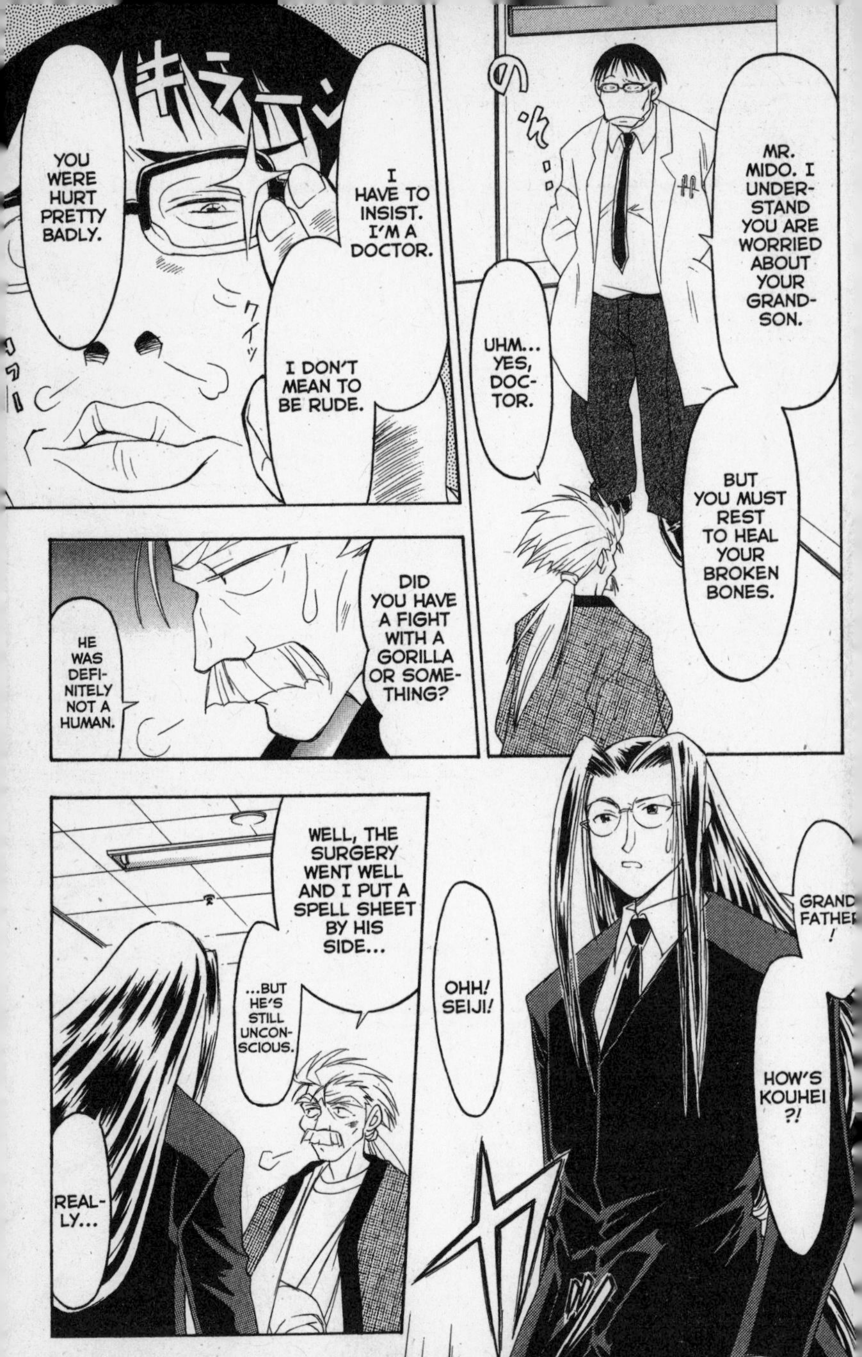
MR. MIDO. I UNDERSTAND YOU ARE WORRIED ABOUT YOUR GRANDSON.
BUT YOU MUST REST TO HEAL YOUR BROKEN BONES.
UHM... YES, DOCTOR.
I HAVE TO INSIST. I'M A DOCTOR.
I DON'T MEAN TO BE RUDE.
YOU WERE HURT PRETTY BADLY.
DID YOU HAVE A FIGHT WITH A GORILLA OR SOMETHING?
HE WAS DEFINITELY NOT A HUMAN.
GRANDFATHER!
HOW'S KOUHEI?!
OHH! SEIJI!
WELL, THE SURGERY WENT WELL AND I PUT A SPELL SHEET BY HIS SIDE...
...BUT HE'S STILL UNCONSCIOUS.
REALLY...

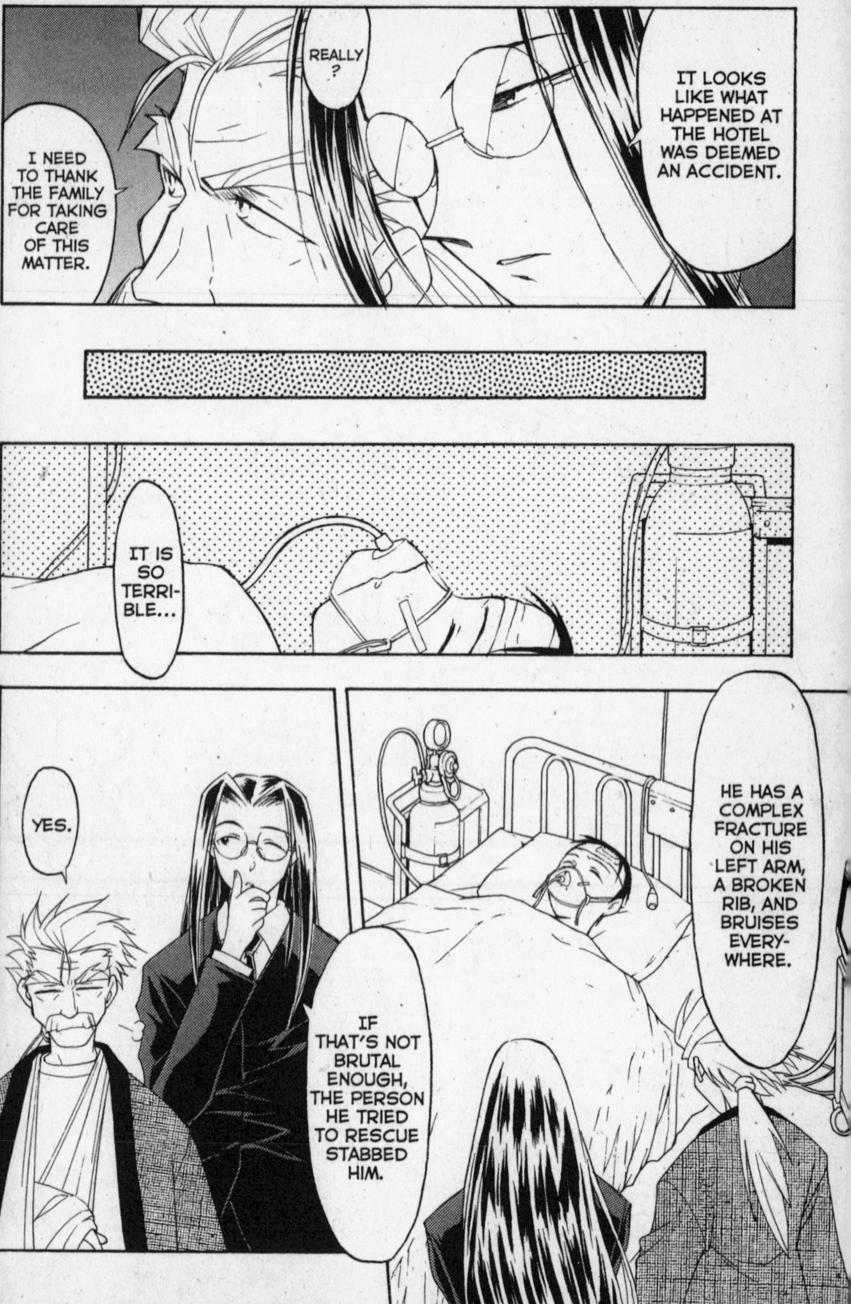
IT LOOKS LIKE WHAT HAPPENED AT THE HOTEL WAS DEEMED AN ACCIDENT.
REALLY?
I NEED TO THANK THE FAMILY FOR TAKING CARE OF THIS MATTER.
IT IS SO TERRIBLE...
HE HAS A COMPLEX FRACTURE ON HIS LEFT ARM, A BROKEN RIB, AND BRUISES EVERYWHERE.
IF THAT'S NOT BRUTAL ENOUGH, THE PERSON HE TRIED TO RESCUE STABBED HIM.
YES.

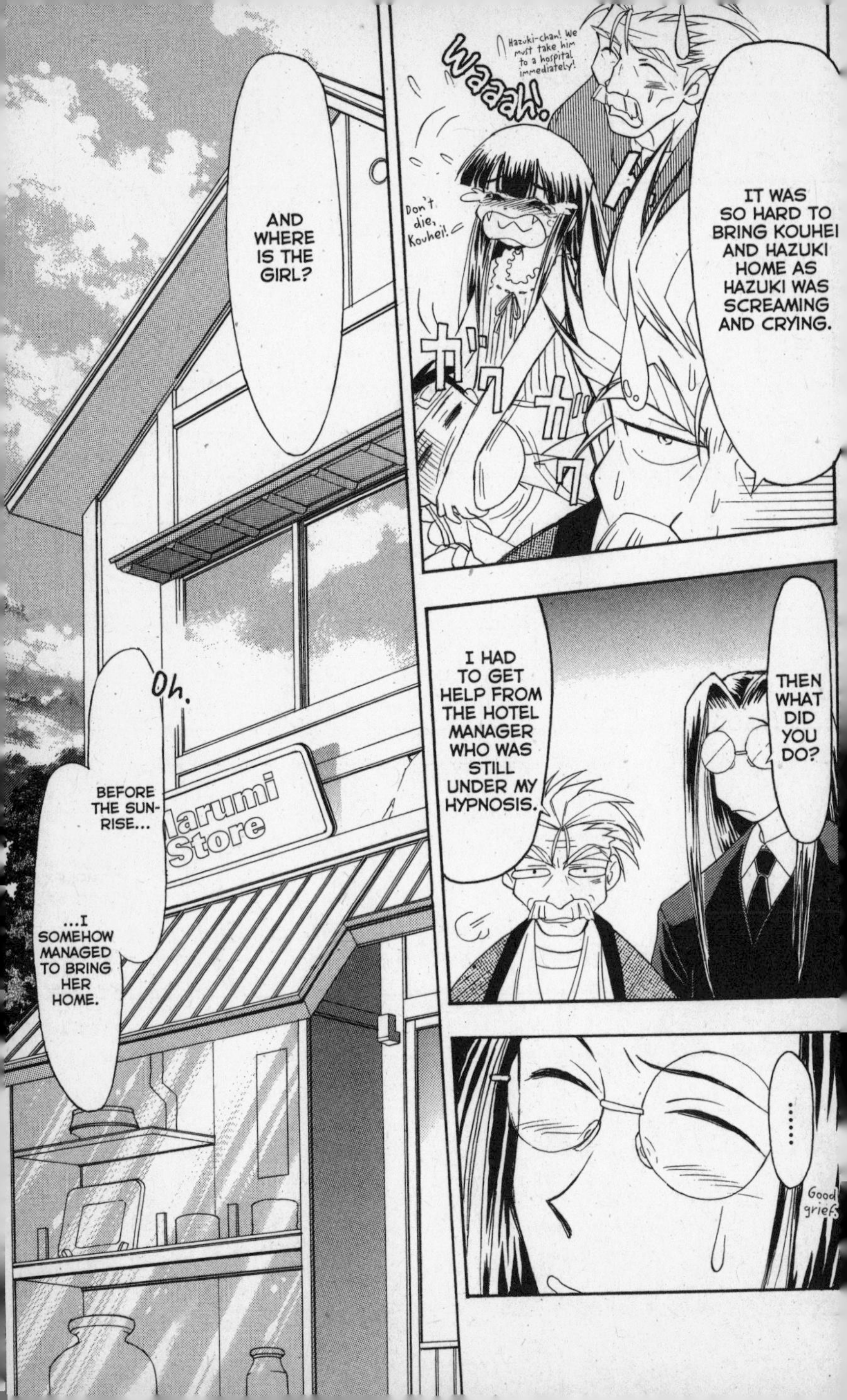
IT WAS SO HARD TO BRING KOUHEI AND HAZUKI HOME AS HAZUKI WAS SCREAMING AND CRYING.
Hazuki-chan! We must take him to a hospital immediately!
WAAAAH!
Don't die, Kouhei!
ガク
ガク
THEN WHAT DID YOU DO?
I HAD TO GET HELP FROM THE HOTEL MANAGER WHO WAS STILL UNDER MY HYPNOSIS.
......
Good grief.
AND WHERE IS THE GIRL?
Oh.
Store
BEFORE THE SUN-RISE...
...I SOMEHOW MANAGED TO BRING HER HOME.

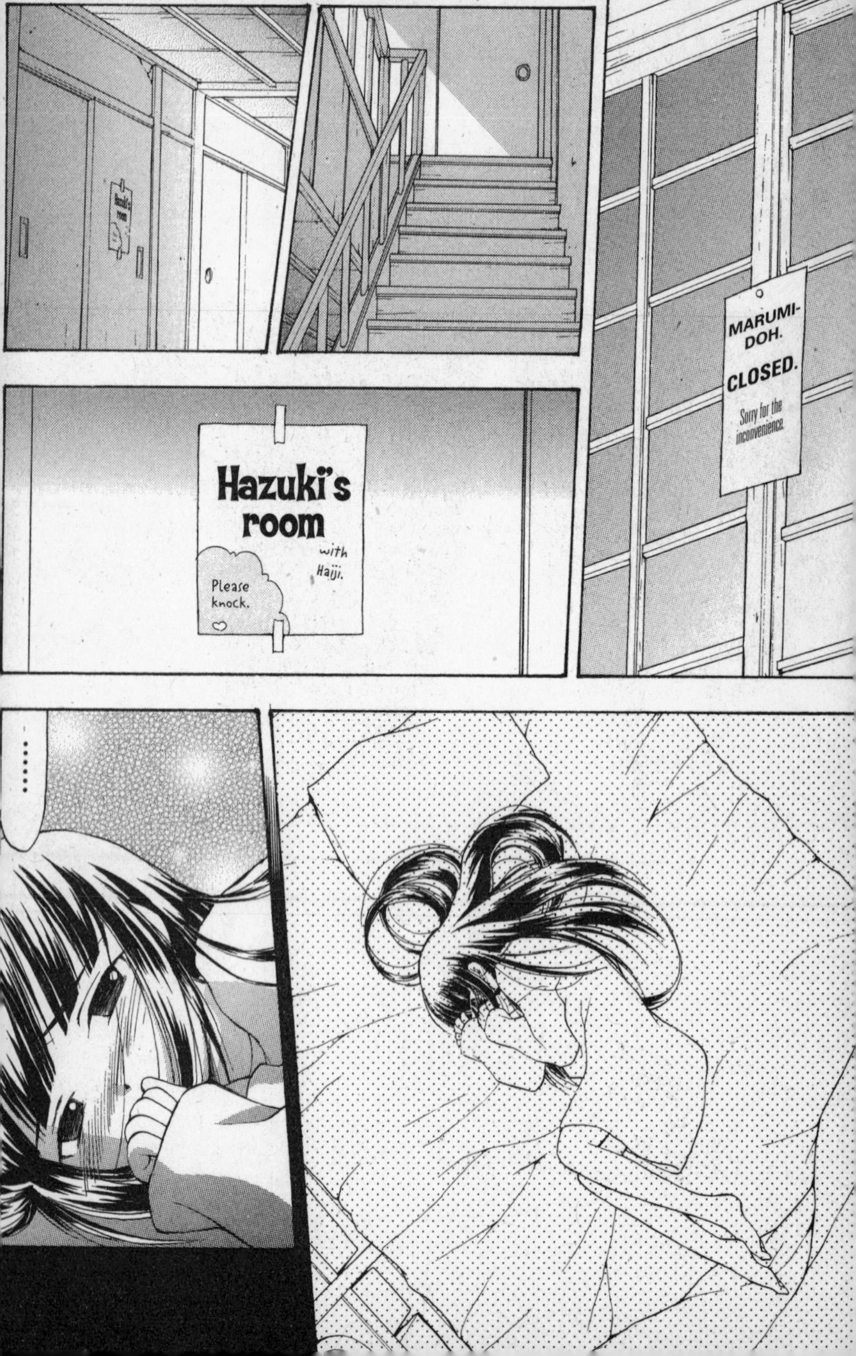
MARUMI-DOH.
CLOSED.
Sorry for the inconvenience.
Hazuki's room
with Haiji.
Please knock.
......

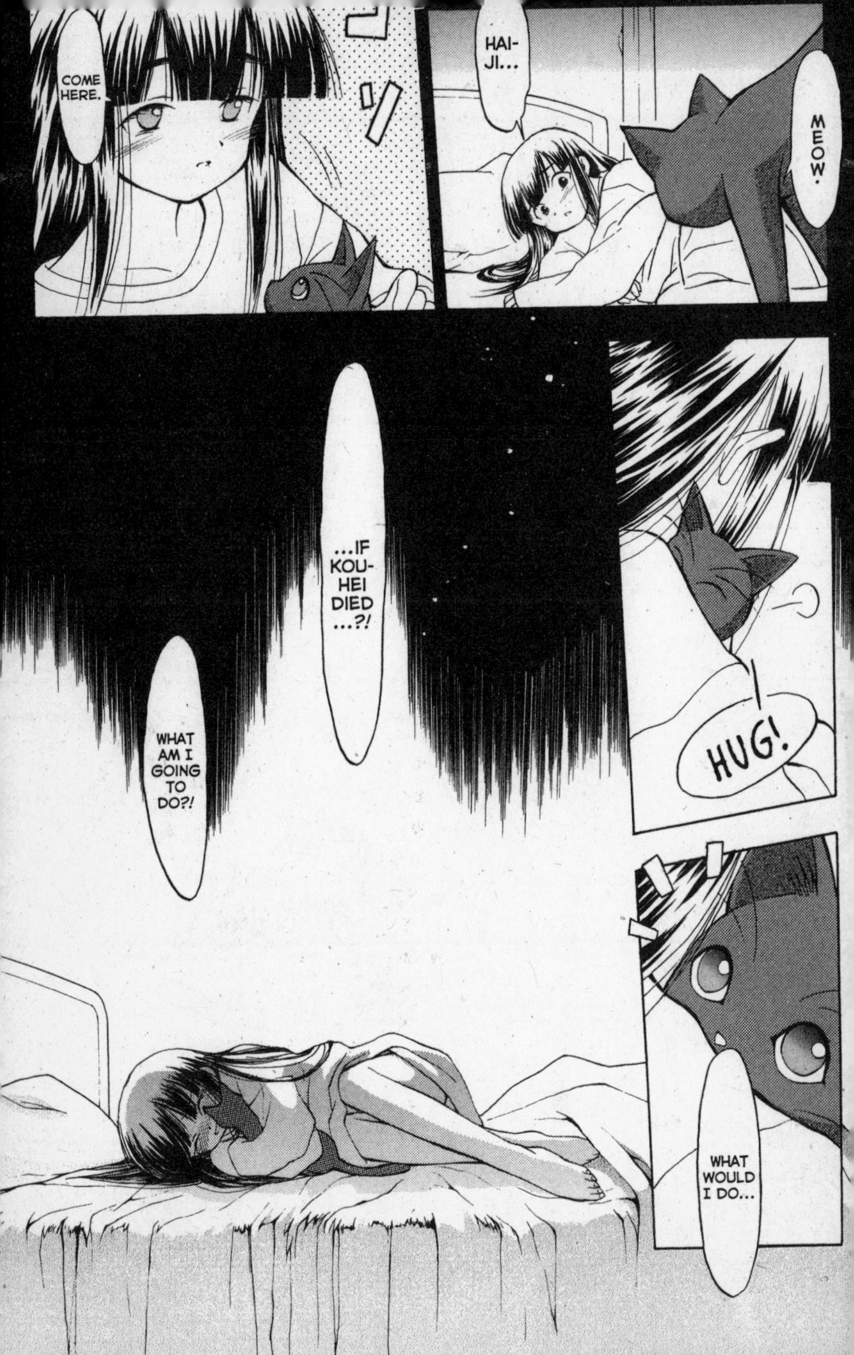
HAI-JI...
MEOW.
COME HERE.
HUG!
WHAT WOULD I DO...
...IF KOU-HEI DIED...?!
WHAT AM I GOING TO DO?!

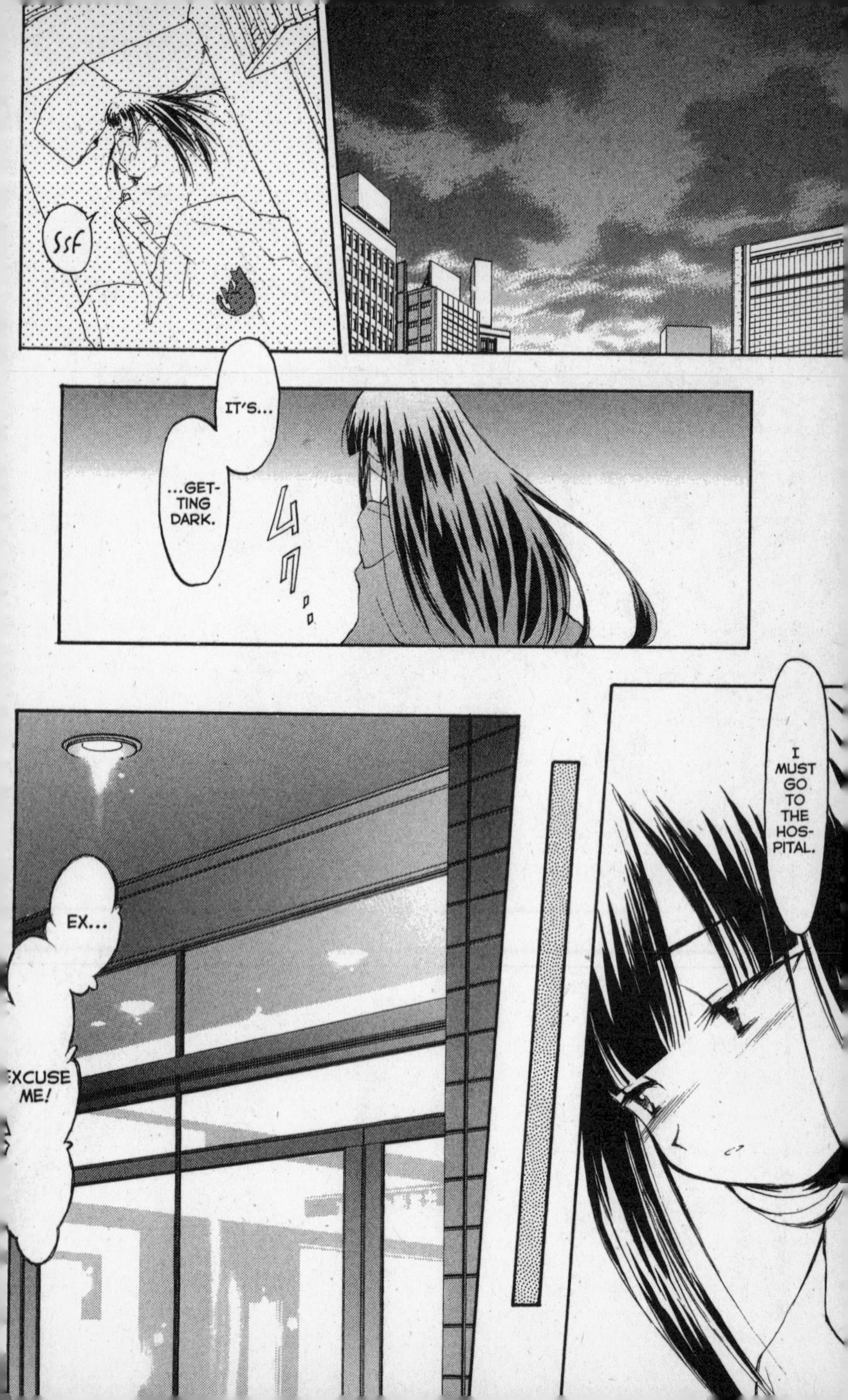
Ssf
IT'S...
...GET-TING DARK.
I MUST GO TO THE HOS-PITAL.
EX...
EXCUSE ME!

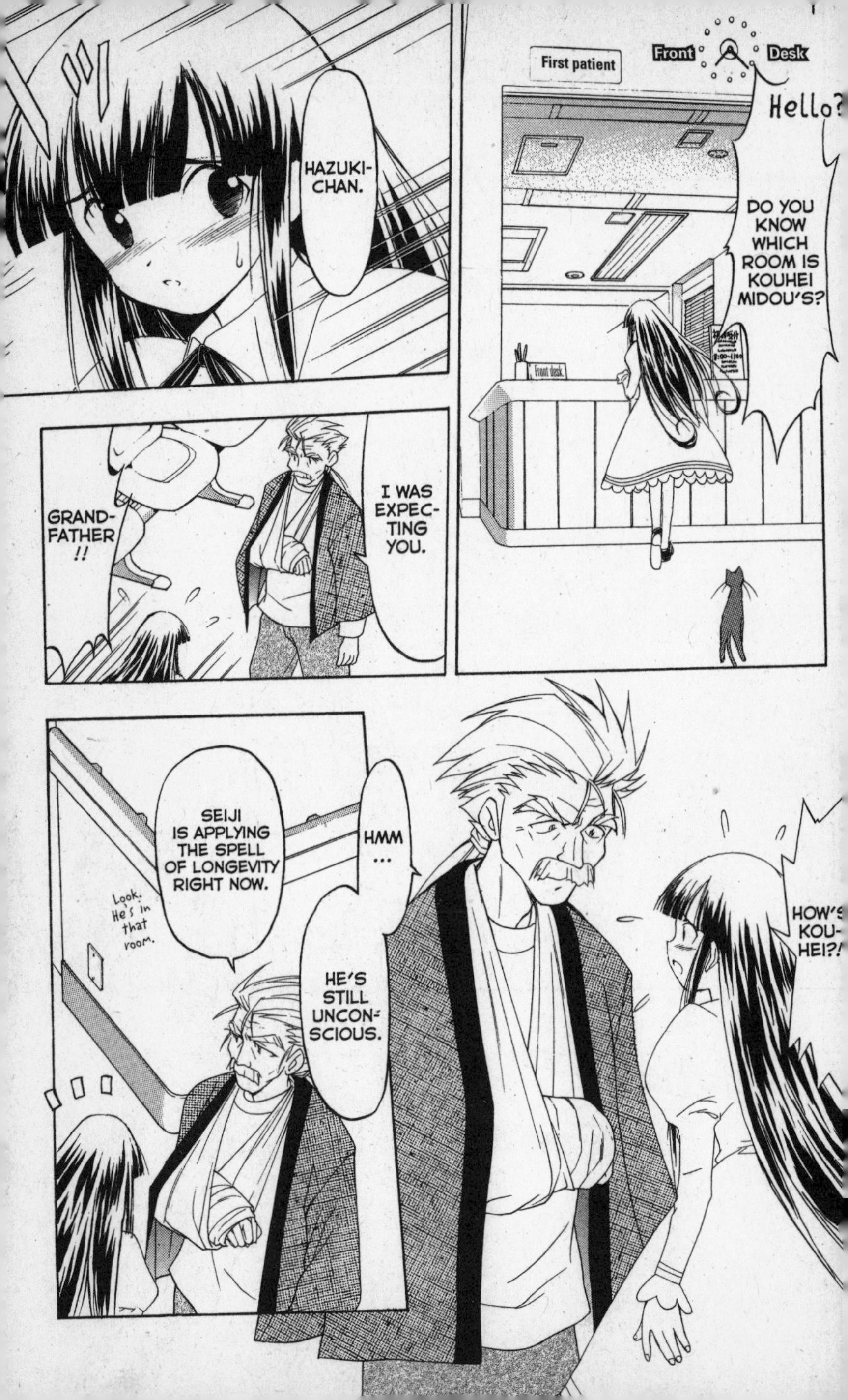
First patient
Front Desk
Hello?
DO YOU KNOW WHICH ROOM IS KOUHEI MIDOU'S?
Front desk
HAZUKI-CHAN.
I WAS EXPECTING YOU.
GRANDFATHER!!
HOW'S KOUHEI?!
HMM...
HE'S STILL UNCONSCIOUS.
SEIJI IS APPLYING THE SPELL OF LONGEVITY RIGHT NOW.
Look. He's in that room.

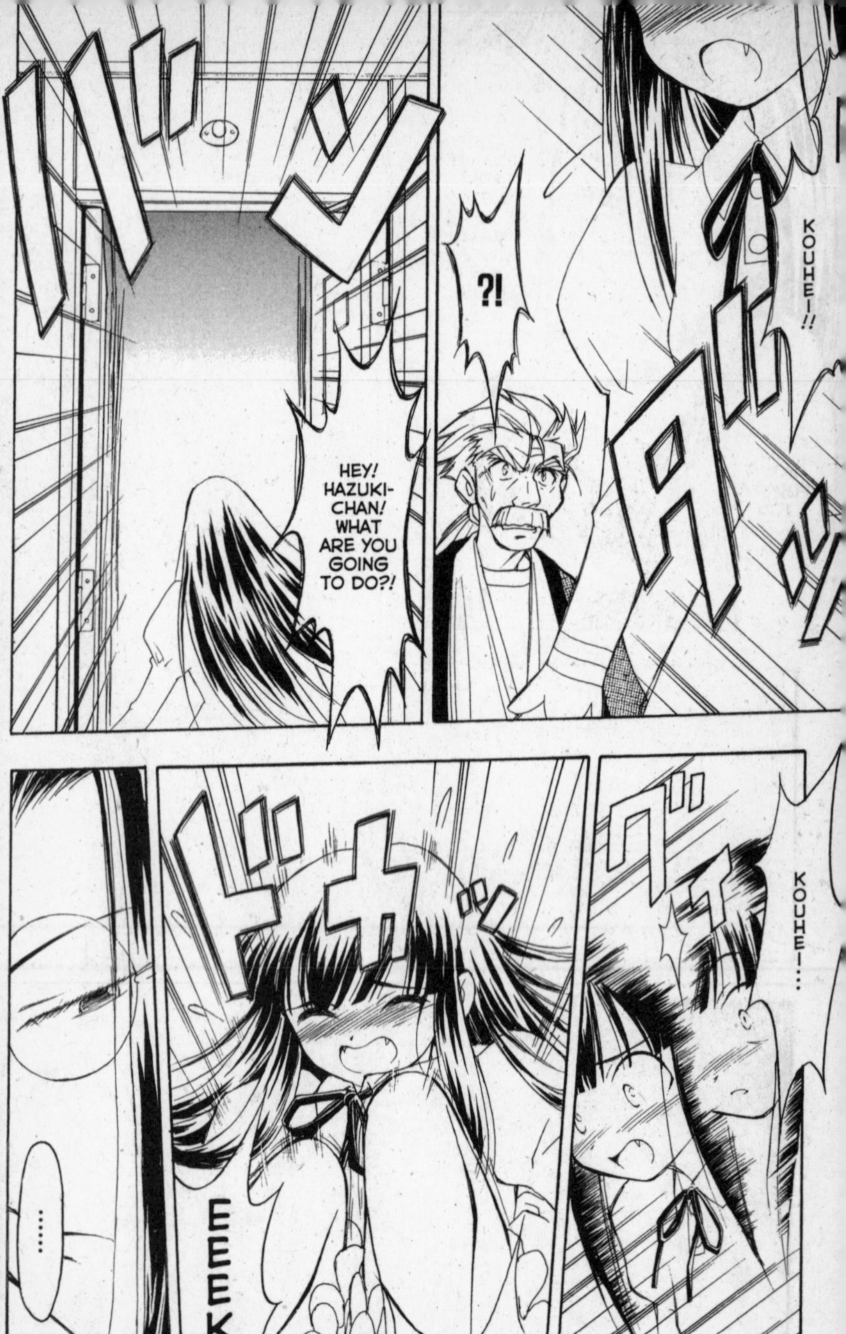
KOUHEI!!
?!
HEY! HAZUKI-CHAN! WHAT ARE YOU GOING TO DO?!
KOUHEI...
EEEEK!!
......

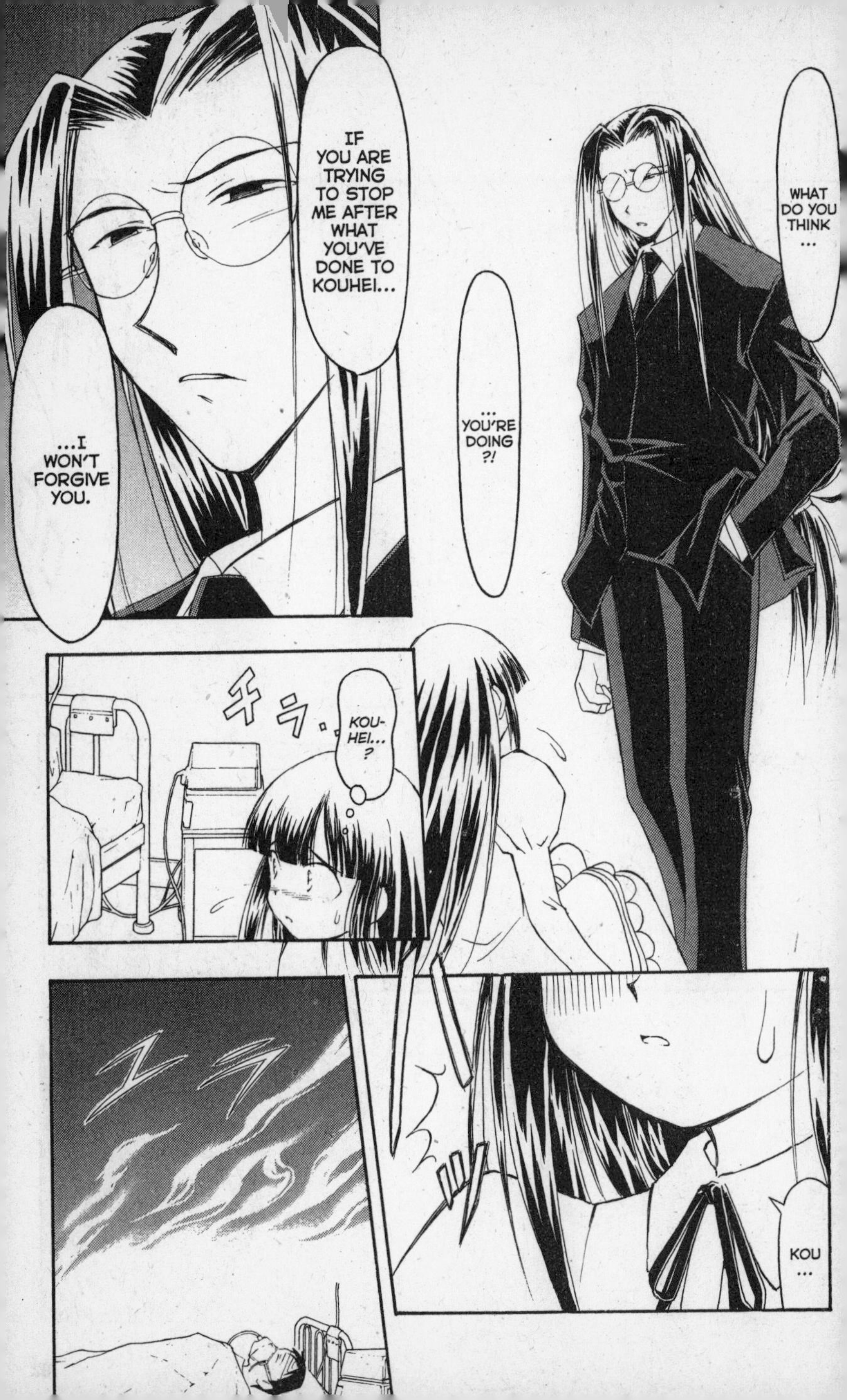
WHAT DO YOU THINK ...
... YOU'RE DOING ?!
IF YOU ARE TRYING TO STOP ME AFTER WHAT YOU'VE DONE TO KOUHEI...
...I WON'T FORGIVE YOU.
チラ
KOU-HEI... ?
KOU ...

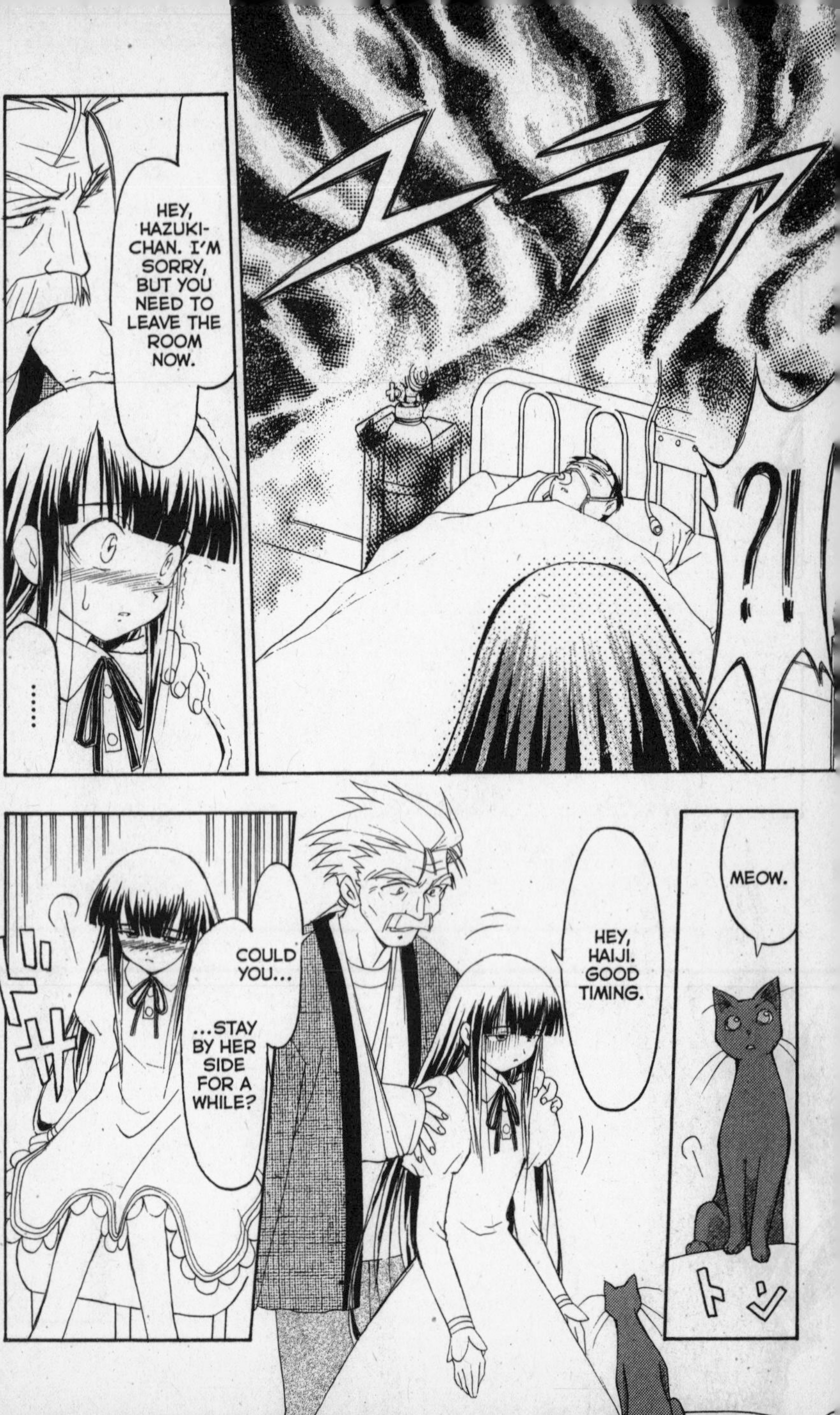
?!
HEY, HAZUKI-CHAN. I'M SORRY, BUT YOU NEED TO LEAVE THE ROOM NOW.
......
MEOW.
HEY, HAIJI. GOOD TIMING.
COULD YOU...
...STAY BY HER SIDE FOR A WHILE?

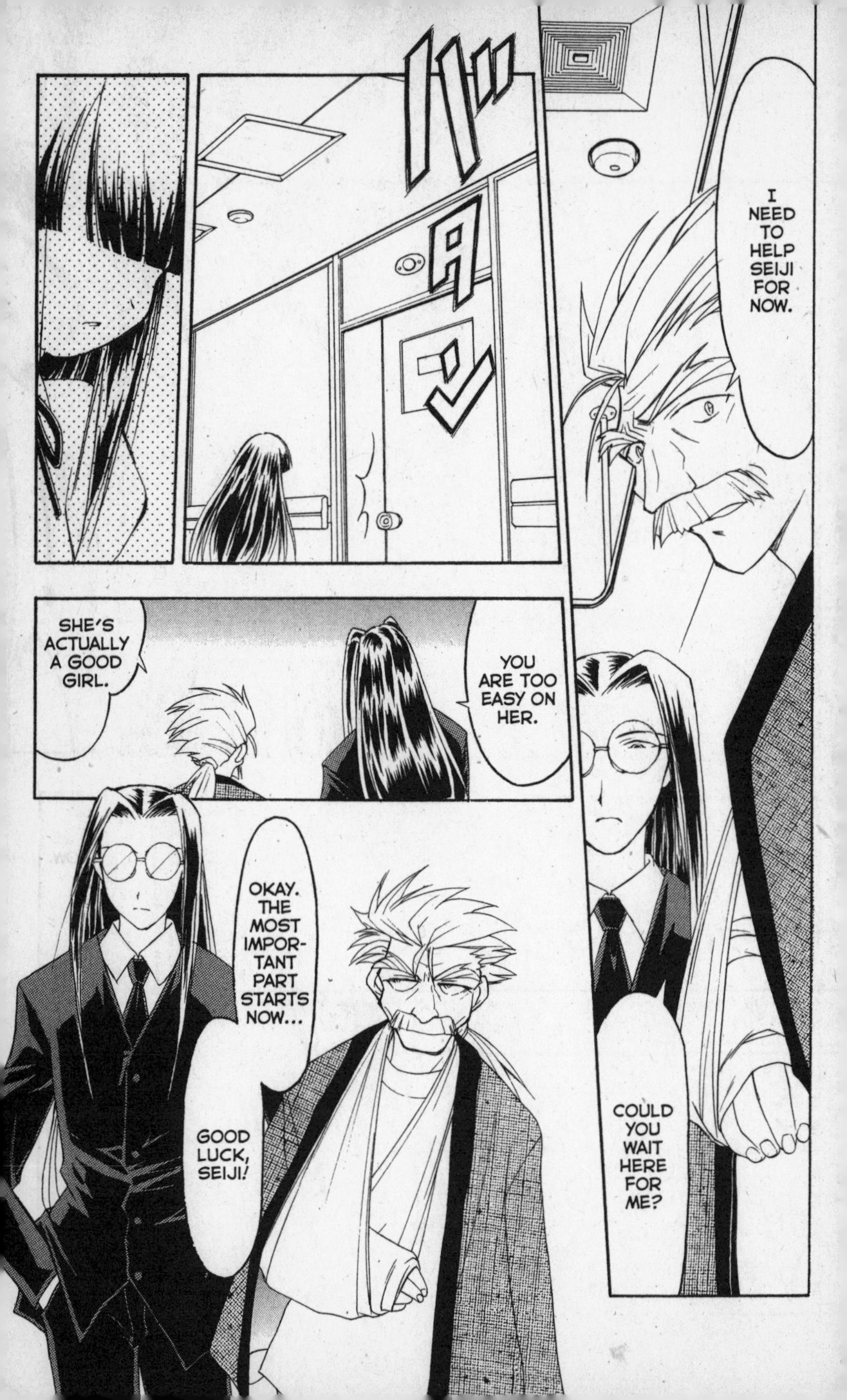
I NEED TO HELP SEIJI FOR NOW.
COULD YOU WAIT HERE FOR ME?
YOU ARE TOO EASY ON HER.
SHE'S ACTUALLY A GOOD GIRL.
OKAY. THE MOST IMPOR-TANT PART STARTS NOW...
GOOD LUCK, SEIJI!

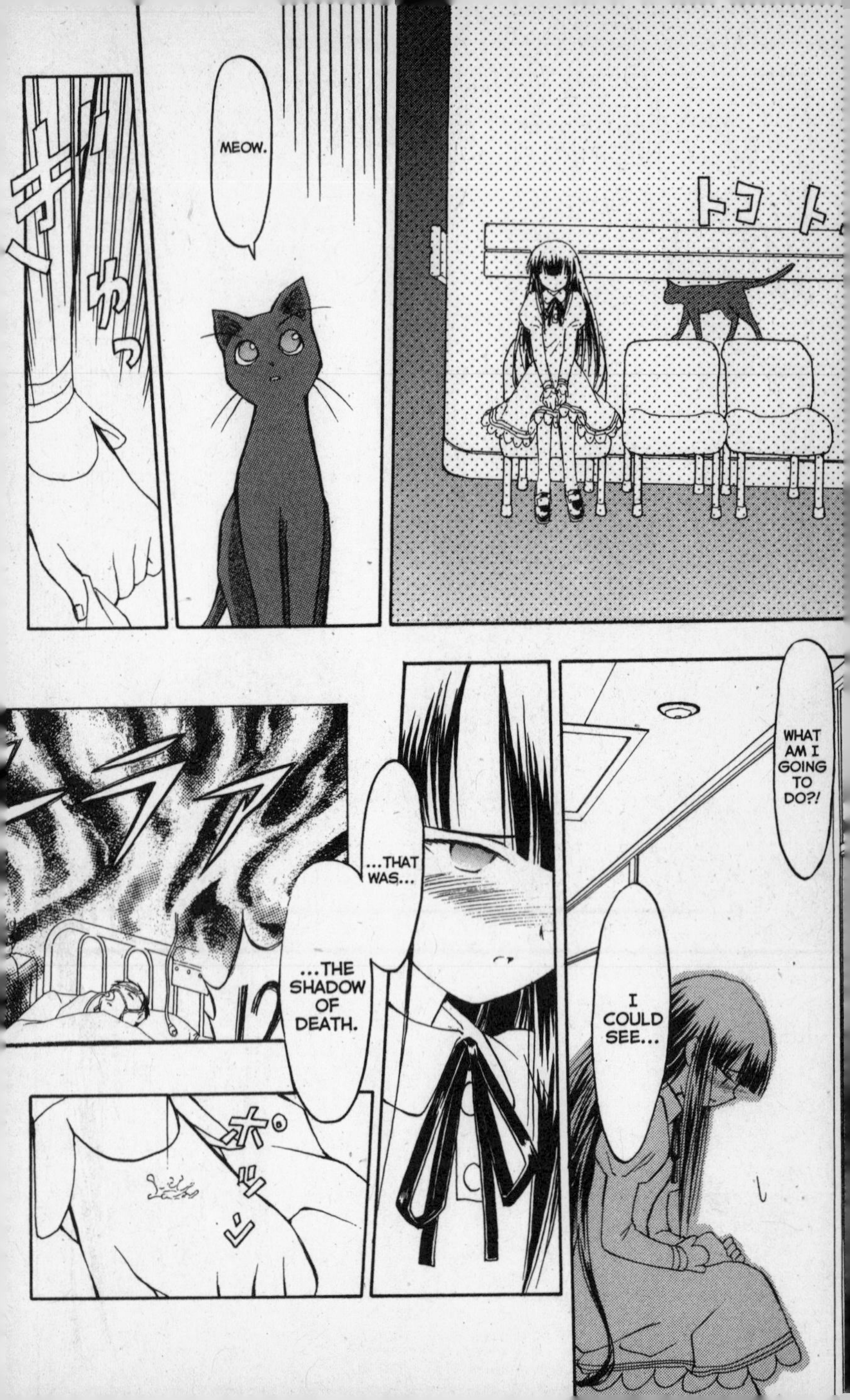
トコト
MEOW.
ぎゅっ
WHAT AM I GOING TO DO?!
I COULD SEE...
...THAT WAS...
...THE SHADOW OF DEATH.
ポツン

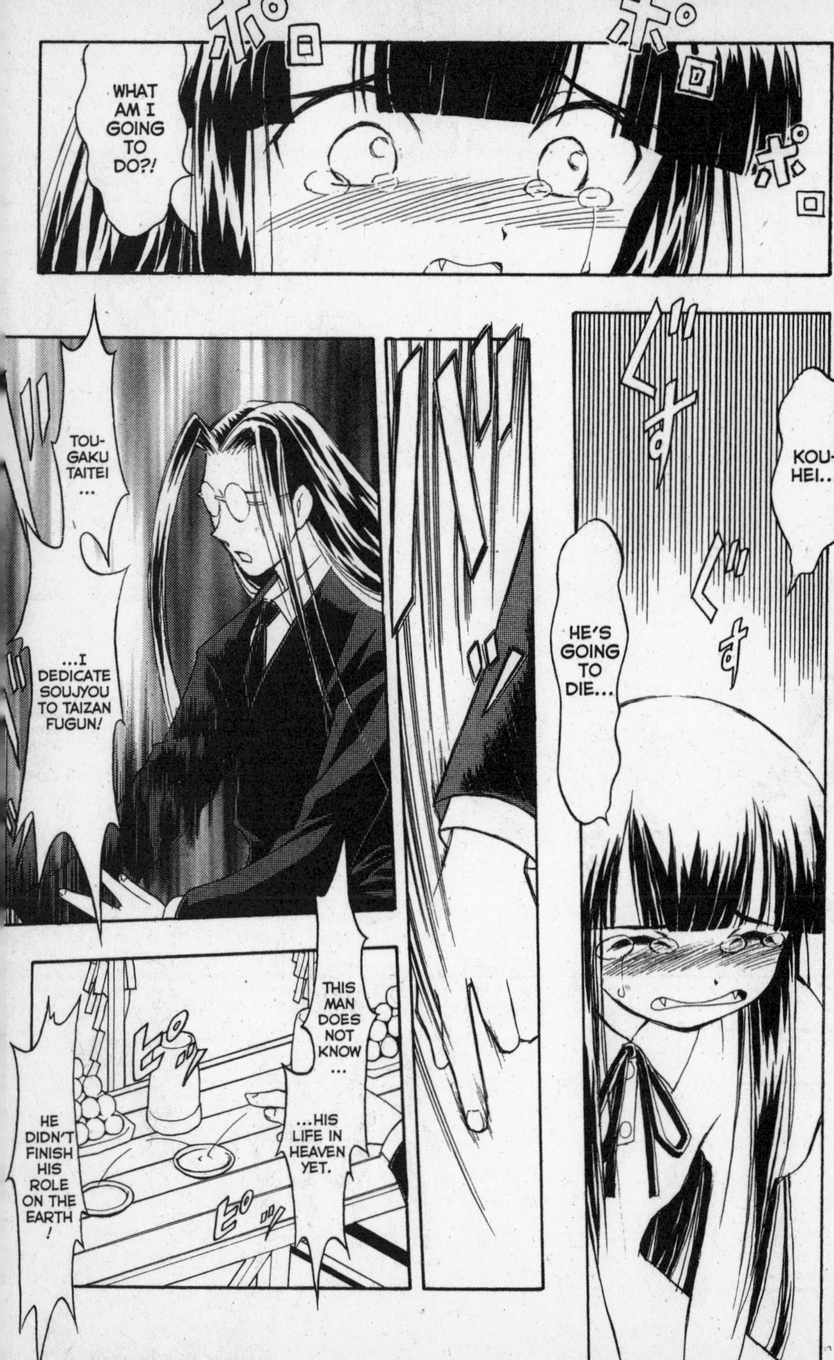
ポロ
ポロ
ポロ
WHAT AM I GOING TO DO?!
ぐす
KOU-HEI...
ぐす
HE'S GOING TO DIE...
TOU-GAKU TAITEI ...
...I DEDICATE SOUJYOU TO TAIZAN FUGUN!
THIS MAN DOES NOT KNOW ...
...HIS LIFE IN HEAVEN YET.
HE DIDN'T FINISH HIS ROLE ON THE EARTH!

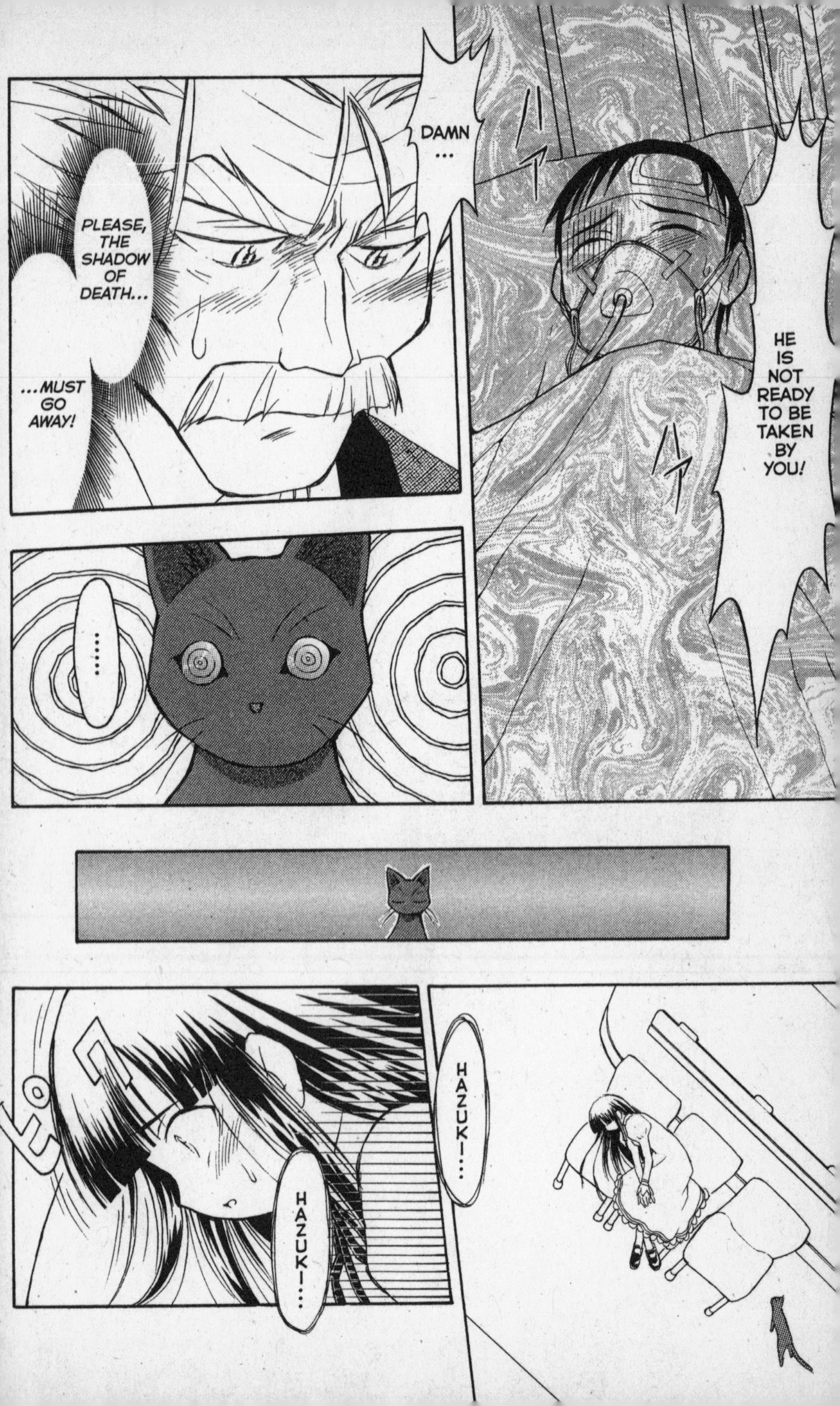
DAMN ...
HE IS NOT READY TO BE TAKEN BY YOU!
PLEASE, THE SHADOW OF DEATH...
...MUST GO AWAY!
......
HAZUKI!...
HAZUKI!...

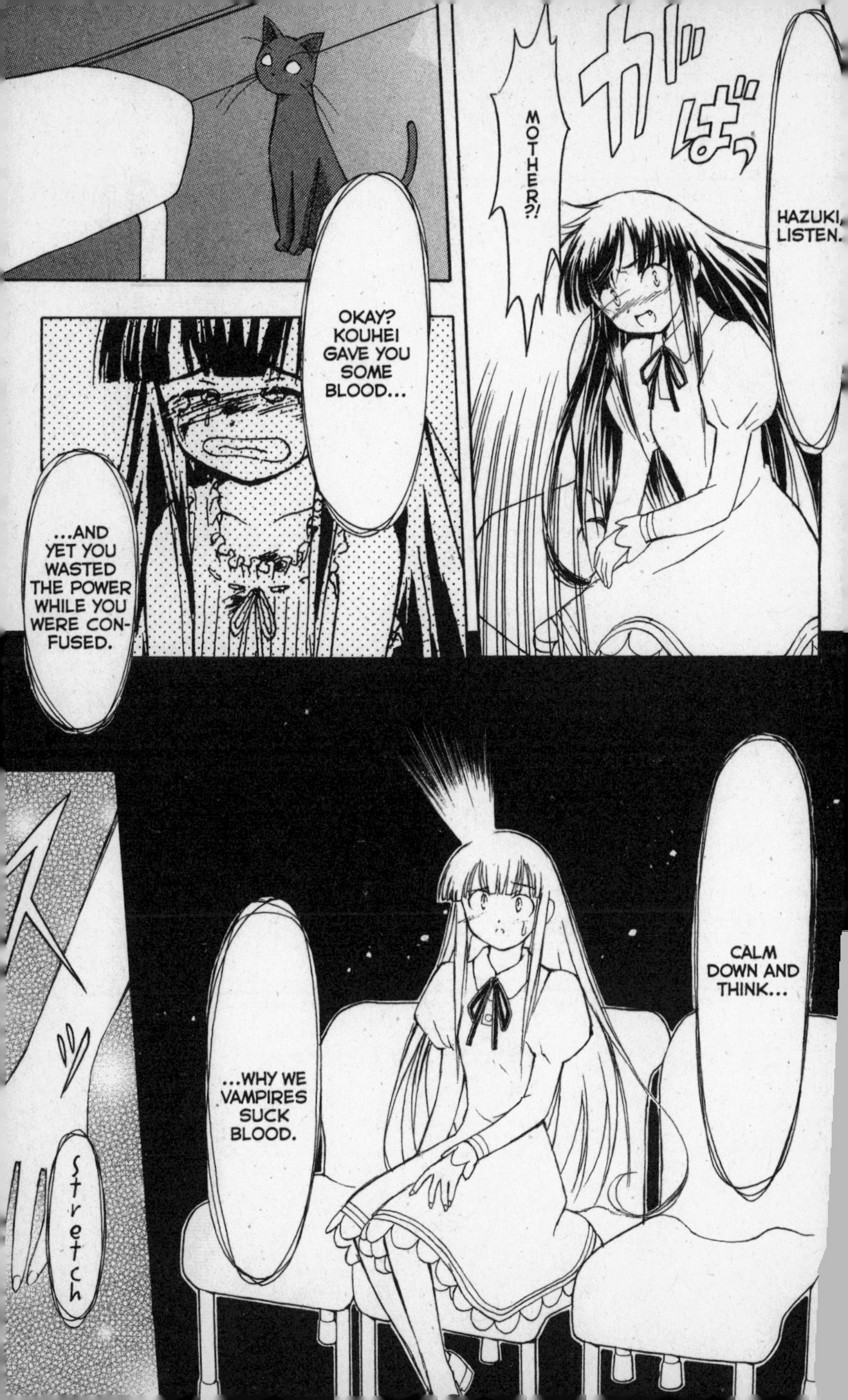
HAZUKI, LISTEN.
MOTHER?!
OKAY? KOUHEI GAVE YOU SOME BLOOD...
...AND YET YOU WASTED THE POWER WHILE YOU WERE CON-FUSED.
CALM DOWN AND THINK...
...WHY WE VAMPIRES SUCK BLOOD.
stretch

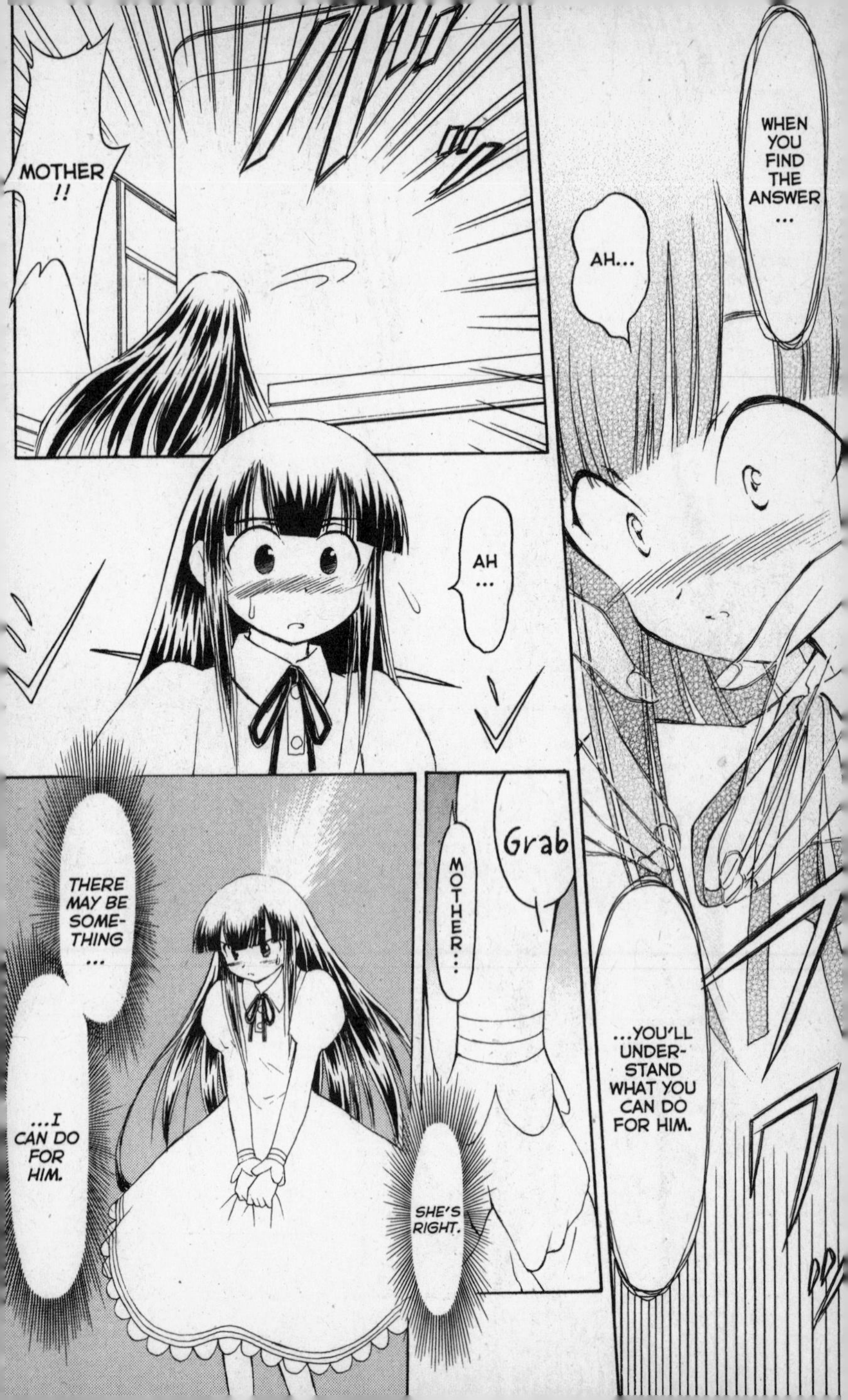
WHEN YOU FIND THE ANSWER ...
AH...
...YOU'LL UNDER-STAND WHAT YOU CAN DO FOR HIM.
MOTHER !!
AH ...
Grab
MOTHER...
THERE MAY BE SOME-THING ...
...I CAN DO FOR HIM.
SHE'S RIGHT.

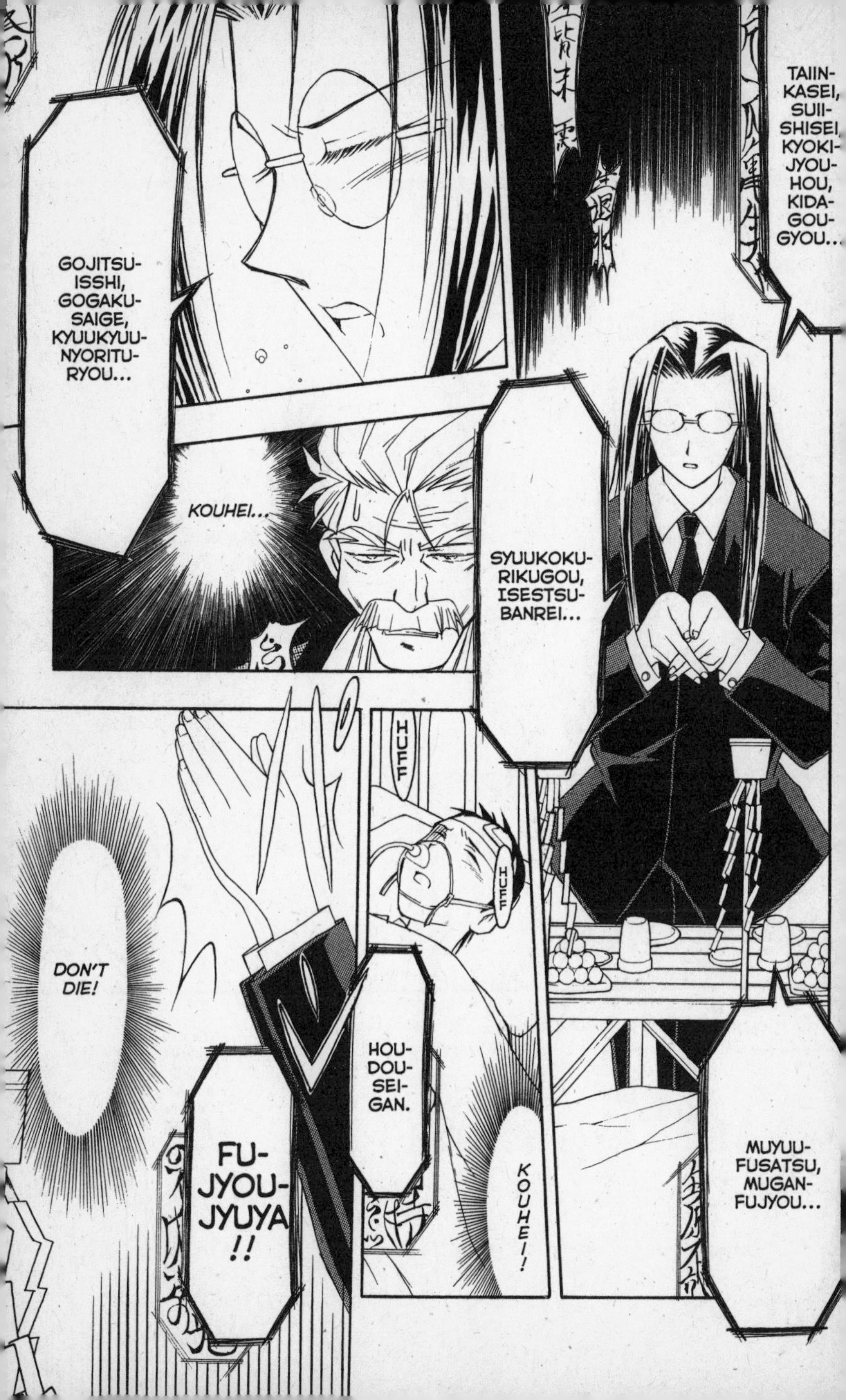

TAIIN-KASEI, SUII-SHISEI, KYOKI-JYOU-HOU, KIDA-GOU-GYOU...
SYUUKOKU-RIKUGOU, ISESTSU-BANREI...
GOJITSU-ISSHI, GOGAKU-SAIGE, KYUUKYUU-NYORITU-RYOU...
KOUHEI...
MUYUU-FUSATSU, MUGAN-FUJYOU...
KOUHEI!
HUFF
HUFF
HOU-DOU-SEI-GAN.
FU-JYOU-JYUYA!!
DON'T DIE!

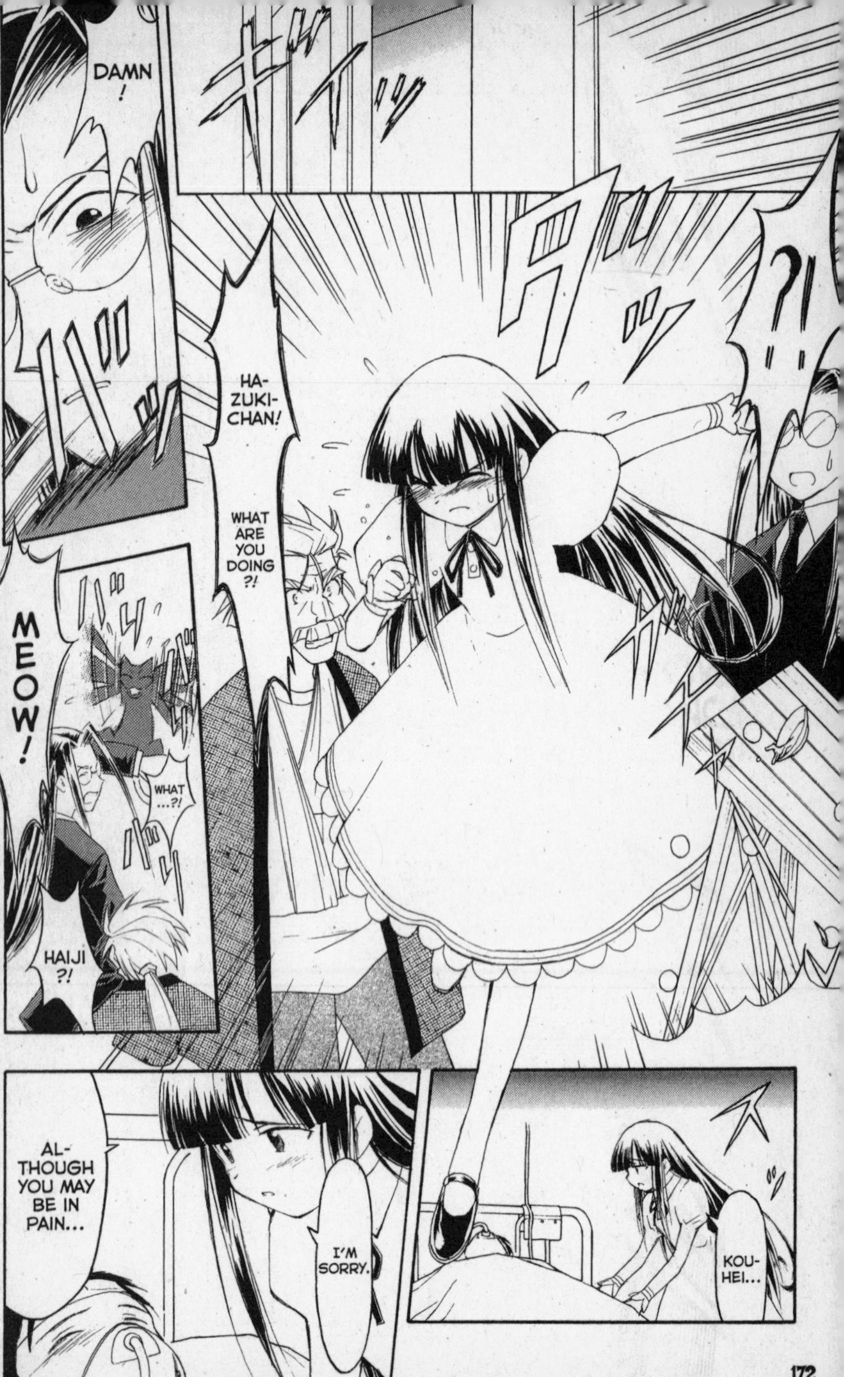
DAMN!
?!!
HA-ZUKI-CHAN!
WHAT ARE YOU DOING?!
MEOW!
WHAT...?!
HAIJI?!
KOU-HEI...
AL-THOUGH YOU MAY BE IN PAIN...
I'M SORRY.

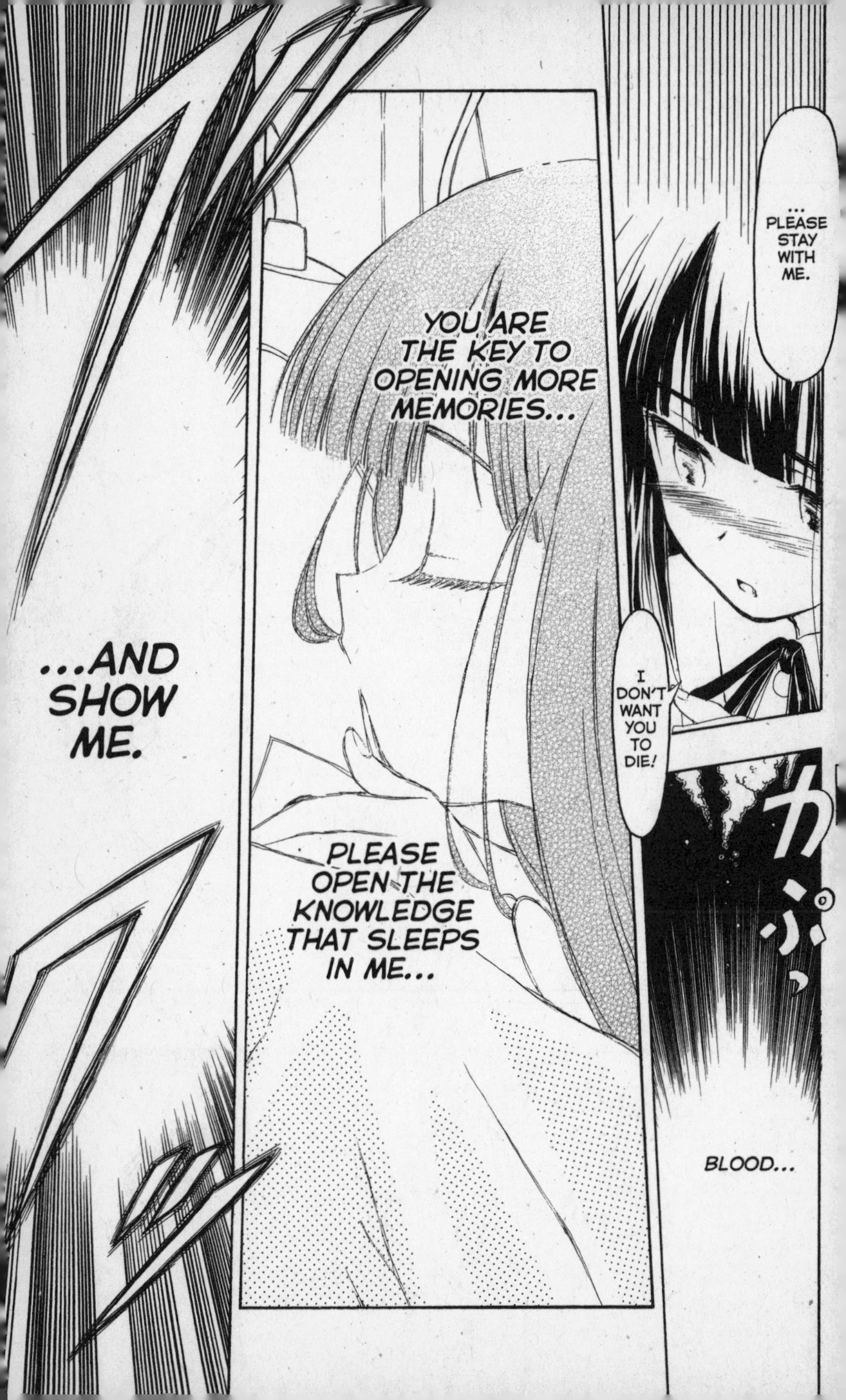
...PLEASE STAY WITH ME.
I DON'T WANT YOU TO DIE!
かぷっ
BLOOD...
YOU ARE THE KEY TO OPENING MORE MEMORIES...
PLEASE OPEN THE KNOWLEDGE THAT SLEEPS IN ME...
...AND SHOW ME.

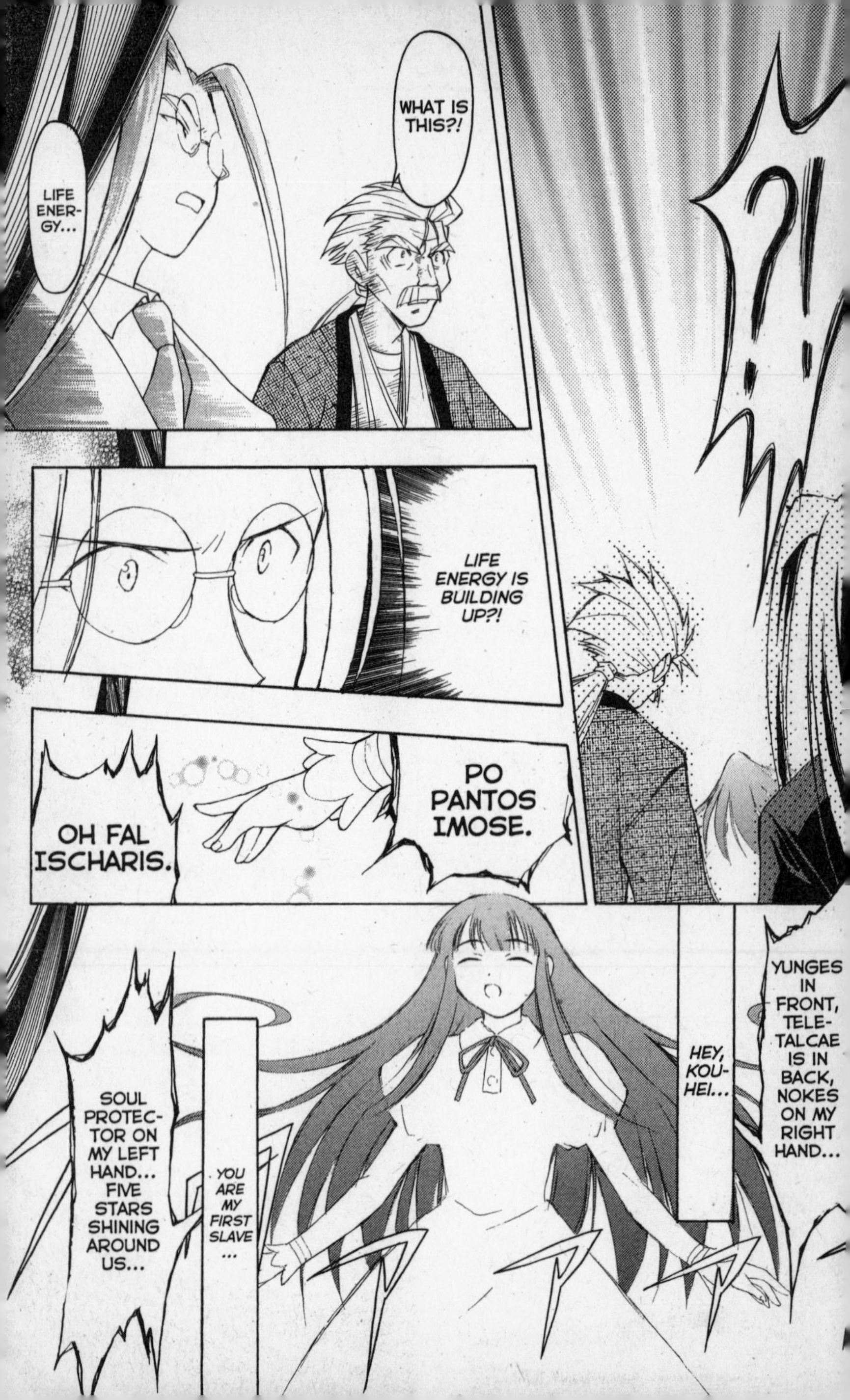

?!
WHAT IS THIS?!
LIFE ENERGY...
LIFE ENERGY IS BUILDING UP?!
PO PANTOS IMOSE.
OH FAL ISCHARIS.
YUNGES IN FRONT, TELETALCAE IS IN BACK, NOKES ON MY RIGHT HAND...
HEY, KOUHEI...
YOU ARE MY FIRST SLAVE...
SOUL PROTECTOR ON MY LEFT HAND... FIVE STARS SHINING AROUND US...

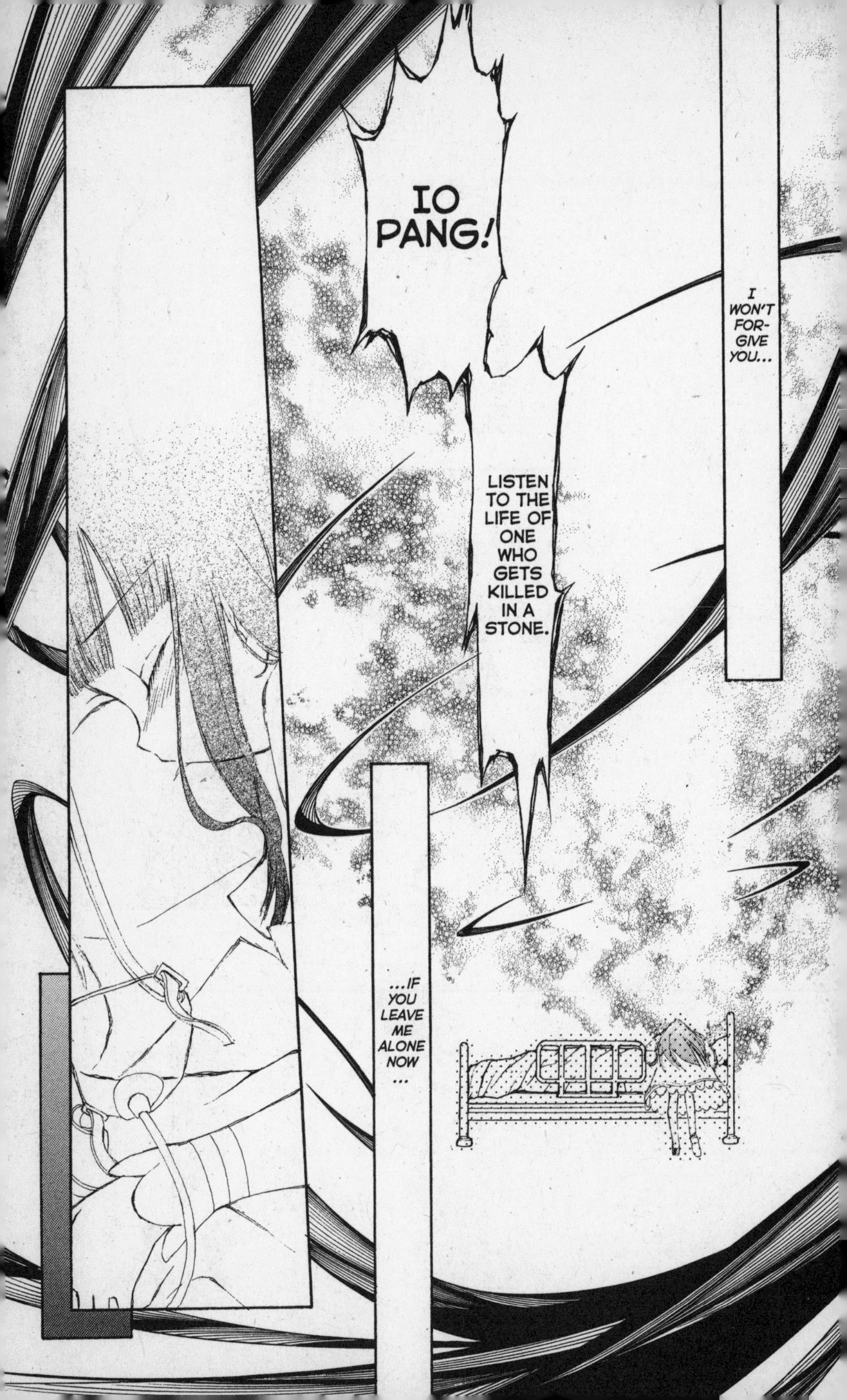
I WON'T FOR-GIVE YOU...
IO PANG!
LISTEN TO THE LIFE OF ONE WHO GETS KILLED IN A STONE.
...IF YOU LEAVE ME ALONE NOW ...

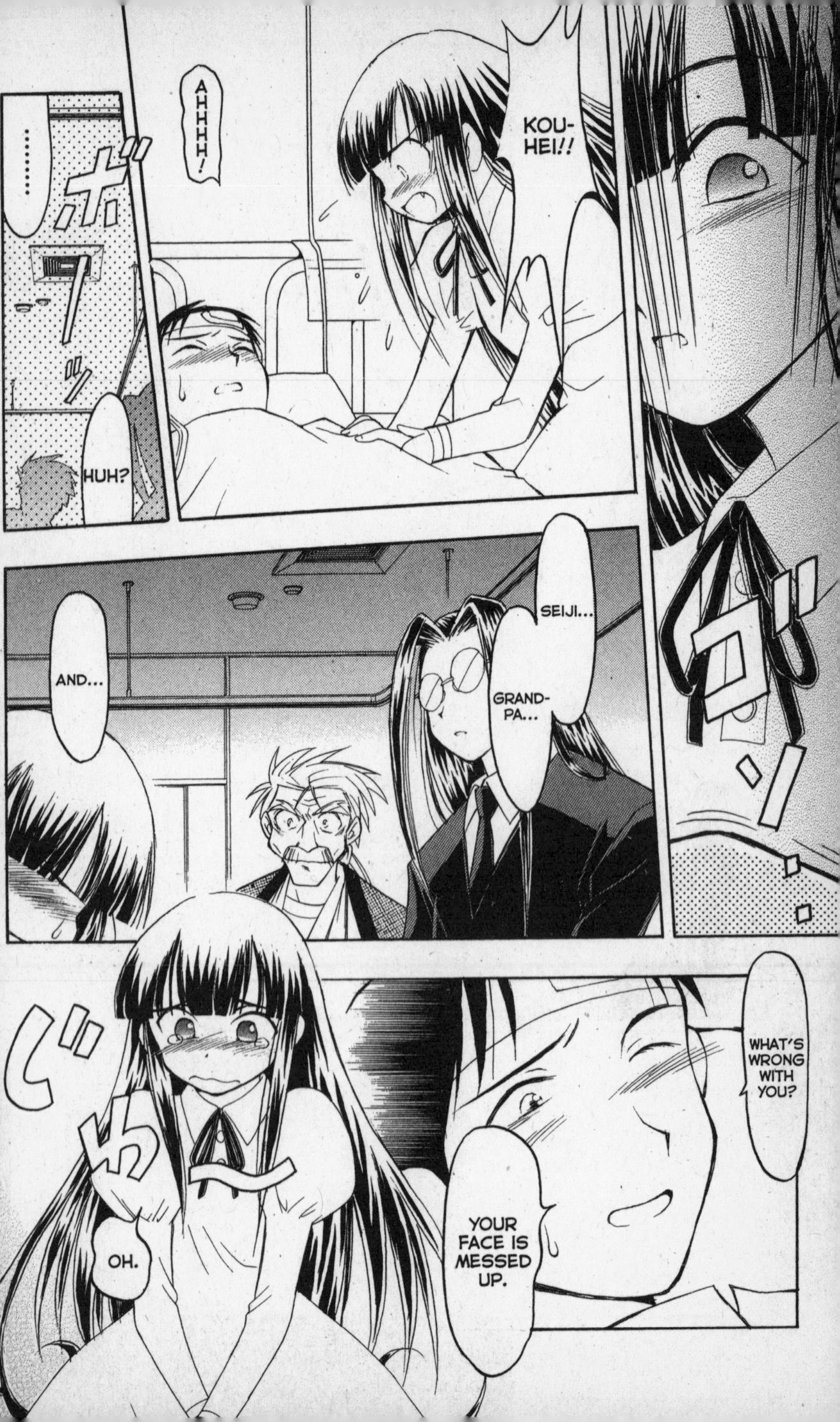
KOU-HEI!!
AHHHH!
......
HUH?
SEIJI...
GRAND-PA...
AND...
WHAT'S WRONG WITH YOU?
YOUR FACE IS MESSED UP.
OH.

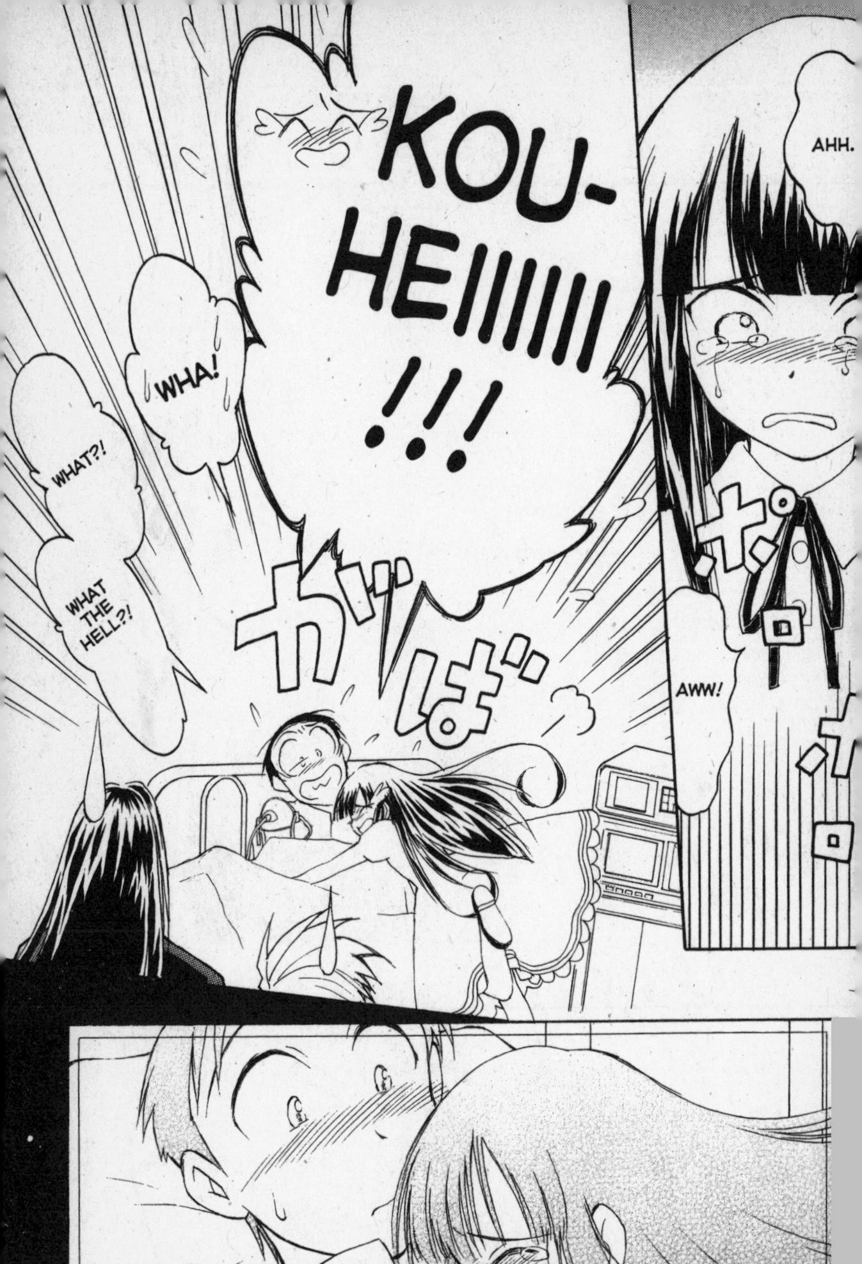

AHH.
AWW!
KOU-HEI!!!!!!!!!!
WHA!
WHAT?!
WHAT THE HELL?!
がば

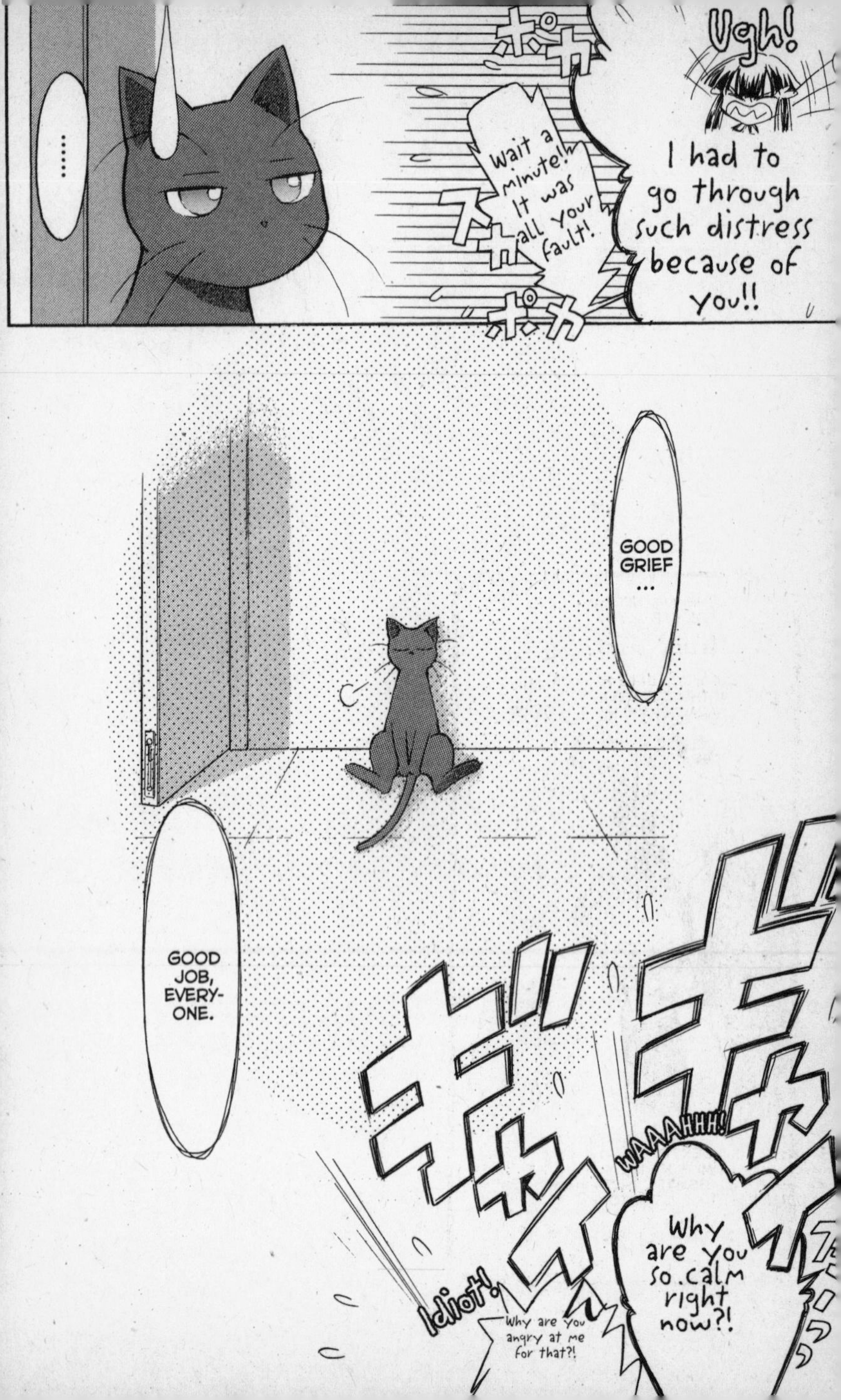

Ugh!
I had to go through such distress because of you!!
Wait a minute! It was all your fault!
……
GOOD GRIEF…
GOOD JOB, EVERY-ONE.
WAAAHHH!
Why are you so calm right now?!
Idiot!
Why are you angry at me for that?!

KOUHEI AND SEIJI ARE BOTH IN THEIR EARLY TWENTIES.

SEIJI IS LITTLE OLDER THAN KOUHEI.

SEIJI MIDO (SAME PRONUNCIATION WITH A DIFFERENT CHINESE CHARACTER) IS HIS PEN NAME.

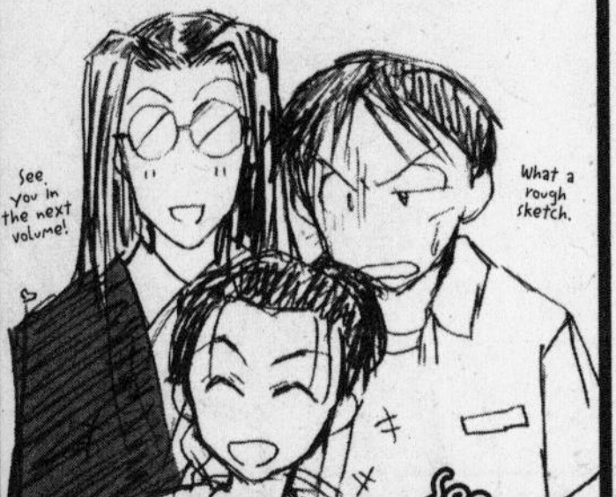
What a rough sketch.
See you in the next volume!
See ya!

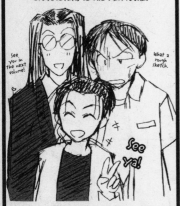

KOUHEI IS STILL A STUDENT WITH A PART-TIME JOB. HIROMI IS KOUHEI'S HIGH SCHOOL CLASSMATE. THEY HAVE A LONG HISTORY.

SEE YOU IN THE NEXT VOLUME!

IN THE NEXT

TSUKUYOMI
Moon Phase 月詠

VOLUME 4

COUNT KINKEL MAKES KOUHEI AND HAZUKI AN OFFER THEY CAN'T REFUSE. HE KIDNAPS KOUHEI'S GRANDFATHER, WHICH FORCES THEM TO THE MANSION WHERE HAZUKI USED TO LIVE WITH HER MOTHER. BUT WHEN THEY ARRIVE, HAZUKI STARTS TO RECALL SOME MEMORIES FROM THE MANSION--AND LEARNS MORE ABOUT HER MYSTERIOUS ABILITY...

TOKYOPOP SHOP

WWW.TOKYOPOP.COM/SHOP

Visit the shop to buy the best manga and merchandise in the known universe!

HOT NEWS!

Check out the **TOKYOPOP SHOP!** The world's best collection of manga in English is now available online in one place!

SOKORA REFUGEES T-SHIRT

LOVE HINA NOVEL

+ANIMA

WWW.TOKYOPOP.COM/SHOP

0 00000 00000 0

- LOOK FOR SPECIAL OFFERS
- PRE-ORDER UPCOMING RELEASES
- COMPLETE YOUR COLLECTIONS

+ANIMA © Mukai Natsumi. Sokora Refugees © Kurt Hassler and TOKYOPOP Inc. Love Hina © Kurou Hazuki © Hiroyuki Kawasaki © Ken Akamatsu. All Rights Reserved.

THIS FALL, TOKYOPOP CREATES A FRESH, NEW CHAPTER IN TEEN NOVELS...

For Adventurers...

Witches' Forest:
The Adventures of Duan Surk

By Mishio Fukazawa
Duan Surk is a 16-year-old Level 2 fighter who embarks on the quest of a lifetime—battling mythical creatures and outwitting evil sorceresses, all in an impossible rescue mission in the spooky Witches' Forest!

BASED ON THE FAMOUS
FORTUNE QUEST **WORLD**

For Dreamers...

Magic Moon

By Wolfgang and Heike Hohlbein
Kim enters the enigmatic realm of Magic Moon, where he battles unthinkable monsters and fantastical creatures—in order to unravel the secret that keeps his sister locked in a coma.

THE WORLDWIDE BESTSELLING FANTASY
*THRILL*OGY **ARRIVES IN THE U.S.!**

Witches' Forest: The Adventures of Duan Surk © 2006 MISHIO FUKAZAWA.
Magic Moon © 1983, 2001 by Verlag Carl Ueberreuter, Vienna.

TOKYOPOP PRESENTS

POP FICTION

For Believers...

Scrapped Princess:
A Tale of Destiny

By Ichiro Sakaki
A dark prophecy reveals that the queen will give birth to a daughter who will usher in the Apocalypse. But despite all attempts to destroy the baby, the myth of the "Scrapped Princess" lingers on...

THE INSPIRATION FOR THE HIT ANIME AND MANGA SERIES!

For Thinkers...

Kino no Tabi:
Book One of The Beautiful World

By Keiichi Sigsawa
Kino roams the world on the back of Hermes, her unusual motorcycle, in a journey filled with happiness and pain, decadence and violence, and magic and loss.

THE SENSATIONAL BESTSELLER IN JAPAN HAS FINALLY ARRIVED!

Scrapped Princess: A Tale of Destiny © ICHIRO SAKAKI, GO YABUKI and YUKINOBU AZUMI.
Kino no Tabi: Book One of The Beautiful World © KEIICHI SIGSAWA.

STOP!

This is the back of the book.
You wouldn't want to spoil a great ending!

This book is printed "manga-style," in the authentic Japanese right-to-left format. Since none of the artwork has been flipped or altered, readers get to experience the story just as the creator intended. You've been asking for it, so TOKYOPOP® delivered: authentic, hot-off-the-press, and far more fun!

DIRECTIONS

If this is your first time reading manga-style, here's a quick guide to help you understand how it works.

It's easy... just start in the top right panel and follow the numbers. Have fun, and look for more 100% authentic manga from TOKYOPOP®!